ENJOY

LEST TOMORROW *FLEES*

THERE IS NO HUMOR IN WAR ITSELF. THOSE WHO IMBIBE OR ARE ASSIMILATED BY THIS TYPE OF HUMAN CONFLICT CAN BEST ENDURE AND PREVAIL WITH A DEGREE OF MIRTHFULNESS.

by
1st LIEUTENANT LLOYD O. KRUEGER
U.S. ARMY AIR FORCE

Herb & Sandy
Though my
generation is
gradually fading
away, we can take
pride in the legacy
we gave the World —
Freedom.

Lloyd O. Krueger
Lead Navigator
95th Bomb Group
May 2001

Printed in Victoria, Canada

National Library of Canada Cataloguing in Publication

Krueger, Lloyd O., 1921-
    Enjoy... lest tomorrow flees / Lloyd O. Krueger.
ISBN 1-55395-108-5
    1. World War, 1939-1945--Personal narratives, American.
I. Title.

D811.K7268 2002   940.54'4973'092   C2002-904436-7

This book was published *on-demand* in cooperation with Trafford Publishing.
On-demand publishing is a unique process and service of making a book available for retail sale to the public taking advantage of on-demand manufacturing and Internet marketing. **On-demand publishing** includes promotions, retail sales, manufacturing, order fulfilment, accounting and collecting royalties on behalf of the author.

Suite 6E, 2333 Government St., Victoria, B.C. V8T 4P4, CANADA
Phone   250-383-6864   Toll-free   1-888-232-4444 (Canada & US)
Fax   250-383-6804   E-mail   sales@trafford.com
Web site   www.trafford.com   TRAFFORD PUBLISHING IS A DIVISION OF TRAFFORD HOLDINGS LTD.
Trafford Catalogue #02-0822   www.trafford.com/robots/02-0822.html

10   9   8   7   6   5   4   3   2

THIS BOOK IS HUMBLY DEDICATED TO A FRIEND, WHO PASSED AWAY MANY YEARS AGO. SHE NEVER KNEW SHE WAS THE INSPIRATION THAT ENCOURAGED MY EDUCATION AND ALL THAT FOLLOWED. I SHALL BE FOREVER GRATEFUL TO ELSIE LOUISE WEINKAUF, ONE WONDERFUL WOMAN, NEIGHBOR, AND FRIEND.

Mrs. Weinkauf lived next door to my parents' home with her family. She was a simple, plain, and very ordinary woman. Despite the limited schooling she had been exposed to, she possessed wisdom and knowledge not apparent to those around her.

During my developing years, this special person took the time to converse with a rambunctious and very energetic kid. We had conversations concerning values, education, development of talents, and the future. She filled in the void that my parents and school councilors created. Her advice, suggestions, hopes and dreams opened my eyes to potentials I never realized existed. My very special friend............THANKS.

ENJOY
LEST TOMORROW *FLEES*

Tomorrows are the collection of hours to be.
Those precious moments when we expect to see.
New things and sights that will bring us glee,
Where all spectacles are enhanced to a higher degree.

Today, right now, is the moment things do exist,
Their presence is here and their actions persist.
We can accept them with smiles or perhaps an upraised fist.
These moments can be embraced while some we choose to resist.

Tomorrow is that time we do not categorically possess,
Though each may think it is theirs, we all have to confess,
All look forward to those moments that do not oppress,
Each wants the best things in life we can possibly address.

Today is now at hand and we are aware what it brings,
Each priceless moment touches us and now exposes all things.
Cherished birds that can soar on their outstretched wings,
Each has their songs that thrill peasants or possibly kings.

We can walk through the meadows or fish its rippling streams,
With very special friends we can talk and share our dreams.
Each one of us can act alone or by choice a member of teams,
We can jot down a single note or can expound with reams.

It takes a lot of living with an abundant amount of cheer,
To bring upon a genuine smile or to erase a person's tear.

Live each single moment that is offered throughout the year,
As though it might be your last, making no room for any fear.

Life will go on with mundane moments and occasionally a thrill,
It is essential to look forward and constantly hoping still.
That our common enemy tires or exhausts his misguided will,
To destroy this precious world and all our tomorrows-kill.

We can mix each of our moments into a harmonious alloy,
Let us preserve what's around us and do not try to destroy.
Why not cherish our friends and their friendship employ,
That the quality of life has but one simple secret - ENJOY.

lloyd o. krueger

TABLE OF CONTENTS

THE PRELUDE

In the process of writing this book, I discovered something about my self that I was never consciously aware of. Humor, it seems, has always been a constant companion of mine, for nearly eighty-one years. I now realize it is a most unusual kind of friend and certainly a welcomed state of mind.

I had always been cognizant that I appreciated good jokes, could see the light side of situations, was known for instigating pranks on friends and had learned how to weather unkind moments with a sense of humor. The interesting reality that this particular quality was an inherent part of my being had been taken for granted these many years.

While writing "COME FLY WITH ME', a story about my nearly four years in the Air Force during World War II, I was constantly discovering the whimsical and ludicrous events that helped me enjoy and, at other times, endure these 1200 days of my life. Each day would be interspersed with moments of mirth, intermingled with the times spent in serious contemplation or performing required duties.

Having stated the above, my memory vividly recalls an exception which will add a better perspective to the days accounted for in this story. While taking an active part in the 35 combat missions against Germany and the three hundred plus hours flying over enemy controlled Europe, I do not have any recollection or remembrance of many moments of foolishness or raillery.

This book will endeavor to record, in some chronological order, the humorous and humanistic incidents that occurred to me and many of my friends. From the moment I enlisted in the Air Force cadets in July of 1942 until I received my Honorable Discharge in October of 1945, I recall with fondness these many memories. All of this, as I look back now, is but a brief instant of time in the 81 years that have been logged by this author.

Most of these moments have special meaning for me and others of my vintage

1

because each is aware of the importance of this period in our country's history. It was a time when our leaders and people possessed qualities that seem to have been forgotten in the ensuing years. Such words as morals, dedication, patriotism, self esteem, duty, principals, determination, respect, and even caring were qualities that have had a constant and insidious decline in meaning since the early 40's.

Though there is no humor in the previous statement, it was made note of to give importance to, and appreciation for, the atmosphere at the time this story takes place. I sincerely believe my generation grew up with a sense of humor that would prove to have a therapeutic effect on each of our dispositions and state of minds.

It is most important to reiterate that the contents of this book, by emphasizing the ludicrous and whimsical moments, may give the false impression of my actual abilities and accomplishments. During these encompassing months, I had been trained as a navigator in the Eighth Air force; flew thirty-five combat missions over Europe (all but nine as a Lead Navigator); and served a stint in the Air Transport Command that would afford me the opportunity to fly all over the world.

I now know that the possession of a sense of humor was not a liability but a magnificent asset. It afforded me the opportunity to overcome an extreme case of inherent shyness. It gave me the confidence to be capable and, in all modesty, good at the responsibility Uncle Sam requested of me. During the three plus years I served in the military, I relied thousands of times on my ability to turn a negative into a positive. I believed most things had a bright side and it was in this direction I usually migrated.

This now is a story of only one, in over 350,000 airmen who served in the Eighth Air Force. A typical young man that answered the call from his country and, like his fellow airmen, put forth his maximum effort as each moment presented itself. Words of this manuscript are predominantly describing circumstances of levity and are jocular in nature. The author, nonetheless, is aware of the 49,000 or more casualties suffered by the men in the Mighty Eighth Air Force. Perhaps it is this somber statistic that has made the special qualities of humor have a particular endearment to me.

One final assurance has to be given to all of the persons mentioned in the ensuing chapters. All incidents referred to are factual and there was no intention to hurt, harm or embarrass any of my friends. It is my hope and trust that they enjoyed each of these moments with the same enthusiasm and zeal as I did.

If, by chance, I've written something that may have offended or displeased one of these old friends, I can only assure them that you only tend to hurt the ones you love............others do not receive this special attention that only fond memories can conjure up.

CHAPTER 1

ONE STEP AHEAD OF THE DRAFT

During the school year of 1941-1942, I attended the University of Wisconsin in Madison as an engineering student. I would be only a first year freshman and eager to start my education. I had graduated from Wausau Senior High School, located in the North Central part of Wisconsin, a full year before. A life time friend, Frank Morman and I had been thrown together in kindergarten in 1927 and had been in every class room, every home room, and had every teacher and subject for the next thirteen-years in the Wausau school system.

Upon graduation this friend, nicknamed "Mope," would start college without me. This inexcusable separation had been forced upon me because of the lack of necessary funds required for a further education. I was now compelled to join the work force during a period that was still trying to pull itself out of the great depression.

My parents did not approve of an education beyond the required twelfth grade and made it very clear to me that they could not, nor would not, have the necessary funds a continued education needed. I was informed, with a degree of haughtiness, "not a single one of my numerous cousins, from both sides of my family, ever wasted their time by going on to school."

Since I happened to be the oldest of four children, I acquired the knowledge of the futility of trying to convince my parents to alter their deep-seated, and often distorted, ideas and beliefs. I was well aware that being the eldest meant I would be the one delegated to break ground for all who were to follow. At an early age I had somehow learned to not make excuses for my parent's lack of knowledge or reasoning and never wasted my time trying to argue or convince them of their erroneous rationale on any subject.

As I look back to 1940 I discovered our country was still trying to recover from a depression that affected all of its citizens. By most standards, my family had many of the stigmatisms that could be associated with being poor. I never felt impoverished for a single moment, primarily because everyone I had contact with, those all around me, and my personal pride dictated otherwise. We didn't have a lot of money, but we always had nourishing food on the table and we were dressed in plain but clean clothes.

I had grown up to accept the haircuts given to me by my Father down in our basement. It was more than adequate and no one ever commented. To not get to go to movies was always accepted as normal. My Mother saw that our well-worn blue jeans were both clean and properly mended or patched.

The neighborhood I was raised in happened to have a predominance of boys. At an early age I appreciated the fact that by participating in sports within this immediate vicinity, these activities not only did not require unavailable shekels, it developed my body and mind and gave me agility and quickness. Without my knowledge, this physical activity also cultivated my pride and gave me self confidence. However, all of the above did little to master a shyness I always possessed while away from my friends.

Now, for the first time, I had to face up to a personal crisis that required me to assert myself if I was to fulfill my desire to get a formal education, something every fiber of my being cried out for. Over a period of many years my next door neighbor, Mrs. Elsie Weinkauf, had convinced me that it was imperative to go on to College or the University in order to develop the tools and skills to fulfill many of the dreams I had confided to her. I was determined to get an education despite any tradition self imposed by all of my relatives.

I came to the realization I could not follow my friend down to Madison and the University of Wisconsin, but rather I would be forced to stay home and work a year to get the required funds necessary to enroll. After two weeks of searching, I discovered that jobs were not plentiful in this town of about 25,000, especially in 1940.

I spent two weeks inquiring about work at dozen of different or likely places, using all of the techniques I had been taught at school. Dress neatly, have your shoes polished, comb your hair and have clean fingernails, be precise in your desires to learn any job, and do not slouch while presenting yourself.

I finally called my Uncle Ed Ronek, a foreman at a sash and door manufacturing company, if it might be possible to get a job for me. The proverbial technique to advance in society would finally persevere . . . . . . .It's not what you know, it's who you know.

The very next day I reported in to my Uncle's Office at Curtis & Yale Woodworking

Plant in Wausau, Wisconsin, my hometown. I was informed I would receive 25 cents per hour as a starting wage but could expect to make 35 cents per hour after my sixth week of employment, providing my work habits were acceptable.

My duties would be that of a flunky, doing numerous mundane chores which required no particular skills, dexterity, artistry, or ingenuity. I would be surrounded by men who had become automated and almost apart of the machines they worked at. The environment I was to work in was a multi floor wood factory building that covered several acres. It was noisy and it was dimly lit.

This manufacturing facility made a variety of different window styles, doors with their jambs and heads, ornate mantels for fireplaces, and other wood products from soft pine, oak, maple, birch, and cherry. I played no part in the manufacture of these products for new homes. I only packaged the finished product, pushed it to a warehouse, stacked paper cartons, and a variety of other humble and ignoble tasks.

I soon became one of the human machines who punched a time clock at eight A.M. and again at five P.M. I felt like a zombie. My work in this factory convinced me that an education was absolutely essential to develop skills to become creative and constructive and to find a future that would prove challenging to my innate talents. During this wasted year of my life I managed to save barely enough for a single year of higher education.

In the fall of 1941 I managed to get my parents to drive the 150 miles to Madison. I had packed everything I owned into a fiber laundry case and a large paper sack. A friend I knew from my neighborhood, George Cormack, suggested I apply to reside in High House in Tripp Hall on a remote corner of the huge campus. This would be a University Dormitory. George would be in his senior year in High House and was enrolled in the Pharmaceutical College. I had been accepted in this dormitory, thanks to this friend. George even worked it out so I, a lowly freshman, would be on the third floor of this huge complex with all of the seniors. I never determined if this was a liability or an asset.

My first four months at the University were spent as a typical freshman on any large campus. George had gotten me a job waiting tables in our large dining room where my responsibility would be serving the same eighteen students at their three large tables. I was away from home for the first time and I now began to feel I had some control over my future and my destiny. Little did I realize how the events of the next few months would change my life and values, and those of countless millions?

On December 7th, 1941, while on a date on the campus of the University in

5

Madison, Wisconsin, I had learned the Japanese attacked Pearl Harbor. Though I was not quite sure where Pearl Harbor was located, I knew it was somewhere in the Pacific Ocean. My date (and future wife) and I soon discovered how personal this terrible news would become.

Late Sunday afternoon on the 7th of December, Norma Ann Schmidt and I agreed to go on a date. Norma came from a little town called Rothschild, just south of my home town of Wausau. I had decided to take this very special person out to dinner prior to going to a movie. Our dinner would be in a quaint little Chinese Restaurant on the second floor on Webster Street, located on the Northeast side of the Capital Square.

We had our own little booth, with a curtain that could be pulled, guaranteeing us of additional privacy. To add to the ambience of this important moment for me, we ate, with some awkwardness, our entire meal with cop sticks. Just as we were leaving, we were told about the news coming over the radio concerning the Attack on Pearl Harbor.

Within hours of the attack we had learned that our new enemy, Japan, had killed two friends we both knew from our home town. Both were stationed at Wheeler Air Force Base in the Hawaiian Islands. Don Plant and Kermit La Vick, both from Wausau, Wisconsin, lived within several blocks of my parents' home. Each had enlisted in the Air Force upon graduation from high school. These young men had been killed by Japanese' fighter planes, strafing the airfield in the first moments of this dastardly attack.

When I enrolled at the University, in lieu of taking a required physical education course, I became a member of the R.O.T.C. (Reserved Officers Training Corp.). Once we realized the significance of the rapidly changing events, Norma Schmidt and I hurried down Langdon Street for the University of Wisconsin Armory. I was aware of a machine they had that constantly received news via ticker tape.

A large group had gathered around the busy ticker tape machine and it was here that we learned of our two friends. The War immediately became a reality in both of our lives. It was at this moment that I knew it would only be a matter of time before my whole world would change. I had already been classified 1-A by the mandatory draft that had been enacted and would only have one year of college behind me. It was obvious to me, and many of my friends, that our country would require our services. Actually, my immediate feelings were such that I wanted to get personally involved.

Mobilization for all Branches of the Service was taking place at a rapid pace. I knew that it would be foolish for me to plan on going back to Madison and start my sophomore year of college. Besides, I had spent my entire savings for the two semesters I had been enrolled and I knew I could not expect help from my parents. Their sentiments and beliefs concerning continuing education remained just as archaic as it had been twelve months before.

When I arrived back home for the summer vacation, I discovered there were many more opportunities to find a job and at a more realistic pay scale. Despite this new knowledge, common sense and being realistic, I knew I could not save enough for another year of school in the less than three months before classes started. At this moment though, I did not realize that once I had finished my freshman year and arrive home for the summer months, my notice to report to the local Draft board would only be a few weeks away.

After declaring war on Japan and Germany, our President, Franklin Delano Roosevelt had the difficult task of preparing our country for the greatest war in history. We were completely unprepared and we were to face two enemies who had been waging war for years. Time to properly mobilize our entire country was at a premium and would have to be our first priority to master.

My father, like many other Americans, served our country in World War I. He was in the 7th Division of the Infantry and fought on the battlefields in France. Several weeks before the end of the war he saw his oldest brother killed at his side. As a youngster I had learned that he had spent endless months involved in trench warfare.

My Dad had been exposed to poison gas during the war and periodically was compelled to suffer and be reminded of this intolerable period in his life. Endless weeks surviving in rat and lice invested trenches, with death sometimes only a shouting distant away, had left him with recollections which time could never erase.

Needless to say, while I was growing up, I seldom heard him speak about this terrible war. Much to my surprise, when my father learned of my pending intentions to enlist in the Air Force, he gathered myself, and my two younger brothers around the kitchen table for the first family discussion I believed ever took place in our home. "What in hell did the "Old Man" have in mind?" were my first thoughts.

My Father, Oscar Karl Robert Krueger, was of German heritage, a kindly man, who possessed a terrific sense of humor. He could also be strict and firm when the situation, in his opinion, demanded it. Though he was only formerly educated through the elementary school level, I found him to be one of the smartest persons I have ever known.

His possession of pure, but keen, common sense permitted him to resolve problems that defied his education. His unsophisticated judgment was seldom in error, with the exception of a continued education. I developed a respect for this man that went beyond a father-son relationship.

My Dad was only about five foot eight in height but he was built like a brick outhouse. He had spent all his life as a plaster, worked ten-hour days, six days a week. His strength was something I never dreamt of challenging. I grew up and learned to accept his only form of a compliment to be, "what kind of crap is that?"

I knew he did not truly know how to display his feelings and I could accept that. Many times, behind my back, I caught him bragging to others about some of his son's accomplishments. The word **crap**, coming from my Father, never carried any vulgar connotations. He just did not understand or comprehend what his eldest son was all about, but somehow I could make excuses for all of this and never let it hinder any of my thoughts or attempts to do anything.

My tiny Irish Mother inherently knew that the pending conversation at the kitchen table would not include her so she immediately vanished. She could not contribute to what was about to take place and she knew that. My Brother Bob was exactly one year and one day younger than myself while Harvey, my youngest Brother, was nearly five years my junior.

The four of us sat around the kitchen table in our breakfast nook. The air was filled with awkwardness as my dad took on a role that was not familiar to me and was most certainly foreign to him. He and I had occasional bull sessions that usually started with an expression containing the word **crap.** This evening would be a different experience that none at this table were prepared for.

I honestly believed my two brothers felt they had done something terribly wrong and were about to learn what it was. I knew my dad was aware of the seriousness of the pending war and for the first time showed some emotion about the future for his three sons. He was uncomfortable as he offered the following words of advice and wisdom. "If you have to go into the Service, stay the hell out of the Infantry." He blurted this out with no preliminary announcement of what this historic rendezvous at our kitchen table was all about. Here, in this breakfast nook, we sowed down at each meal with few words ever spoken. Now, for the first time, we felt we were going to be lectured to.

He then spent several long minutes looking back into his memory some twenty years and finally caught us by surprise once more. "Don't ever be stupid enough to volunteer for anything. It will get you killed every time." His memories of the type of war he had experienced gave him a very strong prejudice that was reflected in his admonition of these words of wisdom. It turned out to be the shortest speech I had ever heard, but perhaps the most profound. The brevity of this gathering was compensated for by the thought provoking message our Father had just left each of us with.

My two brothers sat with their mouths opened, neither one quite sure what had just taken place. Though they were relieved that they had not been reprimanded for something they might have done, I know at this moment they were not cognizant of the gravity of the situation.

I now quietly explained to my Father what I believed my situation would be. I wanted him to know my hope had been to go on with my education, but now this would not be an option. I assured him that I would try to get into a different branch of the service that did not include the Infantry and I would keep him apprised of what my decision would be.

Since one of my dreams, at this point in my life, was to become an aeronautical engineer, I had no difficulty in deciding to enroll in the Army Air force. My two younger brothers, Robert and Harvey, some time later, both enlisted in the U. S. Coast Guard, as their time to be drafted approached. For whatever reason, they obviously preferred to wear a sailor's suit, with its bellbottom trousers, that required the opening of 13 buttons every time they went to the "head".

Shortly after war had been declared, Chief of Staff of the Army Air Force, General Henry "Hap" Arnold, eliminated the requirement that every cadet would be required to have two years of college. What would be substituted for this requirement would be a comprehensive qualifying test that each cadet would be expected to pass. This removed the only obstacle I had known about for my being able to volunteer for enrollment into the Air Force.

Early in the morning of July 23, 1942, I decided to head for uptown and the main Post Office. I had seen that each branch of the service had Recruiting Booths set up to handle the many young men trying to enlist. I decided to do this entirely on my own, both to display my independence and partially to once again declare I am of age to be responsible for my own actions.

Though I had already made up my mind to enlist in the Army Air Force, I approached the two enlisted men, who manned the recruiting desk, as someone who was just seeking information. The entire moment did not truly seem real to me. On one hand I was aware of the seriousness of what I was about to do, while on the other I was excited about being on the brink of a new adventure. I walked into a large room and confronted the two recruiters with both an air of confidence, tinged with a small amount of timidity.

Two individuals were standing before posters and displays showing fighter planes racing across the sky as well as several pictures of young handsome pilots with their helmets on with goggles shoved up on their foreheads. These airmen were spit and polish from one end to the other. Each had several row of ribbons on their chest and the sleeve of their shirt was covered with hash marks, indicating a rank I did not know anything about. They had creases in their trousers and shirts that could slice a loaf of bread. Their shoes had a shine that nearly turned them into mirrors. The only thing I seemed to have in common with them was our haircuts. I also had a crew cut.

These two recruiters had been well trained to act as a team. One of these individuals was rather short and stocky while the second was about six foot with a trim build. As soon as one finished a sentence the other would blare out either positive justification to join the U. S. Army Air Force or negative reasons of why you should stay out of the other branches of service. From a negative side they made mention of the Regular Army, the Navy, the Coast Guard, the Marines, Submarines, and even the Merchant Marines.

The predominant point they made was the duties and glamour of going through aviation cadet training and ultimately becoming a fighter pilot. I was to find out later, perhaps over 95% of the individuals who signed up, thinking they would become a hot shot fighter pilot, would end up in one of the hundreds of other sections of the Army Air Force. I discovered years later that this system was all part of the master plan to rapidly develop the Air Force. They knew that for every man that flew there would have to be about a dozen individuals required in non flying positions.

I listened to the pitch of these two airmen for about twenty-five minutes and then requested permission to enlist. I got so carried away with their pitches I did not have the presence of mind to ask them why in hell weren't they pilots? Within minutes I had signed away my freedom for the next three and one half years.

In time I would realize moments when there were doubts about this momentous decision, yet there were other instances when I knew I had made the right choice. I never dreamed of the unique significance that my simple signature had on the document placed before me. There would be no turning back from this moment on. I was to await further orders that I was told would arrive in the mail. No one bothered to inform me that at this period the Air Force was accepting applicants faster than they were building facilities.

It was only two days later that I received a letter congratulating me upon being selected to report to my local Draft Board for assignment to the U.S. Army. I had previously been classified 1-A, so I knew I would ultimately receive one of the special invitations. Despite this knowledge, I was surprised to open this significant piece of mail. My decision made two days earlier, however, took care of one of my father's requests. My theater of operations in this war was to be in the skies, not in trenches dug into the earth.

I now had the obligation to explain to a member of the Draft Board that I no longer was available to be inducted into the Army. I proudly declared I was now a member of the Army Air Force and would be called up shortly. Needless to say, he was pissed. I was emphatically informed that some individual, who had been placed on a stand-by list, would now have to be moved up and take my place. The red faced civilian ranted and raved at me for ten minutes. I pretended I was sorry.

GEORGE CORMACK

Many months would pass before I would receive my shipping orders to report to the Army Air Force. In fact, it was not until January 17, 1943 that I would leave home and begin my training. It was during this period that a good friend of mine, dear old George, once again played an important role in my life.

George Cormack, my former roommate at the University of Wisconsin in Madison, was home on leave. He only had a single half semester of work before he received his degree in Pharmacy. While we both lived on the third floor of High house, we mutually agreed to move our desks into one room and our beds and dressers into the second room.

The result of this arrangement had a synergistic effect, especially for me. We rode herd on each other to devote quality and adequate time to study and to hit the books. My year working at Curtis and Yale Woodworking Factory had done nothing to cultivate my study habits.

In order to fully appreciate George, it is imperative that I give a brief description of this special friend, approximately four years older than me. George is the type of individual you really have to get to know before you can truly appreciate his many attributes. Your first impression of him would almost certainly be negative, a mistake many people made by not getting to observe his pertinent and sometimes peculiar, but also precious qualities. He was extremely forward, opinionated, and could often be very curt in his replies. George could be classified as truly one of a kind.

It is difficult to describe my friend. He was about 5'-9" tall with a build that made him look shorter. George had never partaken in a single athletic event in his entire life and could be classified as a klutz when it came to any sport. His body was soft and extremely non muscular. His hair was uncommonly thin and it required special attention to get as much mileage out of each single hair while being combed. George's feet were too large for his robust body and it seemed impossible for him

11

to not announce his approach by slapping each shoe to the floor while he walked across the room.

George had been the senior pharmaceutical student at the University while I was a lowly freshman in Engineering. We became friends when he discovered I also came from Wausau, Wisconsin and lived only a few blocks away from his parents. George, by nationality was Scotch. It is important to note that this friend of mine was very Scotch. The trait of being frugal, almost beyond belief, was one of the key ingredients that made him unique.

George had 20-400 vision, a handicap that contributed to his facial appearance. His corrective eye glasses took on the appearance of the bottom of two coke bottles. Without the extremely thick lens in his glasses he would be blind, for all sakes and purposes. On many occasions, while George would be in the shower, I would move his glasses only a few inches on the dresser so he would think he had forgotten where he had left them.

Despite all of the above, I was very fond of this special friend of mine. He was the type of person many would shrug off, especially if they did not take the time to get to know him. This however would be their loss.

As the war went on and most of George's friends were enrolling in the various service branches, he also tried to enlist. This vision abnormality was to keep George out of the service, much to his dismay. He tried repeatedly to enlist in the various branches of service, only to be rejected because of his vision. With corrected glasses he was able to function as well as anyone, but despite this fact, he was even turned down by the Red Cross.

While I was impatiently waiting around, George was attending summer school to get his last credits for graduation. He invited me to come to Madison, stay with him once again, and get a temporary job. I decided to do all of the above, just to break the monotony of what seemed like endless waiting for my orders from the Army Air Force.

My job in Madison turned out to be working the night shift at Oscar Mayer Meat Packing Plant, a fairly good paying job for a neophyte. George's dorm room was on the far side of the Campus while my job was on the extreme opposite end of the city. My duties required I work on the night shift, from 7:00 P.M. till 4:00 A.M. Though my particular job did not have a formal title, I believe the word flunky would be apropos.

I was given assignments in all parts of this huge packing plant. All rooms or areas in this extensive meat processing conglomerate seemed relatively small because of the excessive height of all of the ceilings. Because the lights were mounted at a more reasonable distance above the floor, the space above always looked like the moonless night sky.

Though my hours of toil were on the night shift, once inside the building it was impossible to ever guess the time of day. The ambiance or atmosphere of this place made you always aware of the smell and the death of all the domesticated animals that were about to enter the food chain.

I had been assigned a small area where my main duty was to clean up stainless steel carts on wheels. These carts were about four foot in length, two foot in width, and about thirty inches deep. The tub shaped conveyance receptacles were used to move meat and waste particles around to various departments.

I was informed that it was my obligation to remove all traces of fat, grease, dried meat or whatever would cling to the inside surface of these unique vehicles that were pushed about the plant. It required soapy water, steel wool, elbow grease and a great deal of perseverance. I sometimes felt that once I finished one of these tubs on wheels, it was now the only clean and sanitary thing in this vast labyrinth of divided space that covered many acres and was considered a large facility.

When I had no carts requiring this special attention, I would be assigned jobs others had not finished or tasks that had been screwed up by somebody. At best it was menial work, work that did not tax the brain. The environment that made up my personal workspace was dingy, damp, and the predominant descriptive word being smelly. The place reeked from the odor of slaughtered animals and the processing of their body parts. The small work area assigned to me was one of the few areas free of carcasses hanging from hooks, each with their hoofs barely touching the floor.

My supervisor was a brut of a man who stood about 6'-4" and was built like a tight end for the Green Bay Packers. He was an extremely handsome guy who gradually acquired the persona of someone becoming uglier with each new assignment he gave me. His face was angular and he had a jaw that looked like it could withstand a blow from a sledgehammer. There was a colorful tattoo of some kind of design I could not distinguish on the inside of one of his huge arms. His sleeves were always rolled up to display this indelible conglomerate of colored pigments.

The second night on the job he walked me over to a large refrigerated room, 90% filled with large wooden barrels. Each barrel contained a variety of cut-up meat, wieners, meat scraps, or just bones, each weighing approximately 150 pounds or more. He simply said to mop the entire floor and walked away. My first reaction was that this was a joke, but I instantly knew what the "Big Guy" was doing. If he was trying to piss me off, he had found the right button to push.

The task required that I mop a small cleared area, tilt these heavy wooden barrels on their bottom rim and then twist them onto the cleansed concrete floor. This would have to be repeated hundreds of times in order to wash or clean the entire floor. My boss reappeared at an inopportune moment. He came up behind me just as a barrel of wieners got away from my grip and fell on its side. Bushels of recently produced little sausages slid across the wet floor.

As I was stooping over these little suckers all linked together by their twisted casings, contemplating what my next move should be, I looked up at this colossus. I instantly ascertained that he was both irritated and also delighted. "Pick up these wieners and put them back into the barrel. What customers do not know will never hurt them." This was uttered while his teeth were tightly clenched. I now felt he had been off into the shadows and had waited for this precise moment.

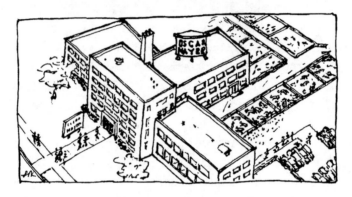

This would be a long night before I made my way back to the campus and George's room. I had been raised by my German Father to recognize any work or task as just that and to diligently continue your efforts until anyone could discern that the job was well done and had been completed. What I was not required to supply with grey matter, I had to compensate for with brawn.

There is one additional fact one must know about my friend George. His sense of smell was as acute as a bull moose during rutting season. This proboscis was always slightly red and I never was sure if it was caused by his many allergies or if he was sniffing out things others were never aware of. It was as though his nose was trying to compensate for his weak eyes.

When I returned to the dorm from work in the early hours of the morning, I would take a shower and then jump into the sack. The sack, in this case, was sharing the same bed in the dormitory with George. I would find my friend asleep since it would be about five in the morning.

Instantly I would notice that my sleeping friend's nose would begin to twitch and get all contorted. He would wake up and grumble, "Kreeeeger, you smell just like that God Damn Packing Plant." Yep, I had to take a second shower and on one occasion a third before I could get under the covers. This did not entirely stop the twitching of my friend's sensitive nose. Even in the darkened dorm room, I could feel or sense the sniffing of my friend's snout.

On the third night of this experience into the real work world, I was told by my titan supervisor to wheel one of my stainless steel carts filled with waste, composed mainly of bones, up to the eighth floor. I then was told to push all of the bony contents into a hole in the floor. This was the chipper and it would turn my messy load into fertilizer that some farmer would later buy.

There was a skinny emaciated older man standing off to one side. He was stripped to the waste with his yellow apron hiding his pants. I noticed this man's rib cage and an almost chicken like breast plate below his unshaven chin. The temperature of this dark space was probably over 100 degrees. No one spoke while the chipper grinding the bones made grunts and clashing sounds as the whirling blades tore into various bony configurations. When a bone knuckle was confronted, it would create its own annoying discord that seemed to make the floor vibrate.

I was surprised that the Big Guy followed me up on the antiquated elevator and watched me empty my load into the noisy chipper. Then it became obvious why he bothered to stalk me through this smelly meat packing plant. When my load disappeared, he ordered me to stay up here and clean my cart by a faucet near this chipper.

Full carts of waste material were all parked around this area and the smell was beyond description. The old man watching this youngster and his supervisor must have been desperate for a job to continue working in such an environment. The noise, the heat, and the smell were almost unbearable. It truly was enough to gag a maggot.

As I stood as tall as possible and with as manly a voice as I could muster, I said, "This cart has to be taken back to my area on the first floor after it is cleaned. All of my cleaning equipment is down there. This place smells rotten and so does your damn job. I quit." At about midnight I was on the bus back to the dorm room and my numerous showers. I'm sure the Big Guy still was standing tall with his mouth open. I was proud of the stand I had just taken and the ride back to George and the dorm did not seem long.

I woke dear George up to give him the news about my decision. I told him I would never go back to the damn place again, not even to pick up any money I might have made. I was compelled to buy a yellow rubber apron and a pair of rubber high top boots when I started, so I didn't expect my check would be worth the trip to the far northeast side of Madison. My Scottish friend ultimately mailed me a check from Oscar Mayer.

I returned to my parents' home to seek less odorous work and to let George devote most of his energies on his books and finals. I still had not heard from the Air Corp but I knew I needed to find some type of job so I could keep my sanity. I also needed money to go out with friends each night. It was not my intention to work right up until the time of my reporting in with the Air Corp, I only wanted enough shekels to entertain myself in the evenings.

"MOPEY"

Shortly after I returned home from my stinky job in Madison, I received a call from my old friend, Frank Morman. I had not seen him for several months so this surprise telephone call was most appreciated. I knew he would help me find things to do with all this free time I had.

"Mopey" meant some very special things to me personally. I knew that many others may have felt he was smug, perhaps arrogant while others surmised he had a haughty attitude and personality. I knew him to be perhaps the smartest student in school, an all conference quarterback on the best football team in the conference, and a friend who I respected for the many positive values he possessed.

Frank got all A's in school with the minimum amount of study. In order to keep pace with him, I had to work my butt off with the books. Unbeknown to "Mopey", his inherent perspicacious abilities would be a challenge for my daily work ethics while in school. His effortless results forced me to get the most mileage out of my limited capabilities during these thirteen years in school. I shall always be indebted to him.

The two of us lived about three-quarters of a mile apart so it was only in high school that we began to socialize. I was fortunate to grow up in a neighborhood with a predominance of boys. We constantly participate in sports with our own neighborhood gang of fellows, such as baseball, softball, hockey, etc. "Mopey" did similar things with the local kids in his community. Once we got to high school though, we started expanding our close relationship to other activities.

While I spent a year at my low paying job at Curtis and Yale, "Mopey" had started his career in Chemical Engineering at the University of Wisconsin. We were

17

now split up for the first time. He was a sophomore when I final got my chance to start school in 1941. Our paths on the campus in Madison seldom crossed so we saw very little of one another.

It would be "Mopey" who would introduce Norma Schmidt to me for the first time. Though she had gone to the same high school, she was a year behind us and I never was afforded the opportunity to get to know her. I knew of her because she had been crowned "Transportation Queen" when the street cars were replaced by buses in Wausau and she also was declared "Donut Duchess" during her Junior year.

During the summer while I waited for my war to start, I received this call from "Mope". Since he was home now after having finished his sophomore year, he thought it might be time to reactivate our old friendship. He wanted to pick me up in his roadster to just go out "beering."

After a few Ballentine Ales, Mopey surprised me a second time when he confronted me with, "How would you like to go get your fortune read. I found out from some of the East Hill gang about this little old German woman who is supposed to be able to read cards. I was told she has a long list of clientele from the East Hill people who go see her often to have their destiny analyzed."

East Hill was noted for the elite and famous of this modest size city of 29,000. This was a part of town that I had little or no contact with. The small city of Wausau was built in the valley of the heavily worked Wisconsin River. Power and energy from the river dictated this unique cities exact location. Choice property on the hill east of town provided the best view of the heart of the city and was bought up by the early leaders, merchants, and entrepreneurs.

Though Frank lived in the south end of town near my parents home, he somehow had broken into the circle of people of means and was able to rub elbows with the "rich and the famous." Many of his friends from high school came from these homes. This is how "Mopey," learned of the fortune-teller and had decided to part with a few shekeles to get his palms read and expose his future. I informed him that I could not afford to have my fortune read, did not believe in it, but would like to go with him as a spectator and as a first class skeptic.

Now, tonight, it seemed only logical that I should be present on this auspicious occasion. The fact that we had had a few beers did not present a problem in finding the house of the fortune-teller on the far west side of Wausau. I had never been to a clairvoyant, a palmist, crystal gazer, or a seer of any kind. The only knowledge I had accumulated in these early years of my life was that they were all fakes and were individuals who specialized in fabricating delusions, hoaxes, and frauds. What do I know?

We approached a very small but neatly kept house that was truly out in the boondocks. The lot size was in proportion to the size of this petite white framed home. We had crossed the bridge to the other side of the Wisconsin River and were now in a part of town I had seldom frequented. The entire street was lined with these neat little cracker-box type homes.

I did not realize it, but "Mopey" had actually made an appointment for this special visit. Because of this, we arrived at the exact time set aside for his "reading". I was extremely nervous because I had no idea of what to expect or just what a "reading" entailed. None of this seemed to bother my friend. When he knocked on the door it was as if he had been there as often as the East Hill clientele. If he had, he never divulged these visits to his old buddy.

A diminutive sort of dumpy looking elderly woman opened the door. At first I looked right over her head until I realized her size. I had never been this close to such a small mature person. She was dressed very plain with extremely thick glasses. She worn some type of cloth around her hair that I have since recognized as a turban. "Vont you plaze cum in" she said, in a thick German accent. As I walked past her, for the first time in my young life I felt tall, even though I knew I was only 5'-8" in height.

This most interesting little person led us into what could be called her dining room and sat Frank down at the circular table that was the focal point of an overly cluttered small space. The interior of this house was very dark and it took some time for my eyes to adjust. I had been relegated to an over stuffed chair in a somewhat darkened corner of this mystical appearing room, a real misnomer because this space felt like it had everything in it but room. The only light was from a hanging ornate fixture with but a single light bulb functioning. This solitary source of light was a 60-watt bulb that sometimes flickered, like it was about to burn out.

I leaned forward so as not to miss a single word or part of the ceremony about to take place. I watched as she shuffled a deck of cards and then place numerous paste boards on the table. She moved them around and by straining my eyes I could see that these cards were not ordinary playing cards.

Each card had different symbols and pictures on them, something completely new to me. I noted that the individual cards had signs of being old, worn and over used. They were like nothing I had ever been exposed to. Before she uttered another word, she moved these cards into several stacks in two different rows. Each had been rearranged several times before it was determined they had finally come to rest.

The first time she spoke at the table was to ask my friend's birth date. I knew he told her the truth when he said, "March 15, 1922." Mopey was born on the Ides

Of March and this had been an in-house joke between us ever since we took Latin together and studied about Julius Caesar.

It was at this time I first acquired the nick name of "Octavianus", the 1st Roman Emperor (24B.C.-14A.D.). I had been assigned this part in a Latin class play, and my friend tried to perpetuate this title. It never stuck but the abbreviation of "Oc" follows me to this day.

I listened intently to what she told my best pal about himself. I could see how she interpreted the pictures on the cards as she moved them about. It appeared each card represented something, like marriage, happiness, hard work, death, travel, etc.

As she talked in this faltering English she seemed to understand "Mopey's" personality, his attributes and his faults. I instantly got the impression that she knew Frank as well as I did. I was becoming more interested and impressed by the minute.

When she finished her reading I was taken by surprise when she turned toward me and said: "Vud you too vant me to read yur fortun." Though she caught me with my guard down, I had already come to some conclusions. My first thought was "To hell with the money, I'd like to know what is in store for this young lad about to go to war."

With no hesitation I had my butt in a chair across from her. Frank disappeared into the dark corner to occupy the chair I had just left. He was still trying to analyze all the mystical information dropped on him by this dwarfish old but most interesting woman.

Once she started reading the cards placed in front of me, I noticed that she seemed almost transformed into an entirely different person. Again the only thing she asked of me was my birthday, June 11, 1921. Under the inadequate light, I could better see these unusual cards. They were not like anything I had ever seen, before or since. I did not know but guessed these cards originated in Germany and were obviously very old, tattered and had seen a lot of service.

The lettering on these cards was in German and I got a little lost at times because of this. The cards were moved about on the surface of this old wooden table in unusual patterns and in various sequences. I could not see any rhyme or reason for the sequences she moved these unique cards in. God, I was impressed.

She had me pegged to a tee when she started to expound on my past. I was especially bedazzled with her guessing that I would shortly be serving in the Air Force, a fact I had not disclosed to her.

"You vil fly in dis wor but you vil cum home safely. The cods tell me you vill be given much mettales." She also volunteered, "Sum day when you cum home, you vil take as my voman a light haired girl you know now." (All of these facts ultimately turned out to be true.) My "voman" would ultimately be Norma Schmidt and she was definitely a blonde. I did receive many metals and I did survive this terrible war.

The climax of this interesting evening came when she told me I could have several wishes. When I expressed the hope that my two younger brothers would return home safely and unharmed from the war, a smile, bigger than her face broke out. I can still see this little old soothsayer, in her dimly lit room, fall back in her chair and let out an unexpected laugh. The degree of emotion she displayed caught me by surprise, as numerous rolls of fat seemed to jump about on her body.

She finally calmed down enough to tell me not to worry about my younger brothers' Bob and Harv. She said they would not be compelled to face dangers and she was most emphatic as she told me not to worry over their stint in the service.

As it turned out, my brother Robert spent his entire enlistment with the U.S. Coast Guards at Great Lakes Naval Station near Chicago. My youngest brother Harvey, also a member of the U.S. Coast Guard, spent most of his time in a lighthouse off the east coast of Maine, shooting ducks and geese with a shot gun he had requested my father to ship to him.

Though I am still a skeptic concerning someone's ability to foretell the future, this night I bought the entire package and was happy I parted with some of my beer money. I left this simple little German lady with the feelings she might have had strong premonitions about the days that lay ahead. I might have been more dubious and doubtful had her comments been negative or demurring.

INTO THE WILD BLUE YONDER

As the summer wore on and fall was approaching, I realized for the first time that I had never been in an airplane. One day I took one of my father's trucks and drove a little over a mile to the Wausau Airport. It was located on the same part of town I lived in next to Lake Wausau, an extension of the Wisconsin River. I had visited the field on several occasion, especially for air shows, but never really hung around.

I met with Archie Towel, "Mr. Aviator" for this part of Wisconsin. He was a good friend of Will Rogers and Wiley Post. In fact, these famous people visited Archie shortly before they died in an accident on their way to Alaska. I explained to Archie that I had enlisted in the Army Air Force, had never been in a plane before, and had aspirations of becoming a fighter pilot once I finished my cadet training. Archie was most interested and said, "Get yourself a friend and I will take the two of you up for a flight for only $8.00."

21

The eight dollars wouldn't be too bad if I could talk good old George into paying his half. I told Archie I would be back tomorrow afternoon with this lucky friend, hoping I could talk Cormack, who previously had expressed his distaste for flying and whose only interest in transportation was trains, to come with me. I then asked Archie Towel, once we were air borne, if he could perform various stunts or maneuvers so that I could get the feeling of what it would be like to be a fighter pilot. He indicated in the affirmative. "I'll see the two of you tomorrow" was his parting remark.

I talked to George for nearly two hours about this wonderful new experience we could have together. He wasn't buying. All the time I worked George over, I was trying to think of someone else I could con into this adventure. My present victim seemed my best hope and I was unloading every conceivable argument onto his disinterested ears. George finally relented and said he would go with me, but only as a favor.

His biggest argument against such an adventure was, "I can get through life without risking my ass in a flying coffin." The next successful accomplishment I managed was to overcome his Scotch ancestry and get him to agree to pay his half of the required $8.00. All the time we walked to the airport I expected him to turn around and go home. I suspect the only thing I had going for this escapade was truly our friendship.

When we got to the airport, Mr. Towel had his all red Waco Biplane sitting on the apron in front of the hanger. He was ready for us. As he walked us around the airplane for his preflight inspection, he constantly explained the reasons for his every move. He stated that this plane was a Waco Model F-3 Biplane and it had a 220 hp continental engine. Underneath the left wing and on the tail was the plane's identification **NC 14082.** A long impressive ornate white stripe ran down each side of the fuselage.

Mr. Towel spent some additional time telling us about the theory of flight. None of this seemed to impress George. I didn't need any help in getting my enthusiasm to a high level but I do believe George was beginning to show signs of extreme hesitation. The most comforting thought I had at this point was we both had given our money to Mr. Towel.

I also was happy when we climbed on the lower wing of the Waco biplane and sat side by side in the front seat, George on the left and I occupied the right. We now were almost at the point of no return for my friend sitting besides me. Archie checked to see that we were properly strapped in before he jumped into the rear seat behind the controls.

The first thing I noticed was the difficulty in seeing out of the plane while being parked on the apron. The slope of the plane only permitted a view of the sky while looking out of the Plexiglas screen immediately in front of us. I could see off to the side, sitting in the right seat, but could barely observe the ground. The upper wing was about two feet forward of the lower wing, with numerous struts and bracing wires between the two. The plane had a tricycle landing gear, commonly referred to as a tail dragger.

One of the men who worked at the airport pushed the propeller around several times and Archie signaled that he was ready to start the engine. After the engine sputtered a few times it let out a sound like a small explosion. Then the engine seemed to cough a few times followed by puffs of black smoke. I could sense the uneasiness of my fellow passenger. This initial discord instantly turned into a loud steady roar.

None of these sounds did anything for George. I could see him fidgeting next to me as we then taxied to the far end of the runway. Before he pointed the plane into the prevailing wind and a take off, Archie made some additional checks of the controls and engine. It was most evident that an airplane is very awkward while on the ground. Dear old George saw fit to remind me of this. "This damn crate will end up being our coffin" was the last thing he said until we finally landed.

Without any further ado, the plane was clumsily turned to point down the runway. As this red plane lumbered down the concrete slab before us, gaining speed with each second, the hair on the back of my neck felt like it was standing on end. The plane responded to each crack or bump in the long slab before us as the engine labored a few feet in front of these two neophytes to flight.

Once air speed had been reached, everything changed. Suddenly the plane was airborne, the ride became smooth, and the engine started to reach a crescendo with an almost musical quality to it. It had the sound of raw power beating and pulling its way through the invisible air.

Our take off was exciting but I knew the best was still to come. Though the sky was almost free of clouds, and the temperature was in the high eighties, I felt almost free of this man made contraption, like I was floating on a cloud I could direct at my whim.

For ten minutes we flew around the vicinity of the airport, over Rib Mountain, over our homes on Weston Avenue on the south end, and then across the heart of our hometown. George looked but did not really see the things I shouted out to him.

As we flew over the center of Wausau, I pointed out to my disinterested friend the Courthouse, the Hotel Wausau, the infamous Curtis & Yale Woodworking Plant, the ball park, and some other obvious points of interest. George did not have the look on his face that he was about to throw up, but he did appear to have an ashen appearance about him. I found it impossible to understand how anyone could not be as excited as I found myself at this moment.

It was about this time I sort of twisted backward to signal our pilot that I thought it time to perform some stunts. The noise of the engine made it impossible to talk, but George seemed to know what my waving arm and twisting wrist meant. Despite the noise of the engine and the rushing air, I thought I heard George say, "Krueger, you son of a bitch." Archie pulled back on the controls so the plane could gain more altitude.

The first maneuver was a slow roll, causing a few of my cigarettes to start falling out of their pack in my shirt pocket, one at a time. It was at this instant that George put his face down into his lap and grabbed the padded edging on the cowling before us. His knuckles were white from the strain he put on them. It appeared that he was trying to actually crush this protective edging about level with our eyes. He did not change this awkward position, with both arms extended so as to grab the plane while covering his ears with his biceps, on the entire flight while the plane went through its crazy maneuvers.

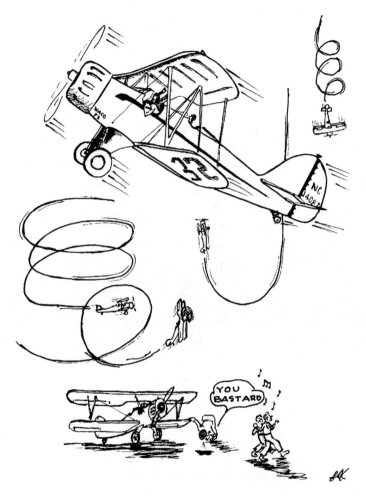

I now was truly sorry I was subjecting my friend to something that frightened him and made him uncomfortable. I put my hand on his slumped shoulder, trying to give him assurance that everything would be all right. I did not know how to bring it to a close since we had no real contact with the pilot sitting less than four-feet behind us in the rear cockpit. The reality was that I truly did not want this experience to come to a conclusion since I was enjoying every maneuver Archey put the plane through.

After several slow rolls, Archie put the plane into some quick snap rolls. This was followed by a loop and another slow roll at the top. Now the Waco went through another maneuver that I later learned would be called a chandelle. We had gained considerable altitude by now as we headed back toward the field. I could see Rib Mountain off the right side of the plane and Lake Wausau below us.

Archie, without any warning, put the plane into a three-turn spin to lose altitude in a hurry. To initiate this spin he slowly raised the nose of the plane as power was cut. Just as the plane stalled out, Archie kicked the right rudder and the nose seemed to just drop down with the earth the only view. We started to swirl in a clockwise direction, at an ever-increasing rate.

Now you could feel that power had been applied and the opposite rudder had been kicked, while the nose of the plane slowly was being pointed skyward. George was only conscience of the uninvited gravitational pulls or pushes on his body.

The engine labored against the change in direction, trying to defy gravity. The view of the earth was now replaced with blue sky as we leveled off. George was missing the best part. Just as I felt we might hit the ground and get splattered, Archie had pulled the plane out into level flight. Right ahead of us was the runway and the end of an experience I shall never forget.

Once we landed and the plane was parked, George finally raised his head and slowly removed his body from the plane. He rejected any assistance I felt obligated to offer. The only reaction I received, as we left the big red bird, was a two-word lecture from my friend. He said, "YOU BASTARD" and then refused to talk to me for nearly two weeks. We walked home in complete silence, I with a mixed feeling between guilt and exhilaration while George wondering how he got talked in leaving the earth.

Despite George's lack of enthusiasm for my maiden flight, I now knew that my enlistment in the Air Force was not a mistake. This new experience of flying left me with a feeling I shall never forget. The prospect that I too might be a pilot some day gave me the necessary motivation for challenges still awaiting me.

NORMA ANN SCHMIDT

The months between my enlistment and my actual leaving for training really dragged by. I started and quit nearly a dozen insignificant jobs during this period. Because of all of the baloney I had been fed at the Air Force Recruiting Office by the two "spit and polished" sergeants, I expected to receive my orders within a few weeks after signing those irrevocable papers that would make me an Air Force cadet.

Time can be both so very precious and also a burden one has to tolerate and suffer through.

It was not my intention to work up to the last moment. All I required was enough money so that I could hang out each night with the gang...I couldn't see the necessity of accumulating any wealth since I had no aspirations to move to "East Hill" or to build up an impressive estate. During these ensuing months my life also got very complicated. The reason being, for the first time in my life, I was dating or just meeting many different girls. I suppose this could be called "playing the field."

My contact with a myriad of girls and being a rank amateur at courting got me into numerous embarrassing situations. There was the problem of, just who I had promised to go with, who I had been with the night before, and, in some cases, just giving the right name to the right girl.

I, however, took none of these escapades seriously as I was only living for the moment. I knew that once I entered combat, there was the strong possibility that I would not be coming home. In reality, the odds turned out to be like the flip of a coin or 50-50 during the time I actually spent in actual combat.

It was about this time that I received a shock, which later turned into a pleasant surprise, from my little Irish Mom. Somehow, she had persuaded Norma Schmidt to come over to our house on a particular afternoon to look at some pictures of our family that had just been taken, primarily because the three Krueger brothers would eventually go into the service.

For seventeen years my Father had made justification for not getting a family picture taken by offering the excuse, "we don't want to spend the money on a picture of the family until we know it is complete." My Mother never bought this argument and now she insisted, with strong and valid reasons, to sit the entire family in front of a professional photographer's camera. The first and perhaps the last family portrait soon became history.

Shortly after this epic photograph was displayed in our living room, I came home one afternoon and received an unexpected surprise. Sitting on the couch with my Mother was Norma Ann Schmidt. My mother had invited her over to see this long over due picture of my parents with their four children, each staring in an awkward pose for the professional photographer's camera.

My Mother and Norma both worked at Wausau Memorial Hospital. Norma was a friend I had met at the University of Wisconsin while we were both freshmen. My good friend, Frank Morman or "Mopey' was the one who first introduced this special girl to me. We got to know each other during the early part of the second semester and we had become good friends.

We had several dates, and because of the pressures of school and the lack spending money, seemed to drift apart. Despite this, I truly had a great admiration for this interesting young woman from Rothschild, a small village just south of my home town and neighborhood. She had completed her freshman year at the University of Wisconsin and was now enrolled in nurses' training at Rochester, Minnesota. She now was home for summer and was about to return to school.

When I walked into our living room this one particular afternoon and saw her sitting with my mother, I almost flipped. This exact moment of seeing her was the first and only time in my life when my emotions and fireworks were on a collision course.

My mother diplomatically left us alone and we had the opportunity to talk once again, just like old times. I obviously have many things to thank my Mother for, but her decision to invite this special person to our home remains the most memorable feat I now can recall.

My mom had already told her about my enlistment in the Air Force and how we all expected my being shipped out very soon. At the end of summer vacation, only a week away, Norma would be returning to Rochester, Minnesota to continue her nurses training so we parted, not knowing when we would see one another again.

Seeing this person sparked a hidden feeling I did not know I processed. On our separation at the University of Wisconsin many months ago, I was unaware just how much of an impression she had made on me. I knew she was the type of person some day I would like to spend my life with, I knew she was pretty, I knew she was bubbling over with a unique personality, I knew she stood out by having her own individuality, I knew she had an interest in nature that equaled my love for the world I lived in, I knew she was very athletic, I knew she enjoyed humor but also serious contemplation, I knew she was sensitive and caring, I knew she was also . . . . "Hell, I also knew at the time I was not ready for any of the things this person exemplified nor was I worthy of her friendship."

It is important to make note of this chance meeting since Norma ultimately became my wife and now my partner for these past 58 years. We both look back on this chance meeting as the luckiest thing that could have ever happened to the two of us. No two people could ever have selected a chosen mate that would be more complimentary than what fate had done for us. History has proven that this relationship had to be something special.

Before we parted this day we both promised each other that we would write and keep in touch. The original spark I had felt after our first meeting was still there. It had not gone out, but only flickered. As it turned out, our entire courtship was to be conducted via the mails. I would not see her again until the 22nd of January of 1944, over eighteen months later, at which time I formally proposed and we became engaged.

During these 18 months we wrote weekly to one another, with occasional telephone conversations. I knew right after I received my Commission as an Officer in the U.S. Army Air Force that I would propose to her. The leave I would get prior to going into combat would provide me this opportunity. Her letters and support played an important part in my being able to endure my early flight training and cadet life.

Shortly after the first of the year, I received my long overdue orders to report for duty. On January 17, 1943, I was to report to a specific office building in Chicago at a prescribed time. This was the gist of this long overdue document. Though the letter was unimpressive, the news was welcomed. I wanted to get on with it.

I knew this next year would be filled with new experiences that I could never even imagine. I also knew I was not alone with these strong emotions over my country about to tangle butts with both Germany and far away Japan. Many of my friends were trying to decide whether to enlist through the regular draft or to volunteer for a specific branch of the service.

CHICAGO

When George Cormack learned of my trip to Chicago, he volunteered to come with me on the train. George had the same intensity of love for trains as his distaste for airplanes. Most of his free moments were spent watching freight- cars being jostled in the marshalling yard or to watch the Hiawatha Special pull into the Wausau Depot, usually within seconds of its scheduled arrival time. It seemed all of the Engineers and Conductors on the railroad knew George. I went with him once and was impressed by all of the railroad personnel he knew and his knowledge about trains.

On several occasions he got to ride up in the engine, to handle the throttle, and to inhale the smoke and soot that this form of transportation emitted. I equated my attraction for these monstrous trains as being comparable to George's disdain to park his butt in the seat of a flying machine.

George was a real asset to have along on my first trip to Chicago. He had been there many times with his parents and often on his own, just to ride those damn trains. The only time I had been on a train prior to this moment was over twenty years ago as an infant. My Mother took my Brother Bob and I back to Iowa to visit her family. I have no memories of this trip.

She had related to me many times how frightened she was and how she went off and left her purse in the depot. Hours later some honest man found her purse, tracked her down and returned it as the train was leaving Chicago. The integrity of this stranger speaks highly of the generation my story is really exemplifying. Today though, I truly welcomed this genuine and thoughtful offer of my good friend George.

In accordance with George's plan we arrived in the "big city" the day before my rendezvous with the Army Air Force. The first thing my older friend suggested was to find a place to spend the night and a place to drop off our simple but adequate luggage. I had what is known as a laundry case, something I used at school to ship dirty cloths home to my mother and she would return it with spotless clothes via this utilitarian case designed to travel through the mails.

On this trip and for the new adventure I was about to partake in, I felt it would be expendable, particularly once I became a cadet. I remembered I had paid a little over three dollars for it. "Hell, $3.00 was only nine hour's of work at Curtis & Yale last year."

I had previously mentioned that George was, by nationality, 100% Scotch and, at this moment in time, he decided to uphold the reputation of his heritage by selecting what I would call a flop-house. The entrance of this dingy "hotel" had an indiscernible amount of welcome. Its location was on some back street within hearing distance of the infamous Chicago El on the fringe of the loop.

The entrance to this abode was about as inviting as being told you had to spend the night sleeping with a pen of grunting pigs. There was a bumish looking fellow sprawled against the building with his legs out over the sidewalk. He was passed out. The culprit was evidenced by a mostly empty whisky bottle sliding from an old crumpled paper sack, both slipping from his fingers and now on the sidewalk.

The clerk behind the desk on the ground floor was a very thin and emaciated bearded man. He had on a dark green celluloid visor that was pulled down to the very edge of his eyebrows. He was bald except for a ring of matted black unkempt hair just above his ears. He wore an unbuttoned old vest with several stuffed pockets protruding on each side of this garment.

The shirt on his frail frame looked like it had never been washed and certainly not ironed. It took on the appearance of gray crepe paper. His obviously unwashed hands were holding a girly magazine. I also noted that the shirt he had on was not been buttoned correctly, something I'm sure was of no concern to him. Where you would have expected a necktie there was none. He sat on a stool but was slouched over a desk, surrounded by a metal cage that was nondescript in neither color nor material. As he offered us a set of keys, he grunted, "Ur room is 313 and the lift dun work. 313 ist down the hull on the tird floor." His voice sounded like the barker at a carnival. Between two of his mustard-colored fingers of his right hand was a cigarette with an inch of ash about to drop on his magazine. These same two fingers obviously had grasped uncountable handrolled cigarettes. It was obvious this weed in his hand accounted for the reverberation in his raspy voice. As we headed for the stairs, we noted the location of the worthless elevator. Looking through the grated door we could see that the elevator cab had been removed years ago.

The narrow stairway that was to be our passageway to the third floor was commensurate with everything we had noted about this hotel that my dear friend George had selected. The dimly lit stairwell exposed an unbelievable amount of dust, dirt, debris, and the body of a single sleeping man that smelled of drunkenness. The environment was enough to gag a maggot, if it could stomach living here. Each inhaled breath carried with it a pungent smell I had never experienced before, perhaps from dried up vomit.

As we rounded the stairs on the second floor we looked down the dark corridor that ran in only one direction. We noted a rat sitting on its hind haunches, wondering why we were invading its territory. With ever step up this narrow dirty stairs I got the feeling we were on a set of a horror movie. The cobwebs were there, only enough light to see what you really did not want to see, and the creaky noises only a worn out stairs has the capabilities to produce.

When we reached what we thought was the third floor, we opened the stair door to a very dark corridor, which was only slightly wider than the stairs. This narrow passageway was illuminated with three tiny light bulbs, spaced evenly down its entire length. A cat suddenly dashed down the stairs we had just left. Even George joined me in being startled. His only comment was the oft repeated "give it a chance."

We found our room by recognizing the number 313, which was barely distinguishable. The six-inch numerals on the wall beside the recessed door had been sloppily painted by some amateurish hand. The numbers seemed to be only a shade darker than the dirty soiled wallpaper. With some difficulty, George got the skeleton type key to unlock our door. It opened into the room, riding on hinges that needed oil to muffle the squeaks they made. We truly felt we were now entering the "inner sanctum."

The room we were to occupy for a single night had a nine or ten foot ceiling. The width of the room was about seven foot while the depth was only nine foot. The proportions of this cell like space was most uncomfortable and the ambience of our room took on the appearance of a large but cluttered closet.

A high narrow window indicated we had an outside room that looked down on to an alley. The window not only would not open, I don't believe it had been washed in years. This really was no big deal since the outside windowsill had over 1/4" of soot evenly deposited on its surface, along with evidence that pigeons constantly roosted and left their calling card there.

The light fixture was attached to the bottom of a large ceiling fan and only one of the three 60 watt light bulbs functioned. The original installation had not come close to locating this fixture in the center of the ceiling. A generous application of oil was something this antiquated receptacle seemed to be asking for as it creaked with each revolution. The mounting of the housing permitted the entire fixture to react as the five blades rotated. It was apparent how dirty the walls were by the several light areas indicating where pictures once hung.

A queen size metal bed, a broken down over stuffed chair with its inwards trying to escape, and a single wooden table were the only pieces of furniture in this den. After nearly ten minutes of silence, I finally blurted out, "Christ George, we can't stay here. This is the worst pigpen I have ever seen. The damn place is musty and it smells like vomit. Look at that thing they call a bed. The springs are broken down and how do we know if the bedding has ever been washed."

Dear old George, in his most proverbial philosophical manner reasoned, "Let's be practical "Oc" (my nickname for tons of years), we're going to be in this place one night and then it is only to sleep. Hell, with your eyes closed you can imagine this to be anywhere you want. Besides, I would rather spend money on some food when we go out to eat. The damn light is so poor in here you can't really see just how bad it is. If this place were lousy, we would be scratching like hell right now." With that last statement I immediately felt the urge to scratch.

I instantly surmised that I did not have the ability to talk George into going to more sanitary environments. We threw our bags on the lumpy bed, never truly expecting to see them again. We retraced our steps down the hall and into the stairwell. Somehow the trip down seemed longer than the walk up.

The clerk, still behind his unimpressive desk, only squinted at us as we hurried to get out on the street. He had been still absorbing the nude picture in the well tattered magazine before him, except now he had added a hacking cough to his demeanor. He looked at us as though we were "queer." This was a look I had yet to learn to interpret.

We spent the next several hours walking in and around the Loop. All of this, the sounds, the smells, and the sights were all new to me. I had never been to Chicago before. "Hell, I had really never been to any other big metropolitan city." I gawked at everything like I had a head of hair full of hay seeds.

Finally I figured out why George picked our residence for the night. It was not only to save money, but the noise of the elevated trains running constantly was like music to his ears. To me it was unnecessary and unmitigated noise. It would not only be the sounds of metal wheels bumping over wide cracks in the rails, it would also be the sounds of sirens, horns, squealing brakes, and yes, during the night, a gun being fired several times.

George now presented me with a real surprise. "I'm going to pop for dinner tonight. I know of a good place my dad once took me and I'll pay the whole tab." I instantly knew that this gesture was his way of telling me what our friendship meant and his way of sending me off to war. I mention this because of the experience I had during the year that we roomed together in the dorms on the campus in Madison. It must be related so as to have a complete picture of my complicated friend.

Just before the end of the semester when we were about to leave for summer vacation, George presented me with a bill for $4.12. I immediately exclaimed, "what in hell is this for?" I was informed that this was the difference of what each of us had spent on one another during the past two semesters. He had secretly kept a ledger in a small notebook with a running account of every cent each of us spent when we ate out, had dates, bought snacks, or popped for anything.

I was never aware that this type of accounting was being carried on. Five cents for a coke, six cents for two postage stamps, forty-five cents for a movie when one or the other was short on change . . . the list went on, with hundreds of separate items noted, each given credit to the person who paid. I had even gotten credit for giving him one shoelace at some time or other.

These amounts were added or deducted, and a running tally was kept on a daily basis. When I received this bill and was told why I owed the sum of $4.12, I was probably as mad at Cormack as he was of me the day he left the plane on our first airplane ride. The reality of this incident was that his calculations were most certainly accurate. I too got over this incident.

I was informed that tonight we would eat at the Bismark Hotel. We would have dinner in the Walnut Room. We were now in the heart of Chicago and I recognized the names of the Walnut room and the Bismark because I had previously listened on the radio and heard some big bands playing there. I distinctly remember hearing the announcer introduce Guy Lombardo and His Royal Canadian Band. My Father's Atwater Kent radio gave me no idea how lavish this place really was.

We arrived at the hotel early, probably before the normal dinner hour, and because George requested it, were given a table right next to a small dance floor and stage.

This had importance only because we were told that there would be a floorshow with entertainment that would take place approximately an hour later. George gave me the word that we would eat at a slow pace, thereby keeping this strategically located table.

Though I felt fairly dressed up, it became obvious as we entered the dining room nothing could have been further from the truth. I had on my clean cream colored shirt with its wide collar, but no necktie. My sport coat, the only one I owned, was now showing signs I was growing out of it. My pants were made of a material that never seemed to hold a press so there was a sort of baggy look to them. The only thing I had on that was almost new happened to be my white saddle shoes. I know I had socks on but do not remember just what they went with.

George, with his pudgy build, had on a suit coat that went with the relatively plain tie he was wearing. The major problem was that it didn't make a great deal of difference what he wore because his general build, his coke bottle glasses, his load slapping shoes all detracted from his garb. Despite all this, George had a certain arrogance about him that demanded both attention and respect. A head waiter escorted this motley pair with all of the dignity usually reserved for some elite couple.

I do not remember what we ordered this particular night from the menu, but I do know I was unbelievably impressed with everything that was going on. I had on the only sport coat whose texture was defined by wrinkles. Even when I unbuttoned it, only half of the creases disappeared. Frankly, at this moment, I felt like a genuine slob in this elegant room with all of its finery. George's appearance was about as tasteful as mine. It did not take a high I.Q. to know why many were now staring at us.

Our waiter was dressed in black tails with the usual neat folded white towel draped over his left forearm. God— —I was grateful that George was going to pay for all of this. I have to confess though, the thought entered my mind that at an appropriate time my friend George would slip away and leave me with the tab, just to make up for his flight in a Waco F3. I then wondered if telling them I was actually in the Army Air Force and they owned me body and soul and they could not make me wash dishes or what ever.

We were given huge menus covered in real leather. Each contained over a dozen glossy pages with entrees that could have been written in Greek or some other language I was equally illiterate with. When I noticed the prices on the menu, for all of the main courses I could hardly read, let alone understand, I almost went into cardiac arrest. I had been brought up on simple foods, nourishment that was noted for sticking to your ribs. I was unaccustomed to see foods tossed into the air and mixed before me, or to see a dish being carried that was aflame.

Whatever food we ordered I remember how nicely it was placed upon the plate and how the waiter would dish us up from behind. Eating helped me forget that others might be watching us. I no longer felt ill at ease. I had an assortment of silverware all around me that only took up space as far as I was concerned. For the next hour we joked, laughed, and reminisced about the year at the University. If people were watching us, suddenly it did not seem to matter.

I guess the waiter asked us several dozen times if there would be anything else. Finally, after the meal and to hang onto our table, we each ordered a drink. I had a bottle of Ballentine Ale while George ordered, with no surprise to me, a Scotch and soda. I had noticed the price for a bottle of ale as costing $6.50. I was disappointed when I discovered it was the same size as we would buy at some tavern on State Street in Madison for only 85 cents.

The other guests in this huge dining room, in all of their finery, soon accepted George and me as something that just happened. I know they wondered how we were given admittance in this most fashionable dining room and to be seated where all in this decorated space would be looking. No one could turn their heads toward the small dance floor where the entertainment was about to start without observing us.

Our table was so close to the dance floor and where the entertainment took place, I could see how a magician did several of his slight of hand tricks. This illusionist was then followed by four girls, who did some acrobatic acts. These gals wore costumes that exposed more of themselves than I could possibly believe would be allowed by law.

What a moment in the sun for this simple lad from the "Boonies!" Their garb, or rather the lack of it, had nothing really to do with their talents. They spun around, bent their bodies till I thought they would break, did splits, cartwheels, walked on their hands, and other acts I have since forgotten about. They were followed by a well dressed man who played a grand piano and sang into a mike.

After dinner and the entertainment, George received the check on a small silver tray. I do not know what the freight was on this exquisite meal and evening of entertainment. I saw George part with what looked like a ton of money. It had a hard time leaving his hand, but the waiter's presence, his statuesque posture, and the stoic expression on his face gave George the message for the moment of truth. Whatever amount he gave the waiter, he had a few bucks change coming.

We left the Walnut Room and as we walked into the lobby of the hotel, George broke the silence by shouting, "That dirty sucker gypped me." I waited at the door as dear old George tracked down the waiter and explained his consternation. I could not hear the conversation that took place, but I could see them pass money back and forth for nearly five minutes.

When George returned and we got out onto the street, I could see that he was still trying to figure out the bill. I could hear him mumbling to himself how much he spent, how much change the waiter gave him, and then he recounted the monies remaining in his wallet.

Again he yellowed out, "That G.D. bastard gypped me again, this time for even more." I persuaded George that he could not afford to go back, that this waiter was an expert. I do not know, to this day, whether George ever got over this experience with a very talented waiter in Big "C."

We walked the streets for several hours, talking, knowing that we would not see each other for a long time, or perhaps ever. Sometime after midnight we found the dingy hotel and climbed the three flights of stairs to our room. The puny amount of light escaping from the hall into our room barely revealed that our luggage was still where we had left it. I mentioned to George that we were just witnessing a miracle. My friend's sense of humor was still bruised from the Walnut Room and our waiter.

A small amount of light crept in through the cracks around the closed transom. The large ceiling fan, in its asymmetrical location, was turned on. It was barely visible in the darkness above the puny light source. It started to groan and was barely able to move the stale musty air about. The noise it made, as it labored through each revolution, sounded appropriate for the ambience of our abode this night. The mounting on the ceiling permitted the fan to develop a secondary movement that would have made you nauseous if the lights had been brighter.

Though the dirty glass in the huge double hung window made it difficult for the lights of the city to enter our room, it did permit flashing colors to be emitted from nearby neon signs. This window was exceptional large for such a dinky room, but it did nothing all night to hinder the unfamiliar sounds coming off the streets below. I lived my whole life in Wausau and had only heard a police or fire truck siren twice.

George and I shared the same lumpy mattress. The moment we laid down we got into a laughing jag. The bed squeaked with the slightest movement, the fan grunted as it labored, we could hear individuals in at least six or seven rooms down the hall, sounds seemed to penetrate the ceiling from the room above us, and sirens entertained us above all of the sounds of the busy traffic as it found its way down our alley and up to our dirty window.

Twice George called for my silence as a nearby elevated train roared by, vibrating everything in the old red brick building. We could not help comparing the moment in this darkened smelly room with the luxury we were surrounded by only a few hours ago. This atmosphere triggered a whole series of memories that would keep us talking throughout the entire night. One could not help feeling the importance of a friendship and the moments, such as we experienced tonight. Over the years we both recalled this evening and all of the events that took place in Chicago.

I do not know if George was cognizant of the importance of his jester to come with me to Chicago. Sometimes these moments are difficult to fully appreciate until one looks back and reminisces. Many times during my days in combat, I would think of those periods of time, just like the one we spent in Chicago. Though George was four years older than me, the differential in our ages never detracted from the many experiences we had together. I am so appreciative our paths crossed and we took the time to enjoy each others friendship.

CHAPTER 2

The orders I had received from the Air Force to report for duty in Chicago were very abrupt with only a date, a time, and a street address. Other than the official letterhead, it could have been just a note from your Mother. I was scheduled to check into a second floor hall in a building on LaSalle Street at 9 AM on January 17, 1943.

Since George and I had spent the entire night before just talking and laughing, this morning we ate a simple breakfast and walked mostly in silence to my mandatory appointment. I did not know too much about the Air Force, but the one fact I was told, once you sign those enlistment papers it was now essential you follow all future orders or be subjected to court martial and other goodies. I had no intention of tangling butts with the military. It was essential to be present and on time.

When we arrived at this mundane looking red brick building, it was obvious that I had not been the only civilian who had enlisted. Numerous fellows, about my age, were approaching this same address from all directions. You could sense the excitement of each individual. Each eyeballed the others, and perhaps, in their own minds, tried to mentally figure how they compared or stacked up with the rest of the pack. This group had come from several mid-west states and it was obvious that we had come from many different backgrounds.

George immediately realized that from this moment on, I would be completely occupied and it was time to say our goodbyes. A strong handshake and an awkward bear hug let each of us knew how the other felt. We avoided staring into the other's eyes because we knew there would have been tears escaping. Sentimentality, for whatever reason, was not to be displayed, certainly out on a street in Chicago. I was going to apologize one more time for the flight I suckered George on, but then I knew words could only spoil this parting.

George, you'll never know what our friendship meant to me. I watched as his billowing profile shuffled and then rounded the corner and disappeared. I took out my handkerchief and did a thorough job of wiping away what I am now unashamed to call tears. I pretended to be blowing my nose. It was not hard to witness most other guys saying goodbye to their parents and be afraid to honestly express the feeling they had at this moment. Machismo was to be the key word on this occasion.

A few minutes before nine, a Sergeant with a chest full of ribbons and an abundance of stripes on his sleeve, grunted out a command that brought everyone into a large hall on the second floor. It appeared that there were over 300 new recruits in this large room, with about a dozen enlisted Army men, barking orders. The huge room was bare of any chairs and a small stage could be noticed at the far end.

My first impression was that our leaders did not appear to be any better organized than this group of neophytes. It took nearly an hour to get some order to this gathering and some specific instructions could be passed on. It also was obvious that I would have to learn how to interpret grunts and groans that seemed to be the accepted way to relay orders. Periodically the whispering and commotion created some back ground noise. Suddenly a whistle would be blown, followed by one of the Sergeants yelling "Shut up."

Most of the men handling us sounded like they were from the south and talked in a slow drawl. They barked orders that sounded as though they had a mouth full of marbles. Nothing would be said in normal tones but every order had a crescendo nature to it. After a few moments, all the pronouncements, commands, decrees, instructions, and orders were bouncing off the four walls and seemed to come from every direction.

In all this confusion I started to look around at my fellow inductees. I was astonished at what I saw. We came in all shapes, heights, and dress. There was also a disparity in our apparent ages. I did not realize at the time that there were no obvious ethnic individuals among this motley looking group. Many years later would I be made aware of the fact that there were no African Americans in all of my phases of training in the U.S. Army Air Force. What a waste of potential talent.

Everyone around me kept whispering, "what did they say?" I was not the only one confused. Eventually, they got the entire group to form several lines parallel with the longest wall of this banquet type room. As each of our names was shouted out, we had to sound off and step forward. Only one individual, it turned out, had not reported in.

NASHVILLE

At this time we were told that we would board a troop train at 1600 hours, and our destination was to be Nashville, Tennessee. From this moment on I had to change my thinking about the clock and how you interpreted time. We will use the 24-hour clock exclusively. We were also informed, from this day forward, anytime we receive a direct command we were to pop to attention and had the choice of only three replies: "Yes Sir", "No Sir", and "No Excuse Sir". This didn't sound too difficult until I later learned these answers would not cover every situation. "La de da for me."

That, however, was the problem of the lowly cadet. We were repeatedly informed that a cadet was lower than a "Yard Bird", whatever that meant. I had known the military was highly regimented, but I never dreamt that here in Chicago, only minutes away from being a civilian, I now was a tiny part of a huge machine. It appeared also that I was not expected to think for myself or to object to any situation confronted with. I was being exposed to everything basically against my very nature.

This motley group was jostled and herded around for several hours and they threw out instructions that few understood or retained. Hell, I didn't even know when I was doing something to their liking. A state of real confusion seemed to be the primary theme on this, my first day in the service. Box lunches were distributed at 1300 hours, and by 1400 hours we were lined up on the street. A group of curious pedestrians stopped only long enough to try and understand what this incongruous mass of humanity was doing. Somehow I had wished the German or Japanese authorities would never hear of this moment.

This unorganized looking group was then marched off to Union Station where we were to board our train for Nashville, Tennessee. We made an unusual sight as we dominated the street in this part of Chicago. This heterogeneous group, supposedly marching, looked like a band of derelict lost souls, being herded down wide Chicago streets. The South side of Chicago probably had seen better cattle drives heading for the stock yards.

We were being led by a handful of the military that now had literally given up on an orderly, precision, and disciplined unit of men who were to be moved from one place to another. I had been in R.O.T.C. at the University of Wisconsin and had been taught how to march. What we were doing was unorganized route step. We were the men who were going to fight for freedom and bring victory back to our country.

I had never really thought about what constituted a troop train other than surmise that it was an ordinary passenger train that carried troops. I could not have been more in error. I now know a better definition for this monster.

A troop train is a collection of assorted, over the hill passenger cars that are connected by worn out couplings, and are pulled by an engine that has seen better days. It is also necessary that each car have several wheels with flat spots on their rims, and not much time would be spent in getting them clean. This configuration would be pulled or dragged over iron rails that were twisting and had voids ever fifty feet or so.

I discovered once the train begin to run, it is relegated to roll on secondary tracks, that every freight or first class passengers train will have priority, and the sidings, where the train will spend most of its time, will be located in rundown neighborhoods. It is also essential to not include a dining car nor any Pullman sleeping facilities as a part of this ensemble. They also discovered that it simplified matters if no provision for feeding the passengers was provided. Finally, most of our trip on these secondary rail lines was through the armpits of America.

The only individual I knew on this whole train was another guy from my hometown of Wausau. Greg Turner and I hardly knew each other before this trip, but the fact that we were from the same town, helped each of us to not feel completely lost. I do not know but I would guess that this is Greg's first time away from home. He stayed next to me like he believed I knew what in hell was going on. By chance, we were assigned to the same passenger car. I'm sure we were both happy over this one small favor. My guess was that he had more hayseeds in his hair than I did.

We had just pulled out of the station, not at 1600 hours, but at 1900 hours, when several different groups of recruits started crap games, poker games, and black jack games. I had not previously been exposed to these games of chance or to any form of gambling, so I found it interesting to be an observer.

The crap game was conducted on the floor at the rear of our car, with a large blanket as the arena for the dice to be thrown and observed. I was hearing a whole new language being spoken, "snake eyes, little fever, box cars, treys, come on baby, etc."

The dices were thrown with vigor, and usually with a series of encouraging words, such as "come on little Joe", or "come on little baby." Others were involved with side bets as one and five-dollar bills were thrown about as if they had no real value. "To let it "ride" meant that all of your winnings were left to initiate the next bet. Certain individuals seemed to roll the dice, while others were just content to place side bets. On the fringe of this active group were the on lookers.

Each of the various card or dice games had one thing in common. The object was to see if you could take possession of the other guy's money. This I learned tonight was called gambling, a favorite pastime in the service. I would later get involved by paying poker. This however, did not occur for over a year and not until I was overseas and in combat.

Greg Turner and I were trying to get some sleep on this swaying passenger car when we were awakened by some loud commotion. Both of us were curious so we walked up front of the car where the noise originated and where some twenty guys had gathered. What we found out was that a poker game had taken place and now a first class fight was taking over between two fellows already in military uniforms.

We saw one individual, a private in the Regular Army, astride another service man. He was pounding him in the face repeatedly. Blood was splattered all over the place. Both of us were surprised that no one made any effort to stop this fight. In fact, many egged it on. The fellow pinned down to the floor was a bloody mess.

When I asked what the heck was going on I was informed that the bloodied guy had been caught cheating at cards. This was the usual justice metered out for this type of sin. My recruiting officers, back in July, had never told me about any of today's happenings when I had asked dozens of questions about the life of a cadet. I found out later that the two individuals involved in this confrontation were in the Regular Army and had been granted permission to apply for cadet training.

Late, on the evening of the next day, our train lumbered into Nashville's Main Depot. We all disembarked from this antiquated monster like each couldn't wait to get this trip behind them.

We were quickly herded into a dozen or so large buses for the trip to our new base. The trip, in a slight drizzle, was a welcome change to the rambling dirty train we had spent nearly twenty-four hours on without food. Each of us now had a look on our faces that was commensurate with our attire. Fortunately there was no welcoming committee to greet us.

I did not know it then, but this base at Nashville was typical of the many that were hurriedly constructed during the rapid buildup for all branches of service during these early days of the war. Though the barracks were not very old, the once white structures were now a dirty grimy gray color.

Coal was used as the source of heat and soot was everywhere. Filthy black smoke, emitted from the hundreds of pot bellied stoves, rose a few feet above the barrack roofs and just seemed to hang there. It took nearly two weeks for the sun to even find this place.

Row upon row of barracks had been built around a large drill field. On one of its perimeters, a huge flagpole had been erected. From the top of this impressive pole flew the largest American flag I had ever seen. This was to be the paramount site for a disproportionate amount of our time. As the days wore on, this parade ground became a nemesis to every one who stepped off the buses this rainy day.

The primary function of this base was to expose each cadet to basic military courses which included drilling, marching, physical exercise, marksmanship, military procedure, first aid, sanitation, care of clothing and equipment, chemical warfare, etc. There was not one thing that came close to flying an airplane. In fact, I truly felt like I had committed a crime and this was some sort of place to make restitution.

The following morning we were informed, due to a snafu, it would be five or six days before uniforms would arrive. This meant that each squad of cadets would drill, march, and function in clothing of every description. The uniform of the day would range from suits, sport jackets, overalls, wool shirts, sweaters, and even a few "zoot" suits.

What a sight to behold. If the Germans or Japanese could witness this they would split their gut laughing. In fact, if the American civilians could have witnessed this debacle, they would not have been able to sleep at night.

The weather and humidity were such that we needed to wear all of the clothes we managed to arrive with, plus anything we could talk a buddy out of. I had a single pair of brown and white saddle shoes when I arrived. They had been polished and were recognizable as saddle shoes. After five days of marching over the gravel covered parade grounds, these shoes took on the appearance of an entirely different style. They appeared to be a single color and the left sole made a flapping noise as I placed it on the ground with alternating strides. "Hell, they were falling apart."

I lived all of my life in northern Wisconsin, a place noted for its cold temperatures and abundance of snow during the winter months. Here in dear old Nashville, I felt like I was freezing everything I owned. Probably the main contributing factor was the high humidity we experienced each day. Intense fog greeted us each morning, followed by a shower of sufficient duration to get all exposed surfaces wet. Mud seemed to belong to this dreary setting.

Needless to say, there was an adequate amount of this soot saturated mud to truly complete the picture. Even the sun did not want any part of this forsaken place. We all obviously had plenty of reasons to bitch and gripe. There also was a sense that the permanent personnel on this Base were enjoying the constant misery being displayed by their charge and the groans uttered constantly.

One of the things that annoyed me personally was the knowledge that I should be able to withstand any temperature Nashville could throw my way, especially coming from Wisconsin. Instead I witnessed most of the locals walking around in shirt sleeves and apparently not minding the temperature nor the humidity. I suppose mental attitude might have had something to do with it.

WE'RE IN THE ARMY NOW

The day after we arrived, about mid afternoon, the barracks I now called home was informed we would be marched to the barber shop. Each company of men was scheduled, and then marched in a group to a long narrow building that held ten barber chairs. They ran us through so rapidly that no effort was made to keep the floor clear of fallen hair. The barbers were ankle deep in hair and, after two or three minutes with each victim, they would shout, "Next."

This whole procedure didn't really affect me too much since I had a crew or butch style hair cut nearly all of my life. The fellows with the big mops, the wavy hair, or cherished curls were the ones I enjoyed watching as they were literally scalped. The ten clippers raced across each scalp, removing any hair that got in their way.

For the very first time I witnessed men with tears sliding down their checks. They wouldn't part with these same beads of moisture for their parents, but they could not conceal these tears when their tresses or curls fell to the floor. As they were forced out of the barber chair nearly every cadet would reach up to the tops of their heads and feel, in disbelief, the short stubble that they would now have to get used to.

Most of us could see the humor in all this and laughed at the transformation of each our heads. However, others took on the look of complete humility and could see nothing amusing in being de-haired. The only thing uniform about this entire motley group now was the top of our heads.

Fortunately, because of the weather, these same bald scalps were covered by an unlimited assortment of headgear. There were stocking caps, tams, felt hats, baseball caps, and one fellow pulled the open end of a wool sock down to his ears with the remainder bouncing off his cheek.

By now the moans, groans, gripes, and complaints were getting to be humorous. All at once it hit me like a ton of bricks. I wasn't in the Air Force. I was in the dame Army. All of the personnel that had been barking orders, giving us instruction, fed us food, or ordering us around were Army, the U.S. Army. It did not occur to me until this moment, that the U.S. Air Force was a separate branch but under the jurisdiction of the Army.

The next day found us being marched off to yet another building, with lines of recruits waiting to get in. This was designated as the day we were given shots to immunize us from scarlet fever, measles, yellow fever, jungle rot, and you name it. Once again we approached our destiny in a long winding line that ended in front of a guy who looked like he might have flunked out of med school.

I never was aware that grown men would be frightened of simple shots in the arm. As they reached a position where they could witness the individuals ahead of them receive shots in both arms, you could hear new assorted groans and moans being emitted. Several fellows actually passed out. This, however, did not let them escape the same fate each was required to be confronted with, even if the orderly had to bend down to administer the shot.

Nearly a week had passed when we finally received the word uniforms had arrived. Once again we would be marched to the warehouse section of the base and, in single file, would enter the bowels of this huge building. A counter that appeared to be a block long was staffed by dozens of workers, part of the permanent personnel. Behind them were bins and shelves containing clothing that had been made out of a single colored material. Every item of clothing being issued would be in olive drab, affectionately referred to as O.D. These men were to outfit us in winter uniforms.

The term "outfit us" was really a misnomer, since each item of clothing was literally thrown at each moving body with little or no regard for size. They would take a quick glance at the next cadet in line and dump an armful of shorts, tee shirts, socks and ties on our outstretched arms. These would be dumped or pushed into a large green duffel bag with our name and serial number quickly stenciled on it. My number on this duffle bag was 16056910, the same number on my dog tags now dangling around my neck.

We were give two brass metal dog tags that contained our name, our serial number, a P in one corner for Protestant, a C for Catholic, a J for Jewish, and our blood type in another corner. We were informed to never take these important tags off our bodies since they would be needed to identify us should we get killed. One would remain with the body and the other nailed to a cross somewhere.

Everything issued was in an olive drab color, affectionately referred to as O.D. color. This type of camouflage made a lot of sense for the Infantry or perhaps the Marine Corp, but why did a hot pilot, 25,000 feet over Germany or perhaps Japan, need this type of protection? With similar hair cuts, the same color of clothing, all that would distinguish us from one another now was our height.

The O.D. shirts and pants were next, followed by an overcoat, a jacket, shoes, and several different types of caps. The only article of clothing that was issued, in which care was taken as to proper fit, was the two pair of shoes we would be given. One pair of dress oxfords was issued and the other was a pair of G.I. Boots. It would be necessary to actually try them on and have some impute as to the precise fit. The G.I. is an abbreviation that stood for Government Issue, a term that we would use for everything we ever received from the Air Force or any branch of the service.

Once we returned to the barracks to try on our "new uniforms", we were told we had the rest of the day to get our clothes "organized" and then line up at attention outside. As we sorted through the mountain of clothes they threw at us, it immediately became apparent that most garments were either too large or too small. Nothing seemed to fit.

Since each barracks contained individuals of all shapes and sizes, many exchanges took place to rectify a lot of the miss-matched items. I remained with only a few problems that I could not overcome.

One of the suggestions my Dad passed on to me, prior to leaving home, was to buy a simple sewing kit and take it with me. He had remembered, from his own experience in World War I. I guess the Army doesn't change much. My kit had a small scissors, several needles of various sizes, a thimble, and spools of several different colors of thread. Olive drab thread was conspicuous by its absence in my little kit. I had been brought up to be both independent and capable, now the moment of truth presented itself.

I cut off 4 inches from each sleeve of my heavy wool overcoat and had to raise the hem an equal amount. I had several pairs of pants that fortunately fit around the waist, but required shortening the length of each leg. I could also handle this, as well as sew on most of the insignia required. The only item I did not tackle was adjusting the sleeves on my dress jacket. This would require the use of an iron and considerably more skill than I possessed. Most other cadet had to use the base tailors, which took weeks to catch up to this needless mess.

The several thousand young men from all sections of the country were broken down into small groups. Each barracks would be called a flight and we would stick together for all drills, functions, or whatever the Army could conjure up. We marched everywhere, and day-by-day this grumbling mass of humanity was beginning to show signs of order.

I had been appointed a Flight Leader, whose sole responsibility was to lead our barracks from one place to another. The fact that I had previously been in R.O.T.C. at college was my primary qualification for a duty I could have lived without. It must have been apparent I knew most of the orders for marching and it would not have been difficult to pick you out of the shuffling group when we went anywhere. Being winter, we were forced to get up in the dark and we were marched back to our barracks in the dark. During the day the sun seldom found Nashville, Tennessee.

DUTIES

Every day certain cadets were given special duties. These duties would take us away from the next day's routine. The duties were described to us as being educational and essential if we were to become officers. In reality, all this turned out to be a crock. My first assignment was 24 hours on K.M. Duty. In the regular Army, similar "educational" duties were referred to as K.P., or Kitchen Police.

Here in Nashville, assignment to KM meant you did all of the dirty works for the mess hall cooks. Someone decided that the Air Force would refer to the identical duty as K. M., which stood for Kitchen Management Duty. All this implied that anyone who was unlucky enough to find his name on the K.M. Roster would have the opportunity to be trained in how to run a mess hall. There wasn't a sole in our motley group who did not know this was rot and the unlucky bastards would spend the next 24 hours doing a crap detail.

Our duty required us to peel mountains of raw potatoes, bushels of onions, similar amounts of carrots, wipe off hundreds of tables, sweep an acre of wood floors and then follow up with a mop, wash stacks of dishes, and scour hundreds of pot and pans. Each of these jobs began, not by being asked, but by a fat mess sergeant screaming at you to move your butt over to a pile of "whatever."

We were required to be on duty for 24 long and seemingly endless hours. The worst part of the whole detail was observing how the food was prepared and the lack of any real enthusiasm on the part of the cooks. One of the most common remarks I was able to overhear was the oft repeated phrase, "what they don't know won't hurt them."

I survived my 24 hours better than most because there was not one assignment requested of me that I hadn't done for my Mother. Only the magnitude was different. I worked with other cadets who did not know how to peel a potato or a carrot. Some had never seen an onion or who hardly knew which end of the mop to hold. By carrying a stack of dishes was probably the greatest weight they had ever lifted. Their 24 shift is a memory they will never forget.

A few days later I had the misfortune of drawing another crap detail. This would be titled Guard Duty, another 24-hour detail. We had to report in to the Provost Marshall Building by 900 hours and we would be on duty until relieved the next day at the same hour. We had heard many rumors about this obligation about to be bestowed on a large group of these new cadets.

There were ten of us on this assignment and each was given pamphlets containing the Articles of War, the Manual of Arms, and The Duties and Obligations of a Soldier on Guard Duty. During the next three hours we were told to memorize all three.

This literature was about as interesting reading as an unabridged dictionary or the Nashville telephone directory. In the process of trying to master all of this dull information, you did not have to be an Einstein to realize it was an impossibility to pack this malarkey in your head.

We were informed that the main part of our job was to police a prescribed area at night and to challenge anyone who was moving about without permission, after taps had sounded. We had two major pieces of equipment, namely a flashlight and a short billy club, our primary weapon. Another duty at night was to check the various potbelly stoves in each barracks in our patrol area to see that they were safely being used.

During the afternoon several of our instructors tried to give us some idea of what to do and what to expect. I now have suspicion of what their true motives were. We were warned that it was not uncommon, after midnight, to expect personnel to climb over the fence on the perimeter of the base and to sneak back to their quarters. Our job was to challenge them and to make arrests.

We were told, "Most of these men would be blacks. These guys are built like professional wrestlers and they carry sharp razors. About all your flashlights will pick up in the dark are two white eyes and a row of flashing white teeth."

Yea, you guessed right. They scared the living hell out of me. I'm not sure about the other cadets suffering this same duty with me, but yours truly did not look forward to the sun going down. My vivid imagination began to go berserk and conjured up every conceivable situation I might find myself in.

Having spent my whole life in Northern Wisconsin, the only Negroes I had ever seen would be the several times a year when the circus or carnival came to town or when the porter might get off from the Hiawatha Train before it pulled out of the depot. I did not know of a single Negro family residing in my home town. Despite this, I had been brought up to judge individuals only after I had gotten to know them. I honestly never tried to prejudge anyone and never considered myself to be a racist. Today however, I let someone plant stupid racial remarks into my head and made their day.

This night I completely lost my sense of values and logic. One of my friends on duty, who also had a blank expression on his face, asked what did I expect? With little or no thought, I blurted out, "In the morning, when they find us, we will be all hacked up in little pieces, spread over half an acre. No one will be able to sort out the right body parts to even bury us." I'm sure my sense of humor did little to ease or eliminate his similar fears.

Before I was to start out on my night rounds, I had made up my plan of attack. I would spend the entire evening of my watch checking potbelly stoves in the numerous barracks in my sector. I intended to be as thorough as possible so as to chew into the hours of darkness. I would make myself as scarce as hen's teeth. I rationalized the logic of this decision by believing the saving of many lives from the danger of a potential fire was more important than catching whoever extended his pass limitations.

My simple motto, for these critical hours of this long night was, "make yourself scarce." I do not look upon myself as a coward, but rather a person who has never been considered being stupid. I also look back now, these many years, and know just how wrong I was. I let myself believe the stereotype picture these instructors had painted, of a group of people I knew very little about.

Another duty that each of us performed, was an activity called Policing the Area.

It sounded like something with real merit. What this instructional course involved was to have hundreds of cadets lined up on the drill field with large metal buckets. Our job was to walk and crawl across the parade grounds and pick up all loose stones and pebbles that happened to be on the surface.

We all were aware of the difficulty of marching over these small objects. These were placed in the containers we dragged along and then deposited in a large dump truck that moved along the line. Tons of stones were cleared from our drill field, making a vast improvement. This seemed to be the first constructive thing we had been engaged in.

The irony of this singularly seemingly worthwhile project was most disheartening. As we lay in bed listening to taps being broadcast to end the long day, the loaded truck of pebbles and stones would be taken back to the parade ground. Here they would

raise the bed and redeposit its entire load evenly over the marching surface. The one and only positive thing I thought about this damn place was now shattered.

At the moment of maximum despair, we all became hopeful when the news raced through the ranks that we would be shipping out tomorrow for San Antonio, Texas or possibly to Santa Ana, California. These two destinations were considered Pre-flight School, the next phase of our training.

The one thing that mattered was just to get the hell out of Nashville. We finally were going to leave this place of gloom and doom and head off to another training facility that at least had the name flight in its description.

AAH HAA — SAN ANN TONE

Exactly one month, to the day, on Feb. 17, 1943, I found out that I would be in the group heading for Texas. I knew California would be a greater distance from Nashville, but at this moment just moving away from Tennessee was paramount. We boarded a bus, supposedly to drive us to San Antonio, Texas. The jubilation on the bus, as we left the confinement of the Army Base, was unfortunately short lived.

Two hours into our bus ride, almost simultaneously, we all became aware that this stupid bus was going back to the same depot we had arrived at twenty-nine days before. This would be another proverbial troop train whose only task would be to take us to Pre-Flight School at the SAACC (San Antonio Aviation Cadet Center). On the surface, this sounded like a simple operation.

The train did not pull out of Nashville until late at night. We were compelled to sit on this stationary train for over eight hours, and then we slowly moved out without any fanfare. Each of its passengers expressed various degrees of glee. All were glad to leave the base that had left us with mostly negative memories.

Few would forget the constant rains and drizzles, the mud everywhere, soot covered buildings, K.M. and guard duty. Also, the constant drilling on the parade field and the hurry up and wait routine we had for a constant diet. None knew exactly what lay ahead, but each was sure that our fortunes had only one direction to go. Many times I had cussed at the two men who recruited me so many months ago.

Our train jostled around for several hours: switching, reversing, stopping, creeping, and making the couplings' clank. We didn't have the slightest idea what the engineer was doing with this antiquated monster. The only fact that became clear, as the sun rose in the early hours of the morning, was that we were parked on the siding in the exact spot where we boarded the train, twelve hours before.

It was shortly before noon when we started to move in a westerly direction, a route that would ultimately take us out of Tennessee. Another fact, I soon learned about troop trains, was: each time you tried to walk down the aisle, the train would lurch forward and throw you into a seat.

It was at times like this that I wondered how my dear friend George had fallen in love with this means of transportation. Then I thought back about some of my dear friend's ideas and I answered my own question by simply thinking "why not?" George had somehow become synonymous with the American Rail System.

Once again, no provision had been made to feed this group of cadets being moved across the country. Many of us were smart enough this time to bring along some candy bars and fruit, but this ran out long before we reached the Texas border. Most of this food was actually eaten before we left Nashville. Occasionally, when the train would stop in some small town, several fellows would hop off and buy cartons of candy bars and sweet rolls if available.

At this time, however, the only thing of importance to each of us was putting distance between ourselves and those soot covered barracks. There were brief moments when it felt like the train was moving at a good pace, then just as suddenly, we would be shunted off onto a siding and begin the waiting process for another delay. The humiliation would be that we would let still another freight train go by.

The first feeling of progress being made was when we realized that we had pulled into Little Rock, Arkansas. Here we stopped long enough for many of us to buy cartons of milk and a variety of sandwiches. The run to Dallas took most of the next day. As one would look down each passenger car, every seat was draped with bodies in vary stages of consciousness. It was impossible to image the various postures different individuals would take to consider they were relaxing.

At the time, I was not at all sure of what the map of Texas really looked like, other than it made my State of Wisconsin seem insignificant in size. I couldn't believe it would take traveling all-night and late into the morning of the following day before we finally arrived at San Antonio.

The four weeks spent in Nashville had seemed like an eternity and the memory of these dismal days was nothing like the picture painted by those two recruiting officers back in Wisconsin seven month ago. The glamorous life of a cadet in the U.S. Air Force was only a dream at this dark moment.

At High School I had gone to the library and read a book about cadet life at Randall Field in San Antonio, Texas. It was here many of the graduating West Pointers came for an advance course in Aviation and their desired to get into the Army Air Force. Many nights I lay on my cot in Nashville wondering what I had done. This would not only be my anxiety, it was the concern of nearly every cadet on this damn train.

We all knew that our signatures on the enlistment papers to be irrevocable and that we would be in for the duration of the war. We had heard that several of the cadets just said to hell with the whole cadet program and requested to be transferred out. This would mean that they would go to some ground school for gunnery, mechanical or specialist training, all depending on their aptitudes. This fell into the master plan of the Air force because they needed bodies for every possible job description imaginable.

I don't believe the sun had made its presence more than three or four times during the past month and the memories that we were to leave behind, would be something each could live without. Later, it was verified, that the Nashville facility was indeed operated by the U. A. Army and not the Air Force directly. At this point in time, the Air Force was a branch of the Army, and it would be some time before they would gain their own complete identity.

In retrospect, it took me years to realize the major problem our country had in going from a peace loving nation basically unprepared for warfare to a country who had not expected to tackle two super powers geared up for war many years ago. Those who had been assigned to handle all these new recruits were only a shade more trained than we. We had no time to be patient. We were given no time to grow up.

CHAPTER 3

It was a tired and dirty bunch of cadets that got off the train and onto buses. Eight or nine large buses wound their way through the city and entered a huge gate, which meant we were at our new home. This was the San Antonio Aviation Cadet Center on the southwest side of this large city.

We were left off in front of clean looking yellow barracks and an abundance of open space. This place was huge and appeared to be diametrically opposite to that place we all wanted to forget. As our names were called off, we were assigned a specific barrack.

Unfortunately though, so many of us were sick when we reached the base, including myself, we were given two days to loaf around our quarters. Hours would have been enough within the confines of this new facility. Everywhere you would glance, you would see "spit and polish." Discipline and orderliness was apparent all over the place. The clean fresh air and the rays of an almost forgotten sun helped to nourish each of our souls and spirits.

All too soon though, we were to get involved in the training program. Our new officers were most concerned and mad that no provision had been made to properly feed this valuable cargo on this two and a half day trip. Chalk this up as another military snafu. From now on we would be under the sole influence of the Air Force and not the disinterested sub branch of the Army.

The Pre-Flight School at San Antonio was as different from Nashville, as night and day. The barracks were two story buildings, with fresh coats of paint. There were sidewalks and large areas of grass, that green stuff, which replaced the dirty black mud of Nashville. We were even greeted by a sun that would not be foreign to this place in the heart of Texas. Cadets could be seen everywhere, each dressed in cotton light tan summer shirts and pants, all neatly pressed with a tailored look. Our group stood out like a sore thumb.

The S.A.A.C.C. appeared very military, with all the orderliness apparent everywhere. Thank God Nashville, Tennessee is now history. At any given moment you could see a dozen or more groups of cadets being marched off in all directions, all in a precise formation. Nearly every group was singing as they passed by. This now was approaching, what I had envisioned as the type of training center I would be sent to. Supposedly, there were approximately 10,000 cadets at this base.

I had certain preconceived ideas about what cadet life should be from the reading of several books about West Point on the Hudson River and the Naval Academy at Annapolis. I had received an appointment to take the exams to enter the Naval Academy prior to graduation from High School from a Representative of Congress, Mr. Gerry Boylow, from the State of Wisconsin.

I rejected this special offer because I knew nothing about the Navy. The largest vessels I had ever been in or on was a row boat and a canoe. I also had a personal problem with the water that I will enumerate at a later time. Had it been West Point I would have considered it, especially since it would have resolved my inability to get help for my education from my parents.

The first thing our new group of recruits accomplished, after our two-day sabbatical, was the issuing of new summer uniforms. This, in itself, was a great moral booster. Once again I had been assigned the duty of Flight Officer for our quarters. We were marched to a building quite remote from our barracks and this afforded our marching unit its first opportunity to break out in song.

The personnel, distributing the various items of clothing, took the time and had the patience to see that each individual was properly attired in well fitting uniforms. Within the period of only a few hours, our group blended in with the rest of the cadets we had seen.

I could hardly recognize the fellows I had been with for the past month. Where there had been gloom, now there was pride. Despondency was now replaced with unashamed gratification. Despair was forgotten as excitement grasped each and every cadet on this new base.

UPPER CLASSMEN

The biggest shocker came as we were exposed to and confronted by the Cadet Class System. Our exposure had been held off for two days because of the health status of this new class of cadets. The class system was really very simple, since there were only two categories, the Upper Classmen and the Lower Classmen.

Immediately, we were informed to which group we belonged. We were instantly made aware of the fact, from this moment forward, our status was about to change drastically. This new experience would change each cadet's outlook on life and his military bearing while serving in the Air Force.

Our metal was about to be tested in more than a subtle way. Like a wave washing over the beach, each member of my class was to be consumed by a way of life we had not expected nor were prepared for. Having read books on our Countries two Military Academies, I had a rough idea about the cadet system. I still was not prepared for what was about to happen.

Whenever an upperclassman addressed you, you were compelled to hit a brace, give your name, rank and serial number; and then do whatever is demanded at the moment. The "brace" entailed assuming a position that was unnatural and submissive. You would pop to attention, pull your shoulders back so that the blades almost touched, while at the same time you would thrust your chin down tight against your chest, and simultaneously pull your stomach in. The hands would be smartly placed along your trousers and your feet would be together. This position was to be held until the command "At Ease" was given.

On some occasions, cadets would actually pass out if held in a brace for too long a period. For some reason, this brace position would shut off the blood supply to these individuals' brain, and they would faint. Our most vulnerable time to be harassed was when we walked alone or in a small group, en route to the PX, the library, or any other place on this huge base. Every effort would be made to travel about during your free moments with fellow Underclassmen.

I had the misfortune of being one of three Underclassmen that was assigned to live on the second floor of our barracks, a place normally off limits for the neophytes. The drop out rate was horrendous at this place so, by the time you became an upperclassman, the ranks began to thin. This accounted for the additional room being available on the second floor, home of all the remaining Upperclassmen.

Each cadet was assigned a cot, a desk, and an open wardrobe, with shelves up one side and a clothes pole across the other section. All our exposed clothing had to be hung up neatly or folded in four-inch increments and stacked in a succinct manner. Your area had to be dust free.

Your shoes were to be shined each day and particularly whenever they got scuffed. All the brass and insignia had to be polished to a bright shine. Soiled clothing had to be secured out of sight in a duffle bag, neatly hung from the end of your bed in a prescribed manner.

I had been brought up at home to do many of these required things, so I had no trouble keeping my area in order. Many of my new friends took days and received many demerits for their inability to adjust rapidly enough. I discovered the best solution was to not touch any clothing that had to be exposed to constant inspections and scrutiny. I did most of my daily living out of my precious duffle bag. It seemed that we never had enough time to do all that was required of us.

Each time I desired to go to my bed or desk, due to the fact that my prescribed abode was on the second floor with the Upperclassmen, I had to repeat the following: "Sir, Aviation Cadet Lloyd O. Krueger, serial number 16056910 wishes to enter the inner sanctum of the Upperclassmen." I would then have to wait until I heard the retort: "Hit It."

Many times, not hearing or given permission to climb the stairs, I would start up. If an upperclassman happened to be upstairs and heard one of us approaching, he would order you to "freeze." This meant you practically had to stop in midair and report that your altitude was 12,000-feet, that is if you happened to be on the twelfth step.

I never appreciated my fortune of having to have this added burden of living above my classmates and with a group of cadets I did not know and whose primary goal was to harass me. Additional moments of my life were taken from me only because I was unfortunately and by pure chance, assigned to live among my tormentors.

The first time we left a classroom and arrived at our barracks to change into athletic clothing, we were told we had but ten minutes to again be lined up in front of our quarters. Fifteen minutes later, there were many cadets not in line. We were given the word that, as of this moment, any cadet not in his right position, ready to march off, in the ten-minute allotted time, would receive demerits. Somehow the next day, and in all future similar situations, few cadets received demerits for this reason. You learned to do things you never thought possible.

The class system would be a part of each cadet's life at the SAACC for the next nine weeks and would follow us through the rest of our flight training. That is, until the system either flunked us out or we were commissioned officers. The only time of each day that we could escape being apart of this unique and different way of life was in our own personal study area and after the bugler blew taps at night. This respite from the class system would last until we heard this same musical sound as reveille was blown each morning.

Mealtime was a particular hairy period, since we all attended mess hall at the same time. You would have a specific table assigned that would have several upperclassmen sitting among us. We were compelled to sit on the outer 2" of our chairs; we could not eat until all upperclassmen were served; had to look straight ahead and rely on your peripheral vision to pass food or to have your fork find a morsel. You then had to lift the fork straight up before your face and then bring it in to your mouth at a 90-degree angle. You had to go through an additional ritual to get anything passed to you.

Any upperclassman could order you to stand on your chair in the mess hall and recite a poem or perhaps sing your high school or college school song for all to hear. It did not take long for our circle of senior citizens to discover that Cadet Krueger could not sing very well. In fact, he could not carry a tune in a leak-proof bucket.

I believe, the only thing that worked in my favor was the fact that I sounded so bad, discretion dictated they hassle me with other tempting methods of torment. The upperclassmen had only their imagination to find ways to harass or annoy the lowly underclassman. Traditional measures to badger cadets would be passed from one class to another. Also, each group would invent or determine new sinister ways to torment the new lowly cadet.

You could, for instance, be stopped anywhere, by an Upperclassman, and asked if you knew how many rivets were in the Brooklyn Bridge? Naturally you would not have this ridiculous piece of information at you finger tips so you replied with one of the usual permitted and appropriate retorts, "No excuse Sir." You instantly knew that this simple run in with this particular Upperclassman meant you would go to the library, on your first free moment, and do research. If you were unfortunate to be confronted a second time without the correct answer, you could anticipate a real going over with a prolonged period of harassment.

This class system had been styled after the same system incorporated at West Point and Annapolis, for their Cadets and Midshipman. Its purpose was to teach discipline, alertness, how to give orders and how to take them, quick reaction and response, and to overcome shyness. Perhaps to an outsider, this entire routine may have seem childish.

Some cadets looked upon the cadet system as just that and requested transfers to other branches of service. This preparation, which followed us through all of our training, gave each a military bearing and a certain pride and self esteem that most will carry with them for the rest of their lives.

At first this rigid system seemed nearly impossible to conform to. Each day it was possible to ascertain the amount of confidence building up within yourself and the feeling of pride taking over. Each Platoon tried to outdo the next one by the way we marched and the way we sang. In reality, few Upperclassmen took advantage of the system by being unduly ridiculous or unreasonable. Most Upperclassmen abided by the spirit of the system.

There were certain parameters to this very rigid cadet class system that protected many of the rights of the lowly Underclassman. The three areas that the Upperclassmen could not invade were the following: They could not touch us in any way, shape or form; they were not permitted to make derogatory or disparaging remarks about one's religious beliefs; and, they could not reflect on a cadet's ethnic background.

HONOR CODE

The very heart of the cadet class system was its honor code:
Cadet Honor was defined as that natural and inherent standard of
distinction, of proper conduct in dealing with one's fellow man.
It is that quality which is so essential to him who is or intends
to be a leader of men in the profession of arms.

Cheating in any form was not tolerated, and anyone violating this basic principal, was immediately washed out and removed from flight training. The Honor system was perhaps the greatest deviation from any educational system each cadet had ever studied under.

All tests and exams were not proctored since each instructor made it a point to leave the classroom after a test had been passed out. Any cadet who cheated was expected to report himself and if he became aware of another cadet violating this code of honor, he was also expected to report this.

In our first days at Preflight School, several cadets were eliminated for this very reason. Others pulled themselves out of the system because they did not desire to be subjected to the entire class system. I honestly believe that those who chose to escape this rigid period in our training would have had an impossible time being exposed to later combat.

We were getting ourselves prepared for insufferable moments in the battles that would take place in the skies of Europe or somewhere over the great Pacific Ocean. At this moment in time, none could know what our minds and bodies would have to endure while flying combat missions.

The final ingredient, in this unique way of life for all who desired to enter the U.S. Air Force as an officer, was the cadet creed each of us had been expected to live by.

THIS CREED IS AS FOLLOWS:

"My bearing is along a course directed toward the
accomplishment of a high mission. That mission
being to raise my earth born soul into the blue
above. To develop honor, self discipline, and
strength of character in myself so that when I am
called upon to defend these principals, I will
neither disgrace my country, my honor, nor my duty.
To this end I will strive honorably, diligently, and
hopefully."

Nearly all recruits were able to conform to this very rigid standard. The early weeks of this system eliminated those individuals who were unable to comply with any of its requirements. Those who felt the system more stringent than they desired or had the capabilities of conforming to voluntarily requested transfers. Some of these individuals were given choices to which branch in the air force they would be assigned. Other cadets would have no impute into their future.

The cadet system was unique because it created an environment of complete trust and honesty. A twenty-dollar bill could be left on your cot for a week and not be taken. You might receive a demerit for being messy, but you would not lose your money. Nearly fifty-nine years later, I am grateful that I had been exposed to this type of standard. A standard, I believe, that is missing from a large segment of our society today.

CHAPTER 4

The preflight training at the San Antonio Aviation Cadet Center had the basic objective to select men for flying status as Pilots, Navigators, and Bombardiers. Individuals that washed out, for one reason or another, would be sent into technical, administrative and service oriented training. Many cadets could not meet extremely rigid physical health requirements, while others had difficulty in learning at a very rapid pace. There were others who met most requirements, but had slow or poor reflexes.

This was a constant worry of every cadet throughout their training, never knowing along the way if they would be eliminated for any of a variety of minor reasons. The constant threat of being "washed out" was foremost on each individual's mind. Most of these young men discovered facts about their bodies, attitudes, capabilities, will power, and determination that few were aware of. Those who successfully completed what was expected of them developed an everlasting pride in their capabilities.

PREFLIGHT SCHOOL AT S.A.A.C.C.

An early part of our necessary training consisted of exhaustive physical, psychological, and mental tests. We spent the better part of two weeks taking the most complete physical I have ever had in my entire life. An inordinate amount of time was spent just on our eyes and our sight. Many cadets discovered for the first time that they were color-blind or had poor depth perception, both reasons for being "washed out."

I discovered that I had 20:15 vision, a fact I was not aware of and also, that my sight was better than average. I was compelled to take the depth perception test four times, not because I had an affliction or problem, but because I had been able to align the two pegs up perfectly each time and with excellent speed. At first this special attention gave me reason to believe I was on my way out.

The test required that each cadet observe two dangling pegs, controlled by two different strings, which extended, perhaps sixty-feet along a lighted tunnel. These pegs were intentionally placed out of alignment, with one or the other in front or behind. It was the responsibility of each cadet to grasp the two lines and adjust these two pegs until he felt them to be in alignment. He would then inform the instructor that the pegs were lined up.

The exact distance that these two pegs were apart would determine how good or bad your depth perception was. Depth perception, for instance, is imperative when landing an airplane. There is considerable distance between a pilot's eyes and the bottom of the landing wheels, depending on the type of airplane of course.

When landing and touching down on the runway, the pilot has to make a judgment of exactly where the tires are in relation to the concrete or grass airstrip. An error could cause the plane to crash into the ground or it could make the plane stall out and consequently bounce, perhaps causing damage or injury.

During the actual physical, I received my next big scare of being washed out of cadets. There were dozens of doctors that checked every part of my anatomy, each seeming to be a specialist. One young doctor had me back against the wall, with my heels pressed against the baseboard, to check my feet. To my amazement, he stated that I had one foot shorter than the other.

First of all I could not possibly see how that could make a difference in piloting a plane or being in any other branch of the service. Secondly, I was not aware of this discrepancy. Thirdly, when I looked down at my two semi-flat feet, I could hardly notice the difference. And Fourthly, I knew the Doctor did not give a damn about the first three observations I had made.

My right foot had a fairly large bump on the top, midway between the toes and the ankle. I was aware of this. Also, I knew why this bump was there, even though I truly did not know about the shortness of this particular foot. In the past six years I had not noticed that my right foot was lagging behind my left one. In a flash, I could see my future in the Air Force vanishing.

The concern on this doctor's face indicated to me that I had to come up with some very quick answers to satisfy his horrendous discovery or I would be "buying the farm", like right now. With my heart pounding and my brain racing up to its capacity, I felt the truth, with some slight distortions, would pacify this doctor.

Nearly six years prior to this day, while going out for football at my high school and as a young freshman, I had an accident. Since I was a 140 pound recruit, trying to make a team in Wausau, Wis., who each year led their conference, the coach did not hold his breath when he first laid eyes on me.

I was issued a worn-out pair of football cleats that had a broken instep and had seen better days. In any case, I played with this pair of football shoes that should have been discarded long ago. On one particular play, while trying to cut through the line as a slippery halfback, I twisted my right foot and went down in extreme pain. I did not realize it then, but I had broken my metatarsal bone in the middle of this foot.

Being young and stupid, I wanted to make the team so bad I never kept off this foot to permit it to heal. I was given an option, which I felt did not cover my problem. I could go to a doctor, but if the foot wasn't broken, my father would have to pay. If the foot was broken my father would still have to pay one half of the cost.

To analyze this option, it would be important to know my father, someone who thought my body was not designed for the sport and someone who did not have money to waste. It turned out that indeed I had broken the metatarsal bone in my right foot.

Instead getting it properly repaired, for four years, each practice and each game, our coach, Win Brockmeyer, personally and methodically taped my foot and ankle. He would not let our trainer handle this problem for some reason. Over a period of time, I learned how to adjust to the constant, but tolerable pain I experienced while playing. I did make the team and, in many games, I played right halfback, along side Elroy Hirsch.

Hirsch ultimately became an All American college player both for the University of Wisconsin and the University of Michigan; a Professional player for the Chicago Cardinals and ultimately the Los Angeles Rams; and All Pro wide receiver. He also is enshrined in the Football Hall Of Fame.

Because of Hirsch's exceptional talent, during 95% of my playing time my only assignment was to block. I personally felt that I was the person who made Elroy "Crazy Legs" Hirsch famous. On many occasions I told him this without ever getting his formal recognition.

Over the years, this broken metatarsal bone remained separated, held together only by the surrounding muscles. Somehow, this problem did not permit the foot to heal properly, thus the slight discrepancy in length. I had played actively in all sports with this broken foot, such as football, baseball, hockey, tennis, handball, etc., and had now learned to live with it.

I informed this young doctor that I had broken my foot many years ago and it was entirely healed. I jumped up and down in my bare feet, somewhat risky, and was able to convince him it now was only a bump, nothing more. Note: I was 69 before I had a surgeon repair this still broken metatarsal problem by chiseling the excess bone away and then inserting a stainless steel screw to hold the still broken bones together. My right foot, sixty-four years later, is now an inch shorter than the left. Who cares, we won the war.

PENNY ARCADE

The psychological and dexterity part of our testing took place in a building that we called the "penny arcade." Dozens of cleverly designed tests were given that required mental skill and quickness of hand. They wanted to test each candidate's dexterity, steadiness when pressure was applied, motor coordination and reaction time to a variety of stimuli.

Simple challenges using pegs of different shapes and colors had to be inserted in a board in a specific manner, and all in a timed period. We were all led to believe that failure in any test could result in being washed out. A place that could have been fun and entertaining was in reality a moment of a series of nothing but one worry after another.

Nervousness was tested by having a rod with a handle placed on a pivot, with the tip penetrating a small opening in a metal plate. Between the pivot and the handle was a swivel hinge. This would exaggerate any movement that the hand might make. Each time the tip of the rod touched the edge of this small hole, a horn would go off and lights would flash, instantly creating additional reaction. The pressure built up because each of us knew what could happen if you failed anyone of these tests.

Coordination was tested by a machine, which had a platter, much like an old fashion record player, that rotated around slowly. On this platter was a small metal disc that would slowly move in a crescent shape slot while the platter rotated. Above this disc that traveled in unpredictable directions was an arm that held a plumb bob type pointer. This protruding arm was controlled by two handles which the cadet could turn in either direction, thus being able to move or keep the pointer over the moving disc.

The primary objective was to keep the pointer exactly above the moving disc, which were both rotating and constantly changing directions. Each time the pointer moved away from the disc, weird sounds would greet the nervous cadet. To achieve success in most of these concocted tests, one had to overcome distractions and to concentrate on the problem before you.

The action created by these two handles that could be rotated in either direction was very familiar to those who knew how to operate certain lathes. The-powers-to-be built in a challenge to these specific individuals by making the directions these handle turned to be diametrically opposite as the lathes they had used.

This "penny arcade," under different circumstances, would have been loads of fun. Instead, each cadet felt his chances of getting into flight school would be hanging on the next test. No one knew exactly how much importance was being placed on each of these many tests we were exposed to. Rumors had it that it could take failure in only a single test to wash you out. In reality I do not believe anyone knew what the standards were.

I never found out what our instructors were ordered to do, since I did pass and move on. I believe the real solution for being successful meant that it would be necessary to relax while trying to master these machines, a near impossible expectation. If an individual were prone to be nervous or goosey, it would be impossible to master the Rube Goldberg devises in this penny arcade.

OFF TO CLASS

The schooling and classroom part of our training consisted of 30 hours of sea vessels and aircraft recognition; 48 hours of code; 24 hours of physical exercise; 20 hours of math; 18 hours of maps and charts; plus physical and the usual military training. The pace that was set was fast and furious. Every minute of each day seemed to be accounted for. After each class we would get into formation and be marched off to another assignment, which could be rifle range, getting haircuts, or still another class.

Our entire routine was a very structured system, and it did not take too long for each cadet to conform. Most weekends we had some free time and on occasion, we even got into San Antonio. There was not too much time set aside for studying, since the essential part of this method of teaching required each cadet to rapidly assimilate the material and move forward. If this technique proved to be too difficult, the cadet would be eliminated from preflight school. It really did not have as much to do with your intelligence, but rather how fast you could pack it in.

GEORGE AGAIN

Right at the height of my training I received a telephone call from my friend, George Cormack. "Surprise, I'm in San Antonio, get a week off and we'll spent some time together," was the gist of his message. My first reaction was surprise, immediately followed by the joy of hearing my old friend's voice once more. These thoughts were supplanted with the realization that I'm in the service with extremely limited freedoms to exercise.

"George, I do not know if I can get off the base at all. I do not have a pass coming for several weeks, but I will immediately go to headquarters and talk with one of my Officers. Give me a telephone number of the phone you're at. Hang loose. I will call you back within the hour, one way or the other."

When all of the dust settled, I felt real fortunate to get an overnight pass, which meant I had to be back on the base by 0600 the next morning. I had explained that my friend had taken a train all of the way from Wisconsin, just to see me. It really didn't cut too much mustard, but I must have hit a sensitive nerve because a pass was written.

I quickly gave George a call that we would only have this evening to spend together and that it truly was a miracle that I even received this. I'm not sure my friend completely understood exactly what my situation was. Luckily I caught a ride into the heart of San Antonio at the base gate and within less than one hour I was able to see this old friend in the lobby of his temporary home away from home.

George was waiting for me at his hotel. It was apparent by the look on his face that he was chagrin. I again explained that peons in the military cannot just get up and take off at will. The best we can hope for is to look on a schedule every few weeks and see if we are eligible for a one day pass or an over night pass. Period, there are no exceptions.

His taste in hotel location and quality had improved considerably, compared with the flea infested fire-trap facility we stayed in on our initial visit to Chicago. Because of his mood during the first hour, I knew George was not at all familiar with military life and the reservations placed on its participants. It was obvious he was happy to see me in uniform and soon his disappointment was forgotten.

With the restricted time together, we had to plan how best to use these valuable moments. It was decided that we would just walk and talk, not spend time going into historical sites such as the Alamo, museums, etc. I knew that my friend was basically a loner and actually visited most cities and sights by himself. He could go and visit the many sights that San Antonio offered on his own once I returned to the Base.

George had never been to Texas before. He had traveled many times with his family to Florida and once to Georgia, but he now was aware of the obvious differences between these three states. He told me he had enjoyed the train ride from Wausau south to Texas, but this was no surprise to me. Hell, he would have enjoyed a train ride through the Okeechobee Swamp in Florida, riding in an old boxcar.

My suggestion was to take San Antonio's famous river walk that has cafes, cabarets, boutiques, and was very beautiful. Periodically along this beautiful walk, they had benches to rest and enjoy the time being spent. This suggestion offered both a unique setting as well as a chance to converse.

I was compelled to give George almost a day-by-day account of my experiences since we both left Chicago. He was not too impressed by the reception I had received in Nashville, Tennessee. I am sure my account of the time spent in Nashville did not do the actual horrible experience justice. One truly had to live it.

He explained how none of the branches of service, including the Red Cross, wanted to utilize his talents as a pharmacist. The primary excuse, of course, was his eyesight. His glasses, though they had the appearance of the bottoms of two old bottles, corrected his visual perception to that of almost anyone else.

His one desire was to serve his country in some capacity. He knew he could replace some able body pharmacist for overseas duty while he served here in the United States. This was just another example of some decisions that were made quite arbitrarily by some individuals, regardless of their practicality.

We spent the entire night just talking and reminiscing. He informed me that he now has his degree and his parents were going to help him buy an existing drug store in Minocqua, a small resort town in northern Wisconsin, about eighty miles due north of my home town of Wausau. We laughed and there were moments when we came close to tears. He gave me the feeling that perhaps I had to participate in this war for the two of us. I could sense that my friend had concern for the days that were before me.

It was four o'clock in the morning when I was compelled to say my goodbyes to my friend and then to take a cab back to the base. The parting we exchanged in the early hours of this morning was not like our separation in Chicago. We hugged each other in an awkward fashion and neither one displayed any shame for the tears that swelled up our eyes. This was a wonderful gesture of friendship by George and I'm sure he knew I appreciated it.

He got to spend a few more days on his own, seeing the many sights in this city with a population of about 750,000 persons. I advised him to walk the length of the River walk, go see the Alamo, there were special areas within the city, like the King Williams District and various old and interesting Missions like Conception, San Jose, and San Juan.

I had hope he could run across someone in this important and interesting city to share these last days he had expected the two of us to commune. Then I remembered that George was basically a loner except for the few of us that had somehow broken through his armor and saw a most interesting person. It would be weeks before I would be contacted by my friend via the mails.

SOUTHERN DRAWL

Several weeks later, I was fortunate enough to get a two-day pass. Now I felt guilt that it had not presented itself earlier so I could have tripled the time with my old roommate. I suppose this is indicative of how things work in the service. Right now the most important and paramount thing is that I get trained so that my country can use my services on either side of the world.

Another cadet and I decided to go northeast of San Antonio to Austin, the State Capital. I was particularly interested in seeing this city because at one time, I, along with Russel "Rut" Weinkauf, a friend, neighbor, and the son of Elsie Weinkauf, the person to which this book is dedicated, had planned on attending the University of Texas, a large and well-endowed school of higher education.

My friend ultimately went to school there. Attending the University of Texas, along with the University of North Carolina at Chapel Hill, had to be discarded by me. I realized that practicality would dictate my attending the University of Wisconsin in my home state, mostly because of the difference in tuition.

Early the next morning, after we had arrived, Austin received a very rare and totally unexpected snow-storm. My friend and I were walking in the vicinity of the University of Texas sorority houses and women's dorms and it provided us with a spectacle I could hardly believe. Coeds, some of whom had never seen snow before, proceeded to roll in it, and rub it on their faces. Several girls came out with containers to gather quantities of snow and then raced inside to deposit this prize in their dorm refrigerators. They hoped they could preserve these beautiful flakes for as long as possible.

Many of these girls had come from southern Alabama and Louisiana, had never had the opportunity of being exposed to snow before, and did not find it difficult to create this unusual scene. I tried to explain, coming from Wisconsin, how we would receive many feet of snow each winter and that the ground would be blanketed with this white stuff for several months. They could not comprehend that the shoveled sidewalks created snow banks so high, that during some winters, we could not see the houses nor the adjacent street.

It was in Austin, while talking with these giggling girls, that I discovered why southerners talk so slow and with a slurred drawl. I could understand a variance in certain phrases and the use of words we seldom heard up north, like "U awl", "go thisa way" or "thata way", " my daddy", grits and many more. Now I uncovered the reason for their cadence. Northerners are forced to slow down when talking with native southerners for the simple reason they just don't **LISTEN** fast enough.

When I finally returned home on leave, nearly a year later, I had picked up a southern drawl. I gradually began to talk like them as a defensive measure by talking more slowly, otherwise you found yourself constantly repeating your every word. My family and friends believed this to be an act, not a transformation caused out of necessity in order to communicate.

UPPERCLASSMEN

By now my class had been made upperclassmen, which greatly reduced the many anxieties we were compelled to live with. On a certain day, at the midpoint of our training, the upperclassmen graduated and my class became the new upperclassmen. We would now assume new responsibilities and our life would also become a little easier. It would be our group who would take on the role of superior beings and could dish out petty annoyances.

Tomorrow the new group of cadets would be shipped in. Today though, for a period of eight hours, we had "Turn About", a reversal of roles between upper and lower class cadets. We could make our former nemesis jump through the "hoop" . . . hit braces, sing songs, recite poetry, serve us food, or any of a number of indignities we had endured.

This reversal of roles was done in a spirit of good fun and it was another way to say good-bye and to wish these fellows the best down the road. Each of us believed we knew the responsibility of going off to war and the consequences of combat.

We had gotten to know most of the Upperclassmen in this class of cadets and, in a sense, were good friends. We knew that someday we might even be flying in combat off of one of these cadet's fighter plane's wing or perhaps sitting side by side in a bomber. As it turned out this turnabout-day, almost universally, the only ones you paid attention to were the upperclassmen that used this class system privilege with discretion.

The cadets who were the abusers of the class system were totally ignored or simply given the title of C.S., an explicit way of saying chicken shit. It was every ones hope that this special type of treatment would open their eyes so that, when they went on to flight school, they would respect the privilege of giving order. This type of class system would continue until we received our commissions.

TRACK MEET

A notice had been posted on our bulletin board that on Saturday there was to be a track meet. Anyone who was interested could enter the ten or twelve different events that had been scheduled. For a variety of reasons this caught my attention.

My High School in Wisconsin did not offer track as a competitive sport. However, I had the opportunity once to travel with a bunch of fellows to Wisconsin Rapids, about 45 miles south of my home town, to see a sanctioned track meet of National significance. Don Gehrman, from Marquette University in Milwaukee was entered in the mile race and sport writers from far and wide would be in attendance to see if the 4 minute mile would be broken.

This would be my very first opportunity to watch a formal track meet and I instantly became interested in each and every event. I enjoyed all of the dashes, the high jump, the broad jump, and especially the pole vaulting. Late in the afternoon the mile event was to be held, but prior to this would be many shorter track events, including relays.

I was interested in this mile run because I had followed the sport news for years regarding the 4 minute mile. There was another important attraction for me because I had been running great distances for years as a therapeutic solution for some damaged lungs.

When I was about twelve years old I had won a mile ice skating race, beating many skaters who specialized in this type of racing. I only owned hockey skates and had never attempted this type of event before. Most of the competitors in this particular event naturally wore racing skates and had a great deal of knowledge about arm motion, turning on the curves, and especially pacing themselves. My specialty was ice hockey.

Much to the amazement of every spectator, and particularly myself, I ended up winning this damn race by shear stamina and determination. Besides winning a blue ribbon I also ended up with double pneumonia and nearly died. I had the misfortune of contacting this infection in both of my lungs before penicillin had been discovered so my recovery was both slow and left me with scar tissue in each lung.

Our Family Physician advised me to run at every opportunity I had so that these lungs could be developed and restored to a healthy condition. From that day on I made a concerted effort to run. Many weekends I would run to Mosinee or to Marathon City, each about eleven miles from home. I usually talked friends of mine to join me, which meant I would constantly have to run back and prod them along.

Now, in Cadets, I found that the position of Flight Leader required me to also lead our barracks on long runs through obstacle courses. This also required me to constantly run back and forth to encourage the stragglers and goof-offs. My fellow companions knew that I loved to run and seemed to have limitless endurance so they immediately encouraged me to enter this up coming track meet.

Throwing caution to the wind I signed up for the mile, never realizing what I had obligated myself for. Late on Saturday afternoon all contestants for the mile run were called to group up behind the starting line. We were ushered in an orderly fashion to make several rows behind this chalk line that would be both the starting point and ultimately the finish line after several turns around the long oval track.

It instantly became obvious to me that most of the participants in this race were fellows who had previously been out for track. They had special light pants and sleeveless tops with lettering on them. Many wore spiked track shoes that at this moment looked awesome. What had I done? I had on my usual tennis shoes and gym trunks I used daily for PT.

By a quirk of fate I found myself positioned on the front line with six or seven others. There were about twenty cadets taking part in this late afternoon event and I could not recognize a single face I had ever seen before. It was at this moment I convinced my self I really did not belong in this race, but what did I have to lose. I would give it my best shot.

Just before the start of the race I noted the guy next to me, with a loud yellow pair of shorts on, doing special stretches and exercises. He was several inches taller than my five foot eight inches and had the obvious appearance that he knew why he was in this race and would wonder what in the hell I was doing next to him.

The gun went off and Cadet Krueger raced away from the starting line like this may have been a hundred yard dash or even a race for the 440. I still did not have enough sense to pace myself as I ran along a track of cinders. I also was not used to the sound being made of all of the pounding feet beating against these black pieces of burnt coal. The only sure thing I noted was to my right and slightly behind me were the flashes of the yellow shorts I could catch out of the corner of my eye.

We circled the track several times, the two of us only a few yards ahead of several others of the pack that started this race. I now knew I was running as fast as I could and I expected my adjoining neighbor or some other participant to overtake me momentarily. As we rounded the last turn prior to the straightaway and the finish line I noted most of the runners strung out over a great distance. However, those damn yellow pants were right behind me.

At this point of the race I no longer could feel my legs or my feet hitting the noisy surface of the track. I only noted each of my knees rising up about waist high, one after the other, and that pair of yellow shorts. Surely he would open up and glide by me were my only thoughts.

At the finish line I noted many cadet spectators had gathered and were yelling and seemed to be waving their arms. Just as I crossed the line and broke a tape that signaled the end of the race, I blacked out and ran down into the cinders. I immediately was carried off to the side of the track and ultimately taken to the infirmary to receive medical attention. I had sustained dozens of cuts and lacerations from the cinder track and I looked like a bloody mess.

I was told I had won the only formal race I had ever been in and I do not know to this day how this was accomplished. I truly have to believe there were some high school and perhaps college athletes who were participants. I also never found out what the time was, though I knew for a fact that it did not ever challenge the record that Roger Bannister ultimately made in England.

GUARD DUTY NO. 2

I finally was given the opportunity to draw that undesirable detail, reverently referred to as Guard Duty, for the second time in my short military career. It had been over a month since I walked the beat in Nashville, with my stubby little nightstick and had gotten the "holy bee gee-bees" scared out of me. The major difference, here in San Antonio, we were given a loaded rifle.

Several factors that permitted me to take on this duty with greater confidence, were the following: first, none of our officers planted erroneous ideas in our minds about the impending dangers we might experience; secondly, the S.A.A.C.C. base did not have a large contingent of Regular Army personnel to contend with; and finally, I had several months of cadet training behind me and felt more confident than on my last debacle.

About three in the morning, while on duty, I observed a jeep approaching in the darkness, with their lights off. I could see, by the dim light emitted from the near by lamppost at my station, that there were two men in officers uniforms. I ordered the men to halt, advance and be recognized. One of the men approached and I again ordered him to stop about four feet in front of me. I immediately recognized him as Lt. Hanson, the Officer Of-The-Day and the person in charge of this particular night's guard detail. He also had been one of my classroom instructors.

We exchanged a few words and then Lt. Hanson asked to see my rifle. At this moment I did the worst thing possible. In stupid ignorance, I gave Lt. Hanson my rifle and was instantly greeted with, "Cadet Krueger, I now have a weapon, what do you have?" I had just committed a gross boo-boo.

Despite the knowledge that I technically had only three acceptable replies to the Lieutenant's question; (the yes sir; no sir; no excuse sir, retorts), I snapped off a nervous response: "Sir Cadet Krueger wishes to know, if you cannot trust your own officers, who can we trust in this man's Air Force?"

If Lt. Hanson had not cracked his familiar face with a broad smile, I am sure I would have gotten my butt really reamed out. What I had done was a cardinal sin in the military. However, tonight I was patiently told about the ramifications of what I had done and that I was never to make this same mistake again, should the circumstances ever present themselves. I was given back my rifle and no mention was made of the question I had thrown back at my superior officer. This was to be the last time I would be required to be on guard duty, both as a cadet and as an officer. In combat this type of duty was handled by the Military Police, with all their specialized training.

On April 21, 1943, we final finished our last class and had taken the last of our many exams. We now had only to wait to find out the results of all of our efforts these last ten weeks of preflight training. Groups of cadets were marched to the Administration Building and were ordered to line up. Each cadet was to make an appearance before the Review Board.

There were five officers sitting behind a long table, each with stacks of files before them. A cadet would enter, stand at attention, and then be given the order, "At Ease." His files would then be reviewed and reported on. There were generally four suggested routes for each cadet: Pilot training, Navigation training, Bombardier training, and a suggestion, for marginal cases, to volunteer out of flight training for some other service in the Air Force.

By mid afternoon our barracks of upperclassmen were awaiting our turn to learn the results. I finally entered this room of destiny, with a great deal of apprehension. I found it impossible to receive a premature clue of my fate by scanning the faces of each of the stern officers before me. I was told to relax, as if that were possible, while my files were explained to me.

"YOU HAVE QUALIFIED FOR ALL THREE BRANCHES OF FLIGHT TRAINING CADET TRAINING" the Officer-In-Charge stated. I was informed I could have my choice. "Pilot Training, Sirs," I replied, before I was offered all the choices. My response had been given without hesitation and before I had realized my present status, I instantly remembered Cadets do not interrupt Officers. All five of the cadre sitting before me had not prepared themselves for my instant retort and each let their face fall into a smile.

After my request for pilot training was duly noted in my files, I was informed that tomorrow I would receive shipping orders for transfer to Garner Field at Uvalde, Texas. It would be here that I would receive my Primary Flight Training. I saluted, did an abrupt about face, and left the Review Board, walking on air. I had just received the best news and confirmation I wanted so very badly. I was about to explode.

When we returned to our barracks, there were very mixed emotions. These feelings ran from ecstatic joy to extreme disappointment. Only one cadet in our barracks would not go into some type of flight training. Several other were disappointed in that they only had the option of going to Bombardier School when their only aspiration was to become a pilot. Our lives became a series of highs and lows. This would continue the entire time I was in the service.

We, who had been through so much together, were about to get separated. Our barracks were having cadets sent to seven or eight different facilities and our paths were not likely to cross again. There were only five cadets, which I knew personally from my class, making the bus trip to Uvalde. Over my years in service, I only ran across two of my friends from this period in my life. Making and losing friend would be a continuing occurrence throughout my stint in the Air Force, something you never got used to.

From this day forward I made a determined effort, with a single exception, to purposely never get so attached to another classmate or fellow crewman that it would affect my well being. Later I would meet this single exception.

CHAPTER 5

Shortly after our noon meal on April 23, nearly one hundred cadets boarded Greyhound buses for Uvalde, Texas, which happened to be only a few hours drive, southwest of San Antonio. The trip seemed especially short because of the obvious excitement of each of these individuals who had survived the rigid ten-week ordeal at S.A.A.C.C.

Everyone wanted to talk at once and the anticipation of finally getting the chance to actually fly. This would be a first for nearly every occupant on this bus. I did not relate my first and only flight in a Waco F3 with my friend George. In fact, I was not particularly proud of my disregard for my friend's fear of flying. Each time I would tend to erase this quilt feeling by reminding myself of his secretly kept accounting system that year at the University of Wisconsin.

Though the constant chatter and all of the varied conversations held our interest, it was obvious, if you took the time to look out of the windows on the bus, the landscape in this part of Texas was changing rapidly. Mesquite bushes were the primary form of vegetation in an unusually flat and dry area. A generous dispersal of prickly pear cactus appeared on most of the land on either side of the buses. I noted that the topsoil in this area of Texas became as thin as the hair on a balding man. Stones and rocks were apparent everywhere.

Periodically we would spot a single emaciated looking cow trying to survive in this harsh part of this State, a State noted for its cattle industry. It was apparent that farmers or ranchers around here did not have to decide on how many head of cattle to put on each acre, but rather, how many acres are required to support a single critter.

Uvalde is a typical small Texas town of less than 10,000 population. Garner Field, the name of our new home, was located some distance and almost directly east of this community. It took on its own identity in this otherwise mundane landscape.

There perhaps was more green grass and vegetation in and about our new Base than in all of the rest of Uvalde and Uvalde County.

To add to the contrast, palm trees had been planted and the entire site was immaculately manicured. There was a staff of over six or seven Mexican employees whose sole responsibility was to take care of the grounds. Few of these men could speak or understand English. Their primary job was to keep this place looking like an oasis, in the middle of an otherwise drab and rather dull environment. They did a magnificent job.

Garner Field had been quickly developed early in this countries war effort. It had been named after John Nance Garner, the two-term Vice President under Franklin Delano Roosevelt, serving from 1933-1941. The facility was well conceived to meet the needs of a primary flying school, and to play an important part in the training of pilots for the war we had just entered.

An entrepreneur, from the area, had foreseen the United States involvement in the war, purchased a lot of land and developed a simple airfield. He gambled on being able to lease this dream of his to the government and he was ready. Years later, I found out this speculation or venture rewarded him handsomely. He had not gone into this venture blindly since he had political clout and was about to get paid back for favors' due him.

The caravan of Greyhound buses went directly to the field, without entering the lazy little Texan town, and parked, one behind the other, on the only road that ran to the center of the barracks complex. Our first view of the place, as we anxiously left these buses, was a complex consisting of single story units. A continuous gable type roof covered the many barracks and kept the same profile as it crossed the breezeways between units.

The basic plan or design for these living units was a huge quadrangle with a large open space in the middle. Sidewalks, under the extensive roof over hang, ran around the extremities of the mall. In inclement weather, one could navigate throughout the complex without getting wet.

There were diagonal sidewalks radiating out from each corner of the quadrangle. In the center of this mall, where the diagonal walks intersected, was a large circular piece of concrete that had a huge aluminum flagpole at its midpoint. A very large American Flag flew from this auspicious location.

REALITY SETS IN

Once we left the buses, we were ordered to line up on the sidewalk paralleling the road. At this instant, we immediately became aware, that once again, we would become Underclassmen. The long line of new cadets was inundated by the Upperclassmen who appeared to be gnashing-at-the-bit to get at us. They did everything humanly possible to make their presence known.

There were many minutes of extreme confusion while we were being shouted at and ordered about. The motivating reason for all of this activity was to intimidate us and to drive home the understanding, for the next month or so, we would be on the bottom of the totem pole once again. I had forgotten about being an Underclassman and was shocked anew.

About the time that all of this commotion had died down, our new Officers began shouting instructions to these new cadets. It was then that I noticed an Upperclassman, with an obvious display of rank, come rushing toward our section of the line. He looked like a roadrunner or perhaps a uniformed version of Groucho Marx. Somehow, I just knew he had a bead on the exact spot I was standing at attention on. My perception was correct. My instant premonition, that I was now in deep trouble, was also correct.

This overly excited Upperclassman did not stop until his face was practically touching mine. At this point he hit the brakes and began yelling. He was so loud and so close I could not understand what he was trying to convey to me. God . . . I felt like I must have just put a hatchet into his Mother's back. His face was flushed and the veins in his enlarged neck looked like they were about to rupture. This commotion got the attention of all of the cadets in the immediate area. Each had to observe this altercation by only rolling their eyes in my direction.

Finally, I ascertained why he had confronted me and why he made a federal case out of a normally insignificant situation. I had done the unthinkable. I had made contact with the grass, this sacred grass. In my haste to line up on the edge of the walk, I inadvertently had my heels protrude over the grass area. I'm sure he was using me as an example and to emphasize the importance of protecting this rare carpet of greenery.

At my moment in the sun though, I felt he had over emphasized this emphasis. I am also sure that my major part in this dramatic episode protected the grass from any in my group, the Class 43J. I am also sure one of my classmates will eagerly await the next batch of new cadets, to find the "lucky" guy with a wayward heel.

When most of the confusion subsided, we received assignments to the various barracks. Each barracks had many large rooms, holding six cadets each. The six cadets assigned to the room I would occupy did not have time to get acquainted, because an upperclassman had entered our abode with typed schedules.

These schedules would become active the next morning. There were several pages of instructions, listing all of the rules and regulations governing us while at Garner field. We would have a few hours to assimilate what had just transpired and then start to enjoy the moment, realizing that our formal training would begin tomorrow. This gave us several hours to release the excitement each Cadet was trying to be nonchalant about.

The Cadets assigned to my unit would be divided into two different Flights. I was assigned to B Flight, along with George Kristy from Marietta, Ohio and Fred Sweeney from Charleston, West Virginia. Our B Flight Instructor would be P. L. Viviani. We had been informed that we would not get to meet him for several days. It would be his charge to teach each of us how to master the art of actual flying a primary training plane.

Life at Garner Field was fast and furious. Time raced by because we were extremely busy, the moral was high, and we were soon to get the chance to actually fly. The Primary Training School was set up be a 10 week course, with a minimum of 70 hours in a 125 to 225 horsepower open cockpit biplanes or low-wing monoplanes; 94 hours of academic work in ground school; 54 hours of military training; and, interspersed in each day, we were required to take part in a variety of physical exercises, including numerous athletic endeavors.

My duties as a Flight Leader had followed me here from the S.A.A.C.C. and once again I would have to lead my barrack buddies to class, over obstacle courses, to get haircuts, to enforce study hour, and to relay to the powers that be any request that would or might affect our small group of Cadets.

The Base encouraged us to participate in volleyball, baseball, basketball, and similar sports. They stressed the importance of each of us being in the best physical shape possible. Formal PT would be both lengthy and strenuous. My weight remained approximately 140 pound throughout my service in the Air Force. Evidently I had developed an adequate balance between the grub we were fed and the energy I expended.

The first two weeks saw all of the class of 43-J settling down to the routine of hitting various classes and subjects and, most importantly, getting to meet our Flight Instructors. The daily regular procedure was designed to keep us busy most of the daylight hours.

My first day on the flight line was with George Kristy and Fred Sweeney, both of our barracks, along with our civilian Instructor, Mr. P. T. Viviani. I never did know what the initials stood for in Viviani's name. All three only addressed him as Sir.

We three Cadets were all short and stocky with a very similar build. We were grateful that at adulthood we finally had reached the insignificant height of five foot eight inches. Viviani however fell several inches short of this modest goal. He was of Italian decent and had moved down here from Houston, Texas.

FAIRCHILD PT-19 PRIMARY TRAINER

Before us sitting on the apron in front of a large hanger was the plane we would receive our instructions in. Prior to our entry in the war and until the year 1940, most young pilots were trained in two seat biplanes. These planes were generally accepted to be the most easily mastered of all airplanes, slow, stable, and forgiving of errors and hard treatment. Soon it was realized that this could breed over-confidence, thus making the next stage in basic training more difficult.

It was because of this philosophy that the Fairchild PT-19 was designed and developed for the Air Force. The plane was a cantilever low-wing monoplane, had a conventional tail unit and a tail-wheel landing gear. The PT-19 was powered by a 130-KW (175 hp) Ranger L-440-1 six cylinder inverted inline engine. The Instructor and student were accommodated in tandem cockpits.

This PT-19 sitting before us was painted blue with the rudder decorated with red and white horizontal stripes. The nose cone was yellow as were both surfaces of each of its wings. A rather large blue circle, with a white star, was applied to the wing. On the other wing were the letters U.S.

To each of us she looked terrific. This plane proved that it was not a lethal instrument of destruction in the hands of embryo pilots, like many had predicted. It had only basic instrumentation and so was unsuitable for blind-flying or instrument flight training.

One of the things we all agreed upon was the fact that this Fairchild PT-19 looked like a miniature modern fighter plane, important to all of us since this was each of our dreams. The biplane that some Cadets trained in, like the Stearman PT-13, was a throwback to World War I. Of course, none of this had any merit and we had no impute into what the Air Force decided in how we would be trained.

Our Instructor was a very serious man and was very resolute when it came to the art of flying. He let us know from the start that he did not want to crank out pilots who would face the enemy and be instantly erased by a more talented enemy sky jockey. He had a sense of humor that was most difficult to locate.

Even when you knew you had performed a great maneuver with the Fairchild PT-19 trainer, Viviani made sure he had on a pensive and sober look. Only after a lesson would he offer belated congratulations or compliments. Because of the remoteness of my instructor in the plane and the difficulty in communicating while flying, necessary time on the ground was spent going over what and why we did the various things. Viviani must have kept notes while we were in the air because he was meticulous and methodical in relating each maneuver, reaction, goof, or accomplishment once we left the plane.

I had several hours of flight time logged during these first few weeks, which I will elaborate on in Chapter 6, when I suffered a very disappointing and almost catastrophic moment in my brief military career. I suddenly became very ill. I woke up one morning, covered with beads of perspiration, a fever of 103 degrees, and my whole body seemed on fire.

I was taken to the Infirmary on the Base and subsequently diagnosed with a severe case of food poisoning, along with about a dozen other Cadets. It appeared that each of us had eaten too large a portion of green string beans that evidently had been tainted or had been contaminated somehow during preparation.

This type of accident was of obvious concern to the Officers in charge of this Base, so consequently we were given the very best of treatment. Most of the ill Cadets were confined to the Infirmary for the better part of a week. This amount of time away from our curriculum does not seem to be too horrendous, but at this particular facility, it turned out to be critical.

Time, desire, and certain abilities are all that each Cadet brought with him when he had enlisted. Our country put a great deal of emphasis on the word and reality of **TIME** because we were now at war with Germany and Japan. Our country had not been prepared for this method and means to resolve differences between nations, so time became very precious.

The recovered Cadets returned to our classes and the flight line a week behind the others. I had been able to do some studying while in the infirmary, but there was nothing I could do about actual flying. Much of this type of instruction did not come from textbooks, but actually from the personal experiences of our instructors.

The pace of what was expected of us, made it extremely difficult to make up this amount of lost time. During this early stage in the rapid training of pilot candidates, there was a shortage of airplanes and instructors. Other branches of the Service suffered similar shortages.

There were pictures showing that the Regular Army started training their soldiers with brooms instead of actual guns during the early days. Trucks would be maneuvered in front of them with large signs that spelled out the word **TANK**. Our peace loving Nation almost had to start from square one to prepare for a war being forced on the world.

I had been granted a special dispensation to study in the latrine after lights were out. This helped with my class work but I still had the impossible task of making up flight training. You had to schedule flights when planes were available, caused by the great demand and availability.

With this type of training, there is only so much you can assimilate on any particular day, making it impractical to have two flight lessons in a row or even an extended one, for instance. My Teachers and Instructors, mostly civilians, did their best to be helpful and they gave me constant encouragement and consideration.

By the fifth week I felt I was finally back into the same routine the other cadets were following. The whole misfortune had been extremely hard, but the total experience of being in flight training, seem to give me the energy to get it done. I knew that with enough desire and willingness, you could accomplish almost anything.

Most weekends we were given a day and a half for relaxation. I was compelled to use most of this time to study and catch up on classroom work. Many of my friends were getting money from home so they could afford to eat off the base sometimes, or to even rent a car and explore the countryside or to cruise with girls they managed to meet in San Antonio. Trips into Uvalde were never a real big deal since there was very little to do, especially for a Cadet who was looking for excitement and a change of pace.

The relatively small city or town of Uvade was similar to most Texas communities of that size. The focal point in town was the courthouse, an imposing structure that occupied an entire block. A ring of several blocks of houses radiated out from this imposing structure. Many areas had wooden sidewalks and most buildings possessed fronts like they belonged on a movie set. I might have appreciated Uvalde more and would be more tolerant of the limited points of interest had I been aware of some of its early history.

Many years later, after I had moved to the State of Texas, I discovered how far back and how significant its history extended. I had known that Texas and Wisconsin were admitted to the Union at about the same time, the year 1845. However, because Texas had been a Republic at one time, it technically is the only State permitted to fly its flag at the same height as the Stars and Stripes. Normally this is not done.

Early history of Texas was influenced of course by Mexico and by Spain. The culmination of most of the early turmoil in this part of our country came to a head soon after the Battle of The Alamo in what is now San Antonio. To this date the actual structure where the 187 men were wiped out by the Mexican Army still is standing and has been made into a National Monument.

Shortly after this disastrous Battle, General Santa Anna and the Mexican Army were defeated for a final time and the land now known as Texas first became a Republic and ultimately a State. Sam Houston first served this State Commander of its Army, then as President of the Republic, then as a U.S. Senator, and finally as its Governor.

Once I tried walking into the countryside between our Base and the town of Uvalde. This proved to be not too inspiring because of the lack of picturesque scenery, and the dominance of the monochromatic color values of only mesquite growing everywhere. I discovered years later, because I never gave this little town much of my attention, that it had a small college. A college of any size would have had coeds. Damn.

One day while walking around the Square in Uvalde, I noticed a young mother nursing her little infant while sitting on a wooden bench in front of a store. She obviously had no compunction about exposing her breast in front of this shy, bashful, and sheltered young lad and damn Yankee.

I had never witnessed this before and now it required some real soul searching. This sight, though unfamiliar, was the most honest and natural thing I have ever seen. I suddenly realized how prudish some of our customs are in this country. Later I would be a witness to similar examples in Europe of people with far less puritanical or sanctimonious attitudes.

WALKING THE RAMP

On my first scheduled pass off the base, once I had caught up with the other cadets, turned into my second disaster. The Saturday morning, prior to going on pass, a most unfortunate situation rapidly developed. During the week I had picked up several demerits for such minor infractions as having a shoe lace come undone at the wrong time; I had my necktie askew; failed to salute an upperclassman fast enough; and some other trivial thing, that could have been any of a hundred seemingly simple mistakes that did not fit into the rigid Cadet Code of Standards.

If a group of Cadets were one minute late for a class period, the entire unit would each be given a demerit. Each Cadet could receive up to five demerits a week and then his slate would be clean for the following period. Anything over five-demerits meant that you were in deep trouble. You had to "Walk on the Ramp" for each excessive demerit received.

"Walk the Ramp" implied a 50-minute march on the diagonal sidewalks and the walks in front of all of the barracks for each hour assigned. There would be a ten-minute rest between each demerit tour. Part of the punishment required each Cadet to have one of our regular parachutes strapped on while walking around the endless configuration of cement walks.

The parachute we used in Primary Training was the type where the chute itself was packed into a rectangular canvas container that would serve the dual purpose of also being the seat cushion while flying in the plane. This meant that the actual pack fell down to the area of your calves and would bounce against them with each step. The parachute harness fit tightly against your chest and back and added to the discomfort for this mode of travel.

There was a certain amount of shame connected with this punishment. The shame being, that you got caught doing some stupid or insignificant thing. I suppose the penance gained from this humiliating act of wasting hours walking a rigid course was the pride one gained for not screwing up again.

You had to look straight ahead, stop at each corner of the walk, turn sharply in a military fashion, and keep a steady pace for exactly 50 minutes. You were not permitted to talk with anyone. Usually, there would be several unfortunate Cadets, spaced out over this boring course, walking away their sins. This particular Saturday would be "yours truly" first and only time required to take part in this form of punishment.

My involvement in walking the ramp occurred when I was compelled to use the third permitted reply, "No Excuse Sir." During the week I had been assigned Cadet-In-Charge of our unit. It was my primary responsibility on this Saturday morning to see that each occupant of this large unit policed his own area and had all of his clothes stored in accordance with specific requirements. During the week, the "Cadet-in-Charge" saw that no Cadet would disturb another during our study hour, our unit was kept clean and neat, and all were in bed at the sound of taps.

The final responsibility of the week for the Cadet-In-Charge was preparation for the early Saturday morning inspection, a white glove affair. Three Upperclass Officers would arrive; you had to pop to attention by your bunk, look straight ahead while they would snoop in every cranny, rubbing their white-gloved finger across any surface they suspected as being dusty.

We believed we were ready, but at the last moment, as the officers approached our unit, Cadet Ketron, my friend from Knockville, Tennessee, had been eating an apple and was unable to finish it. He quickly placed it under the overturned waste paper basket, chancing that they would not look there. Wrong. One of the Upperclassmen accidentally bumped the basket, exposing the apple core.

This horrendous discovery was noted and the blame automatically was charged to the Cadet-In-Charge, which is noted on the bulletin board. At the moment of discovery of this apple core, I noticed Cadet Ketron, this special friend of mine from the hill country of Tennessee, was about to step forward to take the blame. Luckily, we were opposite one another in the room so that he could look into my eyes. Without causing undue attention, I blinked, squinted, and contorted my eyes and nose as a means to inform him not to say anything.

To own up to this incident would only have meant that both of us would be out on the ramp. This incident cost me five demerits, because it was interpreted as trying to fool the inspection team. These demerits, added to the four demerits I had picked up on my own volition during the week, meant that I would have to walk off four hours before I could go into town.

I walked my tour and late in the afternoon, it did not take too much of a decision to utilize the remainder of my pass in the sack and not go into town and do some additional walking. The calves of each leg had become swollen and sore and my ego had been badly bruised.

This method of metering out punishment tended to keep us all on our toes and, though it seems they emphasized trivial things, we were all to learn there really are no minor or puny things when it comes to flying an airplane. Each week the number of offenses decreased and the efficiency and appearance of the cadets showed obvious improvement. We were developing pride, not only as a personal thing, we also took pride in the entire unit, the Class of 43J at Uvalde, Texas.

The class-work we were assimilating was both interesting and pertinent. In nearly every class we had civilian instructors who were conscientious and well informed. The material was covered rapidly, with little time spent in class reviewing past work. Nearly each day we would have an examination in one of the many courses we were taking and, in most cases, they would not be announced in advance. Since most subjects were of interest to me or fell under the umbrella of my engineering background, I was doing quite well, academically.

A week after I became an upperclassman, I had another hairy experience. Four or five of us left our study desks one evening to go to the coke machine for a break. Our returned nickel told us that the machine was empty. This machine, one of the first dispensers on the market, was a simple circular tub that held the "Mae West" type coke bottles.

As the hole in the top cover moved over a full bottle of coke, the nickel permitted its removal. The corners of this antiquated contraption were used for storage of additional bottles. When the coke delivery-man came, he would fill the machine with these bottles and put new ones into the corners. He had not been around of late so we had a crisis.

I discovered that I could reach through the three-inch diameter hole, work my hand into the corner, and with my fingers I could manipulate a full coke bottle out. The whole process took a minute or two while my arm and hand were submerged in very cold ice water. I had removed a coke for each of my friends and was about to retrieve one for myself, when a jeep suddenly drove up with one of our officers. He not only was an officer, he was Officer Of The Day.

By this time my hand and arm had become swollen, both from the cold water and the fact that I had numerous cuts and scratches caused by sharp protrusions of metal. As he approached, my arm was in the machine, nearly up to my armpit. I just knew I was doomed. Instead, Lt. Urban stated: "Cadet Krueger, do you think you could find another coke in that beast?" After my reply of "Yes Sir," I ripped my arm out with his prize and proceeded to get the next one for myself. We all drank nervously, until this intruder drove away. I had lucked out. He did, however, require each of us to deposit a nickel into the machine as he did.

Actually, I only ventured into Uvalde a few times. This small community had very little to offer cadets who had been confined to the base for several weeks at a time and were looking for some degree of excitement or entertainment. I had grown up to not depend on movies at a theater, mostly because I never seemed to be able to afford it. Though they were free on the Base, few seemed worth the time to watch.

I did appreciate waiting for the buses to show up at about 10:00 P.M. for our return to the base. Diagonally across from the bus stop was a small white unpretentious Baptist Church. The parishioners were African American. Each evening that I waited for my bus, I could hear the music and singing emitting from this simple structure. Loud clapping and jovial sounds made the air vibrate, even at this bus stop. There were times I thought I could actually see the walls of this church respond to the energies and enthusiasm of the members of this congregation.

I wished I had had the nerve to go over to their church and had entered. The spirit and sounds of enjoyment were completely foreign to me, but I knew they were obviously created by sincere free spirited people I knew little about. At this point in my life I was completely ignorant and unaware how African Americans had been and were continually being treated in our country. I came from a home and upbringing where I could not look down my nose at anyone.

CHAPTER 6

When I first arrived at Garner Field, our early days were spent getting oriented, starting ground school classes, and just generally getting adjusted to the many demands placed upon each cadet. On the fourth day, I was scheduled for my first exposure to flying. The moment of truth for my dreams and the primary reason for joining the Air Force would now be at hand.

INTO THE AIR

At 1030 hours, Cadets Kristy, Sweeney, and I had to be at the main hanger in flight-suit. We would meet our flight instructor for the first time, P.L. Viviani. He, as were most of our teachers and instructor, was a civilian. Viviane was extremely short, as noted before. The word short, being defined, more accurately, as only about 5' 4".

He was very trim, dark complexion, and very Italian looking. He had a sense of humor but also an indiscernible air about him. It was hard to know exactly what was on his mind during periods of silent. We all respected him and believed it was his job to turn out the best pilots he could and he would do everything within his power to do so.

This new primary trainer, a Fairchild PT-19, was parked on the concrete apron near the hanger and we were about to meet and get acquainted with her. Instructor Viviani spent the first hour walking us around the parked airplane, explaining what the various components were and the essential points necessary to check each and every time when you preflight a plane prior to takeoff.

As we walked around this plane, I could hardly keep my hands off from her. I could hardly believe we were actually going to be given the chance to learn to master this beautiful airplane. Then, to make this moment in time even more memorable, I was informed that I was to be the first to go up, the other two would get their initial ride right after lunch. All I knew at this particular time was, let's get on with it.

The first thing Viviani wanted me to do was to put on my seat pack type parachute. He proceeded to show me how to properly adjust all of the straps so that it fit snug, a necessity, should you have to bail out. It was difficult to walk with this cumbersome chute on, let alone climb into the front seat. I learned about walking while wearing this type of parachute when I had to erase four demerits. The chute is actually meant to be a seat cushion that fits in the simple metal dish in the plane.

Once I snuggled in and secured myself with the seat belt attached to the plane, Viviani checked everything to be sure he wouldn't lose me, should he decide to roll the plane over. Though I felt restricted in movement, I immediately sensed that I was about to realize a dream I had thousands of times. The word excitement hardly seemed appropriate at this moment. My ride in a plane months ago, with my friend George and Archie Towle, was an entirely different emotion.

There were no defined runways, only a very flat grass field that was about a hundred yards wide and four or five hundred yards long. The term grass field might not be a good description since it looked more like a mowed hay field with patches of dirt taking up about fifty percent of the area. It had a row of scraggly looking small Texas live oak trees on each edge of this field, which I surmised were meant to be windbreaks.

Viviani taxied off of the concrete apron near the large hanger and slowly maneuvered the plane to one end of the meadow before us. I could feel that the brakes had been applied as he pushed the throttle forward, making the engine belch out a roar before me. For a moment I thought this little plane would vibrate itself apart.

My instructor now turned the plane into the prevailing breeze and facing the long grassy area before us. The plane started slowly at first, on this grassy carpet, and then picked up speed as Viviani pushed the throttle forward. The noise seemed to increase at the same rate our speed changed. I could watch similar controls move in my front seat section of the plane. All at once the bumpy ride over the tufts of grass was replaced by the feeling of being airborne.

This moment in time on my very first flight in the PT-19, was the first of several real thrills I would experience. Instructor Vivian flew around the area of the field for about twenty minutes, making me aware of the important landmarks so I would know how to locate the field and will be properly oriented in my home flight area. A few miles from the field I could see the small town of Uvalde. It was approximately four miles due west of my new home.

The surrounding countryside appeared to be more blase' from the air than it did while riding our bus, except for the very small area immediately around Garner Field. It looked like a little green jewel and really out of place. Once you left the immediate area of our Base, I realized that patches or clearings you normally would expect grass to be growing, like I was familiar with in Wisconsin, would be rocky barren land. Grass as I knew it, was foreign in this part of Texas. Most of these open areas had a variety of different cactus struggling to live.

It was at this point that I was told to gently put my right hand on the joystick and both feet lightly on the rudder pedals. The joystick is a simple lever control in an airplane that operates the elevators by a fore and aft motion, and the ailerons by a side-to-side motion. The rudder pedal controls the rudder, the movable vertical plane in the tail section.

The next thing I heard was Viviani shouting that I should take over. I was to have control of the airplane. This was something I had not counted on, especially on my very first ride. It was difficult to communicate with your instructor in the back seat, but there was no mistaken about this new order giving me the chance to control this plane for the first time.

Cautiously, I stared to gradually feel what each of these controls would do. If I pulled the stick gently back toward my lap I made the nose rise. Conversely, when I pushed the stick directly away from me, the nose lowered. What I was doing was moving the elevator on the horizontal stabilizer in the tail section of the plane. As I pulled back on the controls, the elevator at the rear of the plane would rise up and the airflow over its surface would tend to push the tail down. This would raise the nose of the plane in a climbing attitude. By pushing the control stick forward, the controls worked just the opposite and the nose of the plane moved downward from its normal horizontal attitude.

I next tried moving the control stick to the right. Immediately the left wing rose and the right wing dropped, causing a bank to the right. What I had done was cause the aileron or small flap on the left wing to move downward and the aileron on the right wing to be turned upward. Once again the airflow over the wing surface would catch these two ailerons and cause a logical reaction. A movement to the left created just the opposite effect.

Viviani now wanted me to try pushing gently on the right rudder pedal. I noticed the feeling of the tail being pushed to my left, causing the nose of the plane to go right. I could notice the flatness of this turn. He told me to turn right again using right rudder with just a little right aileron. This caused a smooth bank to the right. To make this turn perfect I later learned that all I had to do was also add a minute amount of rudder to raise the nose since a plane has the tendency of losing altitude during a turn maneuver.

It became immediately clear that the slightest movement on any of these controls caused instant response from the plane. I knew that my instructor's hands were very gently on the controls with me. I also knew that if I tended to move too fast, I could feel his restraint. The key was a soft touch with gentle and delicate movements.

Before we landed, I had the chance to try moving the joystick to the right and to the left several times while also using the rudder pedals. The PT-19 reacted to the slightest movement of my right hand on the joystick and to my two feet on the rudder pedal. How you moved the ailerons, elevators, and the rudder determined the every movement of this plane. This was the primary key to flying.

This day would be the only time I would not land the aircraft by myself. Landing an aircraft is one of the more difficult operations each of us will have to master. All of the above mentioned operations will have to be considered, plus the use of the throttle with the left hand. I fooled with the controls enough on this first lesson to realize that mastery of this plane required coordination, finesse, concentration, and practically zero muscle.

I went to lunch, bubbling over with excitement and tons of things to tell my two friends, Cadet's Kristy and Sweeney. They would get their turn in a few hours. Flying has to be the most exhilarating thing I have ever done. To rise above the earth and get the feeling you are nearly defying gravity and can maneuver through this almost invisible atmosphere with the freedom of our feathered friends. Defying gravity, however, is where all of our training and subsequent skills will be required. Each of us also knew that gravity would be only one of our enemies once we graduated.

I had the opportunity to go up one more time with my Instructor before I was taken out of circulation by my week spent in the hospital. These seven days, I found, would be very difficult to make up. The demand on all the available planes and the instructors during the daylight hours would make it nearly impossible to get a chance to fly extra hours or even fraction of hours.

A day or two, of rainy weather, would raise havoc with this rigid schedule of each cadet getting in their required flight time. Each day Viviani would try to give me an additional ten or fifteen minutes tacked on to my scheduled lessons, just to give me more air time. I also had the opportunity to fly a couple of times either early in the morning or late in the afternoon.

A big thrill I experienced was on my first flight after I got out of the Infirmary. We took the plane up to an altitude of about two thousand feet and Viviani proceeded to demonstrate how to put the aircraft into a spin and then to recover from it. This is, perhaps, one of the most important skills a pilot can know, since most problems in flight may require recovery from a spin.

THE SPIN

When you desire to practice a spin, the first instruction I was told is to have enough altitude for the number of turns you plan to make. Being somewhat of a coward at this stage I slowly climbed to 4500-foot altitude above the ground and leveled off. To initiate a spin the joystick is pulled back to nose the plane up in a modest climb, at the same time the throttle is pulled back to reduce power. What you are literally doing is putting the plane into a stall. At the instant the nose of the plane starts to fall earthward, you kick the right rudder to have a right hand spin, or left for the opposite.

Usually for this maneuver, you align the airplane up with a road or the edge of a field to have some type of a reference point. If you plan a half turn spin, a one-turn spin or a two-turn spin, it is not necessarily essential but nice to know at what point the spin was started. This is particularly true for a new student pilot.

The instant the plane reaches stall-speed, the nose will drop and you are aware the plane is starting to nose downward. It is at this same instant, you get the first sensation you are being left up at altitude, while your plane wants to leave you. Your heart and intestines are going through similar gyrations. You immediately feel the pressure of your seat belt on the top of your thighs.

While the nose drops the right rudder is instantly kicked and the nose begins to spiral in a clockwise direction. Slowly, at first, the plane starts spiraling to the right. Each fraction of a second, it picks up momentum, at the same time you can noticeably see the earth approaching in a twisting pattern.

To pull the plane out of a one turn spin, for example, about 10 degrees prior to aligning with the road that you used as a reference point, you would simultaneously push the joystick forward, kick opposite rudder (opposite to the direction of the spin), push the throttle forward to increase power, and then with a great deal of effort, you pull the stick back into your lap. This all is happening simultaneously.

The thrill comes from the increased noise, the movement alternately between earth and sky, and the feeling you have lost complete control of the situation. You are now aware of gravity. For an instant you feel yourself being forced down into your seat in the change of direction. The plane first straightens out and then gradually noses up from the diving attitude it was in. As soon as the plane starts to leave the spin behind, you lower the nose to put the craft into a level flight attitude or a slight climb, depending on your intentions.

It may take a dozen or more of these spins before you feel comfortable with it and have the confidence to kick the plane into a spiral, just for the thrill of it. Many practice sessions are required to perfect this maneuver, but none will ever be the same or provide similar sensations, as that first one.

Hours are spent practicing flying in a large square pattern, using a road or highway as a reference point. Exact altitude has to be maintained throughout each maneuver and coordinated turns are essential. This does not sound difficult until you take the wind into consideration. Each turn will be different since the wind may be in front of you, behind you, or from either side of you on each of these separate maneuvers.

Each day will also be different from the previous one, since the velocity of the wind will change as well as its direction. This same type of lesson is practiced over and over, using the familiar road, and turning continuous lazy S turns. It requires constant thinking and a sensitive feel to keep the plane at a consistent altitude. The added problem is the fact that you are continually making turns to the right or left as you maneuver the plane through these S curves.

This all requires banking to the right or left, maintaining constant altitude while the wind direction effects each direction of the plane differently. The S curves have to be identical and uniform even when the wind may be pushing you or your plane is nosing into it. I found this invisible wind was the culprit that caused me the most problems and was hardest to master.

Each day we flew, Instructor Viviani had me practice landings, take-offs, banks, stalls, climbing or descending at a constant rate, S-turns, etc. During these ensuing weeks, I discovered that Viviani sometimes had a very short fuse. If things did not go exactly as he desired or if I did not react as quickly as he wanted, he would rapidly move the joystick from side to side, hitting me on the inside of each knee. This punishment, though physical, had a greater effect on my feelings. I gave it my absolute best to please this little Italian and to master the machine that gave us flight. This was his way of demanding perfection.

EMERGENCY LANDINGS

Regardless of the maneuver I was undertaking, I was told that it was always mandatory I have an emergency landing area in mind, just in case I needed it. This was an added thing to occupy your mind while trying to master the technique of flying. This training was important for obvious reasons, but it was not always easy to think about this particular aspect of flying when most of your concentration was taken up with keeping the plane completely under control.

One particular day, Viviani unexpectedly turned the key off and cut the engine.

The first sight you're greeted with is a stopped propeller in front of you, followed by the feeling the plane is about to stall out. I instantly put the plane in a shallow dive to maintain air speed, and I started a slow turn toward a distant field I had picked just for such an occasion.

I had maneuvered the plane so that I would approach this field in the down wind direction, with enough altitude to turn into the available wind and still have enough of the field left for my landing. Whoopee. It appeared that I was doing everything perfect in this emergency approach. I just knew that Viviani would be proud of me. Wrong. The one mistake I made was that this field was covered by a flock of small goats, not noticed until I had the plane in position for my perfect landing.

Viviani turned on the ignition, started the engine, gave it maximum power, and took the controls away from me. Once we got up to altitude, he started yelling. Though he is sitting in the cockpit behind me, I could make out most of what he was yelling about. I did not have to hear or understand all of his words. I knew what I had done wrong.

In his frustration, he started to waggle the joystick with unusual vigor. My reflexes had developed to the point where I was able to spread my legs and let the spent energy of my instructor merely fan the air. Chalk one up for Krueger. Wrong again. Viviani immediately rolled the plane over, so we were flying upside down, and proceeded to rap my knees with the control stick.

I discovered that it was impossible to spread the old knees hanging by my safety strap. The mistake I made this day, I shall never forget. I did, however, receive an apology from my instructor, upon landing. This innocent lesson I learned today taught me to be more thorough and meticulous in my every action.

On May 20th, we taxied to the end of the runway and were about to take off. Viviani informed me that he was going to leave the plane and this now, would be my moment of truth. Today I would solo. Most of my buddies had experienced this thrill a few days before. I patiently listened to their excitement each day in the barracks. Now I was to have my chance. Viviani assured me I was ready and that I was to take the plane up for a half hour flight, doing whatever I desired.

SOLO FLIGHT

I pointed the plane down the axis of the runway. I raced down the grassy and bumpy surface and was airborne in less than one minute. I had not given myself time to think about what this moment really meant. I slowly climbed to about 2,000 feet and leveled off. I looked behind to reassure myself that Viviani was not there.

Though the cockpit behind me was empty, I could feel his presence. I could also ascertain, on the plane's controls, that his light touch was missing and I alone was in this plane.

With this realization that I was actually alone in this little blue plane, I let out one hell of a scream. I did not know a reason for this outburst, or if it had any real significance. I knew only that my dreams for the past several months had come to fruition. I was alone in this plane and was the only person who could make it respond and react to my every wish.

Just about this time I suddenly began to realize that there was no one to back me up should I make a goof. Even though your instructor is present, you never feel him on the controls. You just know he is flying with you every second. This realization suddenly sinks in and it leaves an empty feeling in the pit of your stomach. I didn't dwell on this feeling for more than a second or two. I still had twenty minutes to have fun and to soak up this unforgettable moment, a moment which can happen only once in your life.

I got the feeling of pride that finally I could do something I had always dreamed of. I was actually flying this heavier that air contraption and I could make it go to wherever I desired, within limitations. I flew over the city of Uvalde for the first time and enjoyed the layout of its streets. I could see the cars and the people, as well as its large courthouse. My watch told me it was now time to return to Garner Field.

The sinking feeling returned, as I approached the field for my landing. Once again I knew I was entirely alone and that this plane would not get on the ground safely without the help of the skills Viviani had taught me. My first solo landing was not one of my best, but it was more than adequate. I attributed this mediocre landing to my excessive excitement.

Viviani, for the first time, showed some real emotion. He displayed a smile that ran across his little Italian face, a face that always looked like it needed a fresh shave. I knew for the first time what was racing through his head. I got congratulated, my hand shook, and a pat on the back, that almost turned into a hug. I still had much to learn about flying, but this moment had to be savored for a little longer.

My classmates in the barracks were happy for me, especially since I was the last in our group to solo. Out of the original six, only one cadet had been washed out, probably an average for each of the units in each barracks. To celebrate on my first day off, another cadet and I went into Uvalde.

Shortly after arriving in town we met a rancher and his young daughter who was about sixteen years old. The four of us made small talk for perhaps a half hour when they proceeded to invite us out to their small ranch, some distance from town.

We rode in the back of a rusty beaten-up old truck, along with a bale of straw and several sacks of some type of grain.

It was not the movie version of a typical ranch, but a small, run-down place that was in a state of disrepair and a facility that provided only an existence for this friendly and generous rancher and his family. I discovered later that few Texas ranches had out buildings like I was accustomed to back in Wisconsin.

Probably the best definition or difference between what we referred to as a farm and here in Texas a ranch, were the buildings. A farm invariably had a large barn designed for multiple purposes such as holding cattle, storage of grain, and a place to keep specialized equipment. A ranch usually consisted of more acreage of land and few if any out buildings.

Having flown over this particular countryside on many occasions, it was apparent to me that this spread, I now was walking across, was all too similar to the many parcels of land I had noted. One could see the relatively small "ranches" fenced in with a little house tucked under several Texas Live Oak trees. In this area, the small ranch houses were dispersed approximately a mile or so apart.

The opportunity to walk around the place, breath fresh air without the pressures of our normal routine, and have the chance to eat a home cooked meal, made this a most memorable day. Most of the cattle I saw on this humble place provided me with the opportunity to study their anatomy. I could see their skeletal structure through their taut hides. These animals had all they could do to just eke out a survival diet from the vegetation available on this stony harsh land.

I must have given away my observation with the expression on my face. Our newfound friend, the rancher, explained that these cattle would be fattened elsewhere, before they would reach a packing plant. In Wisconsin farmers would be elated to state how many cattle their land would support on a single acre. Today I would discover that this rancher would be grateful to have a single critter be able to survive on many acres of the land he owned.

This small white house looked like it had but two bedrooms, a modest sized living room, a kitchen of about the same size, and a room that could be considered multi purpose since it acted like an entrance, a pantry, a closet, and it had a stand with a wash basin.

The floor-boards in the kitchen were worn but it was obvious they had been scrubbed thousand of times. Though very humble, this home was cozy, clean, and comfortable. The large table had been set for six of us since they also had a young son of about five years of age. There were bowls of potatoes, some type of greens, baked beans, and a platter with two different types of sausage on it. We also were to be treated to some homemade bread we could smell as we entered the kitchen.

After we ate a nice dinner, Roseleeta, the rancher's young daughter, walked my friend and me around this modest ranch. Walking down one of the many gullies and across some of the land covered by small mesquite trees I got to see many strange creatures that would be foreign to someone from Wisconsin and the North.

I saw my first rattlesnake coiled next to a large rock. I knew that it was only prudent to not disturb this reptile while it was sun bathing. We watched from a very safe distance while this interesting snake shook the rattles on its tail. I would estimate that if it uncoiled itself and straightened out, it would approach four foot in length. We have this same type of snake in Wisconsin and I gave them the same respect as I was doing now.

Changing my direction I stumbled upon an armadillo. I had seen pictures of this prehistoric looking critter, but now I saw it waddling along to avoid my curiosity. I slowly walked behind this timid and usually nocturnal edentate mammal. I was fascinated by its bony armor plates moving as it tried scampering away. I got too close as I followed and it suddenly stopped and curled into a tight ball. As I finally satisfied my curiosity and was walking away, this little wonder once again took off to find shelter under a large and thick bush.

I was surprised how rapidly it could move when it had a mind to. I had read somewhere they should not be handled without gloves since they are known to transmit some type of virus which could cause leprosy. Roseleeta said she never heard of that and informed us she has picked up dozens of these little rascals.

With all of my interest in this newfound nature, I soon discovered I was alone, since my friend and Roseleeta had other things to discuss. As I lifted up an interesting piece of weathered wood that now had caught my attention, I made a new discovery. I had uncovered several large scorpions. They scrutinized me by curling up their long tail and just stared at this startled Cadet.

Once again I had to rely on my exposure to pictures I had seen of these and the knowledge that they were dangerous. This is one insect I do not believe exists in Wisconsin. I observed their elongated body with the segmented narrow curled tail. I was aware that this unique tail had a venomous stinger at its tip. They also had claws extending out in front of them which added to their unusual appearance. I carefully lowered this piece of weathered wood to its original position and decided I was no longer interested in it.

Perhaps the most fascinating discovery I made this day was my first encounter with a tumblebug, a large beetle about the size of a mature June bug. The male is black and about .8 of an inch in length, while the female is slightly smaller and gray in color. I was told they were often called dung beetles, and I was soon to find out why.

The thing that makes this beetle unique is the fact it has the habit of carving out a one-inch diameter plug from cow dung. They will then roll this plug across the ground, causing all corners to break off. Soon it becomes a perfect sphere. One beetle will ride on the side of this slow rolling ball with the axis beneath it, while the other partner will walk on its front legs with the hind legs pushing the ball forward.

The interesting phenomenon about this particular beetle, they seem to be able to direct this ball of dung around stones, pebbles, and other obstacles until it reaches a specific small hole in the ground. As they enlarge this hole to handle the ball of dung, it gradually drops into the earth. Once it arrives at a designated place, the female beetle deposits eggs into this sculptured wonder.

I sat on the ground and watched this entire incident repeated several times. I could not believe an insect, like a simple beetle, could have developed with this amount of know how. I quickly thought of the performance a simple spider displays as it weaves a complex web.

Next to a large rock I noticed a patch of very fine sand that had numerous small conical depressions in the surface. Quite by accident I saw a tiny ant walk into one of these depressions. As it tried to climb out, I noticed it continually slipped toward the apex of this cone. Suddenly, something broke through the sand and pulled the ant from sight. I watched this same interesting event happen sever times.

I took a small twig and exposed a small little insect that had a single claw like arm. I found out later they were known as ant-lions. The sand was extremely fine and each little grain is almost a perfect sphere. This is what quick sand is. As the ant tried to escape, the ant-lion flicked sand up to the top of the inverted cone and they acted like ball bearings, making the ant slip down so that the claw could grab it.

I could have spent many more hours just nosing around this otherwise drab environment. My friends ultimately persuaded me to get off the ground and get a life. They thought I was wacky devoting a disproportionate amount of this beautiful day to a group of dung beetles, or whatever. I have never regretted my interest and curiosity in all forms of nature.

Things that they hardly noticed were of interest to me. Everywhere I looked I saw prickly pear cactus, several yucca plants, and soaring in the sky were Texas vultures. Most other birds were only indigenous to this part of our huge country. "What's not to wonder about and like?"

UPPERCLASSMEN

In the interim, my class has become Upperclassmen, and I had been promoted to an Echelon Sergeant. My new duties required me to lead the entire cadet group in our barracks to and from classes, direct them in calisthenics, and lead them over obstacle courses, etc. This afforded me the opportunity to get to know my fellow classmates better and a chance to build on my confidence. I enjoyed my class work, and the grades I received in each of these courses were a reflection on this interest. I was one happy cadet.

The next few weeks my flight time was spent flying solo and practicing the variety of maneuvers required for specific flight tests. On occasion, Viviani would ride with me to show this new young pilot something different or to check up on my flight habits or proficiency. He would not tolerate sloppiness in any of the various required training exercises. Often he would break my bubble by showing me ways to improve certain techniques.

As we approached the final weeks of our training, you could sense the gradual increase in the excitement level among the cadets. We were beginning to take cross-country trips in actual formation with our PT-19s. We all knew we were not able to take on the enemy as yet, but each had the feeling of accomplishment and it would now be only a matter of time.

During our final week, the second week of June, one by one we each were scheduled to take a test flight with one of the Air Corp Lieutenants. This would be our check ride to see if we were ready to go on to Basic Flight Training. Again I would be next to the last in our barracks to get assigned for this check ride.

My ride for this final check was a successful one, so I did not worry about if I would pass and go on to Basic, it was only wondering where I would go next. I knew my academic side of our training had been excellent since I received nothing but A's or the simple word Pass on the almost daily tests thrown at us. My interest in engineering and my single year of college had truly been an asset.

CHAPTER 7

Now that we have finished our formal classes and had taken our last test flight, we knew it was only a day or two away from announcing when and where we would be stationed next. On June 14, 1943, I received notice that I was to report to headquarters at 1400 hours. I did not have the slightest idea of why they wanted to see me or for what purpose, since none of my buddies in our unit had been called. Perhaps I was to be the first to find out where I would go.

When I arrived I discovered six other Cadets from other barracks who were to attend this meeting, each of whom were also in the dark, like myself, about this special order. Though I did not know any of the other fellows, I recognized each of them. We sat in an outer office, guessing and prognosticating about where we were to be sent next. Each of us knew that we would move up to more powerful airplanes, requiring new skills we all looked forward to.

After about a twenty-minute wait, we were asked to enter a large office in a group and be seated in front of five officers. Seven chairs had been carefully placed in a straight row. The C.O. of Garner Field began the meeting by welcoming us and then lost no time with his explanation of just why we were all present.

BOTTOM DROPS OUT

Colonel Rogers stated, "As of yesterday, all Air Force Bases have been notified of the necessity to increase the numbers of Cadets entering Navigation Training. This change in policy was caused by the unacceptable losses experienced in Europe due to the method of attack by the German Luftwaffe. Frontal attacks wounded or killed many of the officers in the nose section of the B-17's, those that were fortunate enough to make it back to their home bases."

"The German pilots preferred frontal attacks on formations because the rate of closure gave the fighter planes additional advantages. B-17 Model E's and F's, which are in combat at this time, do not have chin turrets with multiple 50 cal. machine guns. The new B-17 G model now has this chin turret with multiple guns. It is being rushed to England at this very moment and the Air Force is rapidly producing crews to man each of these new bombers."

He went on to say, "The Army Air Force was making up the loss of First Pilots by moving up the co-pilots, but they were facing a dire shortage of trained Navigators to compliment these crews. The order had been sent out to search for any personnel who had qualified for Navigation Training but were not in the program. You young men may not be aware of the fact, but Navigational Training mandates a very special and demanding type of prerequisites that each of you possess."

My heart was sinking. Were they going to pull us out of Pilot training now and make us become Navigators? Colonel Rogers now hit us between the eyes. "You seven cadets at Garner Field were the only ones who had qualified for Pilot, Navigation, and Bombardier Training. The decision has gone out that you will be pulled from your current program and be ordered to attend a Navigational School on selected different bases."

We seven just sat there stunned and waited an order to be dismissed. We all were bewildered and shocked. I could not believe what I was hearing nor could I comprehend the logic behind it. It felt like somebody with a 12-gauge shotgun had just blown away my dream of being a Pilot. I could feel my stomach churning as I tried to visualize exactly what I had just heard.

It was obvious we were not to be given any input into these orders, and the many apologies we received from our officers did not make this moment any easier to accept. I just could not visualize being anything but a Pilot in the many days that lay before me. My one-track thought process had not allowed room for this devastating news.

The Colonel did state, as we left his office, "Should the situation change over in Europe, there always is the possibility you can return to the States and continue you Pilot Training." "That was Bull Shit and he knew it," I said under my breath. We each kicked at the ground and swore as we parted for our individual barracks. This was one dejected group of Cadets. When I got to my barracks and informed my classmates, I received only sympathy that did nothing to ease my current feelings for the Air Force.

On the morning of June 16th, our small group was put on a bus and headed back to San Antonio. The seven of us rode in almost perfect silence, each in our own thoughts. How could one moment be so good and the next one so bad? It was easy to see that each of us, in the eyes of the power to be, were mere numbers and that our files contained a lot of statistical data that would determine our future and our destiny.

Feelings and emotions had no part to play in the decision to alter these seven young Cadet's dreams. Why should the fact that we had qualified for each of the three positions on fighter or bomber planes be held against us. It did not seem fair. This was a word I would learn that is not apart of the military and war in general. I thought this was the lowest point in my young life. I again was to be proven wrong in the days still ahead of me.

We had another surprise awaiting us once we arrived back at San Antonio. We were not taken back to S.A.A.C.C. where we had previously been stationed, but rather too another section of this huge Base, an area I was unaware existed. We were assigned tents to live in, and were told that we would remain here for the next scheduled class of Navigational Student Cadets. We discovered we had just missed the last class moving out by a week. Because of this, that at a minimum, we would be here in these damn tents for at least two months.

TENT CITY

This section of the Base had row upon row of nothing but tents. They looked new, but they were still tents. Streets had names so this area took on the irrefutable and appropriate name of "tent city." The moral within this city was at understandably and unbelievably low ebb. In a situation like this, I can now know how the proverbial service man's oft used expression, "situation normal, all f**ked up" came from. I later was to hear this phrase, along with "hurry up and wait", describe most situations we were periodically confronted with.

"Tent City" had all the appearance of something hastily erected and could be torn down and moved in hours. Each tent was approximately twelve feet square, with six or eight cadets assigned to each. There was a center pole that was about five-feet higher than the outside walls, thus the canvas roof took on a conical look.

The general appearance and atmosphere were comparable to the impression I received when I arrived at Nashville, very depressing. Bunks with mattresses that we had been accustomed to are now replaced with army cots. A simple canvas layer, supported on each side by wood rails, was meant to be a substitute for springs and mattresses. My current moral did not need this ambience.

Fortunately, we seven cadets that had left Garner Field at Uvalde, shared the same tent. Two other tents held Cadets in a similar situation, those who had shipped in from other Primary Pilot Schools. Misery likes company. However, most of the other tents held disgruntled Cadets who had washed out of either Pilot or Navigational Training for one reason or another.

We had been told that those who had scored the highest rating on the many preliminary tests we had taken could enroll in Navigational Training. Up until now the Air Force had let this special group enter whatever flight branch they wanted to be trained in. Now this choice would not be granted to the group who accomplished the best test results, they would automatically be sent to Navigational Training Centers.

All other washed out cadets were being held here until the Air Force decided where they would go. Their moral was even lower than ours, if that could be possible. We, at least, had been assured of remaining in the Cadet-Training program and were still Aviation Cadets.

Our little group was told that we would be taking several additional classes, such as math, military science, and Morse code, but that we would be given a generous amount of liberty. This, of course, meant that we would be able to get into San Antonio, a rather large and beautiful city.

My first reaction was this would ease the pain each of us was going through. The fallacy and the reality soon became apparent when I realized I couldn't afford, on my pay, to make too many trips into the city. The cost of buying meals away from our encampment would break my measly bank.

I am not ashamed to admit I spent the greater part of my first three day in "tent City" periodically crying and feeling sorry for myself. On the least little provocation I could feel my eyes swell up and sometimes tears would make their way down my cheek. It felt like my whole world had come crashing down. My dream of becoming a fighter pilot dashing across the skies of Europe had just been smashed. This was the greatest disappointment I had ever been the recipient of.

The hardest part to accept was the fact that it was not something I did or did not do. In fact, I was being punished because I had, in reality, done too good in these test that the Air Force used to evaluate us. A decision I had no input with had just determined what my fate would be.

Later I was to learn, that this is exactly the situation each time I was scheduled to go on a combat mission. I was never given any impute on whether I desired to go or even just where we would go to drop a load of bombs. I would never be consulted when a target somewhere in Germany was to receive a visit from the Eighth Air Force.

I was never going to hold enough rank or have anyone care about what was bouncing around in my head. There were millions in the Service, both in Europe and somewhere out in the Great Pacific, whose only reply to any order would be the expected "Yes Sir."

We all believed, by escaping our miserable quarters and getting lost in San Antonio, these next two months would fly by. This lovely city, on the edge of the Hill Country of Texas, would help make our situation more tolerable. It did not take too long to bust this bubble.

A very obvious flaw in our thinking suddenly appeared. Most of us, at least in our humble tent, did not have enough money to go into San Antonio too often because we could not afford to buy food. At least on the Base they had to feed us. The pay we received was only significant when you ate your meals on the Base and did not have outside expenses.

This realization dictated that we had to get acclimated to brown canvas, hard beds, and a smell appropriate to the ambience of this ungodly place. I found out later that a few of my friends told me that they got money from home or some other source I was not aware of. I knew that if my Father would not or could not give me money to go on to college, he sure as hell would not send me money to fight a war.

SAN ANTONIO

When I finally ventured forth and went into this unique city, where the Alamo is located, I discovered I enjoyed going alone. I did this because I liked walking to and in the many parks and especially along the River Walk. I also spent many of my days walking through purely residential neighborhoods. Most of my friends did not get a charge out of this type of entertainment, which pretty much determined my solitude. I knew I could not pay to entertain myself or to eat in any fancy restaurants. Hell, I couldn't eat in inexpensive ones.

There was another factor that dictated my actions. I desired to be alone in my own thoughts. I was going through a difficult time and this was my way of meeting it head on. I needed time, to organize my thoughts and to make something positive come out of one of the most negative experiences of my life. Many things I knew I could resolve by laughing my way through them. This was not one of those situations.

I felt very fortunate, during this undesirable interlude, when my moral was at its lowest ebb, to be located near such a city as San Antonio. Instead of a beautiful and interesting city, I could have been out in the boon docks somewhere, with no possibilities. My destination could even have been Nashville, Tennessee.

The only pleasant memory I had of Nashville was that each morning on one of the fellows radio we heard a young woman sing requests to anyone fortunate enough to call into the station. Her name was Dina Shore. She would talk to those who called in before singing their request. At the time Dina was a local young woman on a small local radio station. It became apparent that someone with all of her charm and charisma would ultimately be discovered on a National Radio Network.

This magnificent city, with a population of over three quarters of a million people, is rich in history, since it can trace its roots back to 1718, which predates the founding of the United States by more than half a century. Six different flags have flown over this part of Texas. It is the only state that can legally raise its flag to the same level as the United States flag. This is for the reason that this state was once a Republic

The influence of the Spanish founders is everywhere, with old and interesting missions, Spanish architecture on many buildings, and the names of many streets, plazas, and points of interest bearing this ancient influence. The population of this city has a very high percentage of people who had come, over the years, from Mexico. Their colorful clothing and their language were most unique to this lad from Wisconsin.

I soon discovered the people of San Antonio be very cordial and friendly. A ritual that I enjoyed, especially on a Sunday morning, was to take one of my lonely walks through a favorite residential neighborhood, know as the King Williams District. Here I found huge mature Texas Live Oaks that shaded the sidewalks and most of the street. I had the feeling of walking down a tunnel of leaves. On either side of these beautiful streets were large and impressive homes. Their yards were profusely landscaped with flowering bushes and hedges created from a variety of shrubbery and strategically planted vines.

It was in this section of town that nearly all of the successful German Merchants and business men had built their dwellings. There was a great deal of German influence in San Antonio, dating back to the days when the early leaders did everything possible to get Europeans to come to this new land. The Republic of Texas encouraged Europeans to settle in this area by offering land and other incentives. Entire communities from Germany, Italy, Czechoslovakia and England put down roots all over this huge state of Texas.

Usually during these walks I would meet families on their way to church. Most would stop and talk, namely asking me where I was from and did I like their state. All of these people of course, were used to various uniformed service personnel. The State of Texas had probably more bases, stations, and airfields from the Army, Navy, and Air Force, constructed all over this large and unique state than anywhere else.

On several occasions, during these strolls, I was actually invited into their homes for Sunday dinner and got to spend the afternoon with their families. This not only was most interesting and enjoyable, but it fit right into my budget. I came from a state in which the majority of the people were of German heritage, so the name of Krueger was not unknown in the many homes I visited.

On three different occasions, prior to placing my feet beneath their dinner table, I was invited to attend church with the families. Because I was not very good at saying no, I not only found myself in church but I would be sitting in the choir. Few of these kind people knew that, number one, I was not a Baptist and secondly, I could not sing worth a damn.

What a poor Cadet wouldn't do to get a good home cooked meal. The up side of all of this was I did get to know many families and a better understanding of just what Texas is all about. I learned the meaning of the term Southern Hospitality, perhaps more than most of the recruits who passed through the south during their training.

There seemed to be a different kind of pride in their State. In fact, on more than one occasion, some were tempted to even brag a bit and inform me that the State of Texas just happened to be the largest of the forty-eight.

Right smack in the middle of town is the famous Alamo, an early mission, but more famous as the fort that defied the repressions of Mexico's self-proclaimed Dictator, Santa Anna. In 1836 a band of 189 Texas volunteers fought off thousands of Mexicans for thirteen days, before they all were killed, to the man. Among the Alamo defenders were such famous men as Davy Crockett, Jim Bowie, and William Travis. Six weeks later, Sam Houston's Texans routed the Mexican army at the Battle of San Jacinto.

In addition to the Alamo, there are four other San Antonio missions that were established by Franciscan friars in the early 18th Century. Mission Nuestra Senora de la Purisima Concepcion; Mission San Francisco de la Espada; Mission San Jose y San Miguel de Aguayo; and Mission San Juan Capistrano, all had their beginnings back in 1731.

The locations of each of these missions were intentionally separated by a days walk. Also, each of these missions, over two hundred years old, provided this lonely, but fascinated Air Force Cadet, an opportunity to walk in antiquity or to just sit and enjoy the pleasant atmosphere. Fortunately I enjoyed walking or just strolling along. I have never minded my own company.

My very favorite spot, and perhaps the place I spent most of my time, was the River Walk. The San Antonio River meanders several miles through midtown San Antonio. A formal path was built along each bank and you could walk under giant cypress trees, flowering bushes, and palms. There were a variety of stores, shops, restaurants, etc. dispersed along each side.

Periodically, along this picturesque trail, one would find little alcoves with park benches or bridges to get to the other side of the meandering stream. I spent many happy hours sitting on these wooden respites, mostly because they were within my meager budget, but also to just watch people. The entire atmosphere along the River Walk proved to be most therapeutic for the mixed up emotions I carried within.

Despite the many wonderful sights San Antonio had to offer, the reality was that most of my time was actually spent in "Tent City" on the base. The main reason for this was the lack of funds required each time I went to town. A Cadet received $75.00 per month base pay and a $1.00 per day subsistence allowance. Even though we earned more than a private in the regular army, it wasn't enough to go out on the town too often. Purchasing food off the Base was perhaps the straw that broke the camels back.

Since my income dictated what I would do and where I could go, the simplest solution was to spend an inordinate amount of time on my cot, in a hot tent. Many of the other cadets were confronted with similar situations, although there were those who could live it up at their own discretion. They were, however, the exception and not the rule. Playing cards and simple conversation would occupy most of our time.

A great deal of these moments, unfortunately, were spent feeling sorry for our selves, since each felt the Air Force had let them down. The moral was terrible and it was reflected in how we looked, dressed, and our general attitude. Seldom did any officers bother to come and check in on us. I suppose we each felt we had been forgotten and no one seemed to really care or give a damn. The only time we would shave would be on the days we went into town or perhaps on a trip to the PX.

There were many times my eyes would weld up when I would reflect on my desires to become a fighter pilot, and then realize that the "fickle finger of fate" had caught up to me. The few tents in our immediate area all contained cadets in my situation. We all knew we were not going anywhere until the next group of Navigational students would be called up. We each would be assigned different navigational training schools to go to so each cadet was aware that we once more would be split up.

Other Cadets on the base constantly moved in and out, since they were the ones who had washed out, just plain decided to quit the spit and polish of Cadet life, the class system, or for one reason or another. They were assigned to dozens of units that required trained men to augment the skills to actually get a plane in the sky and off on a combat mission. Many ultimately remained in flying status because they went on to Gunnery School.

Others would eventually get into mechanical work and some into clerical jobs. Our country, now at war, had to take drastic measures to fill all of the hundreds of different jobs required. Logic would make it obvious that all the men who volunteered for the Air Force would not proportion themselves so each and every required position would be filled. There were duties few would seek out, but this did not lessen the importance of this task or assignment.

Many days it would rain or have lengthy showers, so the doom and gloom feeling would be most predominate. The sound of the drops hitting the canvas and the mud everywhere did little to make the situation more tolerable. We were not confronted with a class system and at times, it appeared, no one gave a damn about us.

Eventually, we took on the appearance of a motley bunch. There were several fellows that temped fate by not shaving for several weeks. I suppose they believed no one truly cared and they weren't even aware that this place existed. Most of us, like me, could go several days without touching a razor and few could notice. The fuss on our faces required a scrutiny we never seemed to be exposed to. We did not look upon ourselves as kids, but we were.

August 24th some of my "Navigator-To-Be" friends received orders that they would be shipped out the next day. Their destination was Santa Ana, California. I envied them for two reasons, the first being, that they were finally moving out of Texas and secondly, I believed this base, on the outskirts of Los Angeles, might be a great place to spend the next several months.

My orders came two days later when I was informed that a group of us would be going to San Marcos, Texas, about 50 miles northeast of San Antonio. This would not be a drastic change in environment, but it would mean I would get on with my training as a navigator.

I only had a vague idea of exactly what a Navigator's duties were on an airplane. Since I had soloed and spent many hours flying around by myself, I knew it would have been helpful to eliminate the fear of getting lost and perhaps running into a serious problem.

When I left "Tent City", there were still two of the original seven from Uvalde that had not been assigned. I never did find out exactly where they went, although I knew there are many other facilities where Navigators were being trained.

In my short military career I was now learning not to get too emotionally involved over the reason why for things and trying to make sense for many of the decisions made, all of which would affect each of our lives. Flowing with it seemed to be the best course to follow. I also could see the disadvantage of becoming too close to any particular person because you would find yourself being split up at the whims of outside forces.

CHAPTER 8

At 1400 hours on August 27, we boarded a bus to drive the 30 miles to San Marcos. This turned out to be a small town northeast of San Antonio. Everyone was happy to get on with it and each knew that this would be an entirely different experience. Despite the short distance, we did not arrive until nearly 1600 hours.

Immediately upon arrival, we were made aware that we once again were Underclassmen and that we would be back to the proverbial spit and polish routine. Nearly every cadet from Tent City had to instantly change our attitude and certainly our appearance. I think each of us, in our own way, appreciated this positive change. Almost any environment would be a welcomed sight compared to "Tent City."

BACK TO SCHOOL AGAIN

Early the next morning, the entire new Class of 44-1-8 was issued three different, but unique, types of watches and over 50 pounds of navigational equipment. We were given a wristwatch to keep current time; a stopwatch to determine accurate intervals of time; and a very special watch, a chronometer with a twenty-four hour face, to keep Greenwich, England time.

This last watch had to be very accurately calibrated to know precisely how much time it gained or lost. Over the next couple of weeks we would constantly determined its accuracy and made note of any discrepancy on a little card. It also would be mounted on springs in a special metal container to protect its exactitude from handling or being bounced around.

It now was very apparent that there was a sense and atmosphere of extreme urgency to get this new class of Cadets trained. They were not going to waste any time in getting on with our specialized military training, especially with the current shortage of Navigators.

Our class was informed that a normal day would have a minimum of eight hours of classroom work and we could expect to keep this schedule six days a week, for the next four plus months. We were also told that there would be many days we would be expected to be in class on certain evenings for tests to be given.

Because of the momentous and essential need for Navigators, this also meant we would have many of our nights devoted to studying the stars and mastering celestial navigation. Since the ability to find constellations and stars are a prerequisite for celestial navigation, we all expected we would venture out at night on many occasions. Ultimately we were given the word that most of the actual flights we would be compelled to go on would actually occur at night. I'm beginning to be thankful each day only has twenty-four hours in it. Before any graduated navigator left San Marcos he would have logged over a 100 hours of flight time.

Within a week or two I began to appreciate the challenge of this exact science. I had a rough idea of the meaning of the word navigation, but I now became aware of the difficulty of practicing this art while flying. In the air we were confronted with constantly changing winds, both in direction and velocity. Fog, clouds, storms, and weather in general, would not always be an ally. In some cases, the weather would be the determining fact whether the plane could even fly.

We were told that the Navigator would use several different systems to ascertain his exact location while in flight. The most obvious was what would be termed visual. This required the navigator to constantly track recognizable landmarks and with this information plot his position. Usually he used what was termed Dead Reckoning where his position was assumed from reading instruments on his aircraft.

The third choice we had was Celestial Navigation where positions were determined from observation of the sun, planets, moon, and of course certain stars. Late in the war a fourth method was introduced and it was called Loran. Long-range radio signals could give enough information that a fix could be calculated to determine one's position.

The instruments we used were delicate and they had to be handled with care. Many of these instruments also had to constantly be calibrated. The normal ride in the plane would not be smooth and would consequently make it very difficult to take accurate shots on stars for celestial navigation.

Then there was the noise of the engines, a real challenge to the thinking process. We also flew in a variety of airplanes, piloted by men who were pissed off because they also wanted to get into a combat situation instead of jockeying a bunch of Cadets around.

One major difference at San Marcos, compared to my pilot training at Uvalde, was that here I felt I was several weeks ahead of most of my classmates, instead of being a week behind, due to my food poison episode. The other factor that made me feel like I had an affinity for Navigation, was two of my strongest aptitudes . . . . science and math.

In the weeks to come I would be taking courses in a broad spectrum, such as the following: various math classes, weather, astronomy, temperature, variation, air masses and currents, electricity, maps, charts, radio, geography, blueprint reading, mechanical drawing, and any other science that would prove helpful.

I found each course most interesting and I was able to appreciate how it fit into the overall concept of tracking where you are going, knowing your exact location, and finding your way back to a specific location.

On September 9th, I, along with two other cadets, took our first flight. We would take off in a twin engine Beechcraft. This plane would be a Beech Model AT-7 Navigator. It was a low wing monoplane of all metal construction, with a semi-monocoque fuselage of light alloy, a cantilever tail unit incorporating twin end plate fins and rudders, and electrically retractable landing gear. This plane was powered by two 246-kW (330 hp) Jacobs L-6 engines. This Model was specifically designed for training Navigators. It was equipped with three positions for trainees and it had a special dorsal astrodome to be used for celestial navigation.

There were three navigational tables and we each were expected to practice the many things we had been taught these past few weeks. Each desk had its own set of instruments, such as altimeter, compass, radio compass, E6B computer, map, etc.

A few minutes after we were airborne, one of my friends got sick and "tossed his cookies" in a paper sack someone fortunately advised him to bring along. This would be his very first flight in an airplane. The ensuing odors made the other cadet nauseous and he also had to relieve himself of his breakfast in a cardboard container.

Our Navigator Instructor, who also flew on this flight, told this last unfortunate Cadet who was suppose to work in the No. 1 desk, to empty his container out of the plane by pouring it through a flare hole on the floor behind the two pilots. This funnel like chute has a cover and was designed to have flares pushed out of the plane, for air-sea rescue, etc.

Just as this cadet started to pour this bilious smelling mess into the wild blue yonder, a back draft deposited the entire contents of his container on the back of the first pilot and most of the instruments before him.

It is important to realize, that this pilot is not too enthusiastic to be flying a bunch of Navigation Cadets around on a training mission, because he also had aspirations of being a fighter plane jockey. With the disgorged breakfast running down the back of his head and neck, he made his exact feelings fill the interior of this crowded plane.

At this moment I was glad that I had enough flight time in and knew that I had never gotten airsick. I was also glad that I possessed a strong stomach and was in the last desk near the back of the plane. The aroma under these circumstances could have gagged an entire army of maggots.

The terrified cadet, with the help of a few rags, did his best to clean off the pilot's head, neck and shirt, and to wipe up the entire area. This cleaning operation was almost an impossible task, but it helped to get the entire situation calmed down and even interjected a little humor into this fiasco on our first training mission.

This was the longest two hours I ever spent in a plane and two of my friends will remember their first flight with mixed emotions. The "pouree" spent several hours cleaning up the plane with a bucket of soapy water, once we landed. The paper bag Cadet managed to get his meal off the plane before the contents eroded its receptacle. This mission, for all sakes and purposes, was a wasted adventure for me, but one that will carry memories.

My second flight was a training mission where we had to follow with our instruments. The pilot flew wherever he desired and it was our responsibility to ascertain exactly our position somewhere in Texas. The windows in the fuselage, where our three desks were located, had been blacked out. We had to rely on instruments alone. Ultimately it would be our job to inform the pilot of a correct heading to get back to our base.

This really is not too different from leading or directing the pilot of the plane, since you use the same type of information to know your position at any given moment. This experience was a technique I would use most times in combat. I would let the pilot do evasive action for long periods of time and then proceed to take over to get our plane or group back on course.

The small community of San Marcos is approximately midway between San Antonio and Austin, the Capital of Texas. It lies just north of Highway 35, a major interstate road that goes all the way North and well into Minnesota. It is a typical Texas small town with its courthouse being the dominant building in the center of the commercial district.

The courthouse occupies a piece of land that contains several normal city blocks. I always felt these imposing structures that signified law and order, defied the many stories I had heard over the years about Texas justice.

A great deal of early Texas history however is connected with this community. Several blocks north of the courthouse and the heart of San Marcos is an imposing hill. This is the location of the Southwest Texas State University. I seldom came into town on the few liberty passes I received, rather I preferred to make the longer trip into San Antonio. I did not learn about the University, with its student body primarily made up with coeds, until years later.

The San Marcos River winds its way through town and is joined by the Blanco River on the edge of this unique community that is near the juncture of Hays County, Caldwell County, and Guadalupe County. At this time in my military career I would have never guessed that fifty years later I would move to Texas and build a home within a few miles of this place.

It is now the middle of October and I have lost many of my friends. Some had failed too many exams, while others could not take the pressure we were under. These cadets would go back to San Antonio and get reclassified. For a few, it meant this would be the second trip back to the Alamo City with those unpretentious tents. My heart goes out to these unfortunate young men who have had their dreams shattered.

The contents of each course would not be the major problem, rather it was the fast and unending pace that we were forced to keep. It was not what you had to learn, but rather how fast you could assimilate it. These days, we not only attended classes during the daylight hours, we were now going to night school to observe the stars and practice celestial navigation. Celestial Navigation required the most exacting skills, but it was also the most interesting, at least for me.

Shooting stars at night meant that we had to identify nearly all of the major constellations so that we could identify individual stars. I enjoyed this new challenge the most, because of my knowledge that ancient sailors were able to travel throughout the world, using these same stars. They did not have the sophisticated instruments we were using, but they had the knowledge of the celestial bodies and the earth. They also would be moving at a snails pace compared to traversing the globe in an aircraft.

At this stage of our training I was eating up each new discovery. I no longer dwelt on the fact that I would not traverse the heavens in a fighter plane, but rather a bomber, either in the Pacific or in Europe. Each day was putting distance between my early dreams and the new challenges I was now facing.

CELESTIAL NAVIGATION

In its simplest form, celestial navigation involves the use of a sextant to ascertain the altitude of a specific star at a given moment. The altitude of this star is the angle between the horizon and the sight line to this star. The process is not all that easy on the ground, but it is almost impossible in the air.

The constant movement and bouncing of a plane makes an accurate celestial reading very difficult and averaging of star shots is required. This requires constant scanning the star and when the sextant is aligned making a mark on a disc. This is done for a full minute, each time making a mark. The reading, or altitude, will be at the concentration of marks, thus averaging the results.

Instead of a steady platform from which to take shots of any given star, the airplane is usually bounced about because of air turbulence. Every airplane is subjected to another motion called yawing, which means it turns by angular motion about the vertical axis. This is so subtle that passengers are not aware of it while flying in the typical commercial airline.

This yawing is significant and has to be taken into consideration when trying to ascertain the exact altitude of a star. This is why it is necessary for the Navigator to have the skill and patients when shooting each of these selected stars as the plane is traveling through the night.

The primary function of Celestial Navigation is to calculate and plot a fix, which will locate your position at any given moment. A fix is determined by shooting three different stars, preferably 120 degrees apart, and then plotting the three resulting lines on your map or chart. Ideally, if you were to have perfect shots of these three stars, the resulting lines would all intersect at a common point. This never happens because of many variables that the navigator has limited control over.

An ideal or realistic fix would be a small triangle that would fit into a one quarter inch diameter circle. You would then assume that your position would be in the center of this small triangle, not knowing which of the three lines may have some slight error in it. You try and shoot a star, make calculations using current Navy astronomical star tables, and then plot the resulting line on your chart, all within 5 minutes.

A complete fix would then take 15 minutes of elapsed time. It is then necessary to correct two of the shots for the element of time, by moving your first shot ahead by 10 minutes and the second by 5 minutes.

Some nights the conditions are so bad that once you start to plot a fix, after all of your calculations, you find that you could literally use it for a toilet seat, because of its size. Obviously, one or more shots are in error and the fix is of little or no value. You never know which of your celestial shots might be in error, thus throwing out all of your efforts on that fix. Sometimes the sky has so many clouds that you may not see an entire constellation, making it difficult to identify the single star visible at the moment.

To give some idea as to the critical nature of navigation, it may shed some light by knowing the following. Should you have a single degree error in flying your course through the sky, for each 60 nautical miles you fly, you would end up a nautical mile off course. Realistically, if you were in error for a variety of reasons, that single degree could just as easily be 10 or more degrees.

Our first celestial night mission for our class ended up with some real bizarre results. When we were briefed before the flight, the instructors intentionally gave us erroneous wind conditions. Instead of the prevailing winds being 15 mph at 90 degrees, from the East, they told us the winds were 20 mph at 180 degrees, or from the South.

All of our preliminary work, done prior to the flight, was based on this information to determine our preflight data. As a consequence, you informed the pilot to fly a specific heading on take off, which in reality was in error. The pilot would be aware of this, but his orders were to rely entirely on information supplied by his Navigator, whether it was good, bad or indifferent.

This is no big problem if your work in flight begins to indicate that the plane is not going where you desire it to fly. The actual flight course being re-plotted is now pulling away from the desired plotted course. At this point, you advice the pilot of a new heading that will compensate for the error in the original heading . . . this is what Navigation is all about.

On this particular mission, the pilots were specifically instructed to do whatever each Navigator directed, even though they knew they were in error. The objective was for each plane to fly to Huntsville, Texas and return to the base, about an eight hundred mile round trip and one that sounded simple enough. Wrong.

Twelve planes took off with their student Navigator at about twenty minute intervals, enough spacing that no two planes would be able to see one another in flight. The night was perfect for flying, with little or no clouds to content with and practically no haze. I was keeping track of all instruments and was working on my first fix. All at once I got a gut feeling something was not going right.

My first clue that something was wrong occurred about thirty minutes into the flight. I noticed that a large city, with all of its lights, was off my left window and it had to be Austin. I recognized the unusual lights only this city in Texas has. I believe they were called sodium lights. It appeared to be only twenty or so miles away. According to all of my preliminary work, using the erroneous winds we had been given, Austin would not even be visible.

My first fix verified that we were a great deal north of the course I had given the pilot. I decided to keep the course until I could figure out a new wind, or in reality, the actual wind by determining what wind would have put us on this erroneous course.

This took another fix and a great deal of calculating. I had to work my way back to the base and our takeoff so that I could find out where we indeed were. I gave the pilot a new heading that would take us over Huntsville and then the proper heading back to San Marcos.

Fortunately, the many hours I had flown over this area of Texas during the brief time of my primary flight training and my one trip into Austin on leave, stood me in good stead. This verified that I knew exactly where we were and it gave me the confidence to pass on the new heading that would take us over our destination and the correct heading back to San Marcos.

There were actually only three planes from our base that ever arrived over Huntsville this night. Two planes were about to enter Mexico when the pilot was forced to intercede and help the Cadets out. Several Cadets got so confused, by the time they realized they had made some serious mistakes they proceeded to make some additional bad decisions and had to have their instructor intercede.

One plane ended up spending the night at Waco Texas, almost 150 miles northwest of Huntsville. Each of us, this night, learned some very valuable lessons. From this moment on, I was determined only to trust myself and to immediately check out any information I may be given to see if it made sense and was logical.

We had many additional night missions, as well as some specific type missions, like dog-legs between three different cities, interception and search missions, dead reckoning and pilotage missions. Each of these trips gave us new confidence in our work and ability to navigate.

I discovered that the harder you tried, the greater the results. The washout rate of my fellow Cadets had been heavy, and the remaining class was now composed mostly of individuals that had the ability to practice a very exact science. Because of the excessive losses in the skies of Europe, the Air Force needed Navigators. I personally found this out the painful way. Despite this fact, it was also mandatory that the Navigator possessed minimum standards so as not to jeopardize the lives of other crewmembers.

On November 30th, the remaining Cadets were informed that we could expect to graduate on January 15, 1944. We still had a lot to learn and more missions to fly, but at least we knew the end was in sight. They wanted each of us to know as soon as possible because it was a tradition to receive one's wings by having a mother, wife, or sweetheart pin them on the new officers blouse.

This would not be my fortune since I couldn't get my Mother to leave the state of Wisconsin, I would be unable to have my Father set foot in Texas for his own reasons, I wasn't married, and my sweetheart was a student nurse at Rochester, Minnesota and would not be able to get time off to travel the sixteen hundred miles to Texas.

These next six weeks would be the time to develop confidence in our abilities and to hone our skills. Our Officers knew that the remaining cadets had demonstrated they had good enough grades to graduate and this special announcement would be also beneficial for moral purposes. I have to admit that our excitement was cranked up a few notches.

On December 4, I went into San Marcos on a very special mission. I was going to a shop and purchase my new officer's uniform. This was big business for this small town of San Marcos. There were several different establishments one could go and purchase a standard and specified uniform. One of my favorite Instructors, an officer, planted a seed in my mind by offering a very logical suggestion.

The Air Force gave each cadet a $250.00 allowance for a uniform, which consisted of an officer's blouse, a cap, two sets of pinks (pants and shirts) and two sets of O.D.(Olive Drab). The allotted monies were ample to purchase a stock uniform that had been factory made according to specific Air Force specifications and have some monies left over.

About this time, my pride took command and I felt that I was worth more than a plain, ordinary officer's uniform. The recommendation I received from my Instructor solidified my resolution to go first class. I went to a tailor's place of business and ordered a special uniform, where all of the seams were invisible and the quality of the finished blouse and the material in the complete uniform was most obvious.

Needless to say, I ran over the $250 allowance, but by a mere $40.00, a decision I have never regretted. Instead of getting these garments off the rack, I would only have to wait less than one week for a fitting. When I went to try on everything, I was amazed that the tailor did a perfect job. I looked like "hot spit."

This tailor had assured me the cost would only be slightly more than our allowance and he was right. The other lesson I learned this day that has stuck with me these many years is the adage "you only get what you pay for."

GRADUATION

On December 12, my Norma's birthday, I took my final check flight mission to Winfield, Kansas. The results were great and I knew that my destiny of being a Navigator could erase some of the bad memories of not realizing my dreams of being a fighter pilot. Each member of a crew had responsibilities that the others had to rely upon, and it was important that proficiency had to be achieved. I felt ready for the challenge. I had all the confidence I believed necessary to navigate anywhere in the world and I now liked and believed in what I was doing.

January 15, 1944 was graduation day. Early in the morning, after breakfast, each of us tried on our new uniforms and paraded in front of one another. The excitement in the air was most ecstatic as we scrutinized each other. Within minutes our barracks looked like an entirely different place. At the prescribed hour, we all marched off to the parade grounds and to the graduating ceremonies.

Many of the cadets had their parents present, while others had wives or girl friends in attendance to pin on their new silver Navigator wings. It would have been impossible to have my new friend and soon to be fiancée here in San Marcos, Texas. Bud Soloman, my good buddy, and I accomplished this prestigious task ourselves. We pinned these silver wings on each other's blouse, as well as the new gold bars on our shoulders and collars.

I would have been pleased and honored to have Norma, or even my friend George Cormack present. I knew my parents would not come since they hardly ever left Wausau, Wisconsin. My father had some of his training here in Texas during World War I, and he swore he never had any desire to see this place again, for reasons he never elaborated on.

Each of us became 2nd Lieutenants and this rank now permits us to place the gold bars on our blouses and our shirts. Since we had known about our graduation date and schedule, most of us had made travel arrangements to take off on the several weeks' leave we were given. Bud Soloman and I had bus tickets into San Antonio where we boarded a train that would get us into St. Louis the next night.

I spent the evening at the Soloman residence, before taking a train to Chicago and my trip to the heart of Wisconsin. We stayed up until the wee hours of the morning while Bud filled his parents in on most of his experiences. Bud's parents were justifiably proud of their son and they informed him of this every few minutes.

At this moment, I felt seven foot tall and had no worries in the world. I was going home on leave as a Navigator and as an Officer, and most of all, have the chance to spend some time with my fiancee'. This time, the trip to and through Chicago, did not seem as long and distasteful.

Many of the dark and negative moments were now history. The past year and a half, since I enlisted, seemed like an eternity, and now, finally, it was all behind me. I was proud of my accomplishments and I was confident in my abilities. At this moment I had no idea as to which theater of war I would be sent, although most rumors indicated we were badly needed in Europe against Germany.

I even had the stupid fear that the war might end before I actually arrived in Europe and got into combat. I will still have to await further orders telling me where I was to go to meet my crew and exactly what type of plane we would be assigned to. I had been informed that these orders would be sent to my parents' home, the address I gave them.

CHAPTER 9

It would be exactly one year to the day when I would again be back in Wausau, my hometown. Though it seemed like an eternity, nothing had seemed to change. In fact, most things were not quite as great as my memory had conjured up or as I managed to brag about to my fellow Cadets.

The longer I was away from home, the better, the greater, the more magnificent things got. My mother's food could never live up to my memories, nor did the maple or elm trees that covered the streets look so beautiful. Despite this slight let down, I was most happy to be home and have these next two weeks off.

WITH MY NORMA

On January 22nd, 1944, Norma came home from Nurses' Training to spend a few days with me. She had left Chicago the night before and would arrive early in the morning. We had exchanged several letters each week and knew the happenings of each other. Now, for the first time, in our abbreviated acquaintance, we would be able to be together and truly begin to know one another.

Our relationship this past year was predominately via the mails. Ink and paper does not relay ones emotions and feelings the same as looking into each other's eyes. Touching one another is another dimension that Uncle Sam and the mails are derelict in conveying. Every minute of the time we would have alone had to be precious, especially since our next separation had many question marks connected with it.

It was not necessary to be a rocket scientist to be aware of some of the consequences of a war. The possibility of even seeing one another again was on both of our minds. This would be a subject that would not be on our agenda to talk or worry about so we both consciously avoided any discussion about those negative ramifications.

The day before Norma was to arrive home, from her Nurses Training in Chicago, I had persuaded my friend, George Cormack, to advance me a loan, so that I could buy an engagement ring. Though I am sure George would not understand just why I hadn't saved up the necessary funds to buy this simple token gesture of a pending engagement, he was most happy to accommodate me. I also have to believe, from experience, that the date and amount of loan was duly recorded in some little ledger as well as the purpose of the advance.

I knew that the value of this ring would not be indicative of my feelings for Norma, but I was sure that the gesture would be an expression of my desires. George accompanied me to a jeweler on the corner of Third and Washington uptown in Wausau. He was helpful in the selection and reminded me that it was not the value that was most important but my personal intentions and feeling that this humble ring would signify if she would accept it. "Where the hell did he get all of this wisdom." I couldn't help wondering.

This tiny engagement ring was placed in a fancy jewel box, elaborate enough that it could have held an 80-carat diamond. Now, this elegant box was burning a hole in my pocket. I could hardly wait for the right moment to pop the proverbial question. I know I walked around with my left hand covering the pocket that contained the ring. Only George knew of my intentions.

Most of the day Norma and I found it next to impossible to find time for ourselves. Everyone seemed to be interested in both of our lives. Norma had been sent from Rochester, Minnesota to a training facility in Chicago. She would now be receiving specialized training in Obstetrics at Lying In Hospital, a part of the University of Chicago. Others were anxious to learn what I was doing and when I would be off to the wars.

Because of this, we had to be content with quick glances, a squeeze now and then, and on rare occasions, perhaps a hug or a kiss. It was after midnight before we found any quality time to be alone. Now was my moment to remove this awkward box from my pocket.

Approximately 2 A.M., on the morning of January 23rd, outside in sub-freezing weather, I asked her if she would consider spending the rest of her life with me as my wife. I do not honestly know what I would have done if my ears had heard a negative reply. All of my thoughts and expectations had been for a resounding yes . . . I was not disappointed.

Now, at this moment some 59 years later, I can still feel the emotion of this significant moment in time. There is so much luck and chance in two compatible people finding one another and ultimately becoming a united team in a most happy marriage. I feel so fortunate.

I think we talked until the sun came up, completely ignoring a cold winter morning in Wisconsin. We both realized that the months ahead would determine my fate, but this did not dampen our dreams for the years before us. There was not a question or doubt in my mind that I had fortunately found the single one person in the entire world I desired to spent the rest of my life with.

This experience of making the commitment to one another cannot be put into so many words because it involves indescribable feelings and emotions. I truly felt like the luckiest guy in the whole wide world. If I had any thoughts this night it might have been the doubt or reason why she would choose me.

Most boys, and I was no exception, got their information regarding the opposite sex, from older guys. This source was filled with obvious flaws. My parents were not capable of handling this subject matter any more than the lads I associated with. I always had a gut feeling, that when the right person ultimately came along, I would somehow know. Tonight, assurances seemed to flow into my very being from all sources possible. "I know." "I know."

For my age, I had a minimal amount of exposure with girls, per se. I had been very active in sports most of my life and had waited, until my senior year in high school, before I had my first real date. This person and I never exchanged an embrace or a kiss. She was a very special friend and pal I enjoyed being with, whether it was bowling, going on a hike, or simply conversing. We enjoyed this special friendship for over a year and a half. Vivian, my friend, taught me to respect and treat girls as my equal, that we had more similarities than differences.

Though Norma and I both attended the same high school, we never got to meet or know each other. I was a grade ahead of her in school, plus my apparent lack of interest in playing the field with girls, each created impossible situations for us to have ever been friends. While we were both in high school together, I did know about her and some special accomplishments on her part that was publicized or talked about.

During my senior year in high school, a fund raising event took place that involved the selling of dozens of doughnuts. I no longer can remember for what worthy cause this money was targeted. Each year they would select a "Doughnut Duchess" and her court, as part of the festivities. For each dozen of doughnuts a student sold, they were given one vote to cast for their favorite Duchess' candidate.

Yours truly sold the most doughnuts in the entire school, completely forgetting that he had to deliver the damn things. In fact, it required the use of my dad's truck, to pick these bulky things up and then to decide where each package of doughnuts should go. I had solicited friends and strangers to buy these tasty morsels, over a three-week period, now I was expected to peddle them in a single day. So much for being a super-salesman.

When it came time to go to the ballot box, I cast my entire allotment of hard earned votes for Lena Kickbush, a classmate of mine who also shared the same home-room. I might just as well have dumped them in the "john," because Norma Ann Schmidt won this special contest. Lena ended up in her court, a distinction that did not make peddling my doughnuts any easier. This was the very first time I got to know a little about a very popular girl in my school.

Near the end of my senior year in Wausau Senior High School, the City of Wausau decided to abandon their antiquated streetcar system in favor of new motor- buses. Once again a contest was held to pick out a "Transportation Queen" who would be an important part of the planned historic ceremonies. I am not sure how this Queen was to be picked or chosen, but Norma again was selected as the ruling queen.

I saw pictures of her and her court in the local newspaper. She was decked out in a velvet robe with a gold crown on her short, cropped, blond hair. The other contestants were again part of her court. Obviously this girl was very popular in her school and in her class.

The thought never entered my mind, why this petite little blonde girl, with an unusually short hairstyle, one who had an obvious bubbling personality, would find a reason to look at me twice. However, all of the above called my attention to the fact that this energetic and vivacious pretty girl did exist.

My inherent shyness was reason enough to eliminate all possibility of attracting any attention over the multitude of guys who noticed the same attributes as I did. Hell, if she had given me the time of day, I truly believe I would not have been able to handle it. I was not among the throng who would visit and sit in the Schmidt kitchen with her mother Olga, just to be near her.

I did not get to meet this interesting person until two years later, when we both attended the University of Wisconsin. Our first meeting almost turned out to be a complete disaster. In the fall of 1941, Wisconsin was about to meet Ohio State on the football field in Camp Randall, in Madison.

This game would be a part of the "Home Coming" ceremonies for the University of Wisconsin. Festivities were to start on Friday evening with a huge bonfire on the lower campus just below Bascom Hall. Here a huge crowd would get whipped up by speeches from the University President, the football coach, certain players, and of course the cheer leaders.

Students at any large University are encouraged to attend all football games and to take part in as many college activities as time will permit. Since I had always been active and interested in sports, it was incomprehensible that I would not go to the game on Saturday nor take part in the Home-Coming Festivities. Besides, I wanted to see Elroy Hirsh, the famous running back I helped to make immortal.

HOW NOT TO WIN BROWNIE POINTS

On the auspicious night before the game, I, along with another lowly freshman, tagged along with four of our senior friends. George Cormack, my roommate, was one of the seniors in this group. Perhaps the first mistake of the evening was made when the six of us went into a liquor store and the each procured three half-pints of Kessler Whisky. Someone, with wisdom in such matters, had rationalized that these eighteen small bottles would be easier to conceal.

The other freshman and I commenced to drink our entire supply of this cheap alcohol, never giving it a thought about rationing it out over the evening or exactly what it might do to us. "Hell, at that time in my short life, I was strictly a beer person." In short order, I had toasted and drank to nearly every occasion and consumed my entire allotment of booze in short order. I proceeded to get more than slightly inebriated, ...frankly, I was drunk.

A few hours into the evening, on one of the busiest corners near the campus, the corner of State Street and Gorham Street, the main thoroughfare between the Capital and the University of Wisconsin, I proceeded to make a fool of myself. The four seniors tried to convince me that I had consumed enough, and it was time to return to the dorm.

I, perhaps, was the last person on the corner of State and Gorham Street this Friday night to believe that. My friends proceeded to try to talk me into returning to my abode, which was a big mistake. I was more than able to resist these four, primarily because of my condition, but mostly because of my strength.

I had always been an athlete in five or six sports each year, so I was in excellent physical condition. (Every summer, for years, I was compelled to work on one of my Father's plastering crews. I had mixed plaster and carried a hod . . . a job designed only for mules.)

In the wrestling match that followed, several of the senior's bottles of Kesslers got broken. Also, in the interim, a circle of over three hundred students surrounded us and prevented the police from getting at this tussle. Finally, my friends got me into a cab and we headed off for Tripp Hall, about four miles away.

I lived on the third floor and it became necessary to ascend the many flights of stairs. The inside railing of this stairwell was supported by metal ornate spindles placed evenly every six inches. It was to be a long and arduous trip up these flights of stairs in Tripp Hall.

My four battered friends dragged me up this stairs, one rung at a time, since I found it necessary to grasp each one on the journey up. They finally got me calmed down in my own bed, where I managed to get violently ill. They surrounded me with numerous vessels.

My roommate, dear old George Cormack, being a pharmacy major, became very concerned with the large amount of alcohol I had consumed in such a short period of time. He was aware that an intake of too much alcohol in a short time could result in death. He called up several of his Professors for advice, but didn't receive any quick cures. I survived the night, but the other lowly freshman, my drinking cohort, looked like death warmed over for the next four days.

When I got out of bed in the morning, one look in the mirror convinced me that I looked exactly how I was feeling. My face had a brown scab over every protrusion where the skin was suppose to cover a bone in my face. I looked like I had been beat up by a bunch of thugs. My stomach had its own problems.

Saturday morning, the day of the big home coming game, I had a class in mechanical drawing. Somehow I managed to drag myself the mile and a half to the Mechanical engineering building and my drafting board. Unfortunately the drafting room was on the third floor. With shaky hands, I got one of my drawings out to tack it down on my drafting table.

My instructor was watching me stumble through these maneuvers. My general appearance was clue enough for him to give inordinate attention to one of his students. Once I had my drawing in some sort of position on my drafting table I happened to look up to the head of the room at my instructor. He shook his head in disgust, and gave me permission to head for my dorm and bed. There was not a reason that I could doubt his logical reasoning.

Besides being unsteady and feeling queasy, with my face covered with scabs from the numerous abrasions I had received while fighting my friends and the road surface on the previous evening, I was sure I could not make it back to my dorm. It was a mile and a half away and ninety percent would be up hill. That concrete pavement on State Street had been not too kind to me. I knew I was a first class mess.

Knowing that I did not feel up to the long trek back to my dorm, I used what little energies I could muster, just to resolve my immediate problem. I came up with a brilliant idea. I walked over to my friend Mopey's abode. He only lived two blocks away in a co-op house he shared with others. I slept until mid afternoon, woke up, and had the slight feeling that I just might live.

Mopey asked me to come with him to Chadburn Hall, a girls' dorm, so he could deliver the Wausau Daily Record Herald to a friend of his. This was the only newspaper for the city of Wausau. This friend turned out to be the former Queen of the Wausau Senior High School.

I now was in the presence of Norma Ann Schmidt, the girl I could only admire from afar. In her presence I had completely forgotten about my appearance and the queasy stomach I was toting around. Mopey did the honors of formally introducing me to her.

Once we delivered the paper, all agreed to go out for a coke. Frank supposedly paired with Norma and me with her roommate, Natalie Johnson who hailed from Green Bay. Norma's first real impression of this shy individual, now in front of her, could not have been favorable. I was on the tail end of a first class hangover and I probably had ten or twelve scabs on my face and hands from the scuffle we had, only hours before. Fortunately my clothing concealed other battle damage.

I truly looked rough and I found out later that this was the exact impression she had of me. Years later I had asked Natalie Johnson what was her first impression of me on this coke date. She didn't surprise me by her honest answer.

We spent several hours together this particular afternoon and I'm sure I did not win any brownie points on this first meeting. Though I technically was with Natalie Johnson on this coke date, I could not help but scrutinize and steal glances at this Schmidt girl from Rothschild, Wisconsin. She was kind enough not to make any comments about my appearance, something I was grateful for.

The thing I became aware of about Norma was her personality. She was blonde and kept her hair in almost a boyish cut, combed back from her smooth and interesting face. Her complexion could be described by the oft quoted phrase, peaches and cream. Her skin sparkled with no blemishes while her eyes truly glistened.

She had an athletic build she had developed by all of the activities she participated in. The single most descriptive word to describe this young woman was the word personality. It just jumped out at you and demanded your attention. I could not keep my eyes or mind off her.

The person I was supposedly paired off with on this coke date was Nathalie Johnson. She was an extremely interesting and very well mannered person., but unfortunately was not apart of a chemistry taking place I could not explain nor did I understand

MY FIRST DATE

Nearly a month had to pass before I had enough nerve to ask Norma out for a date. Much to my amassment, she accepted and went with me to a dorm party on Picnic Point, a scenic peninsula that protrudes into beautiful Lake Mendota. This time I made it a point to be more presentable, both in appearance and manners. I assured her that what she now saw was the real me, that it was not a habitual thing for me to get bent out of shape.

During this date, I suddenly realized the importance of getting to know more about this person. I was well aware of the fact, that I was a neophyte at this sort of thing, and that it would take many more experiences before I would consider myself a true connoisseur.

I did manage to make a real boo boo in that we spent an inordinate amount of time talking about her cousin, Karl Hummel, a good friend of mine. I'm sure she could have cared less about the many boy-scout outings Karl and I built our own lean-to shelters together instead of sleeping in a usual tent. Perhaps that conversation might have been better than just talking about myself.

Over the ensuing weeks we had several dates that gave each of us an opportunity to discover one another. Then, I almost blew it again. I proceeded to do something I knew absolutely nothing about. I invited Norma to an all campus dorm formal, known as the Pan Hellenic Ball. It was to be held in Great Hall in the Memorial union, a place I had yet to peek into. She accepted.

Now was the moment of truth for me. George informed me, after I told him I had invited this special girl to a dance, I would have to rent a tuxedo for this occasion. It wasn't just a dance but rather a Ball. To make my picture more realistic, it is important to know that I had never, in my entire life, gone to any dance before, most particularly the Annual High School Prom. Now I am told, with my limited available funds, I have to rent a formal garment and all of the accessories.

This type of rental place is not hard to find near a large campus. The person who waited on me must have instantly realized he was dealing with a first class sucker and or klutz. This astute clerk immediately informed me, "If you rent formal clothing more than three times, it will cost you less money to actually buy it. You have to purchase most of the accessories anyway, so now you would have a formal outfit you can use as often as you desired." Since I had great aspirations at this moment, it did seem to make some sense.

"Something else I would suggest, you should purchase tails, not a tuxedo. Tails can be used for more formal occasions. If you decide to buy these clothes, I will sell you the more expensive tails for the same price as the tuxedo." My first reaction was, "vat a deal I'm getting." As good as I am at all mathematics, I hadn't started to add up these variable figures being thrown at me for the various items, especially when the cost for each article of clothing is preceded by the word only.

My sales clerk is a middle aged Jewish man, nearly bald with very thick lenses in his glasses. The rims were equally thick in a black color. The thing I remembered most about him was that he constantly held his two wrists against his chest with his open hands sort of hanging toward me. His accent was definitely Jewish and I had trouble not mocking him.

Despite my meager resources, somehow I rationalized that during my four years of college it would make sense to make this horrendous purchase. I purchased the whole bag. I bought the formal tails, pleated white shirt, a cumber bun, a black bow tie, special buttons, cuff links, thin black socks and a pair of shoes I thought I never would be caught dead in. These shoes were black patent leather and when I held one up to get a better look at my purchase, I could see the lights on the ceiling of this store and the design in the square metal ceiling panels.

Unfortunately this entire decision had not been made with my friend George Cormack. Somehow my roommate, a senior Pharmaceutical student, had never seen fit to purchase any of the stuff I brought back to the dorm to show him. All my enthusiasm was instantly shattered when I opened all the boxes and packages to show to my buddy.

George Cormack, my dear roommate, thought I was out of my gourd. Despite this reaction, he did remind me that one additional purchase was necessary . . . I was to contact Norma and find out what type of corsage she would prefer. "What the hell is a corsage," I shouted. I now began to realize I'd gotten over my head. Then it hit me like a ton of bricks . . . "I DON'T EVEN KNOW HOW TO DANCE."

I had accumulated zero time on the dance floor, and was sure my exposure to athletics would be of no help on this particular night. I also knew I would expose my lack of talent when she discovered why I was never known as "twinkle toes." George couldn't help me with the dancing problem though he did get another senior to explain to me some fundamentals. This did nothing but confuse me more.

The evening of the big dance, George and two other seniors, who regularly attended formal occasions, helped to get me into these ridiculous garbs. When I finally observed myself in the only full-length mirror in the dorm, I could hardly recognize myself. I looked both stupid and suave. "What in hell had I gotten myself into?"

I slowly walked the two miles between our Tripp Hall and Chadeburn Hall, Norma's residence, with two other fellows obviously going to this same dance. I kept pace with these two dapper guys, pretending this was just another dance I was going to.

Actually, I was imagining horrible things with each step I took. The only consolation I could come up with at this moment was that someday, I could be buried in this ridiculous looking attire. At that moment I noticed that my two traveling partners each had on tuxedos, not tails.

I approached Norma's Dormitory, on the corner of University Ave. and Park St. and realized there were other "turkeys" dressed in formal attire. They also were about to pick up their dates. I held back long enough to listen and learn the magic words. "Will you please inform Gladys Milligan that her escort Joe Blow has just arrived." For a second, I almost felt like I was in control of my destiny. Hell, I could do that.

I walked over to the desk in Chadeburn and requested: "Would you please inform Norma Ann Schmidt that her escort Lloyd Krueger has arrived."

After a wait, which I felt was entirely too short, I immediately spotted her descending the main stairs. She was the prettiest girl I'd ever seen. She was wearing a blue-velvet formal, whose hem dragged on the steps as she came down. Her golden hair was worn in a boyish short hairstyle, and it just glistened like a halo. I even noted the tiny purse she grasped on this dramatic decent into the lobby of Chadbourne Hall with her right hand gently sliding along the curved railing.

As she glanced toward her escort, she honored me with a smile I shall always remember. She reminded me of Cinderella. For the moment, I forgot the main purpose of why she was dressed so formally. I had completely forgotten that I was standing there staring at her in my formal tails. I only could feel how fortunate I was in being her escort this special night. I was so nervous another girl had to help pin on the corsage I brought with me.

We walked the three blocks to Memorial Union, looking every bit as sharp as Ginger Rogers and Fred Astaire. Great Hall, in the Memorial Union, was a most luxurious ballroom. I was more than impressed. A large band was the focal point on the wall opposite the view of Lake Mendota. I remember the wood dance floor did not give the soles, of my new patent leather shoes, the feeling of comradeship.

This highly polished surface was actually slippery and I could feel myself making minor adjustments in my step so I wouldn't slip and make a royal ass of myself. Numerous chandeliers hung from the ornate ceiling and were dimmed while the orchestra played. I could not believe I had volunteered to come to this place. I no longer felt like an Arthur Murry, but rather a klutz from the boondocks.

The room was filled with dancing couples, all dressed in their formal attire. I only recognized a few faces and I honestly believe I was the only damn freshman on this slippery dance floor this night. Between the emotion of my consciousness about my lead feet and the sensation of holding the prettiest girl on the dance floor, I was almost beside myself. I wanted the evening to end and I wanted the evening to go on forever and ever.

Somehow, someway, we got through the evening. I almost prayed that the orchestra might play a minuet, an especially slow dance in three quarter time. I felt a slower musical number played by the orchestra would make me less conspicuous. I just knew every eye, in this place, was staring at one clumsy dude. I took a solemn vow that I would never get myself into a similar situation again.

The fact that my dancing partner, on this particular evening, did not make me feel like a complete ass, was one of the many attributes I would see in her. I will never be sure what all went through her mind this night, but the entire event made an indelible impression on me.

We did manage to sort of dance, we spent some time communicating with other couples who perhaps appreciated conversation to tripping the light fantastic, and Norma and I ventured out to the balcony to look over the moonlight making its marks on the surface of Lake Mendota. You could see the silhouettes of many sailboats anchored to several docks that protruded out into the lake.

Over the remainder of the school year, we saw each other several more times. The pressure of school, exams, and my financial straits did little to promote this interaction. Norm's schedule was perhaps more constricting than mine. We were not to see each other again until the meeting my mother arranged, prior to my enlistment. These however, were all lasting memories now.

BACK TO THE PRESENT

Norma had to return to Chicago, and school, and my remaining week of leave flew by in an uneventful manner. Now, for the first time, I felt I had a selfish reason for making it through this damn war. There could now be a future that had the promise of something important.

I was now going to return to duty with many new thoughts and feelings, which were entirely foreign to me. My priorities were jumping all over the place, with no rhyme or reason. Somewhere, down the line, I've been told that this is what they refer to as "falling in love."

The thought that we two were now engaged gave my every reflection of her in an entirely different perspective than what I had always been accustomed to. Now, during moments of introspection, for the first time the words we and us would find their place in my mind instead of just I or me.

My shipping orders required that I report to an Air Force Base in Alexandria, Louisiana for reassignment. Train tickets were included with the order to report in on or before February 1, 1944. This required my boarding the evening train out of Wausau by January 30.

Once again I wondered just what my friend, George Cormack, saw in trains and how he could get his butt in an uproar over this method of transportation. "Oh well . . . different strokes for different folks."

The one positive thing I knew, I would arrive in Louisiana feeling dirty, bored and tired. Trains seemed to make a long trip seem even longer. Though the landscape seems to race by when you look out the dirty windows, it still doesn't jive with the hours of elapsed time it appears to take.

CHAPTER 10

I arrived in Alexandria, Louisiana, late on a Friday night, February 1st. I was surprised that the Air Force had sent a car with someone to meet me. This had never happened before. I guess I have to get used to being an Officer. I was taken out to the military airfield, some six or seven miles west of the city. Alexandria is a fair sized city, located almost in the geographic center of this boot shaped state.

I did not notice a lot of actively on the base, because of the late hour, but I was certainly catered to once I arrived at the main reception center. There was a packet, addressed to me, awaiting my arrival. I had been assigned a certain room in the B.O.Q. I had been in the military for nearly a year now and had been exposed to numerous new terms, systems, and ways of life. This was certainly one I had never heard before.

This was an entirely new term to me and my inquiry as to what in hell it meant brought a startled look on the face of the enlisted man behind the desk. Though I was dressed in my uniform, it didn't mean that I had mastered everything in this Air Force. I learned that these initials stood for Bachelor Officers' Quarters. He assumed I must have qualified since I did not have a woman on my arm or within sight.

For the first time I began to realize that many of my fellow officers were married and had brought their wives down with them. They would have to be housed elsewhere. Had I goofed? I knew that the relationship between Norma and I had not progressed to this stage and more time would be required for our engagement to mature. Each of us, though we did not talk or dwell on the subject specifically, felt that she had to finish her Nurses Training and I had a war to take part in. "First things first."

On Saturday morning, I noticed on the bulletin board, the complete list of names of all of the new crews. The notice stated that all personnel would be arriving over the next several days and it would not be until February 8, before each crew would arrive and be assembled. The old "hurry up and wait routine" again. I did manage to write down the names of the other three officers, who would be in my crew, as well as the names of six enlisted men who would complete our team.

Periodically, I would inquire at the desk to see if they had arrived. Late in the afternoon, Lt. Ray Weakland showed up, our new Bombardier. Fortunately they had put us in adjoining rooms, which, I suppose is logical. His door was ajar, so I knocked and introduced myself.

I would occupy the nose of the B-17 assigned to us with this Bombardier. I think Ray was happy to see me because he appeared to be as much of a neophyte, taking on the role of a newly commissioned officer, and could use some companionship at this moment. You could be certain of this since he still had his grommet in officer's cap, something no Air Force crew member did, much to the chagrin of officers in the Regular Army.

Lt. Weakland, whose complete name was Walter R. Weakland, hailed from Barnesboro, Pennsylvania. He was married, expecting a child, and he appeared to be several years older than most of the other officers I had met. His face did not present the boyish look most of these new airmen had. He was slight of build, had a distinct gaunt appearance to his face, and he had rather dark and deep-set eyes. He appeared to have very pronounced wrinkles on his rather thin face.

I was informed that he had spent several years as a noncom in the Army and he now was having a hard time believing he was finally an officer in the Army Air Force. He made the mistake of replying "Yes Sir," and "No Sir" to me several times because of the time he had spent as an enlisted man. Each time we would laugh about this and I knew with time this habit would gradually be forgotten.

My first observation told me that he was extremely reserved and quiet, something I knew I could compensate for. Some of these first impressions I had made of Ray, would later come into play, as our crew got into actual combat. I did not discern the same attitude and feeling I had for this important moment in time, a period in which each of us would be going off into a war we knew little about. Ray seemed to have a sort of cavalier type of disposition without any outward appearance that would support this demeanor.

I was to learn I would never completely get inside of Lt. Weakland's head and know what he might be thinking or what he would prefer to do. I did find out that he had hated being an enlisted man in the service and he said he would have resigned if the damn war hadn't started. He had applied for Cadets and was surprised when they sent him off to the S.A.A.C.C. in San Antonio. He told me he was flabbergasted when he had qualified as a Bombardier because he thought he had screwed up royally.

We went to the mess hall, had supper together, and became better acquainted. For about the hundredth time, we were informed not to miss the special stag- party they were having at the Officers' Club tonight. Lt. Weakland and I finally found the club and cautiously entered.

We were a part of a large group of new personnel, joining the Officers of the permanent staff. The Officer's Club was a rather large and well designed facility, the best I had seen thus far. Ray and I both commented on the unusual amount of excitement and buzzing going on as we went into the bar.

Upon inquiring, as to why there appeared to be so much enthusiasm for this particular night, we were told it was in anticipation of the floorshow that would start within the hour. This special entertainment only took place every month, but tonight's show was to be an extravaganza, a "piece de resistance."

Ray and this naive lad from Wisconsin, were about to get the shock of their lives. The word got passed around that we were about to be entertained by six female dancers, flown in from New Orleans. All of this sounded quite innocent enough and could possibly be interesting, even to these two young warriors to be.

Quite by accident, Ray and I "lucked" out, and I use this term with some reservation. We found seats in the front row of the developing circular space being created for the "dancers" in this large room. These girls, as it turned out, were really prostitutes. Their talent, as dancers, certainly left room for improvement, even to the point where one could question if the word dancer would profile what they were trying to do.

Of the six girls that slithered onto the dance floor in their flimsy and gaudy costumes, only two seemed to be what these untrained eyes would call fairly good looking. One was stocky enough that I believe she could have challenged any officer in this room to an arm wrestling match and won. Two of the dancers could honestly be said to be over weight, in fact almost fat. The sixth and final gal, perhaps the youngest, was actually skinny. A dance team they were not. No choreographer would have been capable of developing a dance routine where these six participants could have performed as a team and then expect to receive raves from an audience who would appreciate talent.

In a matter of five-minutes, they had gradually peeled off their already scant, but garish garments. These mediocre dancers suddenly turned into completely nude women, something these eyes had never seen. Ray Weakland, despite the fact that he had been married for several years, appeared to be as uneasy as the kid sitting next to him. "God, I sat there with unbelieving stares, my mouth wide open, and I wondered why this was happening to me." This was a sight that my mother and dad had not prepared me for.

Long ago one of the older kids in my neighborhood had shown me a "girly magazine" that had pictures of partially clad women in a variety of poses. This, at that time, would be classified as a dirty magazine and I would have been disciplined had my parents known about it. Tonight, what my innocent and virtuous eyes were seeing was down right distasteful to me and to my new friend Ray.

From the second rate information I had received from the older guys in my neighborhood, who were prone to exaggeration, and from pictures I had run across, I had a pretty good knowledge of what the anatomy of a woman was. Now, only a few feet away I was able to see perhaps four or five variations of this species of human. Their gyrations and suggestive moves only agitated certain body parts making the entire spectacle look ridiculous.

These "entertainers" began to make contact with their audience and seemed to prefer the officers with the highest rank. Thank God I was only a 2nd Lieutenant. They would rub their breasts in the face of some Colonel, sit on the lap of a Captain, and other "things" only a perverted mind can conjure up. I almost tossed my cookies.

Ray and I slipped out of our chairs, trying to look nonchalant, and worked our way to the bar, where we were out of sight of this spectacle. Those we left in the entertainment area apparently found this phenomenon we just witnessed, enticing, fascinating, stimulating, and perhaps, captivating. Their laughter and yells was as disgusting to me as the antics of the six prostitutes.

One of the gals, who looked like she might have been the youngest, appeared bashful, shy, and extremely awkward. She was the skinny one. This must have been the very first time she was sent out to take on the role of a dancer cavorting in front of hungry and ravenous eyes. A Venus de Milo there was none.

In twenty minutes or so, the formal show was over and I made the mistake of thinking things would settle down to a normal routine of just plain drinking and conversations. What I wasn't aware of, until later, was that these six gals had been paid to mingle throughout the officers' club, still without clothing. Whoever was on the committee to engage this spectacle certainly were not an officer and a gentlemen.

When I happened to glance over toward the poolroom and sighted one of these women imitating Minnesota Fats, I decided to get the hell out of the officer's club entirely. To this day, I cannot understand the purpose of this night and why someone felt it necessary to expose all of these new Officers to such a spectacle. The more I thought about the entire incident, the less respect I had for the individuals who took on the role of a deprived animal.

It was totally repulsive, distasteful, and detestable. For some unexplained reason

I had been brought up in a family, neighborhood, and among friends where this type of behavior was completely foreign. Perhaps I was a prude and simply out of step with the other men from around the country. Lt. Ray Weakland was as upset and uncomfortable as this tyro in the real world.

Monday morning, Feb. 4th, I finally got to meet our two pilots, who had just arrived. Our first pilot was Lt. Frank Heuth Cobb, Jr. from Crown Point, Indiana. He was over 6'4", well built, had red hair, wore a permanent smile and was obviously the largest Irish person I had ever met. His full face was covered with freckles from ear to ear.

He wore his grommet free Officer's cap at a distinct tilt, which made him standout. He had a loftiness and an arrogance about him that defied the knowledge that he also was a newly appointed Second Lieutenant. He not only exuded the trait of being a take charge guy, he personified it.

The first and most dominant impression I had the instant I met Lt. Cobb was that he presented an air of cockiness and self-assuredness. He looked like he should be our first pilot and the leader of our crew. His unequivocal red hair and the complimentary freckles adorning his face only supplemented his aura of obvious brazenness.

Lt. John D. Waddell, Jr. was from Hendersonville, North Carolina. He had a lithe build, almost identical to the crew's Navigator, 5'8" tall and about 145 pounds. Dan, the name he preferred to be known as, was the epitome of a true Southerner. Despite the fact that I took an immediate liking of him, it took me days before I could understand and comprehend what he was saying. "What ~ ya ~ awl ~ doen?, took an elapsed time of over a minute.

Most of my training had taken place in southern Texas, but Dan was from the SOUTH. An immediate kinship developed between Dan and me when we compared backgrounds and discovered we both had fathers in the construction business, we had started college, and we were active in a variety of physical sports.

Within minutes I realized the two of us had similar standards, interests, likes, and values. I felt an instant gratification for having someone to go and share my war with. I honestly could feel the warmth and comfort with this knowledge and belief.

It became immediately obvious, that the four Officers, making up this new crew, though we all came from east of the Mississippi River, namely, the States of Indiana, North Carolina, Wisconsin and Pennsylvania, still had unique differences in the way thoughts were expressed, attitudes, and dispositions.

This in itself would have no real significance. The differences in each of our personalities, backgrounds, and temperament made this crew unique on to itself. We were thrown together by fate and were now expected to perform in war as a competent, well-oiled machine.

Each Officer had received specialized training necessary to carry out all required functions expected of them. If each of the other three individuals received the same intensity of training as I had experienced, then I knew we would be ready for any eventualities. I was both proud and confident of my capacity and expertise to navigate any damn bomber anywhere in the world.

REMAINDER OF CREW

On Tuesday morning, February 5, we finally got to meet the enlisted personnel that would make up our entire crew. These six individuals would be our gunners and each would have an additional specialty mastered. Lt. Cobb, Waddell, and Weakland were as anxious as I to meet the remainder of our family.

Our Engineer and top turret gunner would be Sgt. James E. Eavenson, from Waynesville, North Carolina. I discovered later that Jim only lived a few miles northeast of Hendersonville, Dan's home. The place he called home was Maggie Valley. He preferred to be called "Jim" and there didn't appear a good reason to create a new nickname for this very serious young man.

Though Jim was the oldest of the gunners, there was not a great spread in age on the entire crew. It appeared Jim and Dan had been exposed or taught to speak by the same English Teacher. I think it would have taken an hour for the two of them to exchange ideas on which major league ball team might win the pennant this year.

As the Engineer and top turret gunner of our crew, Jim had a great deal more responsibility placed upon his shoulders than the other gunners. He would constantly be checking and listening for any malfunctioning part of this complex bomber. He had been trained to take care of minor defects or glitches of our plane during any flight. He also tended to be the herdsman for the other five men who would man the protective guns on our plane.

His southern drawl was equally as profound as Dan's. In time I finally did learn to understand this new language, of the two men from North Carolina. A fleeting thought passed through my mind, "What in hell would a native from the State of South Carolina sound like?"

Sgt. Quentin L. Newswanger from Quarryville, Pennsylvania would be our Radio Operator, as well as another gunner. With a name like he possessed, it was not difficult to give him the nickname of "Newsy." He had a personality which gave every indication that he could care less what you called him.

He was the shortest of the entire crew, but rather stocky in build. He also had the distinction of being the most talkative. Newsy would laugh at anything and at any time. These distinguishing character traits would set the mood for the rest of the gunners. I found out later that he was an only child of a single mother who happened to be a schoolteacher. I don't believe there was a time when I didn't see that ear to ear smile take up most of his face.

Sgt. Frank J. Tomsey hailed from Endicott, New York. The fact that he had inherited genes, which kept him diminutive, relegated him to occupy the ball turret. If we could accept Newsy as a Nickname, then the name Tomsey defied being tampered with. His slight stature made it possible for him to crawl into the ball turret and ride for hours in a fetal position. His job was to protect the belly of our B-17 with his twin 50-caliber machine guns.

Something I did not know, until over fifty-six years later, that originally Sgt. Fleet had been assigned by the Air Force to be our ball turret operator and "Tomsey" would be our waist gunner. When Sgt. Fleet tried to enter the ball turret, he found it impossible for psychological reasons to do so.

All the other gunners tried to help him master this problem and develop the necessary fortitude to enter this tiny sphere. It was at this time that Sergeant Frank J. Tomsey volunteered to take over this important task. I shall always respect the "guts" he displayed when he willingly volunteered for the least welcomed job on a B-17.

The ball turret subjected the gunners, who were assigned to this revolving sphere, to the most brutal exposure to the elements and to the enemy. I have the utmost regard for these brave small men, who had to fight their war five miles up, confronted with fifty degrees below zero temperatures, in a cramped position sometimes for ten or twelve hours, and could only escape their cage with loads of luck. Special honors should have been presented to anyone who flew as a ball-turret operator.

Though it took all these years to know the true facts of why "Tomsey" occupied this position, I admired him from the moment I met him. He was the smallest, not in height but in stature, of all the crewmembers. He was reserved and reticent, but he left us all with the knowledge that the protection of the belly of our plane was in good hands. Though he was quite, when he spoke one could have guessed he came from New York.

The two waist gunners for our crew were Sgt. I.J. Ellender from Sulphur, Louisiana and PFC Herman R. Fleet from Houston, Texas. Though both of these men theoretically had come from the South, fortunately neither one spoke like Dan Waddell or Jim Eavenson. I do not know if it would have been possible to handle a situation if all four had the same lazy tongues.

I never did know what the initial J. stood for, but I later discovered that the initial

I. was for Iver, a name he did not seem to like. He was the largest of the six gunners and he seemed to be content with the simple nickname of I.J.

He was particularly handsome, tall, with a well, developed body. He tended to be especially quiet, a mannerism that distinguished him from most of the others in this new crew. I suppose you could say he was the diametrically opposite of "Newsy."

Private First Class Fleet, with a first name of Herman, immediately was affectionately called "Hank." I do not know why Hank did not have a rank of Sergeant. Perhaps he "screwed- up" somewhere along the way and got himself demoted. Rank did not seem to have much importance on our crew, so I never bothered asking him.

Like Sgt. Ellender, Hank also did not make waves. When the moment of truth presented itself, once we were assigned a B-17, Pvt. Herman exposed his problem of entering the ball turret. Obviously, Pvt. Fleet was claustrophobic and could not tuck his body in such tight quarters. Sometime later other problems would present themselves.

The last gunner, but only because he rode in the tail of the plane, was Sgt. James J. Argyrakis from Chicago, Illinois. He was greeted and recognized by the other gunners simply as Jim, just like Eavenson, or on occasions unpretentiously as J.J. On occasions, I heard some of his fellow-gunners refer to him as "The Greek."

He was of medium height and build, and was agile enough to crawl back into the tail section and man the twin machine guns. His job was to protect the rear of the plane and the formation of bombers. Jim epitomized someone who came from a big city, like Chicago.

His position in the aft part of the plane would also be in a very claustrophobic environment, one that required a very special individual to handle. He faced rearward in a kneeling awkward position. He depended on the other gunners shouting out the directions of attacking enemy fighter planes to be effective. He was isolated and depended entirely on the intercom system to feel apart of the crew.

We had six gunners, each from a different State, and each varied in stature and personality. They came to us with nicknames already assigned by their fellow gunners. I believe each of us represented a different ethnic background. We now were ready to confront a common enemy as typical Americans, a hodgepodge that represented the world. I guess you could say we were a typical bomber crew.

The excitement of meeting the individuals who you were going off into combat with obviously diluted the knowledge that you truly knew nothing of one another. It was like getting to meet a distant relative you had never seen before and now suddenly there he was. We each had different responsibilities and had separate and distinct training. As a new team or crew we now had to put full trust in the capabilities of each of its members. At this moment I was naïve enough to have complete assuredness in each of our abilities.

WE FINALLY GET TO MEET THE LADY

February 10th was our big day down at Alexandria, since this was when we had our first opportunity to meet the "lady." The entire crew had to rendezvous at 1000 hours on the flight line for an orientation meeting. Each of us, with the exception of our two pilots, was to be introduced to the "queen" for the first time. Lieutenants Cobb and Waddell had prior training in this bomber, the B-17, shortly before they arrived to join the other crew members.

When I approached her, I could see that she had some years and perhaps a goodly number of sky-miles on the old body. I'm sure the B-17 Model E was a war weary plane, returned from combat action. Nevertheless, she truly looked beautiful to me. Her shape and her general profile left me almost speechless. I had never been this close to such a functional looking creature. Yep, it was love at first sight. This plane sitting before us now may have had some vintage on her, but this could not conceal her lines and size.

The "lady" was dressed in a dull olive drab color and had a very weather-beaten look about her. The only scintillating thing about her was the sun bouncing off her Plexiglas nose. She was somewhat larger than I had imagined, but her overall trim lines gave her a very proportioned look. The ten machine guns sticking out, in all angles from the fuselage, made her look ominous and menacing. "What's not to like?"

She was affectionately called the "Flying Fortress" but most generally recognized as the B-17. The particular plane we were now scrutinizing, was a Model E. This version of the B-17 had now been retired and replaced in combat by the Model F. Despite this, only slight modifications had taken place.

The fact that this vintage B-17 was now relegated to a category considered obsolete did not dampen my spirits this morning. The entire crew took on the same superficial curiosity, their eyes jumping over every section of the plane as they wended their way through the interior. Each crewmember knew there would be a particular niche or place, just for them. Each, with our own specific talents and training, needed this complex piece of equipment, to mold us into a complete team.

The better part of the next hour was spent getting acquainted with this bomber. No one was rushing us. I sat at my desk and tried to imagine being airborne and in combat. When I swung one of the two 50- caliber machine guns assigned to the Navigator and I observed the size of the belt of ammunition arching its way toward the floor, it made me feel invincible.

All of these early impressions were to be blown to hell, once I experienced combat. Today though, I knew we had ten of these impressive guns aboard and I couldn't visualize a German fighter having the audacity to challenge a formation of numerous B-17's. Ignorance is certainly bliss.

The aluminum skin that rapped around us gave the feeling of comfort as it defined our tight little quarters. I later would find out that this covering did nothing to change the minus 50 degree temperatures we would experience in combat. Also, pieces of flak would pass through this thin membrane, without giving up any of its velocity. These were all experiences that would have to wait until later. Our eyes could see only positive things this morning. The entire crew was "gnashing at the bit" to lift this big bird into the air.

Shortly after lunch the entire crew again assembled at the B-17 assigned to us in preparation for our first flight. I truly had no idea what to expect. All of the different planes I had the opportunity to fly in, up to this juncture in time, could be tucked under either one of this plane's wings.

We had not been scheduled for any particular destination, but merely to get acquainted with this aircraft. Both Lieutenants Cobb and Waddell had been previously checked out in this plane so they did not exude the same enthusiasm the other eight crewmen displayed. Though they were more reserved, I'm sure each of them had a certain amount of apprehension since the total number of hours they had flown in a B-17 was minimal at best. I never did know if they even had ever flown together before this day.

Lt. Cobb asked for my opinion on where I wanted to plot a course. I suggested we head out over the Gulf of Mexico and try out our guns. This appealed to everyone. I also stated that he could fly anywhere he wanted to and I would keep track of our position. I would give him a heading home any time he desired to return to Alexandria. This last statement, without realizing it, was my initial indoctrination and commitment as the new crews Navigator.

As each engine was started, the roar was not only heard, but felt. The four 1200 horsepower engines made the entire plane vibrate. Slowly we worked our way down a secondary runway to the far end of a huge concrete ribbon. After taking off and landing the little PT-19 on grass strips at Uvalde, Texas, this runway looked like a sea of concrete.

Cobb and "Waddy" ran through a complex check- list prior to taking off. Finally, after each individual engine had been "revved-up," we heard the command, "Ready for takeoff." Slowly we started to move.

As graceful as the B-17 looks in the air, racing down a runway she feels like your riding on the back of a pregnant rhinoceros. The plane seemed to accelerate at a snail's pace, the vibration felt like we were about to lose something, and the noise of the four engines was deafening.

Finally, as the end of the runway was about to catch up with us, the big bird groped its way into the air. Once we gained adequate altitude, the landing gear retracted and the throttles could be cut back, the noise level reached a sustained pitch where the engine noise almost took on the characteristics of a musical sound.

We climbed to an altitude of about 5000 feet and leveled off. I gave Cobb a heading of 200 degrees and told him I would just follow our flight from here on. In forty-five minutes we flew over Lake Charles, Louisiana, approximately 100 miles from our base. In a matter of minutes we could see the coastline of the Gulf of Mexico, just south of Port Arthur, Texas.

Cobb headed the plane due south for about twenty minutes and each crewmember had a chance to fire his guns. Because of the urgency to rush new Navigators into combat, I had never been sent to gunner's school. This would be my first chance to not only see a gun of this size, but to fire it.

Lt. Weakland showed me how to activate this potent 50 caliber weapon. Our plane took on a whole new series of sounds, as well as the smell of gun powder. The old lady developed a different set of vibrations while the guns chattered away. I owned and fired shotguns and high-powered rifles, but this was something else.

Lt. Weakland, the Bombardier, used one of my guns for this practice exercise. This version of the B-17, as well as the Model F, did not have a machine gun in the nose. This fact, is the reason I was sent to Navigational School and why I was present today, wearing a pair of Navigator wings.

We had been told the Model B-17G would be the first bomber that would receive a chin turret, with two 50-calibre guns installed below and operated by the Bombardier. It was discovered this added protection, from the usual frontal attacks preferred by the Luftwaffe, would make a formation of these plane more difficult for our enemy to be aggressive.

By firing these guns out into open space, we could not begin to imagine what the real world of combat would be like. "If you don't aim at anything in particular, it's impossible to miss it." The real test would have to wait until we flew over the continent of Europe and face our enemy, the German Luftwaffe.

Cobb turned the plane northward and we headed back toward the coast. At the same time he nosed the old gal down in a gradual decent until we were almost on the deck, in this case the water. Weakland and I had the best seat in the house, looking out the Plexiglas nose. Cobb leveled off and we skimmed a few feet above the white tips of the moderate waves. If we had lowered our wheels, I believe they would be spinning in the water.

The plane roared its way toward the Louisiana coast at 180 miles per hour. Occasionally Cobb lifted the bomber over oil derricks, which just happened to be in our path. Workers on these rigs waved and did not appear to be shook-up by the near miss. I would wager a guess that this idea of buzzing rigs was not original. Other new crews, taking their first fling in a B-17, were also full of "pee and vinegar." This was a way of showing off.

I worked out a heading to our Base and in less than a half hour we could see the field. When we landed, our wheel wells had pieces of seaweed hanging out. Our prop wash must have pulled it up, as we were tempting fate. Flying this low was a juvenile act and can really be seen as bordering on stupidity. Today, it seemed the thing to do. Cobb's lack of discretion was not noticed this day, only his ability to handle the Flying Fortress.

Though none of us, including myself, put any credence on this incident, later I would realize the poor judgment and discretion displayed by our first pilot in taking the unnecessary risk by tempting fate. I discovered later how similar daring feats took the lives unnecessarily of many crewmembers. Flying, not to mention combat, is a most unforgiving science and discipline.

ANALYSING THE CREW

During the next two weeks, we had the opportunity to get to know each other on an informal basis, since we had a lot of time to kill. As officers, Cobb, Waddy, Weak and I spent nearly our entire daylight and evening hours together. It did not take long for Dan Waddell and me to migrate toward one another. We seemed to have many traits in common. The one major difference between the two of us was the fact I could spit out a sentence 6.2 times faster than Dan was ever capable of.

Some of the similarities were our participation in athletics, attending college, both having worked in the construction field, politics in general, and our outlook on life. We only analyzed the Civil War on very rare occasions, and then it would be in jest. Dan had a much deeper feeling about religion than I did, so it was a subject he seemed to understand was worthy of being avoided by both of us.

Cobb would be another story. He was 6'4" tall, with a build and physique that were impossible not to notice or be envious of. He had red hair and a complexion that went with it. He was loud and very talkative. He made his presence known in any room he entered.

Some of the traits that started to separate Cobb from Dan and I was the fact he did not drink any liquid that had any alcohol content, he did not smoke, and he did not gamble with cards. He obviously was not aware of some of the important things in life.

Another thing that put distance between Cobb and the two of us was each time we had to walk anywhere. He consistently had such a great stride and pace Dan and I would be left in the dust. Both of our butts were built so close to the ground we found it impossible to keep up with him. We both decided it would have been easier for him to adjust than for either of us.

A distinctive feature that made this rather tall pilot attract attention was his flaming red scarf, which he constantly wore. Even for his size, this neckpiece was especially long. As he walked at his usual rapid pace, the rear portion of the scarf would almost flap behind him in a horizontal position. He took on the appearance of a giant "Snoopy", as he strode about the base.

Cobb was a purist and it would be inevitable that he would have a very hard time finding friends of similar persuasion, especially in the Air Force. He also had the unusual habit of walking around the barracks naked at the damnedest times.

This would be particularly annoying when he would walk next to table of several of us playing poker. "Christ Cobb, get some clothes on", would be the first criticism uttered. He would come back with, "I'm just letting my pores breath", as he slapped his bare chest with both of his hands and keep on doing his thing. I honestly believe he was unaware of any of his idiosyncrasies.

Lt. Ray Weakland was not an easy person to figure out. He appeared to have many moods and I found it difficult at times to truly understand him. There were times I felt very close to Weak and there were moments when it seemed impossible to share his thoughts.

I knew that he had been married a few years and he and his wife were expecting their first child in several months. The forced separation from his wife had to be especially difficult for him, perhaps the main reason for Weakland's various moods. Despite all of this, I probably was closer to Ray than any other crew member.

While here at Alexandria each member of the crew had to attend various classes or exercises, depending on their specialties. I went with Ray on several occasions when he was required to practice simulated bombing techniques, using the Norden bombsight. In one of the hangers they had set up special equipment that could simulate the real thing.

We had to climb to the top of a high scaffold on which there was a large platform. On this platform they had a seat with the bombsight mounted similar to that in the nose of the B-17. Below, on the floor, actual photographs of terrain would be projected. The landscape would move below the platform, simulating actual flight, at various air speeds and altitudes.

A distant target could be selected in the bombsight. By entering altitude, a wind factor, the chosen ground speed, and the course we were flying, it was possible to determine the exact moment for bomb to be released. At that precise instant, a large plus sign of light would be indicated on the moving map below. When the bomb hit the terrain, the map would stop moving. The distance between the lighted cross and the chosen target indicated your error.

For some reason, Ray never seemed to have his heart in these interesting practice sessions. I found this exercise both amusing and most challenging. Ray insisted I give it a try on several occasion, much to my delight. I can modestly state, that for one reason or another, I got better results at working this contraption than Weakland. Actually I felt it important to know as much about his equipment as possible, should it ever become necessary in combat.

On an actual bomb run, the Navigator and Bombardier had to work together. Prior to the bomb run, the Navigator would give much of the information the Bombardier required to be registered into the Norden Bombsight. It would be the Navigator's job to determine ground speed from the actual air speed, our exact altitude at any given moment, the current wind direction and velocity, and the direction the plane was flying in.

On the actual bomb run, as we turned on the I.P. (Initial Point) toward the target, the Bombardier would use all of this information to determine the exact heading the plane should be on. It would be responsibility to guide the pilot and plane on a course that would take us near the target.

At this point, the Bombardier would take over the plane by using the automatic pilot on the bomb run, adjusting our course so that the dropped bombs would score. Getting bombs on specific targets was essential after the tremendous risk getting the planes deep into enemy territory.

I did not know at this time that only the Lead bombardier would have the sole responsibility to ascertain the exact moment when the entire formation of bombers would release their bomb load. All other bombardiers would instantaneously drop their load when the Lead Bombardier's bombs left his plane. Most would in reality be "toggliers."

On the occasions when Ray took off with "Waddy" and me, he would blend in as soon as we got him to imbibe. Alcohol can truly have beneficial medicinal value. "Waddy", a nickname I felt more appropriate than calling him Dan, and I can attest to this little known phenomenon. When Ray got some of this nectar in him, he was transformed into an Officer with a personality. At these times he acquired a sense of humor we rarely saw and he actually became very talkative.

It seems that all my life I've had been blessedly fortunate in always having great buddies or friends that I felt especially comfortable with. Dan instantly filled this welcomed criteria. We felt comfortable with each others company and we could converse by the hour on any subject we might happen upon.

We obviously did not agree on most of the ramification of the Civil War and on occasion I would be called a "Damn Yankee." This would usually be done in jest, just as my reference to his being a "Rebel." Our political beliefs and opinions seldom got in the way of any of our serious discussions.

Dan had gotten married a day or two before we flew off to combat but these few days of married life did not make him an expert or someone I would seek marital information from. Though neither one of us ever attended church during the many months we were in combat, I knew Dan had a closer affiliation to a church back in Hendersonville. I had many conflicting thoughts about formal religion but I also felt this was a very personal thing. We both stayed away from spiritual and theological subjects.

It is always difficult to analyze one's self. Lieutenant Lloyd O. Krueger was a young lad who truly was leaving the only environment he ever knew. I had never been out of the State of Wisconsin. Despite this, I was well read, loved all forms of mathematics and science, had played and excelled to a high degree, considering my height and weight, in many contact type sports like boxing, hockey and football, as well as baseball, softball and tennis.

The one sport I was not good at, in fact I could use the word lousy at, was basketball. All or most of the sports I personally liked were what I refer to as contact sports. In basketball I was continually being called by the referee for charging, pushing, hacking and blocking.

At that period of the game, only four personal fouls were permitted before you were ejected from the game. My love of trying to dribble through an opponent and not around made my talents seldom appreciated. In pick up basketball games I invariably was the last person to be chosen by the captains of the two teams about to do battle.

I had worked hard for my father since I was a young lad. This work entailed mixing plaster, carrying large amounts with the use of a hod on my shoulder, loading and unloading heavy scaffolding, and other equally mulish duties. I had developed both muscles and a build I was proud of.

I had excellent speed and more than adequate endurance. I could be called very shy, yet did not hesitate to step forward to be counted or to express myself. I believe I went out of my way to be liked or to take an interest in others. I was very competitive in everything I attempted.

I could also say that I was very opinionated, an attribute I never was sure if it would be considered a positive or a negative. I had a hard time concealing my feeling once someone did things I did not approve of or perhaps disliked. I appreciated challenges and believed, like my father, I possessed a great deal of common sense.

It took a fair amount of negative outside influences to get me mad, but it took an equal amount of time for me to forget or forgive it. I seemed to have the ability of putting a humorous or friendly face on nearly everything that happened in my presence. Sometimes this would be to the consternation of others I happened to be with.

All of the mentioned attributes of the four officers helped to homogenize the four young men who came from different sections of the country, different backgrounds, and who each had their own idiosyncrasies. We were all trained by the Air Force but we certainly were not carbon copies of one another.

I do not feel capable to analyze the Enlisted men of our crew because I had not gotten close enough to any of them to give an honest or intelligent appraisal. Because of my training and duties, I did not even have a great deal of contact with most other officers during flight.

The officers and enlisted men lived in different sections on the base and the chances to socialize was indeed limited, and in reality, frowned upon in the Service. There were moment when scheduled for a practice flight and we had some time, we did get to horse around with one another. Unfortunately, these moments were too rare.

I did on several occasions take "Newsy" with me on pass, primarily because he had asked to do it and we always managed to have a good time visiting London together. I found out fifty some years later that I had been know as "The Kid" by the enlisted men, but never in my presence. Nearly all of them were older than me. I perhaps looked younger than the twenty three years I had just logged.

Had circumstances been different, I'm sure I would have appreciating knowing each of the other members of my crew in a more intimate way. Time and priorities has a way of dictating most of our decisions and actions. I do not know what kind of intimacy other crews developed between the officers and the enlisted men, but because of impending events, our group never did achieve the comradery I had wished for and I felt was possible to experience.

As this story progresses, it will become most apparent we had limited time that we would be together. In reality, we would only fly a total of three missions as a single unit. The brief amount of contact with the gunners on my original crew is something I have always regretted. Once again, fifty-seven years would elapse before I could learn new and unknown facts about each of these men.

We had been thrown together, supposedly to fly as a crew against the German Luftwaffe, and these plans of our Superior Officers would never permit this to come to fruition.

CHAPTER 11

On February 27, 1944, our crew, along with the many other crews, shipped out to various bases. The Lt. Cobb crew had orders to go to Grand Island, Nebraska and would be temporarily assigned to the 2nd Air Force. Many of the other crews went to Kearney, Nebraska, approximately thirty-five miles away. This would be our last base assignment prior to being shipped overseas and combat.

When we left for Grand Island, Nebraska on February 27, I sincerely believed we would be at the base for only a week, two at the most. Once again I could be considered an eternal optimist. The Base was located a few miles northeast of the city of less than 30,000 people. It was classified by the Air Force as an Assembly Base, a place where crews gathered just prior to being shipped off for combat.

The city of Grand Island is located about 140 miles west of Omaha, is almost in the geographic center of the United States, and was dull. Since the size of this mid western community was approximately the size of my hometown of Wausau, I felt somewhat conformable with the lack of entertainment facilities.

The Assembly Point and Base was the largest employer in town. Despite the obvious boost to the local economy, many people complained and griped about all of the military in their city. Many years later, I found out, these same people complained when the Air Force pulled out. This would be typical of many areas that were selected for military bases throughout the country.

Instead of the seven or ten day stint, it turned into a thirty-three day ordeal. Basically we were to be assigned a new aircraft, calibrate instruments, and take off for Europe. The reality to the entire situation was that our country was trying to move forward faster than all of individual problems could be resolved.

Despite the fact that each of us was anxious to get on with it, it was important to learn to accept each day as it came. The single most important thing each person in the service learned, and I believe this to be a part of all branches, was the old "hurry up and wait" routine.

YANCY HOTEL

Shortly after we arrived in Grand Island, "Waddy" and I discovered the Yancy. This was our affectionate name for the Hotel Yancy, located in the center of town. It was neither large nor impressive, by most standards. Here, however, it was the hub for excitement and living it up. For "Waddy" and me, it offered a place to live, to eat, to drink, to meet, and to fall under the classification of "a home away from home." Many other airmen would also be grateful of the Yancy's existence.

About this time, Norma informed me that her brother was stationed at this very air base. Sgt. Edwin F. Schmidt, and his wife Sally, lived in town, off base. Ed was a career airman, who had entered the Air Force several years prior to the war. It was not difficult to track down Norma's brother, who I had never met, and inform him that it was my intention of becoming his future brother-in-law.

Sgt. Schmidt and I hit it off instantly. Ed enlisted in the Air force many years ago and was about twenty-nine years old. After he left high school, he spent many years traveling around the world while working for the Grace Lines, sailing on ships to far away places.

I had learned from his youngest sister, Norma, that he was an avid iceboat sailor. He had built his own iceboats and skimmed across the lakes in Wisconsin during the winter months. Sgt. Schmidt was rather short and had a stocky build. He had served in many branches of the Air Force, but was now into the new refueling service.

I met with Sgt. Schmidt and his wife Sally on several occasions. However, my first meeting with Sally was the most noteworthy. I had been invited over to their house on a particular evening for dinner and to meet Sally for the first time. With the boredom of the base and the monotony of the dragging time, I accepted this invitation with great expectations. I had been told that the meal being served this evening was to be a spaghetti dinner, something I had not indulged in since I left home.

Late in the afternoon of the day of the dinner date, Ed and I left the base for the dear old Yancy. I had offered to buy Ed a drink or two and we would get the chance to get better acquainted. I was not sure that Ed put the same importance on drinking that "Waddy" and I did. In any case, we went to the bar I had spent the most time at. My appreciation for a nice drink is not necessarily an honorable distinction to have accomplished, but rather an assessment of the situation of the moment.

For several hours, Ed and I conversed over several drinks. We seemed to have lost track of time, something not too difficult while drinking and conversing. Once we became aware of the hour, we started for the little apartment he and Sally were renting.

At this point in time Ed did not seem too concerned about the fact that we were already over an hour late. I also do not believe either one of us was feeling too much pain. However, Ed was struggling under the illusion the entire situation was funny, an attitude which would be on a collision course and much to the dismay of his wife Sally.

When we arrived at the apartment, Sally met us at the door. It was most apparent as to what had happened, but this certainly did not justify our tardiness. Sally was torn between being cordial and affable to me while being genuinely pissed at both of us. Sally was a more mature woman than her age, was slight of build, and did not have the ability to hide or conceal her inner feelings.

She had a way of contorting her face so as to make it impossible to know exactly what might be going on in her mind or exactly what she might utter at any moment. Despite all of this, she made us aware that we were in the dog house.

She had prepared a spaghetti dinner which she had to keep in readiness for nearly two hours. You would have to know Sally, to appreciate the intense stares she could generate. Her glances could penetrate like laser beams. She did her best to smile, while her checks were drawn tight. She saw no humor in the situation, whatsoever. Ed did not help our cause by his steady laughing and snickering at Sally's reaction.

Fortunately, his glow of the moment got him through the dinner, though I knew that before this night was over he would have to pay. I had brought a bottle of wine along, but needless to say, it was never served with this particular spaghetti dinner.

Sally survived and we eventually became very good friends. The three of us had gotten together on several more occasions, prior to my shipping out. I took special precautions that the previous incident would never happen again since I truly blamed myself.

OUR NEW BABY

On March 17 we were informed that our new plane had arrived. It was a B-17, Model G, complete with the new chin turret. It was shiny silver aluminum and had not been painted the usual camouflage olive drab. She was beautiful. Seeing this plane parked on the concrete slab, with the sun bouncing off her metal skin, was like opening the best Christmas present you had ever received. She was ours and we were about to take possession.

A few weeks prior our particular plane had been manufactured by the Boeing Aircraft Corporation in Seattle, Washington. Her Order Of Manufacture would be Number 3662 and this particular airplane Number would be Boeing Number 7807. However, the number painted on each side of the huge tail would be 297334.

I later became aware, that B-17's were also being assembled by the Douglas Aircraft Corporation and Vega, known as Lockheed. Our plane would be forever known as number 297334. The complete number is actually 42-97334, with the 42 indicating that this Model B-17 G was designed in the year of 1942.

The plane had actually arrived at Grand Island on March 3rd and had been parked at a remote spot on the Base. Once we knew which plane would be ours, the crew was rounded up and we immediately went to find it. The entire crew of ten spent the next hour and a half crawling all over our new baby.

We had been introduced to the B-17 F down at Alexandria, but this plane was to be ours to fly and fight in. It had just come off the assembly line where hundreds of dedicated people were pumping out these planes at an unbelievable rate for the war effort. This was like smelling the odors of a new car.

I'm sure each of the Lt. Cobb crew had similar emotions about this new plane assigned to us, however, I felt like I had been given a new, but expensive toy at Christmas. I walked around the plane several times, dragging my hand over the cold but smooth aluminum skin. Every rivet seemed to have a purpose.

I admired the graceful lines and the contrasting awesomeness of the thirteen 50 caliber machine guns protruding from the fuselage. The four huge engines, with their shiny three bladed propellers, only added to the effect of one potent piece of equipment.

Obviously, we were "gnashing at the bit" to get off the ground with our new toy. We were informed that over the next two days we had to calibrate all of the instruments on the plane. This would require us to fly for part of this demanding exercise and to calibrate other instruments by swinging the plane on the ground. It would be a tedious task but one we knew was most necessary.

We did, however, get the opportunity to take a two-hour flight in and around the Grand Island area. The fact that we knew this was the plane assigned to us made this brief flight something special. The powerful four Wright Cyclone Radial Engines purred like a kitten as we traversed the Nebraska countryside. In too short a time we were ordered to return to base and park our new baby.

The following morning, Lts. Cobb, Waddell, Weakland, SSgt. Eavenson, SSgt. Newswanger, and Lt. Krueger took the plane to a remote section of the base on an unused runway. It was not necessary for the rest of the gunners to be subjected to the "swinging of the compasses." I had to have Cobb face the plane in various directions that I requested.

Most of the instrument calibration was required for navigational instruments, both for the Navigator and for the Pilots. The metal in the plane and the operating four engines would affect these instruments. Each plane would be different, so this would be a task each bomber crew would undertake. This would be a responsibility assigned primarily to the Navigator.

An airplane can have all the grace and beauty imaginable, but while maneuvering on the ground she is like a genuine "klutz." In order to swing the plane about, only the two outboard engines are used. In conjunction with engines number 1 and 4, the right and left brake is applied. For example, to move the plane forward both engines are revved up. To turn left, the pilot will advance the throttle on the right engine, number 4, and apply left brake. It will be just the opposite to make a right hand turn.

Each new position or direction, I would verify what our compasses read in comparison to the actual known direction. Slight corrections could be made by adjustments on the compasses, but each time we headed in a new direction, it would affect previous changes. The procedure required that we keep turning the aircraft until its compasses read as accurately as possible.

Once we reached this point, I had the Pilot now move the plane to each of the four major compass directions and instead of making adjustments, I only noted the discrepancies by a plus or minus and the amount on a small card mounted near each compass.

This is a difficult procedure to do since an airplane, especially a large bomber, is next to impossible to maneuver on the ground. It is hard, just using the two outside engines, to get the plane in motion. One of the brakes has to be set while the opposite engine rotates the plane around the immobile tire. Jerking and excessive noise are the paramount results during this lengthy procedure.

Sometimes the plane would turn too far and we would have to start all over. I guess I was the only one who appreciated what had to be done and the necessity of being accurate. It was a boring morning for the other crewmembers subjected to this ordeal. Several times I was asked whether we were about finished. The natives were getting restless. Our Radio Operator, "Newsy," had the chance to check out some of his equipment, as well as the Bombardier. Finally I informed everyone we could terminate this vexing ordeal and call it quits.

After lunch, the remainder of the crew joined us for our first flight in 297334. We had to check additional instruments while in flight, but it afforded each member of our new team the opportunity to see how the plane responded. Once we finished "frogging" around with the required flight patterns necessary for the calibration of instruments, we ventured forth on a short mission of our own.

I gave Cobb a heading for Sioux City, Iowa, a flight of only 50 minutes. We then headed south to fly over Omaha and then back to our base. The trip was long enough to satisfy each member of the crew that we would accept the gift of this plane and to call it ours. I now was assured that all the instruments I would be required to use were in working order and I knew each of their limitations.

More waiting was required before we would receive our orders to ship out. "Waddy" and I had rented a room at the Yancy Hotel so that we could stay in town. We did not want to keep making the long drive back and forth to the base each day. Instead, we would telephone into headquarters for any instructions. If they required that we report in, we would rent a cab for the trip. It would be almost as cheap to rent the room as it was to engage a taxi cab several times each day.

I believe the excitement of going to combat made us restless. Just biding our time by staying on the base did not seem to cut it. Each airman was restless and our superiors, being aware of it, were most lenient with passes and how we saw fit to pass the time. I know also that they were well aware that many of these men now on the Base would never come back, once exposed to combat.

One of the problem's "Waddy" and I had, was the difficulty of buying straight bourbon, our drink of choice. Because of the war, often times it was difficult to find exactly what you wanted, and when we did, it was necessary sometimes to purchase a "package." Buying a "package" meant that for each bottle of bourbon we purchased, we had to buy a bottle of rum. This rum, labeled "Casablanca" was cheap "rot Gut." At the end of several weeks we had stashed away many bottles of this rum. We had a problem, since we had no idea what to do with this supply that was now building up.

Around the middle of March, we expected each day to take off on our next assignment, which would be combat. Rumors were flying around "like mad." The people in town would constantly tell us that none of the crews would be leaving. The civilian seemed to know more about our status than we did.

All of this uncertainty created real problems for "Waddy" and me. Many times we would check out of our hotel room, go to the base, and find out that our orders had not come through, according to the latest rumor. Each time we would have to pack up our numerous bottles of "Casablanca" and store it in a large closet at the hotel. Later, each day, we would have to register again for a room.

SEMI PRIVATE ROOM

One day, after we had checked out, "Waddy" and I returned to town, only to find the hotel had no available rooms. They told us not to worry, because they should have something available later in the evening. This particular night, when I happened to be bent out of shape, I somehow managed to get myself back to the hotel. The clerk told me they did not have a room, but that they would set up a bed for us. "Waddy" later decided to go back to the base and leave me in town.

Since it was very late and I wasn't too confident of most of my faculties, I had them direct me to the assigned room. The room was dark, but I was only interested in hitting the sack. I undressed down to my shorts and jumped into the bed the hotel had prepared for me. I fell asleep and was completely out, until sometime late the next morning.

I had been awakened by strange and unusual sounds. With some determined effort, I managed to get one of my eyes open. Even with blurred vision, and a fuzzy head, I was able to see the predicament I had gotten myself into. I was lying on a cot, in the middle of a large banquet room, and seven or eight waitresses were setting up tables for an upcoming affair in the hotel. When they noticed that this body had some life in it, I could hear chuckles, snickers, and murmurs.

My clothes were scattered and dropped just where I had taken them off many hours before. Fortunately, I was covered with a sheet and blanket, since I usually slept in the raw. I will never know if I had rolled over with the sheet in disarray or not. My predicament only brought smiles to each of the women placing the silver around each setting.

In any case, I did manage to get one of the women to collect my clothing and place it upon my cot. I felt like a one armed paperhanger as I tried to dress myself under the covers. I couldn't get out of this ungodly dilemma fast enough.

UNEXPECTED PASS

On March 24, instead of shipping orders, we were told anyone who desired, could get a four-day pass, starting early the next morning. This came as a complete shock to me, but certainly a pleasant one. I got on the phone and called Chicago. I was not able to reach Norma immediately, but I left a message and someone said they would track her down.

Within ten minutes she called me back. I then explained to Norma, that prior to shipping out, we had received a special four-day pass. If she could get time off, I suggested we both go north to Wausau, taking the train out of Chicago.

Norma managed to get the time off from nurses' training so we agreed I would join her in Chicago and we would both take the train north to our homes. Both of us appreciated this last chance to see each other again. Without talking about it, we both knew, this could be the last time we may ever see one another. This final contact for the two of us, prior to my venturing into the unknown, had more significance than I wanted to think about.

At the same time I called Norma, Lt. Dan Waddell gave his fiancée a call in Hendersonville, North Carolina. Claire agreed to fly out to Omaha, Nebraska, where Dan would meet her. During these brief four days, the two of them got married. This would be a most pleasant surprise for me on my return to Grand Island.

Claire and Dan had known one another for many years. Claire was very southern, pretty, and petite. When she talked, you had no doubt she was born, raised, and educated in the south. Between Claire and Dan, because of the time it would take to spit out words, an hour could be wasted, of their four-day pass, just greeting one another. The two of them went off to Omaha and had a two-day honeymoon.

The three days we had together helped weld the feelings Norma and I had for each other. This brief and unexpected leave gave me the chance to say my good byes to my parents and my sister and two brothers. I had been contacted by several aunts and uncles and received much advice I could have lived without. Norma and I returned to Chicago and I then transferred to a train heading for Omaha, Nebraska and then my base.

I returned to Grand Island Army Air Force Base at Grand Island, late on the evening of March 29. Lt. Cobb told me that we would be taking off in two days. We finally were going to head for Europe. Things would be hectic these next two days since there was much to get accomplished before we started overseas.

The most important matter concerning "Waddy" and myself, was to get into the Yancy and bring back all of our rum. We managed to take a single B-4 bag filled with carefully rapped bottles. The remainder of this "joy juice" we decided to leave in our room. When we left for the field, one last time, we looked back at this old hotel with mixed emotions. The memories, that we could remember, were mostly fond ones though in reality I felt it was a month wasted.

Dan had to say his goodbyes to Claire, and I made one last telephone call to my parents and to Norma. Tomorrow morning early, on April 1, 1944, we would leave this Assembly area on the first leg and head for Bangor, Maine.

This first leg will be a nice practice navigation exercise for me, since I will have the help of all of the radio signals plus familiar maps of eastern United States. Once we head across the ocean, my work as a Navigator will take on a more difficult role when celestial navigation will come into play.

Each phase in my military career seemed to terminate at a point where moving on to the next stage became something to look forward to. I constantly enjoyed new experiences and new challenges and the unexpected that would lie ahead most times only added to the adventure I now found myself on.

CHAPTER 12

April 1,1944, everything is in readiness for the first leg of our long trip to England. Today we will head for Bangor, Maine, our last stop in the States. I have plotted a course that will take us just north of Chicago, within sight of Detroit, over Buffalo, N.Y., and near Rochester in the same state.

"Waddy" and I managed to sneak our B-4 Bag, with the Casablanca rum aboard, thus taking care of the most important item. We had heard it was difficult to find most drinks in England because of the war. Hopefully, someone will be desperate enough to want to purchase or swap something for the cargo the two Rum Runners are carrying.

There was genuine excitement among the gunners of our crew. These individuals were still getting to know each other, just as we four officers were doing. The crew, made up of ten young men, from all sections of the country, were now prepared to fly to Europe and to take part in this terrible war.

This was something that not one of us would choose on our own volition, yet each had volunteered to serve in this time of need. This perhaps, was the most common thread that ran through the group, who hailed from eight different states.

We all were happy that we had been assigned a plane and were going to fly over to England. We had heard that many crews would be sent to the East coast and would await a ship to take them across the Atlantic Ocean. Others would go via South America and Africa to make this same trip to get to a base in England.

Before we took off, Lt. Cobb stated, that he would like to deviate slightly from the course I had plotted, so that we could pass over Crown Point, Indiana. This was his hometown and he had called ahead to let his family know we would be passing by. This would be no big deal for me since this small Indiana city is about ten miles south of Hammond and Gary, Indiana, both contiguous to Chicago. Shortly after takeoff, I gave Cobb a heading that would take us over his home.

When Cobb stated he would like to fly over his hometown, what he really meant was that old number 297334 was about to buzz his home. As we approached the city from the west, we dropped down to the lowest altitude required to miss the highest obstacles. We had absolutely no difficulty on each of the three passes we made over the house tops to identify his mother.

She stood in the center of a large lawn, surrounded by dozens of neighbors. She was not waving a handkerchief, like most mothers might have done, but rather a large white bed sheet. She was surrounded by perhaps a dozen neighbors waving their arms. I have never met Mrs. Cobb, but I could see that Lt. Franklin Heuth Cobb Jr. had much in common with his mother. I could hardly believe the enthusiasm being displayed with the flapping sheet, nor the effort exerted in saying goodbye to her son and our crew.

Just before we made our first pass, the pilots intentionally had all four engines out of perfect synchronization. This would create additional noise and vibrations. We found out weeks later, many windows cracked or were broken in this section of the city, due to the buzz job. The entire incident only took seven or eight minutes away from our flight plan, but I'm sure it made a conversational item, for years to come.

A correction of only 2 degrees, from my plotted course, put us back on track and our rendezvous with Bangor. We flew over Rochester and could see Syracuse, New York off our right wing. The plane touched down at 1630 hours, actually several minutes prior to our anticipated arrival. Despite the buzzing of Crown Point, we averaged 215 miles per hour ground speed, thanks to a favorable wind. I wish each of us on the plane, could have buzzed our hometowns.

April 2nd, and we have a day off. We were told that mechanics were going over our new plane after its first regular flight. It is important to have everything in perfect working condition, since our next three legs, on our long journey, will be over hostile land or the Atlantic Ocean. I don't mind this slight delay, as long as it's for a good reason.

Once again I had a chance to visit with Norma's older brother, Sgt. Ed. Schmidt. Just before we took off from Grand Island, I had the opportunity to get off a last minuet phone call to Chicago and my Norma. During the conversation and our good byes, she mentioned that her brother had just been transferred to Bangor, Maine.

She had no idea I was about to go there on our first leg, since these were secret orders. It was by pure chance and luck I came by this knowledge. Once we arrived, it didn't take too much effort to track down Ed. Schmidt and arrange to meet at our new B-17.

He's in an air-to-air refueling unit in the Air Force, and has temporarily been transferred from Grand Island to Bangor. It's quite a coincidence that the two of us should be together at several different bases, especially since we're in completely different units.

Ed managed to take a slew of great pictures of our new B-17, the crew, and me. Since I didn't own a camera, I appreciated having a record of this moment in time. He later sent me a copy of all of these pictures of our new lady, which the crew unanimously decided to name "HAARD LUCK." I will elaborate on this choice of name later.

GOOSE BAY, LABRADOR

Early in the morning, on April 3, we took off on our next leg. Today we would land at a huge facility in Goose Bay, Labrador. The base is just west of the small Canadian town in Newfoundland, and is approximately 100 miles inland from the Atlantic Ocean. We had snow on the ground at Bangor, but we were not prepared for the snow we were about to see on this next leg.

Our flight path took us over the Anticosti Islands in the Gulf of Saint Lawrence. From this point on, we had nothing but raw wilderness below us as we flew over the eastern tip of Quebec Province and the Province of Labrador. Once we left the United States and began flying over Canada we never saw another city, town or even a settlement. This entire area was completely covered by forests and was obviously void of any signs of human habitation.

Looking down during the flight, one could only see snow that covered the forests and the hundreds of tiny lakes. One of the gunners claimed to have seen a lone moose plowing through the deep snow, which is more than I had noticed.

When we approached the Goose Bay field, we were instructed to land on the main runway, No. 28. The multiple runways at Goose Bay were the longest and most impressive ones I've ever seen. They were all defined by the tremendous amount of snow surrounding them. All runways had been shoveled and in most cases only concrete being exposed.

The man in the tower was most explicit when he instructed our approaching plane, due to water and ice on the runway, we were to touch down on the right side of this huge concrete slab. On our base leg we could see a snow bank on the right side of this runway. It looked like it may be over twenty-foot high. The runway had been recently plowed and patches of water were visible.

For some unknown reason, Cobb set the wheels down on the left of center section of the runway, which meant we rolled through large puddles of water. We could hear some objects hitting the airplane but it was impossible to see what the problem was. Chunks of ice floating on the water were ricocheting off the left wing, just outside my navigational window.

Once we stopped at the end of the runway, we were directed to follow a jeep to a revetment so that we could park the B-17. Snow banks on each side of the runway, the perimeter strips, and around our revetment, were over twenty feet high. And I thought we had snow up in Wisconsin!

We parked the plane and got out into the cold air. Immediately it became apparent our new plane had sustained some damage. Chunks of ice had been kicked up by the prop wash and beat the hell out of the underside of our left wing. It was indeed in need of repair. No one asked Cobb why he did not follow instructions because we all knew he probably felt worse than we did. I'm sure somewhere down the line he would have some explaining to do.

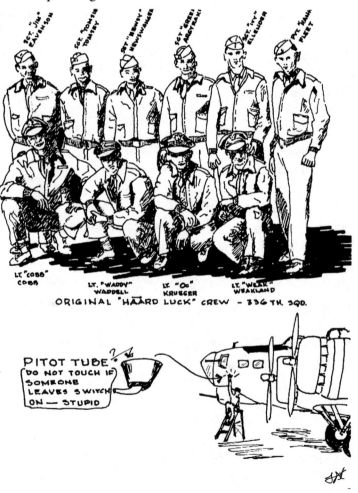

ORIGINAL "HAARD LUCK" CREW - 336TH SQD.

164

There was a lot of activity around the plane, unloading of bags, checking the amount of damage, etc. In the process of trying to help, I picked up the canvas pitot tube cover, with its little red flag. It was lying on the runway apron. My intention was to climb the ladder, which the mechanics had wheeled out, and place this cover over the pitot tube. The pitot tube is an instrument which points forward along the fuselage and its function is to ascertain our air speed while in flight.

I reached up and grabbed this metal projection and at the same time, used it to help pull myself up to the next step at the top of the ladder. Someone had inadvertently left an electrical switch on, which made this air speed indicator red-hot. It was impossible to immediately let go of the hot tube until I could get my entire weight back on the ladder. All of the chords in the palm of my left hand immediately contracted, pulling all of my fingers into an involuntary fist.

A Staff Sgt. from the Base immediately took me in his jeep to the Infirmary for medical attention. The doctor and nurse gradually got my fingers straightened out and dressed each one separately with ointment and bandages. The pain was something I could have done without. Because of the profusion of bandages, my left hand was now prepared to go out into the cold Labrador air, without a mitten. I had been given several pain pills to help with the discomfort I was experiencing. I suppose I could have suggested some spirits that would have made these many pills unnecessary.

Several days were required to repair our damaged left wing, something I had in common with old No. 297334. Four small sections of new aluminum panels had to be riveted to the underside of the left wing. Also some dents had to be removed. My handicapped left hand did not hinder my activities during the four days we were required to remain at Goose Bay.

We learned today about a B-17 going down about twelve miles from this field. This had happened several days before we arrived. By the time a rescue unit with dog teams reached this crew, who also were on their way to combat, all ten crewmembers were frozen to death. Their bodies were scattered over many miles between the downed plane and the base.

They had made the terrible mistake of leaving their plane. Had they remained inside the downed bomber, all might have made it. Instead, they believed they could walk the twelve miles to the base. This decision did not take into account the depth of the snow nor the many obstacles in the dense woods.

They also made another mistake by not keeping together. They left the downed plane in several small groups, struggling through impossible obstacles until they could move no further. It had taken days to find all of the ten bodies.

We discovered that the permanent personnel, at the Officers' Club, guarded their liquor supply like it was liquid gold. About the only thing we could buy was a type of beer I had never heard of, and I consider myself to be somewhat of a connoisseur. "Waddy" and I said to hell with them, we had our own stock. We had forgotten just how bad the Casablanca rum really was. To make matters even worse, we found out that the Base was out of coca cola and did not expect a shipment for several days.

We went to the mess hall and appropriated a gallon can of tomato juice. Using brand new galvanized metal cups, from the mess kits we had been issued, we mixed a generous measure of the rum with some tomato juice. The combination got to taste better after the third or fourth drink. We lightened our B-4 load somewhat by disposing of four or five bottles with the crew.

The word had gotten out, that we had this rum and several of the Base Officers wanted to buy our entire stock. They were willing to pay "Waddy" and me twice what we remembered this stuff cost us. Our final decision was to part with only about half of our bottles. If things got that bad this close to the United States, perhaps we ought to hang on to it. We did.

The next morning, six or seven of us woke up with first class headaches. In fact, you could even label it as a hangover. The most startling thing we observed was the condition of our new galvanized metal cups. We had not cleaned them out from the night before.

In the process, we found that the combination of our rum and the tomato juice had eaten most of the galvanizing off the metal cups. They looked disgusting. I couldn't help wondering what this horrible mixture had done to our stomachs. I now had a perfect clew as to why our heads and other parts of our anatomy were out of synch.

GONE FISHING

The next day, April 6, we walked over to the Red Cross facility on the base, to play some ping-pong. They informed us that they had fishing gear, should we like to give it a fling. Goose Bay is located on the southwest shore of Lake Melville, right where the Churchill River dumps into the lake. We were given the necessary fishing tackle, a shovel and a heavy metal ice chopper. The one thing, that all agreed on was totally lacking was warm clothing for the wind we were to discover on the lake.

We walked across the snow-covered ice for about a quarter of a mile, stopping at a spot that all agreed would be prime fishing territory. A wide area was shoveled off, exposing the ice. Some of the fellows started to chip an eight-inch diameter hole in the ice.

When they got down about a foot, they were forced to enlarge the hole to a diameter of about eighteen inches. I sort of supervised and acted as a straw boss. I had my bandaged hand sticking out so all could notice that I was incapacitated.

The diameter kept increasing as the depth of the hole went down. Everyone was pooped from chopping or shoveling out the loose ice. Just about the time everyone was ready to give this up as a bad idea, I volunteered to use my good right arm to take a turn. I had ice fished back in Wisconsin and I knew you could ram the heavy iron chopper into the hole with only one hand. I slammed it down into the ice pit and the sucker just kept going. I had lost my grip on this heavy tool as it finally had broken through the ice. It sank out of sight. We now had a six-inch diameter hole at the bottom of the two and a half foot thick ice sheet.

A few of the fellows baited their hook and took turns tempting whatever might be lurking in these cold waters. We were very fortunate that the only things that bit on our bait were small fish, about three inches in length. We knew we could not get a large fish through the hole we managed to chop, but the fish we caught were ridiculous.

So much for these wild, romantic, virgin-waters in the far north, I could have done better in a small pond in Wisconsin. I had to go back and apologize to the Red Cross people that I lost their chopper. I had made sure that my bandaged left hand was visible at all times. My apology was accepted.

That night we had the opportunity to meet a real rugged looking trapper. This fellow had just arrived and the Air Force was putting him up for the night, in our barracks. It was interesting to listen to him tell of some of his experiences in the wilds of this remote section of Canada.

He had about a dozen beautiful cured pelts. Several were sable and the one that caught my eye was a snow white fox pelt. This old trapper turned his nose up at the Casablanca rum we offered him. He said he doubted that the Native Indians would even try it, and they weren't usually fussy.

As soon as it was dark, on the evening of April 7, we took off on our next leg. This would be a 1500-mile flight over the Labrador Sea and the Atlantic Ocean to Reykjavik, Iceland. We took off at night intentionally because it is essential to use celestial navigation for this dangerous trip.

At this latitude and in this section of the world, the ordinary compass in our plane proves to be completely useless. This is because of the magnetic north pole and the problems it causes. So much for all of the instrument calibrations we had made.

This would be the acid test for Krueger the Navigator and all that I had been taught at San Marcos. I had to start off this flight, and the challenges it offered, with a very bad left hand. The doctors had bandaged each of my fingers separately, making them fan out. I found it impossible to handle my sextant with this injured hand, the most important and absolute essential piece of equipment for navigating in our plane this night.

I begin to wonder if it had been a smart idea to tell them I was ready for the next leg of our journey. I know we could have delayed our take off until my hand healed. Because I didn't want to reveal the condition of my hand to the nurses lest they suggest a delay in our take-off, I planed for the removal of the bandages once we got into the plane, thus keeping our flight on schedule. We already had lost several days due to the damage on our new baby. Despite all of this, I knew this would be the biggest test I would ever face.

The first thing, after I gave Cobb a heading to fly, was to ask Lt. Ray Weakland to remove all of my bandages from my hand. He then used about one tenth of the bandage material to redress my left hand. There remained a pile of gauze on the floor, enough to stuff a pillow.

With my fingers now tightly bandaged together, I could now slip this hand through a strap and grasp the sextant. I could hold it long enough to take shots of the many stars I would shoot this long night. Though the hand hurt, other pressing matters kept my mind focused on the task ahead.

MOMENT OF TRUTH

This mission would be my moment of truth, as far as my new crew was concerned. I had to prove that I was their Navigator, and that I was also capable. Tonight, each of our lives would be on the line, should this plane not reach the tip of Iceland. Ditching in the North Atlantic Ocean would have only one outcome, with each of our fates being determined in only a matter of minutes.

The nine-hour trip would be a real bore for everyone but yours truly. Our Radio Operator would be put to work on occasions, but the rest of the gunners would just have to sweat out the trip. Most of the time, the pilots would put the plane on automatic-pilot, making occasional changes due to the precession of the gyro. I would call up to the pilots if I felt a change in course might be necessary. We had a complete blanket of clouds between us and the iceberg infested seas below. This condition would remain with us for most of the flight.

About an hour out, the Radio Operator was able to pick up some music and sent it to each of our headsets. During one of the moments, when I was "busier than a cat covering crap on a hot tin roof," the radio blasted Woody Herman's version of

"Caldonia— What Makes Your Big Head So Hard."

It was at this moment that I lost my cool. "Turn that G.D. radio off "Newsy", I can't think with that stinking noise," I shouted into my mike. With all of the pressures of what lay ahead, I found that I was letting the roar of the four engines annoy me. This was a completely new experience for me.

I began to realize the difficult task of taking repeated shots of the stars, doing the required math, and then plotting these fixes, all the while my head felt like it was shoved inside a pail while someone was pounding on it. Suddenly I realized that this was my problem and not anyone else in this plane. I had to learn to work under these difficult conditions.

The plane was constantly bouncing around each time I tried to take shots with my sextant. This made me conscience of the possibility that I could make erroneous shots and end up with worthless three star fixes. If this happened, I would lose over a half hour of work with little or no results. Fortunately this night, my fixes were within the limits of what would prove useful.

About three hours into the flight, Sgt. Eavenson yelled into the mike that something funny was going on in the sky off our left wing. Flashes of brilliant light were racing across the sky. It was as though huge patches of irregularly shaped fluorescent objects were dancing about. Sometimes they would merge and at other times they appeared to almost bounce away in new directions. There were brief moments when these luminous splashes of light disappeared entirely.

It was both eerie and beautiful. There were short periods of time when the inside of our plane would light up. None of the crew had ever seen anything like this spectacle, and had no idea on what was going on.

Being raised in northern Wisconsin, I knew these were the Northern Lights. The technical name is the Aurora Borealis. Though I had witnessed this spectacle many times in Wisconsin, never with the brilliance we were now being treated. I had never seen such a luminous spectacle as we were privileged to see this night. There were streamers and arches of brilliant light in this otherwise pitch black night sky.

I was questioned on what it was and what was causing it. Though I knew its name and that it was electric particles in the air, I was not capable of giving the crew a scientific explanation for this unique occurrence. Once most of the crew knew what this spectacle was, they stared out the only three windows in our plane at the exhibition off our left wing in this night's sky. Unfortunately, I could not dwell on this phenomenon because of more pressing problems.

Occasionally, the sky above us would have large areas of clouds, making it very difficult for me to identify constellations. This then would make it next to impossible to identify individual stars that I needed for navigating. On several shots of these doubtful stars, I just had to make an educated guess on what was available in any particular quadrant or section of the night sky.

I would then make calculations accordingly. If I made an error in identifying a specific star, it would show up when I plotted the results, and then perhaps the entire fix would have to be discarded.

Adding to all of my problems, Lt. Cobb was becoming most uneasy and getting very edgy. I'm sure the bad decision on the landing at Goose Bay, and subsequent plane damage, did little to fortify his confidence. I had to give him compass directions that made no sense due to the effect of the magnetic pole and to the unbelievable strong winds. The winds were stronger than I had ever experienced before. We were living in an age when nothing was known of the excessive winds later referred to as the jet streams.

Lt. Cobb continually contacted me, through our intercom, asking if I was sure of our course to Reykjavik. Each time I would answer back in the affirmative, even though he now started to plant a seed of doubt in my mind. The compasses before him in the cockpit were useless for him tonight. I do not believe he fully appreciated this fact. There was an increasing tone of sarcasm with each contact I received.

The apparent course to Iceland, discounting variation, wind, etc., was approximately 45 degrees. The course I told Cobb to fly and to maintain was something like 76 degrees. Cobb knew if he plotted 76 degrees from Goose Bay, it would eventually take us toward Norway or even Ireland. He also knew that our fuel supply would run out long before we reached either of these two countries.

In order to maintain a true course to our final destination it was necessary to point the plane additional degrees to the right to compensate for the extreme winds our plane was being subjected to. I also believe that Cobb trusting his erratic and worthless compass in front of him.

CONFIDENCE

Each time I had to assure Lt.Cobb that my fixes placed us on the planned course to Reykjavik, it seemed to add to the pressures I was under. Each fix took approximately a half hour to shoot, calculate and plot. As soon as I finished one fix, I would immediately start the next one. I did this hour after hour.

It did not help psychologically, during these trying moments, to know most of the others were either sleeping or listening to music while my head was spinning with the current responsibility of keeping track of where we were and were we were going. I also knew it did not help for me to feel sorry for myself when all my talents were being tested.

I was aware, because it had been hammered home to me at San Marcos, that for each single degree we would be off course, our error would be one nautical mile for every sixty nautical miles we flew. That single degree error, on our entire flight, would amount to missing Iceland by over 40 miles. The reality of our situation remained, that if you were in error by a single degree, you could be in error by perhaps ten degrees.

About this time, I remembered what one of my most respected instructors back at San Marcos had told me. "Develop confidence in your ability to Navigate. Remember that you are the only person, and I mean only, in the plane you'll be flying in, that has this knowledge and training. Believe in yourself." I finally barked in the mike, "Dammit Cobb, sit back and relax. This plane is heading for Reykjavik." I think my stern reply took effect because Cobb no longer titillated my nerves with his apprehensions.

We flew close enough to be within sight of the tip of Greenland, but the cloud cover below us took this important landfall away from me. Any help I could get to verify my work was always appreciated. I knew, should we be in trouble, a forced landing on Greenland might have saved us. Tonight we would not need this emergency windfall.

I did know for a fact, that with luck, when we got near enough to Iceland, we could pick up a meaningful radio beam. The needle would swing in a wide arc, but at least you could gage the approximate direction of this important signal. It would be only a matter of a few hours and the sun would rise.

Early on the morning of April 8, I gave Lieutenant's Cobb and Waddell an ETA (estimated time of arrival) for Meeks Field as 0832 hours. With a ton of confidence I added: "You can start a gradual descent in 45 minutes. This will put us at the right altitude to enter the air traffic pattern." Now that we were close to Reykjavik, I had the positive assurance from the radio directional compass, plus all of my other aids. I just felt the need to show off, prior to our crew spotting the coast of Iceland.

Cobb made radio contact with the control tower at Meek Field and entered the traffic pattern. Our landing was not particularly good, resulting in six or seven rough bounces. The plane settled down and gradually rolled to a stop at the end of the runway. I make mention of this landing and the one at Goose Bay, only because it has an important bearing on future events that were yet to take place.

When we reported in to operations, we were informed that we would take off for England on April 10, giving us a two day lay over in this very different part of the world. Iceland is a Sovereign State with strong ties to Denmark. The land is very rugged, since it is composed of a series of volcanic tablelands. There are exposed lava beds that do nothing for the landscape.

We were told that all incoming crews were restricted to the base until our departure on the 10th. "Waddy" and I felt it equally important that we see something of Reykjavik, so we kind of slipped away from the Base at Meek Field. We spent nearly two hours in this capital of Iceland, a city with a population of approximately 40,000 persons, before the Military Police caught us. They were very kind to us, by simply demanding we get our butts back to the base and stay there. In fact, they provide taxi service for this short trip.

While we walked the streets of the residential area of Reykjavik, we did spot several groups of girls ahead of us. All of them vanished as we approached. They seemed to be very shy. I found out later, with this permanent American Air Base so close to the city, parents probably advised their daughters to keep some distance between them and the American G.I.'s.

At a much later date I was told that if any of the permanent personnel at Meek Field got an Icelandic girl pregnant and did not desire that they be wed, they would be compelled to pay this unlucky girl and her parents the puny sum of $800.00. This doesn't make much sense, but I guess it's believable. A lot of unconcerned American servicemen left a trail of deserted children from one end of the world to another, without even glancing back. This would be yet another terrible and tragic cost of war, something none of us can be proud of.

OFF TO ENGLAND

On April 10, at 0700 hours, we took off for England on the fourth leg of this long journey. Our destination would be Nutts Corner, Ireland. It would be a flight over water of only about 540 miles, while the entire trip would be slightly less than eight-hundred miles. We directed the plane to a landfall at Stornoway, Scotland that is located on an island in the Outer Hebrides, at the Northern part of Scotland.

We then headed almost due south to the airfield at Nutts Corner, just about twelve miles north of Belfast, in Northern Ireland. Once again we experienced a mediocre landing after our relatively short trip of seven hundred plus mile flight. This is the third landing in a row that Cobb had trouble setting the plane down. I do not believe other crew members were aware of these landings, they only were happy to have completed the flight.

Once we landed and were cleared through operations, we received the biggest shock of our new careers. We were informed that we had to release our new shiny B-17 over to the Air Force and that it would be reassigned to one of nearly thirty five Bomb Groups on Bases over in England.

I couldn't believe what they had just told us. I felt like saying: "You can't do this." I stopped because I knew that their wish was my command. All of us were stunned. For me it was the second time I had been slammed in the solar plexus in less than a year. The Air Force I was willing to put my ass on the line for did not seem to care. "What in hell happened to the words understanding and compassion."

I had grown so accustomed to this beautiful airplane and truly believed I would fly in it until my tour was over, I had been shot down, or blown out of the skies. This order had never entered my mind and I was numb that I would never see this special plane, Number **297334** again. The thought of some other uncaring crew, looking upon her as just another B-17, was on the verge of being more than I could handle, especially after our long and tiring trip.

I do not know if I shed a tear because of this news, but I do recollect I felt like I had lost a very precious part of my life. I was pissed enough that I know it harden me for some of the decisions I would have to make in the days ahead or situations I found myself in. I was now determined I would not let them crap on me again or get to me.

Though we had received orders that all crews were restricted to the base, because of our present moods, we found no trouble in disobeying this order. Within an hour of arriving, "Waddy", Weakland and I went under the fence, which surrounded the airfield, and headed toward Belfast.

We got on a highway that would take us south and started to hitchhike, believing we would get a ride in a hurry. We did not know if this was an accepted form of traveling in Ireland. We discovered though, each vehicle that came down this lonely road was loaded with people.

We later were told that no one would think of using a vehicle with only a single passenger aboard. Petrol was at a premium all over England and it was even worse in Ireland. We kept walking south and thumbing anything that came along.

Finally, a fairly large bus stopped and offered us a ride. It was partially filled with coal miners, returning home after a long day in the mines. They were tired looking and most were covered with coal dust. Once we got settled on the bus we three were accepted as welcomed Yanks. When we first came on board, these tired miners stared at us in disbelief.

Immediately the atmosphere changed on the noisy bus and we knew we were welcomed. We talked with many of these miners and were able to understand them, despite their thick Irish brogue. It seemed that they rolled their tongue on every other word. The whites of their eyes were exaggerated because of the black coal dust deposited on each of their faces. Their white teeth took on importance when they smiled or laughed.

I happened to be half Irish from my Mothers side of the family. My grandparents were named Curtis and Mullins, respectively. Right now my Irish heritage became more dominant over my German ancestry. When these Irish coal miners turned to talk to one another, we could not understand a word they said.

Before we arrived in Belfast, we did manage to get them to sing with us "My Wild Irish Rose" and McNamara's Band." The trip on the bus seemed to be over too soon, due mostly because of the rapid and unexpected friendships we developed.

The bus, we were so fortunate to have gotten a ride on, took us near the center of Belfast, the largest city in Northern Ireland. It has a population of over 440,000 people and only slightly smaller than Dublin, in size. Though one half of my heritage was Irish, I felt like I was in another world when I tried to communicate with these lovely people.

Wherever the three of us went, we were welcomed, accepted, and asked to join in their activities. It was obvious they did not get a chance to meet too many Americans, due to restrictions on the Base. We knew we had no business in this city tonight, but not one of us gave a damn, especially since they saw fit to confiscate our plane.

Many wanted to know how we were permitted to come into Belfast. Our illegal entry only made us feel special at this moment. Ray Weakland had a certain amount of anxiety until we got a few drinks into him. My present attitude and mood made me feel I was right where I belonged this night.

The first stop for us was an Irish pup where we had a sandwich and our first crack at their famous whiskey. Both of these attempts to ingest nourishment agreed with our palates. We were told that we must attend the weekly dance in a large ballroom nearby. This ballroom was in the basement of a rather old hotel.

IRISH JIG

By the time we got there, the place was really hopping. The room was especially dark, with the main source of light being reflected off a moving sphere of small mirrors. The light seemed to jump from hundreds of sources, and reached out in ever corner of this large room. Small squares of light in constant motion, hopped off faces and clothing. It took awhile to get used to the effect caused by this moving source of reflecting mirrors and the constantly changing visions around the darkened room.

Everyone appeared to be having a jovial time. There was a constant muffled sound caused by the hundreds of different conversations, isolated laughs, greetings of newly recognized friends, and noises associated with happy people.

The orchestra, at the far end of this ballroom, played many recognizable American tunes. Dan, Weak, and I stuck out like a sore thumb. We were the only persons in uniform in the place. There could have been other service men present from the permanent personnel of the Base at Nutts Corner that were in civilian clothes. This did not seem important at this moment in time.

I appreciated just watching and listening this unique group of happy people. This airman had no intention in going onto the dance floor, especially with my reputation of tripping the light fantastic. My last "dance" was with Norma at the University, a century ago and it still left me with a few negative thoughts.

Time, being grabbed by a jovial large Irish lass, and Irish whiskey eroded any reluctance I may have had. Before I knew it, I was pulled into a long line of people. I was taking part in the Lambeth Walk, a dance the British people loved.

Because of the late hour, the alcohol, the shock of being on the dance floor, and finding myself in the midst of several hundred happy strangers in a foreign land, I suddenly lost most of my inhibitions. The darkened dance floor gave me the false security that no one would notice me making a fool of myself.

Much to my amazement, I found that I could "put my right foot in, and shake it all about." I could even do the same with my left foot. I watched everyone's movements, and did the best I could muster, by imitating them, always a few seconds behind the others. The primary obligation was having fun, and I suppose some of my antics added to the enjoyment of any who glanced my way.

I was pulled, yanked and maneuvered about this large floor until I thought my legs would come unglued from my hip sockets. Despite the ordeal, I truly enjoyed this moment with my Irish ancestors. My impression this night, of these jovial people, was that they appeared to be small in stature but each possessed a huge heart.

Sometime after midnight, two girls, who were cousins, invited us to their home for some tea and food. They gave the three of us the impression that it was only a five-minute walk, over the cobblestone streets of Belfast. It turned out to be about two miles.

I enjoyed the walk on the damp cobblestone pavement and the hollow sound of our voices bouncing off the brick walls of the buildings that lined the street. In the distance we could hear the musical sounds of a horse clattering across these shiny cobblestones while pulling a small cart. It broke the silence of the night with its wheels with metal rims.

The unusual part of this incident, I shall never forget was the sincere hospitality shown by these two new friends and the mother they woke up at two o'clock in the morning. She made us tea and offered us several different kinds of crumpets. An American mother, whose daughter would bring three strange servicemen home at two in the morning, would still be bouncing between the floor and the ceiling.

The sun was coming up when we somehow arrived back at the airfield. I don't believe "Waddy", "Weak", or I are really sure exactly how we made it back. Somehow we had gotten under the fence and we ultimately found our assigned barracks. Just why we were never disciplined, is a mystery. Despite all of the unknowns, I still have this entire evening as a lasting pleasant memory. This diversion helped to make me soften my feelings toward the men who, without out any sentiment, separated our crew from its own personal B-17, number 297334.

On April 11, we were told all of the crews in our group had arrived safely from the States. Tomorrow the twenty plus crews would be sent to England and be dispersed to the various combat units. The crew of Lt. Cobb were to be assigned to the 95th (H) Bomb Group at Horham, England somewhere in Suffolks. At this point I didn't have the slightest idea where Horham was located, nor did I know anything about the 95th.

While we were biding our time, I got the bright idea to hunt down some four-leaf clovers while we were still in Ireland. As I grew up in Wisconsin, I was led to believe that to find a four-leaf clover, meant you would have good luck. This day, I had a gut feeling that somewhere down the road, each of us would probably need more than luck, to see us through the months ahead.

I had often heard my Irish Grandfather talk about shamrocks and the luck of the Irish. I did not know it at the time, but the shamrock is a trifolium leguminous plant and does not have the usual four leaves, which I had been told would favor you with good fortune. Despite this technicality, I can still hear my little old Irish Grandfather say: "Me Laddy, you find a fier-leaf clover and sure 'n begorry the sun will shine on you all day."

I searched for over an hour, when suddenly I stumbled on a small patch of clover with some plants having the four leaves I desired. I found ten of these little rascals, one for each member of our crew. No one turned me down.

I pressed and dried my specimen for several days so that it would be preserved. I then placed it on a small square of cardboard and covered it with the transparent wrapper from a package of Old Gold cigarettes. (I still possess this four-leaf clover, 58 years later.) I'm really not superstitious or a believer in luck, but what the hell, I'm here eighty-one years and counting.

On the morning of April 12, over two hundred American Airmen were bused to Bangor, Ireland, about a two-hour trip. Here we boarded a large ferry, which would carry us across the North Channel and into the Irish Sea to England. This was a new experience for most of us, since many came from landlocked states. Because we passed close to the Isle of Man, we could see land in the distant for almost the entire trip. Our destination was Stone, England.

The crossing was uneventful because the sea was relatively calm. We all displayed a degree of excitement in that we knew we were inching our way toward our final destination.

Each moment seemed to bring on a new experience by the people we met, by the different scenery we were being exposed to, and the knowledge we were constantly moving farther away from each of our homes. Once we departed the boat, we were put on buses for a short trip to Stone, England. Each moment exposed everyone to new sights that none in this caravan had ever seen before.

The countryside of both Ireland and England was different from anything I had ever seen in my country. There were no large areas or fields fenced in with barbwire. Large farm barns and silos were missing from the landscape. Instead we saw small cultivated fields or grassy meadows defined by hedgerows. These divisions that delineated each section of land were sometimes piles of stones or rocks, some were masonry walls made up of the same material, but more often they were simply a hedge of different types of bushes.

The homes were small compared to what I had been accustomed to. Most had thatched roofs and were quaint and truly beautiful. Near every small home would be a garden, both with flowers and with vegetables. Few failed to wave at us as we passed in our bus. I had seen enough to wish and hope that some day I could return and visit both of these English speaking Countries.

CHAPTER 13

Once we were billeted at Stone, England, we were told we would remain there the next four days. A small amount of this time was devoted to Anglicizing this heterogeneous group of Americans. The several hundred men that had just blown in from the States came from every nationality imaginable, we spoke dozens of different dialects, and we have very diversified backgrounds.

We had come to help the British stop the horrible aggression of the German war machine, but we were also inundating this tiny island with a culture shock. Most of us, who now found ourselves in England, have hardly seen most of the United States.

For many of us, we were just beginning to understand and appreciate the diversification of our own country. There were a few individuals that came with a great deal of baggage, like racial prejudice, class distinction, rudeness, and peevish manners. Fortunately, these individuals were definitely in the minority.

"AYE SAY OLE CHOP"

We spent time in controlled bull sessions, where we were told a little about the British people, how they tended to be very reserved out of necessity, and recommended methods to gain their friendship. My only knowledge of a typical native of this beautiful Nation was from scenes or parts in American movies. The British people were portrayed with the same accuracy as what the film industry did for the American Indian, the cowboy, and the Negro.

I knew I had much to learn and to assimilate. The history of the British Isles went back before the time of the Romans, but it was a mottled past. There were spans of time with greatness and there were also historical periods that were malicious and heinous.

Mastering the skies over Eastern England became an obvious priority. We had to learn how to fly in British air space, with horrendous amount of air traffic. We had to learn how to drive in a country that decided the right seat of a vehicle is the proper place for the driver. Their automobiles were designed to put importance on ones left hand to manipulate the cars, and the wrong side of the road is the right side.

We had to learn their monetary system, like tuppence, hay penny, quid, pound, sixpence, or guinea. There would be Irish, British, and Scottish pounds. At this time in history the British pound was equivalent to $4.035 in American money. Later it became apparent that we never truly understood the value of the British pound. When we played poker we tended to throw this pound around like it was a single American dollar.

We were told, and I'm afraid most Americans never learned, that the pub is a meeting place for the entire family. It is not a place where you barge in and try and see how much you can drink in the shortest period of time. The pub, to the average Englishman, was almost a substitute for the daily newspaper.

In this pub they would sip on their "bitters or milds" (both warm beers), they would discuss the day's happenings, politics, the health of neighbors, children, flowers, weather, you name it. Some would take part in throwing darts, as individuals or as teams. Here they could purchase fish and chips, a unique combination to savor and pacify the palate. In some respects, these pubs were not a place to escape to but almost a necessity in order to keep abreast of the current or daily events.

Two of the most flagrant violations of good etiquette that the Yanks were guilty of, are the following: not respecting the natural reserved nature of these people and to flout the monies that their American wallets may contain. You did not look over an Englishman's shoulder and try and read his newspaper. You did not saunter up to the bar and immediately get involved in random conversation. You did not throw money around like it had no value. We had arrived in a similar, but very different world than most of us were familiar with. The differences were subtle and sometimes refined.

Americans were prone to complain about the lack of ice or refrigeration in the pubs, inns or restaurants. They made fun of the oval cigarettes and the tobacco that was in them. They could not understand why they used their forks upside down or the limited types of meats that were available. They complained if the coffee did not taste like they were accustomed to.

Though we spoke the same language, to some degree, we had many different cultural habits that would require each, to learn respect. To be different did not necessarily mean that one person or the other had iniquitous habits or traits.

Few could know the suffering and sacrifice made the previous four years as this small County took on the prowess of the German war machine. England, alone felt the wrath of the Nazi bombs. With loyal support from her colonies, England met the daily challenge of the German Luftwaffe. All of her Allies on the continent had been overrun by the Nazis.

Prime Minister Winston Churchill had the Americans pegged fairly well when he said, in his raspy-gravelly voice "The Americans are over fed, they are over paid, they are over sexed, and they are over here." Sir Winston Churchill was always noted for his witticism, but he also had a reputation for being very astute.

To resolve this subtle difference between the two cultures would require that the peoples of both countries bend and be tolerable and try and understand and appreciate, not the differences but the uniqueness we had to offer each other. We were in a common fight to defeat a mutual enemy and it was essential for us to depend on one another.

HORHAM IN SUFFOLK COUNTY

On April 17, the Lt. Cobb crew, along with five other ten-man teams, left for our new base at Horham. Early in the morning we boarded a train for the relatively long trip to the southeastern portion of England. Riding on this train would prove to be a very different experience from those we were now growing accustomed to in the USA. I honestly could not imagine a mode of transportation being worse than the current system in the United States.

The passenger cars were divided into compartments that had two wide seats facing each other and were completely enclosed. Each compartment had access directly to the outside. Actually, there were several different types of these compartmented passenger cars, with varied seating arrangements. Once the train started to move, you were compelled to remain in your chosen compartment. Obviously there were advantages and disadvantages to this system.

Each car was connected to the adjoining one by a coupling consisting of a large three-link chain. This appeared to be a simple but certainly adequate means to hold the train together. There were huge metal plungers that spaced the cars and absorbed the normal shock of two cars moving toward one another. I believed the British train ran much smoother and made less noise than the trains I had been on in the States.

My experience found that it proved a very effective means to do the job. The train rode a great deal smoother than what I had experienced on the many compulsory train trips I found myself on these past two years. These passenger trains in England were considerably cleaner and kept up in a state of good repair, despite their age. I do believe even dear old George Cormack would have approved.

This particular train, that we were on, was a regularly scheduled run, so it meant that we stopped at many small towns to pick up new passengers or to let others disembark. We all found the English countryside to be interesting and beautiful.

The farms were very small, well developed, and usually defined by hedgerows or rough walls of accumulated stones. Many of the farmhouses had thatched roofs of straw, something I had never seen before. We saw small herds of cattle, some pigs and many sheep. The key word, that epitomizes my memory of this beautiful countryside, is the word NEAT.

The small towns we slowly passed through had many homes with little or no yards, very crooked streets, and usually a small church as its focal point. Most yards were defined by various type of fencing material and all seemed to have had some sort of landscaping.

The two observations I had made were that the British people appeared to love the outdoors and they obviously enjoyed flowers. Almost every abode had beds of colorful flowers and most windows were adorned with window boxes that held blossoms of every hue.

Traveling in this part of England, it was hard to image that these people had been at war with Nazi Germany for nearly five years. The countryside seemed so peaceful and its inhabitants so compatible with the view from the window of our moving train. Occasionally, we did see signs of different military vehicles or personnel, but never in a panic situation.

Ireland had declared its neutrality and consequently did not suffer the wrath of the German Luftwaffe and there was little possibility of being invaded. Despite this, Ireland was involved because many Irish workmen traveled to England and worked in the many factories producing necessary war materials. There were also many volunteers in the various British units.

OUR NEW HOME

Late in the afternoon, our train stopped in the small town of Diss, where the sixty anxious airmen stepped on to the platform. Six large army trucks, with canvas covered bench seats were awaiting our arrival. Each crew, along with all of our baggage, climbed into the back of a designated truck, and sat on one of the two hard benches that had been installed alongside the truck bed. Great pains had been taken to eliminate springs from this vehicle or any padding on these seats.

The mottled camouflage canvas cover made it dark inside, and it contained the excited sounds coming from its cargo. The small convoy wended its way southward, to the modest little community called Eye, where it turned in an easterly direction. Only those seated at the very rear of the truck could truly appreciate the changing view. In a little over twenty minutes we arrived at Horham, our destination.

It was apparent, as we passed through the minute village of Horham, a ten-minute walk would cover most of the streets. We were to learn that size has nothing to do with quality. We would also learn to appreciate what the people of this small community would mean to lonesome Americans, thousand of miles from their homes.

The 95th Bomb Group, with its runways, buildings, planes, and thousands of personal, was located only a short distance away. These people had accepted and adopted these young men and women so far from their homes. I found out later that many of the permanent personnel would almost be adopted by some of these English families

We soon discovered that our new airfield was different and quite spread apart from the deliberate compactness of the American Air Force Bases. This place, like the other bomber bases carved into the English countryside, was designed intentionally to make it difficult for the German Air Force to hit or destroy more than a small section of the installation.

Several of the American Bomber or Fighter Air Bases, had been former R.A.F. Installations. Others were developed out of rich English farmland, taking over several family farms in the process.

Our field, which covered over five hundred acres, came in contact with several small English villages. Many of our service roads were actually part of the existing country roads, where civilians, farmers, school children, and others could be seen daily. Farmers worked many of the fields adjoining our hardstands where the planes were serviced. Some fields, within the runway complex, were also planted and cropped. Every effort was made to fully utilize the available land for the war going on.

95TH BOMB GROUP

The heart of this complex installation was the lengthy main runway. There also were two shorter secondary landing strips crisscrossing almost at the center of the main strip. The landing and take off facilities were approximately two and a half acres in size. The primary runway was a concrete ribbon laid out in an approximate East-West direction and was about 300 feet wide by nearly 7000 feet long.

Connecting the six ends of these three runways was the perimeter track, which encircled the entire field. It would be along this perimeter the B-17s would maneuver to get into position, for controlled takeoffs. The many bombers would lift off every thirty seconds, on a typical bombing raid.

Branching off from this perimeter track was the numerous hardstands for individual or groups of B-17s. It was at these hardstands that the bombers were parked, serviced and maintained. Some hardstands accommodated four, six or even eight B-17s, while many were designed for a single aircraft.

At each of these hardstand would be facilities for the ground crew. This team of experts worked throughout the night, keeping each plane repaired from battle damage, replacing engines, patching up flak or shell holes in the aluminum skin or parts that were torn off. They refueled each plane and loaded the designated type of bombs. They worked in rain, snow, blistering heat, and in extreme cold to keep these planes in readiness.

The team of men, who worked at these hardstands, all specialists in a variety of the skills required, put forth an unbelievable amount of effort to keep the bombers air worthy. Not enough accolades could ever be given to compensate them for their talents and dedication. They sweated out each mission, not only for the return of their plane, but the ten men who would face the common enemy.

I know, during my tour of duty, I perhaps did not appreciate completely, the importance of their dedication. I suppose each of us got somewhat lost in our own little world or were too young and immature to fully see the entire picture we were an intricate part of. There were many who believed the fly boys got all of the glory. This was true to a point. The men who went on mission were also the ones who did most of the dying. It took each person in this war to contribute his or her talent so that the final solution would be the results of the entire team.

Bombs and explosives were stored at a remote section of the complex, in an isolated area. The 95th Bomb Group had experienced a tragic ground accident right after they arrived in England and prior to settling in at our base at Horham.

On May 27, 1943 at near by Alconbury, while the ground crew was checking over plane No. 229685, the bomb load exploded, killing nineteen men and seriously wounding another twenty. This B-17 actually disappeared, leaving only a huge crater in the earth. Four other planes were crumpled into unrecognizable junk, while eleven other aircraft were damaged severely and would not fly again for many months.

The 95th Bomb Group consisted of four Squadrons. These were the 334th, the 335th, the 336th, and the 412th. Each of these Squadrons was billeted in separate locations, and isolated by enough distance to maintain their own identity. There were many cultivated farm fields or woods between each of these Squadron locations. The Cobb crew was assigned to the 336th Squadron, which was located on the far west side of this entire complex.

The Officers and the Enlisted Personal were quartered in different sections within each Squadron area. Our living quarters would be a Quonset hut, constructed with corrugated metal and completely lacking in architectural design or style. They were heated with coal fired pot bellied stoves and had a noticeable lack of fenestration. There was very little effort to design into these huts the normal comforts of home.

Somewhere along the way, I had been told, "home is where the heart is." Since my entire body had been assigned one of these huts, it behooved me to call this dim, smoky, unattractive place, "home." Since the structure was a Quonset hut, other than at the ends of this monster, there were no walls to hang or put things.

The interior was either too hot or too cold. Several pot bellied stoves had their own characteristics, none of which are complimentary. They were usually out, and when they contained burning coal, they smelled and were too hot to get close to. The illumination within this environment was terrible. An inadequate number of low wattage light bulbs, hung from the ceiling. One had to go outside to write a letter or, if you were fortunate to receive one, to read it.

Having stated all of this, I now need to explain each of us appreciated the meager comforts available to us compared to what most of our buddies in the Army realized. Trenches, fox holes, mud, rain, tanks, cold and even snow drifts were all words each could use to describe their accommodations. We would have warm beds and prepared hot meals.

There was not any available space on the limited wall area that did not contain pictures of loved ones. More generally there would be hundreds of pictures displaying the talents of such artist as Alfredo Varga, George Petty, Gil Elvren and Milton Caniff. Clipped out pictures from magazines displayed such favorites as Betty Grable, Lana Turner, Rita Hayworth, Francis Langford, Deanna Durbin and Hedi Lamarr.

One of the first things it became important to discover was, "where is the PX?" This is an abbreviation for the Post Exchange, the place where you would go to purchase cigarettes, candy bars, toiletries, etc. It did not take long to figure out a weak flaw in how the PX operated. The day-to-day clerks behind the counter were enlisted personnel.

"CASTELLO"

One individual, who attracted my immediate attention, was a private who hailed from Brooklyn, New York. This one of a kind individual, who looked exactly like Lou Castello, from the Abbott & Costello Act, had a body that made a definite statement. Bluntly speaking, it gave him an unmistaken short and dumpy appearance.

His speech gave away the fact that he hailed from Brooklyn and his chubby little face noted that he was an Italian Catholic. His jet black hair was oily and combed straight back. It did not take any effort to get to know and like this very special experience behind the counter of our post exchange.

During this period of our history, we could buy an entire carton of cigarettes for fifty-cents, or a single pack for just a nickel. Most of the major brands were available. A candy bar would also cost just a nickel, but the unique thing about this chocolate bar was that it completely filled a larger paper wrapper. Candy, though, would be semi rationed and not always available. You would be permitted only a few candy bars a week.

If you got to know "Castello", for want of a better name, since I never did learn his real handle, you could over-come rationing by telling him a dirty joke. He constantly would greet you as you approached the counter with, "Hey tigah, hav ya hoid this one." He would then proceed to unload a joke or story that would be filthy 98% of the time. If you lingered for a while, he would entertain all who would listen or react to his lowly, but different sense of humor.

Because of his one-dimensional sense of values, it was possible to double your ration allowance automatically by simply relating a joke or story to him. The Officer's Club provided "Castello" with a military vehicle (large truck) to go into London each Friday to track down and purchase any type of liquor he could find. Because he was so successful, I do not believe there was any other Bomb Group who had an Officer's Club with a better stock of alcohol.

On these trips to London, Castello would also conduct business for himself. He would find good linen sheets for the bed, he would find linen pillow cases, he would bring back interesting items that would be practical gifts to send to loved ones, and he procured items one could not even get on the black market. These items were sold, not over the PX counter, but on the Q.T.

The Brass of the Base knew about "Castello" and some of his shenanigans. I'm sure they turned their eyes because of his other values. Each week he took another vehicle and rounded up enough fresh eggs so that any personnel going on a mission could avoid eating powdered eggs. This simple act would not mean a great deal to anyone who had not experienced the powdered eggs of World War II.

All my life I had been brought up to eat anything served to me. Now, for the first time in my relatively short life and the fact that I was away from home, I discovered a food I learned to live without. Powdered eggs, when prepared as scrambled eggs, ended up with a green hue. They tasted like crap and they had a texture that defies description.

I only ate breakfast on the mornings I would be scheduled for a mission. On all other mornings, I would sleep in and forgo my favorite meal of the day. If we had to fly, we would get a three A.M. wakeup nudge and, with eyes half open, we would wend our way to the mess hall.

On these mornings, I would order three or four fresh eggs, fried over easy with fried potatoes. I knew I would not be able to eat again for twelve to fourteen hours and I knew this meal would hang around. I also was aware this could be my last meal.

To this day, if I were to be shot at sunrise, for whatever reason, and was offered a last meal, it would be: "Three goopy fresh eggs fried over-easy, and broken over fresh fried potatoes, and slightly seasoned with salt and pepper." Upon completion of this very special requested final meal I would only say: "fire away." At the 95th Bomb Group my only remarks of gratitude would be: "Thanks "Castello," for liberating me from those damn powdered eggs.

Though each member of the flight crews in a particular squadron were housed in a specific area where we had Quonset huts where we slept, there were other buildings and places of importance. There were mess halls where we would eat, clubs where we could get a drink, where our plane may be parked, or perhaps where we would be briefed. We all knew this Base was more complex than this. At various times we often were required to track down certain structures for various reasons.

The following is a partial schedule of the many diversified buildings or structures required on a typical Bomber Base. There were twenty-six B-17 (H) Bomb Group Bases in the 1st and 3rd Air Division in the 8th Air Force. All of these fields were located in the southeast part of England, and each was fairly similar to the 95th B.G. field at Horham, in Suffolk County.

It is also important to realize that there were additional fields for the B-24 (H) Liberator, all of the Medium Bomber Bases, and the many Fighter Plane fields. All required similar faciliies as listed below:

Armory maintenance	Fire tender shelter
Pyro store	Floodlight trailer
Blister hanger	Squadron & Flight Office
Free Gunnery Teacher	Barrack Huts
Fuel compound	Flight Officers' Quarters
Maintenance Staff Block	Station Offices

Guard Houses

Picket Posts

P.P. Officers' Quarters

Components Store

Main Workshops

Dinghy Storage

Parachute Store

Bulk Petrol Installation

Static Water Tanks

Latrines

Gas Defense Center

Fire Tender House

Speech Broadcasting Bldg.

Lubrication & Inflam. Storage

Photographic Block

Crew Locker & Drying Rm.

Armory

Sleeve Streamer Mast

Control Tower

Mess Halls

Flame Float Storage

Barber Shops

Chaplains' Facilities

Briefing Room

A.M. Bombing Teacher

M & E Plinths

Gas Chamber

Sub-station

Radar Workshop

Maintenance Unit Armory

Squadron Armories

Dump

Hangars

Battle Headquarters

Pump House3

Beam Approach

Bomb Sight Storage

Special D.C. Test Facilities

Crew Briefing Room

Bomb Stores

Fused & Spare Bomb Stores

Component Storage

S.A.A. Store

Sea Marker Storage

N.C.O. Club

Officers' Club

Hardstand Shelter

Laundry Facilities

In the same general area, North and East of London, there were also most of the R.A.F. (Royal Air Force) facilities. The logistics to coordinate all of this air traffic was tremendous, especially because of the close proximity of all of these various airfields. Much of the best farmland in England had to be sacrificed for these bases and the extreme effort put forth by the Allies. I never hear a single complaint from our Allies and friends, the British people.

Many American Bases had been transferred over from the British Air Force, while others were constructed as the war progressed. This area of England was chosen for several good and logical reasons, namely its location in relation to Europe, but also the intense air traffic would not be over larger cities.

Though each Squadron was separated from one another, all were within a mile of the field and Headquarters. The Flight Officers were housed in a separate area from the Officers who were permanent Personal, as well as their gunners. Segregating these various different groups tended to break the large number of personnel on this base into smaller groups.

This also gave everyone a chance to get to know the men in your Squadron real well. There, however, was a negative side to it. When one of your buddies in an adjoining barracks, or perhaps, in the next bunk, had to cash-in his chips, it made it very personal. Though this occurred much too often, this was something none of us ever got used to.

Each Squadron was within a one-minute walk of some English farm or rural cultivated field. Nearly all of the narrow country roads were scenic to walk down. In contrast with my home State of Wisconsin, the farms here were very small and each had land divided into five to ten acre plots. Many of these fields were defined by hedgerows of rock, knolls of earth, trees, or simply bushes.

There was an obvious lack of barbed wire fencing. I found, on my numerous walks through this countryside, the scenery and the people to be both friendly and comforting. I ultimately found I need solitary walks down these restful surroundings just to collect my thoughts and to sometimes recharge my battery.

HORHAM, ENGLAND

The small community of Horham had a special homey atmosphere to it with its brick, stucco, and half-timber homes. There were several pubs within walking or cycling distance of our base. The people from this beautiful little community had accepted these Yanks and made us feel at home.

In the center of town was a unique signpost with four panels pointing in the cardinal directions. One panel had the communities of Eye, Yaxley, and Ipswich. Another, pointing in the opposite direction had Wilby, Worthingworth, and Framlingham on it. Mounted 90 degrees on this same post was a sign with Redingfield, Bedinfield, and Debenham. Opposite this panel would be the fourth, with black letters painted on the white background. Here you could find the direction to Stradbroke, Laxfield, and Hadesworth.

Many American G.I.s, as some would refer to us, would annoy our British friends in Horham by mispronouncing the name of their village as "whore ham." All in all, they learned to understand more about the Yanks than perhaps we did about them. Though I had opportunities to visit other 8th Air Force Bases, I did not see one I would have exchanged with.

Within days, each of us settled into a variety of routines, each designed to make life more tolerable. The English weather has always been noted for being on the border of miserable. We had the high humidity to constantly contend with and the ever-present fog seemed to obscure the beauty of the countryside or the direction you might like to go.

Rain and showers occurred often enough to help the surrounding crops and the many flower gardens around us, but it also was the culprit that could produce mud. We were to learn that the weather also made our main mission for being here, more dangerous and hazardous, and at time impossible.

There were many days when we actually saw the sun, and I do not know a more picturesque place to be on these occasions. Often "Waddy" and I would appropriate a bike, since we never did own one, and take long rides through the countryside. I had never owned a bicycle in my entire life so this was a rare treat I always enjoyed.

Perhaps this is not an entirely true statement. My father had made the mistake of buying a single second-hand bike for my brother Bob, exactly one year younger, and myself. Bob immediately claimed it as his sole possession, never brought it home, had a secretive hiding place for it, and made sure I would see him ride past me on rare occasions. I truly was so involved at this time of my life I could have cared less about that damn bike. However, I did not want this indifference of mine to be too obvious to my kid brother so he would continue this meaningless charade.

At night I often sat on the bank of a hedgerow, under a large tree, and just listen to the songs of the British nightingale, a member of the thrush family. On these nights, the war would seem remote, and my thoughts would drift homeward. Many times I would share these moments with my best friend "Waddy", Lt. Dan Waddell. More often though, I would wander off by myself and find an appropriate spot to flake out and drift off in my thoughts.

I honestly cannot say I dwelled on being homesick per se. I seemed to require this type of time with myself to help and keep putting things into a perspective I could handle. For the first time in my life though, I found myself thinking about a single other individual. This would be the person I had become engaged to and someone I truly did not get to know as well as I would have liked because of this damn war.

These secluded spots on some little insignificant English winding road afforded me cherished moments that I know helped me keep my sanity during the days I flew in combat. I had friends that did everything in their power to not be alone. They needed constant fellowship because they could not handle dwelling on the exposure we would be subjected to. I could relate to this also.

CHAPTER 14

The morning of April 20th, one of our gunners came dashing into our barracks with the news he had spotted our old airplane, B-17 No. 297334. It was parked in one of the remote hardstands and it had been strictly luck that Sgt. Thomsey spotted it. Our plane had been taken away from our crew when we landed at Nutts Corner, Ireland and we were advised that we would be assigned another plane at the proper time.

The chance that this particular B-17 ended up on our field was very remote, since there were over thirty other bases where it could have been sent. We all agreed that Lt.Frank Cobb should immediately inform the "Upper Brass" that we would appreciate getting this Flying Fortress back, since we had all fallen in love with her.

Lt. Cobb was successful. In a matter of hours, this plane could have been assigned to any one of a dozen new crews. Needless to say, every member of our crew was elated over something as trivial as getting the original plane assigned to us returned.

In reality, each new B-17 would be identical as it left the Boeing Plant in Seattle, Washington. A little of my skepticism about any sentimentality that the Air Force might possess had now been recouped or at least partially retrieved.

For the next two weeks, we all attended several classes and flew four or five practice missions over the English countryside. On one of these flights, our crew ventured out over the English Channel so that the gunners could fire their machine guns. We also practiced formation flying with six or eight other B-17s on different occasions.

As I would later learn, tight formations had the best chance of surviving German fighter planes. These formation practice flights were the means of gradually getting us prepared for combat and our first mission. I honestly believe the 95th Bomb Group, by stressed the importance of formation flying and insisting on it, was able to accomplish more than many other Groups.

A great deal had to be learned about new systems of sharing the crowded airspace, approaching and recognizing our base at Horham, weather conditions and its related problems, emergency procedures at airfields along the East coast of Suffolk County, and the perfection required in tight formation flying.

We had to learn about splashers and radio bunchers. Nothing could be taken for granted while flying in a limited air space with several thousand bombers and fighters struggling to get into formation.

The 95th Bomb Group put an inordinate amount of emphasis on each and every plane, flying on a combat mission, to fly in close proximity to the adjoining plane. Any one of these basic lessons could mean the difference between making it back to our base, ditching in the sea, or getting shot down over Europe.

A tight formation would concentrate all of the available fire power on any attacking German fighter plane. I later noted that should a Luftwaffe pilot have the choice of diving into a well disciplined Bomb Group with each bomber pulled into a concentrated formation or a Group that was stretched out and not compact, they would chose the later. I believed the 95th Bomb Group exemplified this theory and took pride in maintaining it.

LONDON, HERE WE COME

Early in May we received notice that several new crews, including ours, would be issued four-day passes to go anywhere we desired. "Waddy", Weakland, and I didn't have any problems with this, since we had already decided to go to London at the first opportunity. This was the moment we had been waiting for.

Early the next morning, a military truck, with its' built in vibrations and hard seats, drove us to the neighboring village of Diss. We just had time to purchase a "London and return" ticket on the L.N.E.R. This was the London and North Eastern Railway, whose primary stops on its route, would be London, Ipswich, and Norwich, while several smaller communities were also favored with service. This station at Diss offered first class and third class tickets. They offered no second-class facilities.

Hell, we didn't care. We would have ridden on the top of the damn train, just to get to London. The passenger cars consisted of separate compartments, which could seat approximately eight to ten people, depending on the width of the individual butt. Additional passengers would be compelled to stand up. There were times, when a large contingent of servicemen went on leave or were returning to base, we would feel lucky to find standing room only.

The small, quaint cars had colored prints of English scenes on the walls and the seats were worn, but fairly comfortable. The war had been going on for this small country for over four years now. Replacing railroad cars was clearly not a high priority. Every ounce of energy in this country was being used to hang on in the war against the world's greatest war machine. It required that stringent priorities be set on what was and wasn't important.

At night all of the windows would be blacked-out for obvious reasons, while the under designed lighting in each car made the ride an eerie experience. Despite all of this, the ride, the stops and starts, were actually smoother than what I had learned to expect on American trains. Each trip brought me a fleeting thought about my friend George Cormack. I knew he had never been to England, but I was positive he would cherish a ride on this railroad and he would nourish every second of the journey.

This first trip to London carried a great deal of excitement with it. The one fact, I personally knew about this famous place, was London had the distinction of being the largest city in the world. This historic place covered over one hundred square miles in area. I had also heard that one could spend his life here and only see a fraction of its sights. If the Germans cooperated, I plan on making several more visits to this fascinating megalopolis.

The word had been passed on to us, by some of the veteran Combat Crews, the gathering place for American servicemen was Piccadilly Circus. This was a large intersection where Piccadilly Street, Regent Street, and Shaftesbury Avenue all come together. If you lost someone, or if you intended to meet someone, this intersection was the place to do it.

This also was the local that attracted most of the prostitutes for obvious reasons. I remembered from some of my reading about World War I that this specific corner in London, Piccadilly Circus, gained notoriety for loose women. Time changes many things, but this market place for the oldest profession still met all of criterion that both parties desired.

The three of us got off at Victoria Station and headed for a Red Cross facility that assisted servicemen in finding places to sleep. We got a large room, with three beds in a very old hotel. The price was right and we didn't expect to spend too much time in this antiquated domicile. We dropped off our overnight bags and hit the London streets.

The first several hours were spent walking aimlessly, trying to get acquainted with landmarks and points of interest. We would explore all of these interesting places on the following days. We did manage to get a map of the city, only to concur that you could spend the rest of your life sight seeing in London. Early in the evening, we had several sandwiches and beers in an old and interesting English pub.

When we finally found Piccadilly Circus, I was both impressed and surprised. This section of the city has most of the fashionable shops and stores, located on both sides of the street. In normal times, Piccadilly would be considered the gathering place for the elite. Though I had been informed, my surprise came when I discovered both the degree and prevalence of these hookers on this famous street. They were everywhere and most were very obvious as to what wares they had for sale.

As you walked down the street and passed some American serviceman, with one or more of these girls, you could catch pieces of the conversations. "Five pounds, you've got to be crazy." "Come on Yank, I'm worth it." No effort was made to conceal the propositions being negotiated by these girls and the many eager Americans who were present.

The many women who chose this means of making a living came in all sizes, appearances, and nationalities. Yes, there was a great disparage in the ages also of this group. I suppose the price they could charge depended on all of their attributes. I also knew that most of these women were driven to this means of making a living because of the war and the times in general.

This famous corner in central London still made an ideal place for American Service Men to meet, should you become separated from your buddies or just wanted to rendezvous with someone from another base. I guess the old adage, everyone has to be some place, applies here. Obviously, the British authorities could do little to discourage any of this. The dire need of so many families and the excessive numbers of American servicemen with pounds in their pockets, plus the inevitable sexual drives of the many, congealed at this particular spot in the world's largest city.

Though the open bargaining between the promiscuous British girls and similarly intended Americans, each with their "over heated engines", provided some entertainment as we loitered in their territory, we had other things to do.

London provided unlimited opportunities to see first hand some of the world's most renowned and acclaimed points of interest. At this stage in our tour of duty, we had no idea how many opportunities we would have to see the sights of this famous place.

Early the next morning we headed for the British Parliament Building and Westminster Abbey. We decided to split up and see each of these structures on our own, since we had different interests in each. It had become immediately apparent to me that the others would not desire to scrutinize or spend adequate time looking at the things I knew would interest me. I would rather see less and observe more by not rushing through this opportunity now before us. We agreed to meet at noon, below Big Ben, the famous clock.

WESTMINSTER ABBEY

Westminster consumed most of my attention this morning as I meandered through every space opened to the public. I was particularly interested in the abundance of artistic woodcarvings. Early in 1944 I had no inkling that someday I would become a registered Architect, my ultimate and chosen profession.

At this uncultured period in my life, I found I did possess appreciation for the style of architecture I was observing in this beautiful building. At this juncture in my life I had no idea most of the structures around me would be known as Gothic Architecture, the pinnacle or zenith in architectural style in my opinion.

I also did not know, during this carefree period of development, that someday I would be an avid wood carver, my ultimate hobby. I spent hours admiring the intricate detail and the artistry in the carvings done over four hundred years before. I even discovered carvings under the seats of the fixed chairs and pews. There seemed to be no surface left untouched by the chisel of the mason or the knives of the wood craftsmen.

Another entirely different facet of these buildings was the beautiful stained glass in each of the side windows. The colors that rays of sunlight emitted to the interior were breath taking. The intensity and depth of each hue, was beyond description. I was less impressed with the religious connotations of all of these artistic endeavors, than I was with the actual abilities of these artisans.

The total harmony of stone, metal, glass, wood, tile, mosaic, and other materials, displayed a real depth of knowledge and understanding. The Gothic Period of architecture certainly was the pinnacle of artistic endeavor. I suddenly got the fear of some German bomb destroying one of these beautiful structures. I was to learn that indeed the British did protect and put in safe storage many of their prized artifacts.

I saw visitors walking through these buildings, not noticing any of the details, only the total effect of all of its parts. They left this magnificent environment, after spending but minutes racing through its space, only to be awed by its size and spaciousness. They could not see the trees, because they only saw the forest. I was to discover later that my two friends fell into this category. Ooze and aahs do not necessarily denote intelligent appreciation for the beautiful and unusual.

The Houses of Parliament and Westminster Abbey had slabs of marble on the floor that literally covered the history of Britain. Many of its Heroes and Statesmen were buried beneath these slabs, with brief chiseled words that alluded to their accomplishments. The crime was to walk upon or over these areas of stone and not pause to look or contemplate the true significance of what had been.

Every niche or undeveloped space along its many walls had meaningful sculpture, put into designed depressions or on free standing pedestals. Each of these statues captured a detailed likeness of Englishmen, who had played apart in the history of this old and significant country. These also were recorded statements of the people, who wanted to honor and remember their heroes.

When you stood and scrutinized each figure, it took little effort to imagine that this statue only captured a split second of time in the subject's historical life. I particularly admired the skills of each of the craftsmen who must have devoted their entire lives to create such beauty. The profusion of art in these magnificent structures moves one to want to assimilate or soak up every expression and detail of the artist's efforts.

Many experiences in life can be best shared with an understanding partner or perhaps a friend. Walking through cathedrals and buildings, such as the ones I was seeing for the first time, should be done in solitary fashion. One had to marvel at the flying buttresses, the pinnacles, the gargoyles, the carvings, and the ornate steeples. It would be unusually difficult to have a friend who would have similar sensitivities to each of the objects being scrutinized.

After lunch, "Waddy", "Weak", and I, decided to visit the world famous Madame Tussaud's Wax Museum. We had been told that this was one place recommended on the must list of places to see. We had received rough directions on how to find this attraction, but in London, this is still a major challenge.

The fact that it was near the Baker Street underground station would make it somewhat easy for this small group of visitors from the 95th Bomb Group because we could always take the subway. Despite all the advice we had received, we decided to walk and see more of London in the process.

MADAM TUSSAUD'S WAX MUSEUM

The museum is about two miles from Big Ben, as the crow flies, but it is about four miles of hard walking by relying on the sidewalks. Once we found the place, we discovered they had a special price for servicemen. We entered this unique establishment, not knowing quite what to expect.

First of all, we came upon a guard, a man in uniform that appeared to be overlooking the lobby. We had been warned, by some of the fellows on the base, that some of the guards were wax figures and others were actually human. We were advised that you could only tell by looking at their shoes. If their footwear appeared to be worn, unpolished, or had creases on the toe, they were alive and capable of answering any question you presented to them. On the other hand, if their shoes were highly polished and looked brand new, they were wax figures, and who would want to get caught talking to a dummy?

The first thing we did was to scrutinize this well dressed, rigid standing guard, with immaculately shined shoes. We obviously believed him to be a wax figure because we proceeded to make uncomplimentary remarks to his stoic face. As we walked away, one of us happened to glance back and see this guard move over to a new location, very much alive. Gotcha!

It became very apparent, as we started through the various sections of this large and unique establishment, that this was indeed a different type of art. A French family had brought to England their talents to reproduce lifelike figures, where every hair is installed, one at a time. Where skin blemishes are recorded and the figure's pose and garb capture the significance of the times. No detail was too insignificant to ignore.

The latest person represented in the gallery, was a life size statue of Joe Lewis, in his usual stance as a boxer. I was extremely impressed with the realism. Franklin Roosevelt in his familiar chair and Sir Winston Churchill, in his statesman like pose with his familiar cigar, appeared willing to carry on a conversation with me.

You almost felt like waiting for Sir Winston to put his cigar in his mouth and take a puff. Each figure, meticulously created in their matter-of-fact pose, represented some noteworthy event or historical happening in the world. It was interesting to note the inordinate amount of American statesmen, noteworthy individuals, or historical events.

There were groups of costumed figures representing the signing of the Declaration of Independence, or the crowning of one of the English Kings. Groups of statesmen would be standing together, each very recognizable. Room after room was filled with these ghosts from the past, each painstakingly created.

In the lower level, an area recreated to look like a dungeon, we saw scenes depicting some of the less complimentary history of these British Isles. Horrible reenactment of beheading, torture chambers with bodies on the rack, and other skeletal creatures chained to the floor or wall. There was a scene where a person was about to be beheaded. The artist captured the expressions of the unfortunate soul, as well as that of the executioner. It represented a period of history that should, perhaps be forgotten.

The three of us decided to return to the Piccadilly landmark by walking south down Baker Street. Suddenly it hit me. In our excitement to see the sights of this famous place, I was visually and mentally ignoring the tremendous amount of bomb damage.

In some areas we walked by, entire blocks had been leveled, where once stood buildings. I had read about the nightly bombing raids by the German Air Force, and I had seen numerous pictures of the British firefighters battling impossible odds to save structures and lives.

Once you became aware of the nearly five years that the German Bombers tried to destroy this largest city in the world, you could easily spot and recognize the scars left by their endeavors. Ton after ton of bombs rained down on London in an indiscriminant fashion. What made it less obvious was the fact that the British immediately cleaned up the rubble.

I found out later, most all of the bricks, mortar, glass, and twisted steel were deposited in the holds of the ships returning to the United States. This debris was used as ballast for the empty ships, which would return another day, with war material.

The next observation I made was that most of the historical buildings seemed to have suffered very little. Many stained glass windows had been removed or boarded up, while some art treasures were put in safe places. I do not know, nor have I ever read, that the German Bomber Pilots intentionally avoided the heart of London or if the British, in all their stubbornness, kept them at bay.

I learned later that the German V-1 and V-2 Weapons had no regard for the value of life or property. These instruments of war were intentionally released with little or no ability to aim them. Their sole purpose was to indiscriminately kill and destroy. Hitler had become desperate. Ultimately, this strategy to wantonly devastating British cities would come back to haunt the German populous as the war wore on.

In our effort to return to Piccadilly, we chanced upon Oxford Street. We noticed a sign directing us two blocks to the west and Hyde Park. This was another place I had read about. We picked the right corner to discover this large and beautiful open park, with its Serpentine Lake, Kensington Palace and Gardens, and its many trees and flowers. As soon as we passed through Marble Arch, we immediately stumbled on the famous "Speakers' Corner".

During the next hour we watched and listened to numerous nuts expound on religion, politics, new theories on evolution, and the eminent end of the entire world. Individuals would stand on a make shift podium while trying to convince a relatively large crowd that they had the answer to any of the day's problems.

The occupant of the podium sometimes sounded like a sputtering and unkempt old bum, while others would be "neatly" dressed in suits that needed pressing but would speak with fluent English. This was almost carrying the freedom of speech to its maximum limits.

Our return took us down South Audley Street and the American Embassy. We could not come up with a reason on why they would want to see or talk with us so we only gave it a passing glance.

By the time we reached Piccadilly Circus, we knew our legs had been over worked. We also were aware we had spent all most an entire day without thinking about whetting our whistle. This realization automatically determined how we would spend this evening in London.

The next morning we slept in late. We managed, in due time, to get moving with some difficulty. The tremendous amount of walking and the evening's imbibing had a great deal to do with our lack of energy and enthusiasm for this new day. However,

each knew we had not come to London to lie around or just relax. Another long walk, to the East, alongside of the Thames River, brought us face to face with the ugly, but famous London Bridge. We crossed over it and returned, never being sure of why we had expended the energy.

We continued down Lower Thames Street, and discovered the Tower of London. We took a tour through this famous landmark and were made aware of some of its history and the important role it played in its distant past. My memory of English history was recalled when I was informed who had been held prisoner here and who had been executed in less than humane ways.

The oldest part of the complex was the White Tower, which dates back to William the conqueror. We saw an interesting collection of English armor in this part of this very old structure. I couldn't decide if it would be more ruthless to be clobbered by one of these ancient weapons of the past or to be blown to hell by our sophisticated new technology. War's sole unequivocal uniqueness is the word progress. Each successive war develops new and better ways to kill, maim, and destroy.

CROWN JEWELS

Next we entered the Jewel House and got to gaze upon the Royal Crown Jewels. I think that I was the only one in the room who was not overly impressed by these crowns, necklaces, wands, and rings. I felt them to be gaudy, over sized, ill designed, and a misuse of some of the world's most precious stones and gems.

I listened to the sighing and the oohs and aahs from the spectators, as they were ushered past this impressive collection, but it did not alter my personal feelings. I felt then, as I do today, that there were more positive and constructive ways of showing rank, quality, leadership, and power. In history, when I was taught about all of the opulence of royalty that had been accumulated on the backs of the peasants, I believe I developed a lasting feeling against the display of this ostentatious way to rub it in.

Before we headed back to our hotel, we took a quick trip over to the adjoining 19th Century Tower Bridge. From its walkway you could look back at the Tower of London and see the Chapel Royal of St. John and the Chapel of St. Peter-ad-Vincula.

From this vantage point you could appreciate the scale of this very old historical landmark. As you gazed in either direction, you saw all of the activity on the Thames River, a main artery passing through this expansive city. It also provided a spectacular view of the London Dockland.

We decide to hail down our first taxicab for the long trip back to our humble hotel and a place to "flake out." This was an experience worth the price. Because of the war and the lack of petrol, there were not many automobiles on the streets. Despite the lack of cars, traffic was still congested, with the double-deck buses, horse drawn wagons and carts, military trucks, and an unusual amount of pedestrians constantly crossing these relatively narrow streets.

The one vehicle that attracted most of my attention was the many predominantly black taxicabs that darted about on every street and alley. Their drivers were constantly trying to drum up business and because they hailed from many different nationalities, they spoke in various dialects.

LONDON CABBY

The typical cab was old but meticulously taken care of. Though the area behind the driver was quite large on first sight, you found yourself really crowded, especially considering they took on additional passengers and utilized several pull down seats. The cab drivers drove too fast for the conditions and seemed to rely on their constant use of the horn to clear the way.

If the street ahead seemed too congested, without hesitation, he would swing the cab up an alley or some secondary street. Next you began to develop the feeling that this driver was intentionally taking a longer route to your destination. Many cabbies were real characters and were fun to egg on.

The additional thrill of taking this first ride with a London "cabbie," was to experience driving on the opposite side of the street and seeing the driver sit on the right, using his left hand to manipulate most of the controls on the vehicle. It all seemed to be backward, compared to what we were accustomed to back in the good old United States.

This typical "cabbie" constantly mumbled with a strong brogue, you could barely understand him when he did speak. He could bring this cab to a controlled halt at the last instant, and would accelerate fast enough to move all of the passengers against the back seat. A ride in a London cab is truly an experience.

We learned later, that one of our earliest observations became a reality. You had to watch where these cabs drove and to learn enough about London streets and points of interest, otherwise they would take you for a joy ride. Their antics of taking winding and crooked little side streets helped to confuse the passengers and increase the fare they charged you.

Sometimes, if you were alert, you would notice passing a particular landmark two and sometimes three times. It seemed to be a game with these polite, but very cunning taxi drivers. I think they were motivated to try and run the fare up and to stick it to these "flush Yanks."

The final observation I made this day was these cabs would drive down a one-way street, in the opposite direction and everyone seemed to tolerate it. It was as though they owned the streets of this city. Each trip I would take in one of these unique cabs would be an entirely different experience.

Trying to communicate, perhaps, was the most frustrating part of each taxi trip, because every cab driver seemed to have a different cockney accent and many were from some English colonial foreign country and spoke with strong dialects.

We decided to leave our cab at Trafalgar Square, where seven or eight streets

201

converge. The most noteworthy characteristic of this intersection is the tall column with Admiral Lord Nelson's statue on top. It now became apparent to us that night had set in and London was to take on a whole new persona.

The entire city of London, as well as the entire country, takes measures that are mandated by war. The necessity of the blackout requires a better knowledge of the streets and sense of direction that the three of us possessed.

As we groped our way toward Piccadilly Circus, it became obvious that special effort had been made to conceal light sources within all of the buildings, stores, and houses. Opaque material had been drawn over windows and most buildings had fashioned some sort type of maze for their primary entrance at night. It would have been very helpful to carry a small flashlight with you on these occasions.

Everyone, we literally bumped into, was most helpful to give you your location or direction to some destination. Twice during this night we heard the sirens, which indicated that German planes had been picked up on radar and were approaching the city. We heard no explosions on either occasion.

The activity along Piccadilly indicated that this was the place to be in London. The "Piccadilly Commandoes" were out in force and prospective customers were in great supply. As you walked down the street, most of the overheard conversations were understandable, without being able to visually see the participants. What was going on blew my mind.

I suppose I would be considered a prude in most circles, but my limited travel and exposure did little to prepare me for what I was witnessing. My life, before enlisting, evolved almost entirely around athletics. None of this was part of the circle of friends I knew or traveled with.

On the streets of London I now was seeing women, probably from the age of 15 to perhaps 40, dressed in what they must have considered the most perversive and décolleté blouse and diminutive skirts that barely coved their posterior. They would sashay up to a potential customer and proceed to try and convince this individual that they would make this the most exciting night of their life.

I observed each episode that I witnessed, both with a great deal of sadness and also bewilderment of actually seeing something I had only heard about through older kids who took it upon themselves to give free lesson in sex education. Despite all my early enlightenment I truly was not prepared for what was taking place this night on the darkened London streets near Picadilly.

Most military bases I had been stationed at, including the one at Horham, required that you leave the post with a condom. M.P.s would check for this, as well as your pass, before you could leave the Base. I had carried the same one in my wallet so long that it formed a perfect circle in the stretched leather. I had only to flash the outside of this pocket bank to the Guards to go on pass.

Since we had to be back at the base tomorrow, we headed for the train station and boarded the L.N.E.R. for Diss and the city of Norwich. Riding the same train we had taken three days earlier was an entirely different experience at night. Our compartment had just enough light, from the puny bulbs, making it difficult to see the people you were riding with.

All of the windows had blackout curtains over them so you could only sense when you passed through small villages. The fact was, the three of us were exhausted from all of the walking we had done, and from the inadequate amount of sleep we managed to get. I suppose we could have returned in a boxcar and it wouldn't have made much difference.

We were met at the train station by a group of army trucks to get us back to the field and to our barracks. These trucks kept a rigid schedule, to meet all of the returning trains from London. I truly enjoyed this famous city, and I now believed that one could spend a lifetime to see and explore all this unique and special place had to offer.

CHAPTER 15

Back on the Base, we flew a few more formation practice sessions, both to get the feeling of flying in formation in close proximity and to learn to contend with the air traffic in this part of England. Most of our crew was getting anxious to start our tour of duty and get on with it.

Each crewmember was to fly a total of 25 combat missions before being sent back to the States. We all knew that this was like a toss of a coin, since statistics indicated we had about a fifty-fifty chance of being one of the lucky ones that would complete a tour.

Just before I left for combat I had the opportunity to meet several from the crew of the Memphis Belle, particularly Lieutenants Robert Morgan the pilot and Chuck Leighton, the Navigator. This crew had been given the distinction of having been the very first crew flying in the Eighth Air Force to have completed their tour of duty, twenty-five combat missions.

Because of the rarity and the difficulty of accomplishing this feat they were honored by taking a tour all across the country. They flew their last mission on May 17, 1943 and were one of the lucky crews who survived those early days of combat.

Early in May, late in the afternoon, Lt. Waddell and I were walking over to the Officer's Club when we heard unusual noise coming from the returning planes of the 95th. They had been on a mission and were just now expected back to Horham. The returning formation would fly over the base and then make a large 360-degree turn as each plane would peel off and make an approach for a landing. If there were wounded or severely damaged planes, these bombers would be given priority to land first.

Today, the welcome sound of your returning buddies sounded entirely different. "Waddy" and I looked up and saw another entire Bomber Group pass behind our Group, nearly colliding. They had obviously goofed up since no other Bomber Group should be in our landing pattern.

As we watched, one of the B-17s had its large tail section break away from the fuselage. This formation had less than 2000 ft. altitude. The plane immediately rolled over on one wing and then nose-dived toward the earth. "Damit Waddy, they're all going to get killed", I shouted. Several airmen left the falling plane, but only two chutes had time to partially open.

We could see falling bodies with partially opened parachutes and we knew there were others who never got out of the plane. The B-17 crashed several miles from our Base but the falling bodies landed near the edge of our main runway. It appeared that this unfortunate plane got into the prop wash from thirty some planes of the 95th Bomb Group and the resulting air turbulence was enough force to cause this unusual failure.

I surmised that the rapid moving turbulent air from the many propellers of the formation slammed into the side of the high rudder section of the plane and tore it from the fuselage. This plane might have had battle damage, with that section of the plane already weakened. In any case, the aeronautical engineers did not design this unique tail section on the Boeing B-17 bomber to withstand this freakish accident.

"Waddy" and I just happened to be in front of the fire station at this moment and as an emergency truck was pulling out, we asked if we could jump on. We made the horrible mistake of going out to where several bodies had crashed into the unforgiving earth. Since this plane was also returning from a combat mission, each of the airmen had on their flight clothing.

It was not difficult to look down at the broken dead bodies and to visually see one's self in these lifeless forms. They looked like ever bone in their bodies had been broken. Their limbs were twisted in all directions so that they took on the appearance of being rag dolls.

One crewman had impacted the hard earth so violently that his head was split open like a broken coconut shell. It was a sickening sight. Not a single sole on this plane survived. There would be ten empty cots tonight.

I vowed, at that moment, I would never go out of my way to visit another accident or a crash scene. The only exception to this would be if I could convince myself I could be of some assistance to the survivors in an emergency situation. At this instant in time I had no way of knowing I would be subjected to the wages of this terrible war on several other occasions.

"Waddy" and I walked in silence to our barracks. Both of us were searching our souls for a reason why this should happen. These young men had just survived a combat mission and now they met their death here in England.

During the next year, I would be able to ask myself many similar questions that would have no logical or sane answer. Fortunately, I soon learned not to dwell on these negative results of armed conflict and the hostilities of warfare.

Perhaps some could say I might have been naïve with this mental game I played with myself, but I learned to function effectively during thousands of moments of living hell. It made no sense to torment oneself over events you could not alter or prevent. Its only consequence could only make an individual less efficient or capable of doing what many expected of you.

MISSION NUMBER 1

On May 8, I get the news that I have been scheduled to fly my first mission in combat. I received a special notification from an officer who tracked me down at the Officer's Club. Normally all members scheduled to fly a mission is through their First Pilot's name. Much to my amazement, the Lt. Cobb crew was not on the board for the upcoming mission. I was to be the Navigator on another crew tomorrow, a crew whom I knew little about. How can this be and why?

This certainly was not how I expected it to be. I believed that our ten-man crew, Lt. Cobb's Crew, would stick together and fly each mission as a unit in our own plane, Number 42-97334. I struggled under the illusion that we would fly all of our assigned missions together, or we would all go down in the same plane. I was surprised, happy, sad, and above all, very nervous. How can one person deal with so many emotions?

Early the next morning I was awakened by the C.Q. (Charge of Quarters) and informed it was time to go. It was only three in the morning. Only a few in my barracks were stirring while Cobb, "Waddy", and "Weak" were deep in sleep. I had spent most of the night with a thousand different thoughts racing through my head and had no answers for anything. I could see no constructive reason for waking up my buddies only to say I'm off on my first mission. I suppose they had their own mixed emotion about my being assigned while they had to wait. What a war.

I entered the latrine with several other men, all in the state of some type of stupor. I received no special attention because I do not believe anyone even noticed that this neophyte was about to go on his first mission. I shaved by looking in a mirror that long ago had given up its ability of throwing back a clear reflection.

I had remembered the importance of shaving before a mission because of the many hours we would have to contend with the rubber oxygen mask rubbing on our face. I did not have the degree of beard many of the others were afflicted with. I was only a stage beyond what many would term fuss.

I tagged along with the Officers of the various crews making this trip today, not completely contemplating what was in store for this greenhorn. Hell, I didn't even know what I should be worrying about or what was to lie ahead for this airman.

As much as I was looking forward to this day, somehow it had sneaked up on me and now I did not feel fully prepared. I would be flying with nine other men who I did not know and somehow this was not how I had imagined it.

A couple of other Navigators, who I knew, were most helpful and concerned. They guided me through this early hour ritual that was required before we even took off. Somehow each of them must have been reminded of their very first mission and felt obligated to repay a kindness they had received from some other concerned friend.

In the cool mist of early morning we all made our way to the mess hall. This morning, much to surprise, I found out we would be served fresh eggs, fixed anyway we wanted them done. This was a perk given only to the crews scheduled to go on a mission. Though I walked into the mess hall with a great deal of apprehension, this would not in any way hamper my appetite.

Though this would be my first recorded mission, and I would ultimately fly thirty-four more, it is not my intention to write about the specifics of all of these combat flights. I have previously written a book in which most of these missions were described in greater detail. This previous book entitled: "COME FLY WITH ME", published by Excel Press/iUniverse, ISBN 0-595-09135-0, contains pictures and details specifically about this part of my experiences.

It covers my contact with the German fighter pilots, the intense German flak over targets of Europe, the destruction of B-17's and planes of the Luftwaffe, the death of comrades and the devastation only war can bring about. Each individual, who flew on these missions, had their own distinct experience because of their position or duty within a bomber and much depended on where their plane flew within the formation.

Here, suffice it to note, only a reference will be made to some combat missions, while others may be described in greater detail. The intent is to describe the humanistic side of the individual crew- members, the part they played as a well-disciplined war machine, and the humorous turn of events that made tolerance of this terrible dream possible.

Though there was a certain similarity in most missions, each one was a distinct event and would be as different as individuals' fingerprints. Such things as the specific target, the distance from our base, the weather, the Luftwaffe, and of course, the degree of the ever-present flak.

Several of us walked in semi silence in the early darkness on our way to the Briefing Room. Each of us is visually in close proximity yet our minds isolated one from the other. We were in our own thoughts about what the next hours would hold for us.

I entered this noisy briefing room that was saturated with a cloud of smoke that hung half way between the floor and the ceiling. It was noisy with excitement and apprehension as I slipped up near the front of the room so I could both see and hear everything.

After this first briefing on May 9th, I learned that our target would be a German aircraft factory, just East of Paris, France. This would not be a typical mission, because of the relatively short haul and the fact that our fighter planes would be able to provide air cover the entire trip. The men around me called it a "milk run." For me, it seemed like an ideal mission to get exposed to actual combat. Each mission, however, has its own hazards and dangers, whether it is caused by the enemy or by some type of accident.

I would be the Navigator on the Lt. W. G. Wood Crew and our target would be at Laon Anthies, France. The only two important things to note about Mission Designated as GSN 127 by our Group, was that it would be my very first one and I would be flying in the very plane assigned to our original crew. It was "HAARD LUCK", plane Number 42-97334.

I had been isolated from my own crew, but the power-to-be did not put me on just any old plane. Though I had never met any of the other crewmembers I felt at home in this special bomber. I would be less than honest if I did not own up to some nervous unknowns within me, this being number 1.

This relatively short mission, both in time and distance, was an ideal baptism for me. I was to get indoctrinated in the basic rituals of a combat mission with most of the negative consequences eliminated. On this mission we flew to our target at the rear end of the formation, we dropped our bombs on an airfield, saw a few support fighter planes escorting us, there were no Luftwaffe pilots that would challenge us, and the amount of flak was almost negligible.

However, I think it interesting to note an incident that occurred on this specific assignment. The engaging occurrence on this mission is not about any member of the crew I flew with, nor even any plane within our 95th Bomb Group. It concerns a friend of mine, another Navigator flying in a B-17 from a different Bomb Group in the 13th Combat Wing. Though the target was recorded in my log as being a "milk run," for Lt. C.B. Rich (the C. is for Clarence, a name few people were privy to) from Dean, Montana, it had a greatlt different significance. It changed all of Lt. Rich's "tomorrows."

Lt. C.B. Rich graduated with me from San Marcos. We were very close friends. He would be assigned to one group and I would end up in another. I did not piece together his story until long after the war was over. It seems this identical mission that would be my first, was also Rich's first trip over Europe. His crew was flying "Tail End Charley", in the rear of their formation, the same position I and the Lt. Wood Crew flew in.

Their plane got hit by flak on the run over the target and was seriously damaged. The entire crew was forced to bail out over the French countryside. Every member of the crew managed to exit the plane, but was dispersed over a large area because of the difficulties in escaping a falling bomber. One by one they left their disabled B-17 and would be scattered over a great distance.

Lt. Rich landed safely and was immediately discovered by the French Underground. He luckily avoided being captured by the Germans, as was the misfortune of the other nine members of this crew. During the night, these brave Frenchmen deposited him in the attic of a French farmhouse. This apparently was the closest and most logical place that the underground Frenchmen could hide him prior to the sun making its presence.

The other members of Lt. Rich's crew were all captured and ended up being Prisoner's Of War. The farmhouse, with Rich in the attic, just happened to be right in the middle of a German Fighter Squadron located on the outskirts of Paris. It, fortunately, was not the airfield our two Groups had dropped our bombs on.

Each day German Fighter pilots would visit the farm family, sit down, and have coffee. They, supposedly, had a good rapport with this family that had been developed over the proceeding two years of occupation. Now this stranger housed in their attic endangered their very lives.

By harboring an American escaped airman would be cause for severe action by the German Authorities and each member of this French family was aware of it. Lt. Rich lived in this attic until rescued by Patton's Army several weeks after D-day.

Years later, on a visit to Dean, Montana, I talked with C.B. about this incident and the coincidence of us starting or ending our combat careers on the same mission and on the exact day. Lt. Rich had been completely surrounded by the enemy until he was rescued. The German Pilots who sat directly below him obviously never suspected.

Each day C.B. would hear the fighters scramble because of approaching bombers in one of their areas they had been assigned to monitor. Many days he could hear formation of American heavy bombers fly over, formation after formation. Sometimes, when he would peak out of his attic window, he could see chaff (aluminum foil thrown out of the bombers) drift lazily down, like a light spring shower.

This farm family was typical of many French people who risked their lives to help. Had the Germans discovered or suspected that Lt.Rich was harbored by this family, they more than likely would have shot each heroic member. Surprisingly, children of this farm family were capable of keeping this surreptitious act from the Germans, for these many months.

Similar heroic actions were taken by partisans from all over France, Belgium, and the Netherlands. Many brave men and women daily risked their very lives to hide, fake passports, give clothing, feed, provide some type of transportation, or in anyway try and protect these unfortunate American and British fliers.

Because of their dauntless and heroic efforts many downed Allies were able to make it back to England or at least escape being imprisoned in some Stalag Luft or prisoner of war camp. A great deal of gratitude is extended to these very special heroes.

FROM HERE TO ETERNITY

On May 12 I am again assigned to another crew for one of the longest and more difficult missions our Group had been assigned to date. I still do not understand why I have been taken from my original Crew. All of my plans and dreams had revolved about flying with the other nine fellows I had gotten to know and like. The rest of Lt. Cobb's crew also began wondering why they could not start their tour of twenty-five missions.

Just four days ago our crew had gotten together and had decided on a name for our plane, good old 297334. We had chosen the name HAARD LUCK. This happened to be a common retort on the Base any time someone might be looking for a little sympathy. The usual reply to one of these sad stories was "Haaaard Luck." It was usually spoken with an obvious amount of sarcasm or disparagement. The other reason for collectively deciding on this somewhat unusual name was a simple paper napkin Lt. Dan Waddell happened to pick up on the night he was married in Omaha, Nebraska.

This small square folded napkin acquired in an Omaha bar had a little girl drawn on it. This buxom and curvaceous little lass had red hair, with a horseshoe as an ornate decoration; she had dice for earrings; she had a left hand monkey wrench in one hand and a four leaf clover in the other: she wore two eight balls for a brassiere; and she wore a bandana around her midriff with hearts, clubs, spades and diamonds on it.

This napkin, that "Waddy" and Claire had saved, had the title LADY LUCKY on it. We knew of two other planes called "LADY LUCK" so we all decided to give our queen something original. With all of this logic, it was only natural that she would here after be affectionately called HAARD LUCK.

Ultimately I was able to buy tubes of oil paint and a few small brushes. I then proceeded to paint, this lovely lass, on the back of all ten of our A-2 leather jackets. The painting would be about 10 inches high. With ten jackets requiring this art, it took some time to get all of the jackets finished. I also started to paint this same little gal on the nose of Number 42-97334.

BRUX, CZECHOSLOVAKIA

On this, my second mission, the wakeup call and breakfast were similar. We all shuffled in the darkness toward the briefing room. There would be little conversation going on, primarily because it seemed each was deep in their thoughts and contemplations. When we finally reached the smoke filled briefing room, after putting away a similar breakfast I had the day before, I could sense a higher degree of concern among the airmen than on my first mission only a few days before. The sound level increased by many decibels due to the myriad of conversations and questions being asked. Most seemed to sense something I was not aware of.

Nearly everyone in the briefing room must have sensed the impending mission. There again was that same layer of billowing smoke, caused by all of the cigarettes, pipes, and cigars, which reached from the ceiling to just over the heads of the gathering crews. It seemed to stratify just a foot or two below the ceiling and the same distance above the heads of the anxious crew members.

Tiny areas of light tried to penetrate this sooty vapor from the dozen or so under powered 40-watt bulbs dangling from the ends of electrical cords. Most men had on flight suits that were unbuttoned because of the excessive body heat in this overflowing room. You could smell the odor of perspiration intermingled with that of the burning tobacco.

I could barely tell where the front of this elongated room was located. The only clue I had would be the direction each of the chairs had been placed. As I moved closer to the front, I could see the map on the wall. It would determine where this group would go today. The map was covered completely by a curtain, placed there to conceal this information, if only temporarily.

The noise from a hundred simultaneous conversations going on was abruptly ended when someone shouted "Attention." In walked our Commanding Officer, Colonel Carl Truesdell, Jr. as this motley group rose to a standing position.

Colonel Trusesdell appeared to be a man of middle age, very stocky, with pitch-black hair parted in the middle. His chubby face seemed to always have a cigar protruding from his lips. This instantaneous moment of silence was broken when the order "At Ease" was given and over a hundred butts dropped into their chairs, almost as one.

Col. Truesdell had just taken over command of the 95th Bomb Group as he replaced Col. Chester P. Gilger. After a few brief words, the curtain was pulled back and there were enough moans and groans to almost clear the air of smoke. A heavy wool string reached from our Base at Horham England to the extreme eastern edge of Germany and the Czechoslovakian border. It did not stretch in a straight line but had several bends in it.

This string ran across the Channel to our European landfall at Vlissingen, Netherlands, southwest of Rotterdam. From there it bent its way between Cologne and Frankfurt, Germany; and continued on to a place they said was Brux, Czechoslovakia, a town about fifty-miles northwest of Prague. There would be a different route described by the continuing string as we left the target and headed back to England.

Col. Truesdell pulled the cigar from his mouth and stated: "Today's target is part of a maximum effort by the American 8th Air Force. Two thousand heavy bombers and fighters will fly out to hit five major synthetic oil plants, four in the Leipzig area of Germany and one at Brux. Targets to be attacked in Germany will include oil plants at Merseburg, Bohlen, Lutzkendorf and Zeitz."

"Our target is over 600-miles in a direct line from our base and we all know that we never take the shortest route. We also know our fighter escort can only help us on the first half of the mission. The rest of the time we will be on our own. Gentlemen, this is the type of target you don't want to go back to. Do a good job this day. Good Luck."

You now could hear a pin drop in this large smelly room. It was obvious to everyone the hours ahead would not be easy ones. Synthetic oil was most important to the German war effort because they had limited sources for the precious lubricant to run their war machine. They would defend these targets with all their prowess and capability. This would be the longest mission attempted to date.

This day would prove to be my first real baptism under fighter plane attacks and the intense barrage of antiaircraft shells at the target. On today's mission, I was to fly with yet another different group of fellows, Lt. Charles Snowdon's crew. Again we would be relegated to the back of the formation in what is affectionately called the "Tail End Charlie" spot.

This position in the formation would prove to be the most hazardous, both from enemy fighter attack and especially from flak. It was also the most difficult location to be assigned because of the accumulative spacing error in the formation. It would prove most difficult to maintain a tight position with the plane off either wing or before it.

The rear of the formation was delegated to all new crews until they could prove they had the ability to maintain a position in a tight formation. This is almost a Catch 22 situation because many new crews were not around long enough to move up into the formation.

I was beginning to wonder if I would fly continually with different crews for all of my missions. "When would I be able to go with my own HAARD LUCK group?" I asked. No one would volunteer a reason for what was going on with me. The most common reply was, "We just do what they order us to do." Again I did luck out by flying in my special B-17 we had named HAARD LUCK. To that extent I felt like a team, my special B-17 with its own personal Navigator.

Shortly before 0500 we boarded our plane. In the early hours of this morning, before entering the nose of this shinny B-17, I glanced up at the tail to assure myself it was indeed old number 297334, the plane I had crossed the Atlantic in. For some stupid reason, I felt this would be a good omen and a degree of apprehension left me.

When I finally climbed into the nose and got situated at my desk, I once again spotted the name and a short note written by one of the "Rosie The Riveter" gals who had worked on our plane. It had been scratched on the aluminum skin in a rather obscure place, perhaps only known to me. It simply said "always come home."

As we crossed the English Channel and for some distance into France, we could see our "Little Brothers." This is an affectionate name for our fighter support, namely P-38 Lightnings and P-47 Thunderbolts. They would be protecting our formation for about another hour and a half. Then they would turn toward England, drop down on the deck, and strafe any target that happened to come within their gun sights, targets of opportunity.

Actually, each fighter group would be with us for only brief periods because of range capabilities. As they would be forced to leave us another group of fighter support would rendezvous with our formation of bombers. Each successive group of fighters could remain with us for shorter periods because of the distance we were from England. Finally, we could expect no more escort protection. This limitation was usually anything beyond a three hundred mile radius from our Base in England.

As I saw the last group of P-47's break for home, I began to have my first signs of nervous tension. I felt we would not be as lucky as the "milk run" I had been on only three days ago. I could feel the necessity to consciously force myself to breath.

I foolishly let my mind try and handle what it would be like to be hit by Luftwaffe bullets entering my little space in the nose of HAARD LUCK. I knew also that all my required missions would not be without the risks that war demands of its participants.

Shortly after the fighter escort broke off, we heard the first reports of German Fighters. They had been waiting for this very moment. The first group of bombers they attacked was directly ahead of us. This would be the 100th Bomb Group that was stationed in Thorpe Abbotts, not too far from Horham.

We could see what looked like over a hundred little bees, swarming through the air space of the Formation barely visible ahead. Large contrail loops swirled in the sky before me. The ten miles that separated us made their formation appear as elongated silver dots that took on the shape of several arrowheads, traveling five miles above the earth. Within minutes our moment of truth erupted with machine gun fire vibrating my plane and shouting on the intercom system. Hell had just broken loose.

We were being attacked from all directions, but primarily from the front. About this time several of the bombers from the group ahead, which had been shot down, were now exploding on the ground below us. We could see several balls of flame and pillars of smoke.

Next I saw my first German fighter plane roll over and spiraled down to earth, with a trail of smoke arcing behind him. A fighter plane raced past my left window while it rolled over to race in a lazy arc away from our formation. I do not believe a single shot was fired at this plane. The noise from the 50 caliber machine guns was deafening.

The only time I would use one of the two 50 caliber machine guns mounted in the Navigator's section of my plane, I managed to make a cardinal mistake. As I tried firing at a German fighter plane, which appeared to be diving toward my right window, I held the trigger for an excessive amount of time. As I held my sight on the rapid approaching enemy, my gun finally jammed in all of the excitement. Nothing happened when I tried pulling the trigger, as the plane rolled away from my window.

I found out later I had ruined the barrel by not knowing you were to only fire the gun in short 8-second bursts. In their effort to speed Navigators to the combat area, we were never given training in how to use the guns in the nose of a B-17, nor any other plane. I truly did not have the slightest idea of what I did wrong and how to fix the damn thing.

On the two practice flights I had where we could use our guns, I only pulled the trigger for a second, just out into space. I immediately could comprehend that the two 50 caliber machine guns, designated for the Navigator, were absolutely useless. Neither gun had the ability to swing and follow a speeding airplane or target.

In addition, the visibility behind these two worthless guns was truly atrocious for the action now taking place before my unbelieving eyes. Now, while witnessing ME 109s and FW 190s flash past my tiny windows in split seconds, it did not take a rocket scientist to realize the impossibility of a Navigator also being called a gunner or having success shooting down an enemy plane.

My experience in hunting grouse, pheasants, ducks and geese told me that these two worthless guns could have been left off this bomber and saved the taxpayer money. I had learned from my father to be successful at bird hunting, you had to aim at the bird, follow it with your sights, move slightly ahead of the target in an even swing, and then pull the trigger. Your lead would be determined by how fast the target would be moving. The Navigator's machine guns could do none of the above.

I made up my mind, that during the heat of the battle, I would observe and note everything I believed to be important on to my charts. I would make note of bombers and fighters that were shot down, I would note the number of parachutes spotted, I would indicate longitude and latitude for each instance, and I would record the degree of flak noted along our course, its location or at the target area. Anything I over heard on the intercom that seemed important would end up on my chart of the mission being flown. To hell with those two damn worthless guns.

The Group ahead of us lost several bombers and I noted that while some seemed to flutter toward the earth like a fallen leaf, others were diving in a lazy arc, and one just exploded into a ball of debris. One B-17 took a spiral course toward its inevitable rendezvous with earth. German fighters were also dropping from the sky, leaving a smoking trail toward the earth. Some broke into dozens of pieces that flew in all directions. I wrote all of this information on my charts with trembling fingers and a dry mouth that felt like I had forgotten to remove the cotton in it.

As soon as the action had started, it stopped just as suddenly. The almost unbearable noise from nearly a dozen machine guns firing simultaneously was simply reduced to the accustomed roar of the engines. Everything seemed to be calculated in degrees of discomfort and torment. Both the mind and the body seemed to rebel simultaneously. There was a lingering smell of spent and burnt powder that somehow mixed with the oxygen we were breathing through our masks.

The planes of the 95th Bomb Group had sustained some damage, but so far, all 36 B-17s were holding their position. The Group ahead had taken the brunt of the German Fighter Plane effort. Suddenly, Lt. Yablonski's plane in the echelon in front of where we were flying veered off to the left and pulled down and away from the formation.

All knew any plane that could not keep up with the formation would have a terrible time making it home on its own, especially from this part of Germany. German fighter planes would find and pick on these isolated crippled planes, invariably shooting them down.

The order had been given in Lt. Yablonski's B-17 to abandon ship, two parachutes were counted by our gunners. Shortly thereafter, the plane exploded in a ball of fire and pieces of the B-17 were thrown in all directions, before gravity moved them downward. Eight airmen would die at the instant of this explosion. I received a report from one of my gunners that he could see the two men floating earthward.

Minutes after we lost one of our own planes, the Germans broke away from our Group and just vanished. For whatever reason they turned away, lack of fuel or loss of many of their planes, their decision was welcomed. Another hour of flying would bring our formation near the German-Czechoslovakian border.

Once we hit our Initial Point and turned the entire formation toward our target, a new hell began to erupt. At first there were only scattered bursts of flak, but as we flew the approximate ten miles to the drop zone for our bomb load, the intensity increased with each passing second.

These bursts of flak took on the shape of an inverted large Y. The entire puff of this explosion would be about ten feet long, with each stem of the Y appearing to be about eighteen-inches in diameter. Each of these bursts would come at us in groups of four or five shells. At the instant the shell exploded, it would throw out thousands of pieces of metal in every direction, seeking something to slam into. As we witnessed these black smoky bursts, we knew the particles of death were already on their way.

Within minutes the sky was now black with hundreds of flak bursts, enough that you could not identify individual shots. It was at this point that you now could actually see flashes of color present themselves at the instant the timer in each shell went off. It was so dark it was difficult to observe the plane next to you.

Every plane was being pushed about by the bursts of flak, and each not in the same direction. The turbulent air, the black menacing smoke, the explosive sounds of shells erupting, the roar of our engines, the sashaying of the remaining 35 bombers, the difficulty to remember to breath, and the heart pounding in your chest made each second seem like an eternity.

Despite the fact you had ten men in your plane and you were apart of nearly four-hundred individuals, you felt all alone and like this terrible ordeal was just happening to you. The sights, the sounds, the smells, the concussion . . . . . . none of this seemed like reality.

All at once I noticed my left leg began to tremble so hard I could hardly keep my heel on the floor. The feeling of hopelessness consumed my mind and every sensitive part of my body. It seemed impossible to inhale enough air to satisfy my lungs. The smell of cordite grabbed my nostrils and created something I had never experienced before. So much was going on it was impossible to focus your eyes on any one thing.

There were moments when I felt like I had forgotten to breath. Many minutes seemed to elapse when everything within my body had frozen in time. I looked toward the Bombardier sitting only a few feet from me. I realized there was nothing he could do for me, nor that I could do for him. This was to be my first experience with genuine fear. I knew somehow I had to learn how to conquer or at least be the controller of this expected fright on my first real contact with hell.

Our run to the target seemed to take an eternity. Though it was approximately a ten-mile leg and our formation was flying at about 180 miles per hour, these were the longest three minutes of my life. Finally I heard the command to open bomb bay doors. Though it was difficult to see in this man created mess, all eyes would be on the Lead Bombardier.

As soon as his load left the lead ship, all other planes dropped their rack of bombs. As the entire rack in the bomb bay released their load, each plane immediately leapt upward about ten feet, not in perfect unison. They were now falling toward the target and we could get the hell out of here. The formation made an abrupt turn toward the west and we moved away while the bursts of flak followed us.

Once we left the range of the anti aircraft guns my tail gunner gave me constant reports of the huge column of black smoke rising from the target area. We had hit their synthetic oil facilities and now the results were rising in the form of billowing black smoke. It had reached our altitude of over 30,000 feet and now the top of this column was being blown to the left. Some of our tail gunners said they could see this beautiful sight when we were nearly one-hundred miles away.

What seemed like a short period of time after we had left the target area, suddenly, the yells of our gunners broke the silence and shouted over the intercom, "Here those bastards come again." The 95th Bomb Group was about to get attacked by German fighters, for the second time. The stupid thought that this did not seem fair flashed through my head until I realized the business both sides were engaged in did not have dispassionate rules to guide them.

I noted on my maps and charts, that we were in the same vicinity of the previous attack. The German Fighter Pilots had time to land, refuel, take on ammunition, and get back into the sky to again greet us. This time, it appeared that they would not be as aggressive, as they were against the Group that led us into the target area.

The 95th received only slight damage on the single pass the Luftwaffe made on us during this latest encounter. I noted only one fighter plane trailing some smoke as it sped away. Our guns were now quite but the smell of powder lingered on. As we lumbered along in the back of the formation we could see only the single vacant spot that the Lt. Yablanski crew had occupied.

Not far from Frankfurt, Germany this crew met its end. Two crewmen, the Radio Operator Sgt. R.M. Harbeck and the ball turret Sgt. G.V. Dimayo managed to bail out and would ultimately become prisoners of war. Pilot Lt. E.M. Yablonski, Co-Pilot Lt.W.L. Corrigan, Navigator Lt. J.F. Madigan Jr., Bombardier Lt. V.F. Humme, Top Turret Sgt. C.R. Lyon, Left Waist Gunner Sgt. L.H. Smith, Right Waist Gunner Sgt. P.R. Neuman, and Tail gunner Sgt. M.B. Cullum all were killed as the plane went down in a ball of flames. There are no words to erase the vision my eyes and mind had been exposed to this day.

This had been a long haul and darkness was beginning to set in as we approached the Base at Horham. We had been in the air almost twelve hours and the look of fatigue was present on every crewmember's face. We had lost only a single bomber and its crew, though many planes would fire off their red flares indicating wounded aboard. The 100th Bomb Group, part of our 13th Combat Wing, would not be as fortunate as the 95th Bomb Group this day.

Tonight I would substitute my evening meal for a drink or two at the Officers' Club. I met "Waddy" and "Weak" there and immediately they started picking my brain about the mission I had just returned from. The few drinks of bourbon and the conversation with my two friends helped to get my nerves reacting normal again.

They could not understand why our original crew was not called upon to partake in a mission, why I had been pulled away from our crew, and why others were flying HAARD LUCK. They obviously were asking the wrong guy.

BACK WITH MY CREW

The very next day I discovered I was to fly my third mission, but this time it would be with my original crew. With two missions under my belt, I practically felt like a real veteran flying with my buddies on their first trip across the Channel. Yesterday's experience kept my mind busy throughout the night, trying to put all that had happened into some kind of perspective.

I was beginning to realize that my destiny would be completely governed by chance and chance alone. There was little I could do to alter any of it. Unbeknown to me, this realization helped to make me tolerate similar nightmarish experiences in the days ahead.

I began to see this conflict as a typical athletic event where, in most sports, you tried to knock your opponent on his butt before he did the same to you. I did not hate my enemy yesterday because I knew he was only doing his required duty for his country. We were invading his air space and his homeland.

When I used to participate in the numerous sports I loved, especially as a little guy, it took additional guts to tackle or block someone who outweighed me by nearly two to one. I caught softball behind the plate for many years without a facemask. I knew that I would occasionally get hit in the face by a ticked ball or even the bat.

I had played semi professional hockey with little or no body protection, in those days, against players that made me look petite. I had even participated in the foolish and senseless sport of boxing. I now realized and believed I had the resoluteness and moral strength to do what the Air Force had trained me to do.

This mission with my crew would be to Osnabruck, Germany and would turn out to be only moderately rough. I know that each member of my crew would not agree with this assessment since they had nothing to compare it to. The flak was pretty devastating, but for some reason, the German fighters did not hit us. I'm sure this was discouraged because our fighter support could stay with us the entire time while flying the unfriendly skies of Europe. Much is owed to our "little brothers."

A REFLECTION

Several things that are about to happen during the next several days are important to note here. One incident will happen on this mission to Osnabruck, Germany and others will surface during the next several days. These occurrences have both validity and importance to try and put these damn hostilities into a more realistic point of view.

I know most things are not just black and white and I also recognize as a young officer I had many built-in deficiencies. Despite all this, I honestly believe the following events noted by this author to accurately portray things in the real world of combat. I sincerely believe it important to state it like it is.

Right after we left the target area I got a call from my pilot, Lt. Frank Cobb. Frank asked me for a heading to Switzerland. This did not make sense to me because we didn't seem to have serious battle damage and we were holding our position in the formation. Most importantly, if we had to leave the formation for whatever reason, and had to head for a neutral country, it would have been Sweden. We were in northern Germany.

I gave Cobb some damn smart-ass answer and never thought anything more about it. I honestly believed him to be only kidding with his usual and normal dry humor. Today, it went over like a lead balloon.

I would only fly two more missions with this terrific group of fellows and that would be to Berlin and a final mission to Brussels, Belgium. On May 19th we had been scheduled to go to the Capital of Germany and all knew it would be a rough mission. This city was surrounded with many antiaircraft batteries to protect this important Capital of Germany and all of its many manufacturing facilities, airports and government buildings.

BERLIN, GERMANY

Soon after our fighter support left us we were hit by the German Luftwaffe. What seemed like an hour was probably less than five minutes. Each of the several dozen fighter planes made several passes at our formation with no observed damage to our Group.

One of my gunners yelled that a German FW190 blew up and another FW-190 German fighter was seen falling out of the sky. Finally we had the sky to ourselves and our formation was able to press on toward the target. As we made our turn from the I.P. to our drop zone we encountered the expected intense flak.

Each of the 32 bombers now opened their bomb bay doors, awaiting the signal from the lead plane. Suddenly, it became obvious that the target area became obscured by a huge bank of thick clouds below us. Normally, if you cannot visually see the target adequately enough to bomb (this was prior to using PFF or radar) you would have an alternate objective.

Today, however, it was decided that our Group would make a 360-degree turn and hope to hit the target on this second pass. This decision was made because it was noted that the cloudbank was breaking up and blowing away from the target area.

It seemed we never got out of the range of the anti-aircraft gunners while making this 360-degree turn. Flak became so intense it now appeared we were on a night mission. There no longer were individual puffs from each of the exploding shells, only flashes of yellow and orange could be seen. Our planes were being pushed and pulled by the turbulent air so that the formation appeared to be sashaying over the Capital of Germany.

All at once our plane was hit on the under side and you could feel the plane momentarily shutter. I did not hear anything special over the roar of the engines but I instantly was aware of my right foot being moved from beneath my body and falling to the floor. I lay there for only a moment or two, trying to twitch my toes or moving each foot. I could move my legs and I did not feel I had been wounded.

Slowly I pulled myself up in a standing position so I could assess whatever damage had been done, first to my body and then to the plane. I looked down and my flight suit from the waist down was covered with large slivers and splinters of plywood and I could see a large wad of fir lining protruding out from an irregular tear in the heel my right boot. It looked serious.

At this moment I had not time to dwell on this because we were in the process of dropping our bombs. I did not feel any particular physical pain or see any blood. What actually had happened was a piece of the flak had blown through the bottom of the nose of the plane and went through the plywood flooring just below where I usually stood. Just then another shell exploded right above us and again the plane shuttered. It felt like the impact momentarily stopped our forward motion. I turned and could see Sgt. Jim Eavenson slump in his seat in the top turret position.

I put on a portable oxygen bottle and went to help him down onto the floor below. He was somewhat stunned but managed to get out of his seat and onto the floor behind the pilots with little or no assistance from me. There was a large piece of flak, nearly the size of a small fist lying next to Jim.

What had happened, this piece of flak hit the top turret at a strut section, sheared it off, then hit our top turret gunner. It passed through the collar of his Maywest life jacket and the collar of his flight suit. The only significant damage it had done was deposited a huge lump on Jim's neck. If the shell had not been spent, it would have taken Sgt. Eavenson's head completely off.

We wasted no time leaving the target area and headed away from the flak. Our number three engine had been hit and the pilots were now feathering its propeller. We had received battle damage but we were still airborne and holding our position in the formation. Suddenly someone announced that one of the B-17s was leaving the formation and had announced it was going to Sweden. Lt. W. S. Waltman had two engines out, was trailing some smoke, and was losing altitude rapidly.

He informed the Group he was going to try and make it to Sweden in plane number 297290 called "Smiling Sandy Sanchez. As I looked out my window to see this plane dropping to a lower altitude, I realized our plane was also pulling away from the formation. I immediately yelled up to the pilots to find out what in hell was wrong. "Waddy" answered my question by saying Lt. Cobb was going to follow Lt. Waltman. I shouted back: "Waddy, do we have mechanical or control problems?" "No, none that I can see." was his reply.

All at once, like a ton of bricks, the many myriad of little happenings began to fall into a pattern and I believed I knew what was about to happen. "Lt. Cobb was going to take the entire crew and sweat the war out in a neutral country," immediately flashed through my mind. "This was not going to happen to me," I told myself.

I reached over to Lt. Weakland and grabbed his 45 caliber revolver (I never carried mine because I believed, had I been shot down and got caught with the damn gun, I would have been killed) and moved up behind Cobb. I informed him he was to turn the controls over to "Waddy" and we were going to get back into the formation. This was a simple and spontaneous reaction.

It did not occur to me that I could be court-martialed for this extreme act or the degree of significance to it. I only knew we were expected to do our utmost to defend the trust that had been placed upon each us. Suddenly my mind sorted through all of the doubts and past observations that had been stored there. I acted purely on instinct since only a split second was required to finally complete the picture composed of a dozen little pieces.

Lt. Cobb must have realized my determination because he neither said anything nor did he offer resistance as we slowly climbed back to the rear of the formation. It took almost an hour before we were in our rightful slot as tail end Charlie for the long trip back to England.

Once I got back into the nose I returned the gun to "Weak's" holster and his: "What in hell was that all about." "I'll tell you later Weak", was my only explanation. I now remembered I wanted to examine what in heck happened to my boot. As I tried to remove it I discovered the rip was about three inches long and it looked like hell because wool had pushed its way though the opening. I found a small piece of flak in the boot but it had not injured my ankle. It must have spun around to create such damage.

All at once I would have sworn I was bleeding from a wound on my back. I could feel the warm blood traveling down my spine and flowing down to my buttock and off my tail bone. I turned to Lt. Weakland and asked, "Weak, check my back and see if you can see anything." His negative reply was followed after he had run his arm down the back of my flight suit next to my skin. He removed it and said, "That's nothing but stinking sweat."

"Waddy" and I made the mistake of not reporting this entire incident during our interrogation. I suppose each of us thought this to be a one-time incident and we never had a real chance to sit down and discuss all of its ramifications. Few in our crew even knew that there was an incident. Even "Weak" and Sgt. Eavenson did not inquire further as to what the commotion was all about.

The next morning our crew was again scheduled for a mission. This time we would go to a target located near Brussels, Belgium. We all knew this would be a short haul and we could expect good fighter support. Lt. Cobb made no reference to the previous mission and I could sense a definite coolness toward me.

I did not find words to discuss or defend my actions of the previous day. I believed my drastic reaction to what had transpired spoke for me. I also did not know the mission to Brussels would be the very last complete mission I would fly with my friends.

On May 24th, just five days after our hectic trip to Berlin, we were schedule to return to the German Capital, only this time our plane would be as a spare. Should some B-17 scheduled to fly in the formation have an engine problem or perhaps a crewmember become sick, they would pull out of the formation and the spare would fill in. We followed the formation until about the middle of the English Channel and were informed we were not needed and should return to base.

Lt. Weakland had already pulled the pins on each of the forty 100# bombs and now it was his charge to reinsert each pin again. He and Sgt. Frank Tomsey worked at this until we arrived back at Horham. We had a full load of gas, enough to have taken us to Berlin, and we had 4000#s of bombs on board. With this extreme weight, we would require every foot of the over 7000 ft. main runway to successfully make a safe landing.

Instead, Lt. Cobb did not touch the wheels down until only 500 yards remained of the runway. Over 5000 precious feet of concrete slab had been wasted before we would make contact. He hit the brakes, both wheels locked, the tires blew, and when we hit the perimeter track the left landing gear was torn off. Instantly the left wing dropped and the numbers one and two engines were partially ripped from the plane.

I had not been watching this landing since I had begun to collect my navigational equipment and stash it away. We all knew we would not be given credit for this mission since we were returning as a spare. It was with this indifference that I packed up much of my gear.

The first I knew of any problem was hearing the screeching brakes, smelling rubber, and then being thrown by brutish force against my right cartridge box, knocking the wind out of me. Because of the angle of the plane it was obvious it would be prudent to get the hell out.

In a dazed state, I released the hatch behind me. Instead of jumping out and dropping to the ground, I had to crawl between the latch edge of the hatch and the grass, which happened to be only twelve inches away. I ran like the dickens, trying to catch up with some of the gunners who were up ahead. We all expected our plane to explode momentarily.

As I looked back, I could see Lt. Cobb trying to get out of the narrow window to the left of his seat. He appeared to have his large body free of the small window but his left foot was caught between the side panel of the plane and his bucket seat. I started back to see if I could help. As I reached the plane I could see Cobb give an extreme yank as he pulled his foot free from its boot and he fell to the ground.

We were in luck. As rescue vehicles and fire engines raced to this dusty corner of the field, it appeared HAARD LUCK had decided not to blow up. We all knew the upper echelon would not be so considerate. Cobb was in deep trouble. We had to inform them of the problem we had five days before because we were now aware that Lt. Cobb needed help that he had unconsciously been seeking for several months now.

Hindsight can be so noble when things begin to fall into place. All of the landing problems we experienced on our trip over to England began to have some significance. Little comments or lack of enthusiasm took on a new relevance as a clear picture was developing. A request to go to Switzerland and an attempt to seek sanctuary in Sweden were momentous pleas for help to friends who did not know. We were also kids, with our own built-in limitations.

It was at this time it was determined both Lt. Cobb and Lt. Weakland had found it impossible to withstand the pressures of combat. The Base Doctors recommended they be taken off flying status. One of our waist gunners, Pvt. Fleet, also became a clerk and was removed from flying status.

Three from our original crew could not adjust to the conditions this damn war demanded of its fliers. They had only endured three missions. A few weeks later our Engineer, Sgt. Eavenson, had a nervous breakdown and he also was removed from flying status. Four of my original crew were now gone and it was obvious new arrangements would have to be made.

Each individual had to discover how to endure the reality of combat. There was no formula or secret that would be effective for every flier or member of a crew. We all came from different backgrounds and we all had been exposed to varied experiences. Most of us were able to adjust to this unreal action, but there were others that mentally would snap if they were forced to continue into situations they could not endure or handle.

In the case of Lt. Cobb, we can look back and see many tell tale signs that should have been plain to see, but being mere youngsters, we were unaware of what must have been going on inside of him. I'm sure even he did not know. Hindsight is a wonderful thing, but it usually comes too late to be of any real help, or assistance.

After the war I tried repeatedly to track Cobb down and apologize for not being there to help. I know I did not totally understand, and I also know, that being only 23 years old, did not give me the necessary wisdom to have been of much help.

Periodically, all of the flying personnel would be taken off flying status and sent to a west coast resort known as "Flak Shack." Here we would have a week to rest, relax, and just unwind from the obvious strain of combat. The purpose was to prevent more individuals from breaking because of the almost daily exposure to enemy fighter planes and the horrible flak. I'm sure each person has a distinct point where even the best of nerves has to say no more.

95TH MASCOT

At one time, a group of gunners at the 95th Bomb Group Base, got together and purchased a small donkey and a very unique cart. I was told it had been picked up in Africa when one of the crew flew over to combat. Ultimately, this donkey became one of the many pets that the 95th adopted. The cart, with its two large wooden wheels and the elaborate seat for two passengers, could be seen daily in and around Horham. There were many dogs and a few cats, but this unique pet attracted most of the attention.

For many, this tiny, friendly little donkey became a mascot of our Bomb Group. Unfortunately, it ultimately died during the summer of 1944. A group of enlisted men decided on a final service this much beloved animal could contribute to the war effort. He would be sent to Hitler's Germany.

They fashioned a special designed service jacket, complete with rows of ribbons, ample rank insignia, and a note to the German people. I believe the note said: *"Ich habe mich verirrt"* which loosely translated means "I'm lost" in German. It was placed in the bomb bay so it would leave the B-17 on a scheduled Bombing Mission.

Just prior to the bombs being dropped, our little friend parachuted to the "Fatherland", along with the note, to whoever discovered this unique intruder. This was not done in disrespect or lack of love for this pet, rather to send a confusing message to our common enemy.

I have no idea what communication it conveyed. The importance may have only been the release of some nervous tension via a small amount of humorous foolery. I do not know where it landed or who discovered it.

OUR SOJOURN

One afternoon, several days prior to Lt. Weakand having to go to the hospital, "Waddy" and I took him along with us, on a bicycle trip, designed to see some of the countryside and to hit a few pubs. "Waddy" and I wanted to get "Weak's" mind off the new problems he was confronting. We did not have to talk about his situation, yet each knew how devastating this must be to him. This would be our last sojourn together.

Our first obligation was to once again appropriate three unattended bikes, with the intention of using them for the next several hours. This was no big problem, since these vehicles were scattered all over the place. These bicycles were usually owned by the enlisted permanent personal, and few ever put locks on them.

We would stop at a pub, have a warm glass of beer and continue down the winding narrow roads until another pub beckoned us. We did this for several hours and were miles from our base at Horham. The moods we were in didn't raise any concern about the fact that none of us knew where the hell we were. This, despite the fact, I had been trained to be a Navigator.

About this time we accidentally stumbled on an American Medical Hospital, about ten miles into our journey. We agreed that this place should have an Officer Club and perhaps we could talk them out of a drink or two.

Once we found the place, referred to as the Officers' Club, we entered and couldn't believe our eyes. There were three doctors reading books and a nurse who appeared to be writing a letter. The place looked more like a library and took on the atmosphere of a funeral home. They did have some sort of a bar at one end and it looked like it hadn't been put to use since last New Years Eve.

We inquired about the possibility of buying a drink. It probably was most apparent, but this trio, who had just barged into the solemn atmosphere of this medical club, did not really need to imbibe in another drink. In any case, two doctors started up a conversation with us, inquiring where we were from, and other small talk. It wasn't long before we had a scotch and soda drink in our hand and the place began to show signs of coming to life.

More doctors and nurses arrived and they seemed to make us the center of their attention. I suppose, the "fly boys" then usually see, are brought in on stretchers or are laid out on an operating table. In any case, they seemed to be most interested in our experiences during combat. Several hours were pleasantly spent with all of these medical specialists.

One of the doctors asked if we would like to try a unique drink they had, called "Special 52." "Never heard of it!" "It" turns out we had to walk over to the Officer's Quarters and at a room number 52. They emerged with a large bottle of grain alcohol. This was mixed with grapefruit juice, taken from a large can that had been appropriated from their mess hall.

The first drink was rough or harsh. It went down with the same ease as if you were trying to swallow a file. The next observation I made was that when I touched my cheek, I could not feel anything. I wasn't sure whether it affected the nerves in my checks or the tips of my fingers. This stuff made you numb and dulled all of your senses. The sensation was different than just being inebriated.

They decided that the three of us had enough and suggested we sleep it off in one of the barracks. We were the last ones to buy that suggestion and told them that the three of us would peddle back to our Base at Horham, wherever that was.

Since they could ascertain that we did not have the slightest idea as to where we were, one of the Doctors carefully drew up a map on the back of an envelope. God, when I looked at it, I thought it might be the plan for a perpetual motion machine. He put down such major landmarks as a windmill, a small pond, a road sign, or anything three tipsy airmen could identify. The only important advantage we had going for us this night, was the moon. It was out and was exceptionally bright. This clear a night is a minor miracle in England.

The group of doctors started us out in the right direction. The hardest part we had to contend with was to feel comfortable on our wiggly bicycles. As we left this hospital area and went off into the night, we knew we would have a real problem or challenge to get the bikes and ourselves back to the base.

We immediately discovered our bikes did not ride as well as the ones we had started our trip with. What we wouldn't have given to have wider and straighter roads this night. We constantly kept peddling into the hedgerows and being spilled off our cycles.

The landmarks given by our former hosts were not as obvious as they were on the crumpled envelope we checked with our cigarette lighters. Part of the problem was the lack of concentration and the need to tangle with all of the bushes along our path. If laughing could have gotten us home, we would have made it easily.

We discovered that if we tried to stay in the center of the road, we would have enough time to straighten out our bicycles before they met with obstacles. Next, we discovered that we could not ride abreast without getting tangled in one another's bikes. We looked exactly like three drunken airmen, riding down an English lane, in the early hours of the morning, and without a single worry in the world.

When we finally got within two miles of our base and we were getting over confident, "Waddy" and I locked handlebars. We both went "ass over teakettle." I flew over the front of my bike and broke my fall by extending my two arms. When the dust settled, I immediately broke out in a laugh, exclaiming that I had absolutely no feeling in either of my hands. "Waddy", I think both of my damn arms are broken." "Waddy" picked himself up and discovered that his bike was a complete wreck.

After looking me over he assured me that the only thing broken may have been my pride. The bike that carried me over the countryside, these past few hours, was also a twisted piece of junk. Both bikes were tossed on the other side of a row of stacked rocks and were immediately forgotten.

"Weak" had survived this collision but had fallen off his bike while just being a spectator. He had laughed his way into a hedgerow. If anything good came of this whole travesty was we had taken his mind off his release from flight duty.

The first mistake we made, after dusting off our bruised bodies, was to try and ride "Weak"'s workable bike, with "Waddy" on the rear fender and myself on the crossbar. Weak convinced us, after three or four attempts, we best hide his bike in the bushes and walk the remainder of the distance. We must have been quite a sight walking through the gate and to our barracks.

The most fortunate thing about this entire episode was the fact that we did not have to fly this day. We woke up late in the afternoon and for some strange reason, none of us suggested we make the long trek to the Officer's Club for a drink.

It may be next to impossible to explain to an outsider the justification of such juvenile behavior on the part of three men who should know better, but there are some things in life that cannot be logically supported or defended.

My memory of this excursion will always recall Lt. Ray Weakland at his very best. On this particular night we took him away from his worries and some of the many problems he was having. We knew the fact that his wife had delivered a little boy, a son he had never seen, did not help his situation. Soon he would be going home and he could be with them.

Though many may rationalize about the morality of drinking and letting one's hair down, I sincerely believe that it was an important outlet for our built-up tensions and the ever realization and knowledge of the possibility of pending death. We all were accustomed to seeing the vacant cots, when four of our friends did not return to our barracks, because their plane was lost over Germany or went down in the Channel.

Within a day or two, new replacements would occupy these same four cots, or on some days, maybe eight cots. We all knew that life in battle had diminutive values. Our particular duty of flying in bombers gave us a mere fifty-fifty chance of going home in one piece. You did not have to be a gambler to know these are lousy chances or odds.

LEAD NAVIGATOR

After my ninth mission to Boulogne, France, Captain Lyle Dallman requested my presence at Squadron Headquarters. This was June 5, the day before D-Day and the invasion of Europe. He suggested that I become a Lead Squadron Navigator for the 336th. He stated they had observed my work on the missions I had flown and it was felt I had the capabilities on taking on more responsibilities.

Remembering what my father had told me, "never volunteer for anything," I was at first reluctant to say yes. Then I realized if they wanted me to fly with lead crews, they would just have to give me an order. I also was well aware that I no longer was apart of a specific crew since we had four dismissed from flying status. I gave

Capt. Dallman an affirmative answer. It was also about this time I was promoted to First Lieutenant

I knew by saying yes that I would be pulled away from my buddies on a permanent basis. This was not all negative, since I had already flown six missions more than my original crew. Besides, my HAARD LUCK crew was now completely decimated by the events that had taken place just two weeks ago.

Most of my missions had been with different crews, so I was getting used to being with strangers. The Navigator for each crew had to attend the regular briefing for each mission and then when the rest of the crews went out to the plane, he was detained in order to be given any specific information he might find useful or important to have. I never truly got to know any of the men I would be flying with.

We, as Navigators, usually arrived at the plane just prior to take off and did not get time to josh with the men. During my next twenty-six missions, I would fly with nineteen different crews. It was only on rare occasions that I went on several missions with the same group of fellows. I somewhat felt isolated, since I did not share most of these undesired experiences we were exposed to with buddies I was real close with.

This whole combat affair was not what I had imagined it to be. I thought that the Cobb crew would fly together and our entire tour of duty would be in "HAARD LUCK," old number 297334. Another fact that helped develop my "I don't give a damn attitude" was the amount of missions we had to fly in order to complete a tour of duty.

When I started with my missions the total number required was twenty-five. After I had flown five missions, it was increased to a total of thirty-missions by General La May. I flew an additional five missions, or a total of ten, and then I was told that General James E. Doolittle had raised the required tour, to a total of thirty-five. At this point, I was sure I would never complete my tour, nor ever see my Norma again.

The duties of a Lead Navigator did not require that I change my habits of how I performed my duties. From the day we headed across the Atlantic on our way to combat I worked as hard as I knew how to collect and pass on information to the pilots I flew with. I was always aware of my responsibilities. I realized I would be the only person in the plane who should know exactly where we were at all times, and which direction we had to take to get home.

Lead Navigators carried the additional burden of knowing additional crewmembers would depend upon them. Instead of having only ten men in your plane relying on your abilities, if you led the entire Group, there could be three hundred and sixty men on the particular mission. Some days you would lead a high or low Squadron, and at other times, you could lead the 95th Bomb Group, the 13th Combat Wing, or even the 3rd Division.

Each duty on this B-17 Bomber has equal importance. Every member of the crew had specific responsibilities and all others depended on them to carry these duties out. The lead plane of the Group, took on the maximum burden of leading perhaps 36 aircraft to the target.

This plane, leading the rest of the formation, avoided areas of possible flak, rendezvous with fighter support, and then have its Bombardier be the one to determine the exact moment, when the bombs are dropped. All other planes opened their bomb bay doors and dropped their bombs when this Lead Bombardier said so.

The Lead Navigator and Lead Bombardier had crucial duties to perform from the minute we left England, meandered our way across Europe, and finally deposited our bombs on some target. Everyone on these lead crews had to perform their duties in a flawless manner if a mission was to be a success. Each of these crewmembers knew and accepted this responsibility.

During the times I was actually on missions, I had no problem in concentrating on my responsibilities. It would be the intervals between these missions when I began to feel almost like a robot, adding up these trips over Europe as if they were just becoming routine.

In my moments when I could contemplate and seriously think about things, I knew the importance of each of these daily risks. I also knew I had no control over the outcome. I suppose my strong belief in the Laws of Probability and Chance helped to alleviate my fears. I had built an invisible shell around myself that few events or friends were permitted to intimately penetrate.

CHAPTER 16

The morning of June 6 was not like any other morning. I knew I had been scheduled to fly by the list posted on the bulletin board at the Officer's club, and I suspected that I would be in a plane that would fly Squadron lead. The big plus in flying up near the front was you were located at the head of the tightest part of the formation and you sometimes took a little less flak. All of these thoughts did not prepare me for this morning's briefing.

From the moment the C.Q. got us up, we could sense that something big was in the air. We knew that our Group was to fly a maximum effort by the number of bodies moving about. Other crews were alerted to stand by for additional flights. The mess crew, at breakfast, was more talkative and even smiled when they dished up our plates. In fact, they sort of placed it on our tray instead of slinging it.

We saw and could hear additional vehicular traffic taking place on the base. In the dark there were distant sounds that we normally were not aware of. Everyone seemed to know something we flyers were not sure of or could only speculate on. There was enough additional and unusual activity and commotion that it attracted everyone's attention.

For the past several weeks the Eighth Air Force Bombers had been hitting targets in the Boulogne, Calais, and Le-Touguet part of France. These were short and easy missions, often referred to as "Milk Runs." Earlier I went on one of these missions and was given credit for one of these abbreviated trips against the enemy.

Once you became a Lead Navigator, you were not scheduled for this type of trip. We only went on the longer and more difficult trips deeper into Germany where our skills could best be utilized. Though this does not seem justifiable fair and impartial, from a logistic and objective viewpoint it made sense and was accepted with pride of our worth and value of each of the Lead Navigators.

We did not know it at the time, nor did the German high Command, that the sole purpose of this constant attention and effort on this portion of the French coast was meant to give the impression the eminent invasion would take place there. This area had the least amount of Channel to cross and made some sense. The consensus among the flight crews was that this was indeed the deducible place to try and get a foothold onto the Continent, but what the hell did we know.

The Germans had to expect a landing at almost any point of Europe, but with limited amount of resources, they had to give priorities to certain logical spots. The Allies were trying to help them decide where additional fortifications were to be built. It would turn out that this effort was completely successful, because Germany was compelled to divide their limited number of troops, over an over extended area. This had been a cat and mouse game for over a year.

Some of the Officers were so excited by the charged and emotional spirit emulating through out the Base, they even dished up, ate, and enjoyed the powdered scrambled "green eggs." I'm sure they were oblivious to what they had just done. This fact only becomes relevant when you know that crews going on actual combat missions could have farm fresh eggs fixed anyway they desired. This incident could be equated to an Infantryman clapping with glee when served Spam, or any service person in the Pacific Theater asking to be dished up the famous Australian "mutton."

Inside the briefing room, the atmosphere was electrifying because the noise level had an unreal crescendo to it. The smoke from the cigars and cigarettes made the visibility in this elongated room down to ceiling zero. The one thing that remained the same as all other briefings was the opaque dull drape that concealed the map on the front wall. This map would indicate where we would be sent this day. A member of the briefing crew was guarding this secret by being sure none got near the curtain to sneak a preview of our target. We would not have long to wait.

When Colonel Carl Truesdell, Jr. and his entourage entered the room, someone shouted, "attention," and instantly everyone "popped to" as a single unit, pushing their heads deeper into the thick smoke that floated in layers. When the same individual yelled, "at ease," the entire audience dropped their butts as one, into noisy chairs. Then, at this next moment, a feather dropping onto a soft pillow could have been heard in the most remote corner of this large Quonset hut.

Before he could speak, Colonel Truesdell had to remove the ever-present cigar from his mouth. Then, with unbelievable calmness he somehow was able to muster, he started the briefing with these words . . . "Gentlemen, this is it. Today the Allied Forces are about to invade Europe and the 95th Bomb Group will take part in this momentous occasion."

- D DAY -

The curtain was pulled back with the same casual motions we had observed on other briefings. What it exposed this day was of more interest than usual. What caught our attention was the fact that the Forces would not land in the Pas de Calais area as most of us had guessed, but rather that part of France that was south of England between Cherbourg and LeHavre. Our guesses were over one hundred miles away.

As we got a very detailed explanation of what was about to take place, we could immediately grasp the logic that went into the determination of where the invasion would be made. The importance for the selection of this part of France was made obvious, once we were told that the entire Cherbourg Peninsula was to be taken as a high priority and as rapidly as possible. Space was required for the millions of tons of supplies and the equipment that would be needed for the days ahead.

The map at the front of this smoky room only indicated the details of our trip to the target and the route we would return to England and our Base. It was not too much different from other missions, at first glance. Further briefing by several other officers went into enough details about the operation we knew would make June 6 an unforgettable day. June 6th, 1944, would be forever known as **D- Day**.

It would not only be FON (Field order number issued by the 8th Air Force) Number 394, GSN (Group sortie number credited to the Bomb Group) Number 145, or Lt. Lloyd O. Krueger's mission number 10, it would be our effort to join forces for the first time with all of the other Services to defeat and end German occupation of Europe.

The magnitude of the thoughts racing through my head could hardly be contained. My gratification this moment, knowing I personally would be apart of perhaps the greatest consequential moment in the twentieth century, made my nerve endings tingle throughout my body. Tears of joy and satisfaction made my eyes swell up and I became aware of my heart pounding in an expanded chest. This truly had to be the real beginning of the end of a war that had been going on so many years.

At the very moment we were learning about this operation, we were told that the invasion had actually started many hours before. Thousands of ships and boats, over 5,000 of them, of every description had sailed from hundreds of English ports and were approaching the French coast as we listened with absolute attention. Many Naval battleships, cruisers, destroyers, and other small vessels, were escorting this armada toward the shores of France and we were going to have a small part in its success.

The plan called for several beachheads to be taken and the troops would fan out in all directions, taking as much territory as possible. Men of the Allied Forces had been secretly preparing themselves for this day and we were assured that they were ready. We also knew the dangers facing them and our need to help.

There was not one body in this room that did not welcome the opportunity to be apart of this horrendous operation. For the very first time I felt we were apart of the bigger picture, not just trying to eradicate specific targets or to let the German populace know they could not hide from the wages of war.

We were shown charts that gave the over view of the entire air operation. Thousands of bombers and a similar number of fighter planes would be in the skies at the same time. The resulting traffic problems would be almost impossible to image. Every single plane and each Group had to be accounted for, with detailed rendezvous points and traffic patterns confined to limited space, and a very specific flow of all planes, to and from the invasion front, had been worked out in minute detail.

The air armada would have thousand of heavy and light bombers, fighter planes, from both the American as well as the Royal Air Force. The bombers had routes that required all three Air Divisions from the Eighth Air Force to takeoff from over three-dozen airfields in East Anglia, fly to the invasion front and then divert around Cherbourg in a clockwise direction for the trip home. The problems of getting this maximum number of bombers into the air and formation, for this single mission, had to be astronomical.

This huge air pattern, requiring a clockwise flow across the Cherbourg Peninsula, across the English Channel, and back to your individual Airfield, was absolutely mandatory. Should any plane deviate from this command and fly counter to the prescribed flow of planes, they would be shot down. Many fighters had been delegated for this specific job, of policing this dictate. All fighter planes carried new identifiable markings that had never been seen before. Someone appeared to have thought of everything.

While each of us had been sleeping, dozens of Pathfinder planes had taken off with their specially trained paratroopers aboard to prepare for the arrival of over 20,000 regular paratroopers to follow. They would drop within areas occupied by German troops marking drop zones or those that were to follow. Nearly half were killed before they even reached the ground.

All knew the elapsed time of this mission could classify it as a "milk run", yet each were aware of the significance and the momentousness of this day and our small part in the operation. About this time, each of the excited airmen in this briefing room received a printed message from the Supreme Commander of the Allied Forces,

General Dwight David Eisenhower. Each had been handed a simple piece of paper. The following is this message, every member of the various branches of the service and support units received:

"Soldiers, sailors, and airmen of the Allied Expeditionary Force. You are about to embark upon the greatest crusade, toward which we have striven these many months. The eyes of the world are upon you. The hopes and prayers of liberty-loving people everywhere march with you. In company with our brave allies and brothers in arms on other fronts, you will bring about the destruction of the German war machine, the elimination of Nazi tyranny over the oppressed peoples of Europe, and security for ourselves in a free world. Your task will not be an easy one. Your enemy is well trained, well equipped and battle hardened. He will fight savagely. But this is the year 1944. Much has happened since the Nazi Triumphs of 1940-41. The United Nations have inflicted upon the Germans great defeats in open battle, man to man. Our air offensive has seriously reduced their strength in the air and their capacity to wage war on the ground. Our home fronts have given us an overwhelming superiority in weapons and munitions of war, and placed at our disposal great reserves of trained fighting men. The tide has turned! The free men of the world are marching together to victory! I have confidence in your courage, devotion to duty and skill in battle. We will accept nothing less than full victory! Good luck! And let us beseech the blessing of Almighty God Upon this great and noble undertaking."

The above order was also distributed to assault elements after their embarkation. Commanders in the Allied Expeditionary Force, read these orders to all of their troops. Each of us, at our June 6 briefing, received a printed copy of this Order of the Day.

The feeling I felt at this moment was like being on a football team that was leading the conference and we were about to take the field for a game that would decide the National Championship. I felt ready and prepared, as I knew each participant did. We had waited a long time and a great deal of sacrifice had already taken place.

This day our mission dictated we fly at a low altitude. This obviously made it possible to witness the greatest armada of ships and vessels of every description. The patterns from the wake from these ships and boats made could have created a work of art on a huge canvass. Our sky was crowded with friendly fighter planes, each resembling an angry bee looking for a victim to sting. Then you could see several large groups of heavy bombers demanding their space in these crowded skies.

The 95th Bomb Group had a target just inland from the beach, off the Channel coast and just north of Caen, France. As we crossed the invasion coast to drop our bombs, British troops were embarking from the bowels of a galaxy of ships of different sizes and shapes. Men were wading ashore simultaneously along the entire length of this selected French coast.

Our Group had to drop our bombs within seconds of a prescribed time, since the men were already in the water. Should this prove impossible, we had a secondary target inland near Caen. (Our Lead Navigator for the Group got our formation to the target area at the precise moment and we bombed the intended German coastal gun installations.)

The Americans landed at Utah and Omaha beachheads and the British and Canadian troops approached the Gold, Juno and Sword beachheads. The actual attack this memorable day was accomplished with 176,475 men, 20,111 vehicles, 1,500 tanks and 12,000 planes. The planning to invade Normandy Beaches was known as "Operation Overlord."

The briefing we received this morning included the usual information which we were given for any other target, with one exception. For the first time we were told to look for anything unusual that the Germans might throw at us. They knew that an invasion of the Continent was inevitable, so it was expected they might have a secret weapon that had been held back just for this occasion.

We were told there could be the possibility of our engines stopping in mid air, or some special type of flak never seen before. This information, in all of its vagueness, only added to the apprehension we already had. Most considered this warning as only another imperilment to be added to the list of ways the Germans wanted to impede our assignment on any mission to the continent of Europe.

Everything about our briefing and this day seemed special and somewhat different. For the first time, I found myself listening to the pilot and copilot run through the "check list" before starting engines. One would read the list while the other repeated each action taken. **Green Flare at 0500 hours**. "**Start engines**"; "**Fire guard posted**" - Fire guard posted"; "**Batteries on**" - "Batteries on"; "**Hydraulic pump auto**" - "Hydraulic pump auto"; "**Hydraulic pressure up**" - "Hydraulic pressure up"; "**Flaps** up" - "Flaps up"; **"Cowl flaps open"** - "Cowl flaps open"; **"Master switch on"** - "Master switch on"; **"Gyros caged"** - "Gyros caged"; **"Bomb bay doors closed"** - "Bomb Bay doors closed"; **"Start number one."**

It was now that we would hear the usual whine and sputter before the engine kicked off with a roar. Each of the four Pratt & Whitney engines was started in a specific sequence. As each engine coughed to a start, a new set of checklist items had to be run through and **repeated. "Booster pump on. Throttle cracked. Fuel-mixture to idle cut-off. Prop high rpm. Magnetos off. Circuit-breakers on. Generators on. Starter on for 20 seconds. Ignition. Prime the pump."** Then and only then, would No. 1 engine come alive.

Immediately, a new set of instructions would flow out. **"Mixture to auto-rich. Check oil-pressure. Stabilize at 1,000 rpm. Check fuel pressure."** Like the previous instructions, these also had to be verified by concurring that the action was indeed taken care of. Oil and cylinder head temperatures on each of the four gages had to ascend into the green arc.

While I was listening to this, I had certain duties that required only secondary attention this day. The trip to the target would be short and each Group had little leeway to deviate from the specific plan of things.

"Wheel chocks locks out." **Flight control locks off."** **"Flight control locks off, exercise controls."** **"Radio on and set."**

Another flare from the control tower meant that it was time to taxi. The right hand of the first pilot would be placed over the four throttles and slowly he pushed the two outside or outboard throttles forward and the 65,000-pound bomber lumbered out of the hardstand toward the perimeter runway.

The left throttle was pulled back and the right throttle was pushed forward. The pilot applied left rudder and a small amount of left brake with his toe . . . tires squealed as the B-17 turned sharply to the left onto the perimeter track. All around this huge field, 34 planes were lining up so that they could be ready to take-off in a predetermined sequence.

The squeal of these many tires against the pavement almost made you feel you were on a pig farm in Iowa. Each plane would be parked slightly askew of the one ahead of it for better observation and then the parking brake would be pressed on. This graceful airplane, while air borne, was a real clumsy klutz on the ground.

Finally the order was given for the actual take-off. **"Tail wheel locked. Parking brake off. Cowl flaps trail . . . flaps up."** The brakes were held as all four throttles were slowly moved forward to the fire stop. **"Release brakes."** The plane slowly moves forward down the 7,000-foot main runway, just thirty seconds behind the

B-17 in front and thirty seconds before the plane behind.

Then the increasing speed is called out in miles per hour by tens . . . **40-50-60, etc.**, until **110 mph** is reached. The red lights near the end of the runway lets you know it is time to lift off. **Wheels up - Climb at 500 feet per minute and hold speed at 125 mph**.

About this time, each crew-member checked in on their intercom and at 10,000 feet, each was told to get on oxygen. The power was reduced to **30 inches of manifold pressure** and **2000 rpm**. Now it was most essential to hold the predetermined heading, rate of climb and air speed to avoid running into one another, especially if confronted with several thousand feet of cloud cover.

Each and every time we took off, the same ritual would have to take place. Today though, it seemed more meaningful, for some reason or other. The thought raced through my mind that we had ten crewmen, each trained to do precise but different duties on this complex Flying Fortress.

It was only a few months before we were scattered around the United States, living ten different and separate lives. In reality, we were actually ten over grown kids or at best, certainly under developed adults. We had been trained (in approximately one year) to be a team that would operate a complex bomber, fighter plane, ship, submarine, tank, or whatever. "Remarkable!"

This was to be a maximum effort with the 34 planes that took-off. We made up the 95th B.G. formation. The 100th and the 390th Bomb Groups each had similar numbers, so that the 13th Combat Wing would leave England today with over 100 planes. Today would be my first as a Squadron Navigator and I would fly lead in the high element.

The take-off and rendezvous with the 390th and the 100th Bomb Group's were routine. This particular day would require near perfect assembly because of the total air activity going on over Southern England, especially in East Anglia. Fortunately the weather appeared to be cooperating, something the English skies normally did not offer us.

With the entire Eighth Air Force, both heavy and medium bombers and the fighter planes, plus the entire British RAF contingent, the skies were very active. This was because all of these formations had targets to hit in a limited area and within a short time range. This made the logistics for this operation most important.

We left England near Eastbourne at about 15,000 ft. altitude, which would normally be considered a low bombing height for typical missions. This altitude would make the actual bombing results more accurate, something that would be imperative for this operation. Our course across the English Channel was south southwest (190 degrees) to a point just west of LeHavre. We dumped our load of bombs at the precise moment on German emplacements along the coast.

We could see the landing craft and the excessive commotion on the water below. From our altitude we could recognize some of the action and activity going on in the English Channel below us. Battleships could be recognized with their big guns aimed toward France. The surface of the water was broken by swirling wakes from both large vessels and small craft. It looked like anything that had the possibility of floating had been moved into the scene below our formation.

If Germany had a secret weapon, they were still keeping the lid on it. For a few brief moments we observed a new and distinct pattern of vertical plumbs of smoke at our altitude, about three thousand feet in length and spaced about twenty foot apart. While the formation flew through this new configuration, our wings cut through these smoky pillars with no apparent effect. This phenomenon we were observing could not be caused by the usual anti aircraft shelling we were used to. If this is the best you have Adolph, bring it on.

About five minutes past the target, we turned at the R.P. Point to a heading of 295 degrees. This took us just south of Rochefort, France and over the Bay of Biscay. We altered course slightly to avoid the Channel Islands of Jersey and Guernsey where we knew we could pick up some flak. Once we crossed the English coast near Weymouth, we turned on a heading of 52 degrees. This would take us to our base at Horham.

When we flew over the Channel, we could see the activity of the Navy and their cargo of Infantry in these thousands of ships of every size. These ships and boats were making unusual patterns on the surface of the water because each had a different function. Some provided firepower, some were loaded with frightened but dedicated men, while others had supplies.

For the first time we could actually see how our Group fit into the whole picture. We did not go to some remote spot in Europe and have a strategic target for our Group to bomb. Today we were a part of an immense effort and we were taking part in a piece of history.

Details of this mission have been related only because it had specific meaning for me personally. Of course the primary importance was the fact that it was D-Day and the invasion of the continent. It was my first flight as a Lead Navigator and it was a mission flown at an altitude where we could witness this memorable operation. It was also the only one of my thirty-five missions where no German opposition was detected, either fighter planes or flak.

There was not one man who flew in these skies over Normandy that was not aware of the action going on below with our brothers who fought on the ground. Our hearts and thoughts were with them because they were about to open the gates to hell and enter.

FOUR DAY PASS

Shortly after this mission, I was issued a four-day pass, which for me meant London. This turned out to be an exciting place to be, since the British people reacted to the invasion with even stronger feelings than we Americans. Their city and country had been in this war for over five years. They watched as London had been devastated by constant air raids, with lives lost and whole blocks of buildings destroyed. These people had been at war with Germany and its allies since 1939. Now we are finally taking back European soil in June of 1944.

Their lives had been completely disrupted by food shortages, spending countless nights sleeping in air raid shelters or going below ground into the subways. Their country had been inundated by the hundreds of thousands of strangers who have landed on their shores and were dispersed throughout the countryside.

They could sense that June 6 marked the beginning of a new phase in this terrible war, one that would put the end of the conflict within sight for the first time. Each knew that there would be more sacrifices required, but they knew the Germans would now feel the full wrath of war. By now they had learned we had made a successful invasion on the shores of France and that this foothold would be the beginning of pushing the enemy back within their own borders.

It was next to impossible to enter a pub and try to buy a drink. If you happened to be in uniform, there was someone who insisted they wanted to treat you to a "bitter or mild." I was proud at this moment to be an American, and equally in love with the British people. There was a strong feeling that we allies were not made up of different nationalities but we were one and the same.

Several times on this leave I almost got my head knocked off by various paratroopers, who had returned from the front. Fortunately, they were looking for any American airmen who were in the 9th Air Force. It seems that some of the pilots from the 9th, who dropped paratroopers or who towed gliders into France, got "chicken" at the last minute and got rid of their cargo prematurely. They forced these men from the sky to land in wrong areas, often in swamps or wooded sites.

Many of the paratroopers were caught in enemy fire while being forced to struggle waist deep in water. Some had been killed as they dangled in their chutes, caught up in the upper branches of tall trees. They were rightfully mad and wanted to express their feelings.

In fairness to many of the pilots of the 9th Air Force, many who flew transport or towed gliders had little or no experience in actual combat against the enemy. There were pilots who obviously got the holy hell scared out of them and were not prepared mentally for the job at hand.

I saw many 9th Air Force Officers with black eyes, cut-up faces or torn uniforms. I'm sure many of these were innocent of what they were charged with, but were not given time to explain. I also saw many paratroopers being incarcerated by pairs of M.P.'s (Military Police). Thank God I had on the right shoulder patch. Our 8th Air Force patch had a large numeral 8 with a five-pointed star in the lower circle and a pair of gold wings, all on a field of dark blue.

The type of patch these irate paratroopers were looking for was really very different than ours. The 9th Air Force patch was not circular like the 8ths, but was shaped like an arrow. There was a smaller white circle with a gold numeral 9 inside. Radiating out from the edge of this circle were golden curled wings. On the top of the circle was a small five-pointed star.

I learned later that some of these pilots in the 9th A.F. who flew on subsequent assignments and had established a reputation of not facing up to the dangers in flying to a drop area, were taken care of by certain paratroopers. The last one to leave the plane would pull the pin on a live grenade and roll it along the floor of these DC47s or DC 46s. While they were floating earthward, they would see the plane they just left, blow up. This account came from a variety of sources.

The Allies had now gained a foothold in Europe, something Hitler never believed possible. You could not help having a feeling of accomplishment, especially when you realized that the Allies had just done the impossible. Each day, by listening to the radio or reading the Stars & Stripes, we would keep track of the terrain that the Allied Forces captured, knowing that we were pushing the Germans back into their own country.

We also knew that each day would put our targets into a more concentrated area or to some more distant place. Now though, for the first time, we could look down the long dark tunnel and see a source of light. Our major contribution would be to diminish the enemy's supplies and to destroy his means of transportation. We also would carry this war directly to the German populous so they would lose their will to continue this senseless war.

I could well imagine the terrible ordeal the men on the ground were facing. Their enemy were ground troops that had fought their way through Europe, had fought on the Russian front, some had seen action in the Spanish Civil War. The enemy of the

Allied troops had been tried and tested. Hour by hour, despite the difficult terrain and an entrenched enemy, these brave soldiers accomplished their objectives against the German Forces.

That night, as I lay on my bunk, I tried to relate what these ground troops were being exposed to. I wandered if they would get bogged down like my Father had been in France back in 1918 and be subjected to trench warfare and all that it entailed. I knew we would receive daily news of the progress being made, territory taken over, casualties, etc. but I knew they could not truly describe what it would be like fighting against that well trained and equipped German Wehrmacht.

I also knew that no one other than a member of a bomber crew would ever know what the true meaning of the word flak meant. Through out my descriptions of various missions I have made mention of this flak, sometimes as being intense and other times perhaps being just scattered or defined as light. All flak is consequential if it comes any where near your bomber.

The Germans developed several different flak or antiaircraft guns that were radar-directed. The most common was the 88mm Flak 41 gun that would be located at or near any target of consequence. They also had 105mm Flak 38 and a 128mm Flak 40 guns. To give some idea as to the size of shell they threw at us the 128mm shell weighed 87.3 pounds, had a muzzle velocity of 2,886ft. per second and could be fired at the rate of 10 rounds per minute reaching an altitude of 48,556 feet.

The standard radar used with AA guns surrounding German targets was the "Wurzburg D" which had a tracking range of 15 miles. With this kind of equipment our formation of bombers could be picked up at our Initial Point, usually eight or ten miles from target, and still be able to track us several minutes after the bomb run and drop.

Each target, depending on its importance to the war effort or probability to attack, had a dozen or more flak batteries surrounding it. Each flak battery consisted of six or eight guns, mostly 88mm and 105mm. Some cities had railroad flak batteries that were radar controlled that could be moved about.

Simple arithmetic would arrive at a figure of over a thousand shells being fired off per minutes as a formation approached a simple target, more at a priority target. Each shell, when it explodes, is blown into thousands of pieces of shrapnel of various sizes. A small piece of spinning metal could tear an arm off or cut a hydraulic line in the plane. A direct hit when the shell explodes on the plane meant it would immediately burst into a ball of flames without the possibility of any survivors.

Once a formation reached its I.P. and turned in toward the target, the Germans knew we would fly on a given course, at a given altitude, and at a given rate of speed.

Their radar gave them all of this information which was immediately programmed into the hundred or more antiaircraft guns. Then they would box in the approach to a target.

This cube of intense flak would be about 2000 feet wide, about 2000 feet high and about 20000 feet deep. Once we hit this solid black box of flak shells exploding it literally was like flying into a black cloud. It would now be dark enough you could see the colorful explosion just as the shell burst. Millions of pieces of flying metal are flying out in every direction.

Spent pieces of this shrapnel would hit the aluminum covering on each plane and sound like we were in a hail storm. If this metal hit us before being spent the aluminum skin would part and let the missile find some target within the plane. The concussion from the exploding shells created so much air disturbance each plane in the formation would be tossed about.

The reality of this situation was like walking out into a hail storm and hoping that not one single piece of ice would touch you. To add to the terror you could throw in the smell of these exploding shells and also the various noises they created. All of these words do not begin to create each moment you are required to spend in flak. It is a living hell I would not wish upon my worst enemy and yet it is a reality we in the Air Force experienced on nearly every combat mission we flew.

There was not a single recorded mission flown by the Eighth Air Force that that wall or box of flak deterred a formation from dropping its bombs on the chosen target. Such words as guts, bravery, heroism, audacity, daring, spirit, courage, or valor are still only words that may not be enough for an individual to weigh the odds and still accomplish the feat.

Each crewman who flew their missions week after week had to learn how to survive a mental and physical hell no earthly thing should be subjected to. Yet, this is part of the definition of war. Freedom is a legacy that all veterans gave the world and its price was tremendous. We must cherish Freedom so no other human will ever again be subjected to demoniac and diabolical anguish.

Though I cannot know this night what our brethren who landed on the beaches of Normandy or were dropped from the skies are required to face, I know they will do whatever is required of them. The Wehrmacht has grabbed a tiger by the tail. We are all pulling for the tiger.

CHAPTER 17

After D-Day, things worked themselves into a routine that seemed to keep me busy. Now, as a Squadron Lead Navigator, I flew more regularly, though usually with different lead crews. Much to my surprise, Squadron Headquarters either "screwed up" or they knew something I didn't.

A few days after we returned from London, Headquarters notifies several of us we could sign in for a four-day pass. This is something you do not argue about or question. In less than a week, I was going to go back to my favorite city in England, the City of London. This is one type of mistake I can learn to live with.

"Waddy", and I left on Thursday morning and stayed in this famous city until Sunday afternoon. This trip would be entirely different. On June 13, London was hit for the first time by V-1 rockets, weapons that Hitler had saved for the invasion of Europe. On the very first night we arrived, the Germans started sending their "Retaliation Weapon V-1" across the Channel to truly begin a desperate effort to alter the outcome of the war.

BUZZ BOMBS

This bomb flew at a relatively slow speed and looked like a miniature airplane. It was a flying bomb. This contraption made a buzzing sound, as it passed overhead. The British people affectionately called this a "Buzz Bomb." The Germans chose London as an early target because the accuracy of this missile is not very good. The city covers an area of over one hundred square miles, a sizable target.

The bomb would be aimed at the center of the city and then its gyro would keep it circling until it ran out of fuel. It then would glide to earth with its one-ton bomb. It did not have a specific target in mind nor did it seem to care what type of havoc it would create. Once it landed and exploded, it could destroy an entire city block.

The Germans named this new weapon "Vergeitung 1," thus the abbreviation of simply V-1. They had 38 launching sites along the European coast of the English Channel, most aimed at London. There were sites in Belgium, Netherlands, and France along the channel because of the limited range of this new missile.

These new bombs were launched from an inclined concrete ramp and aimed toward logical targets, mostly large cities. Once launched, it could fly across the Channel at approximately 400 mph and would reach an altitude of about 2000 feet. The majority of the V-1's were launched at night, though you could expect this visitor at any hour of the day.

By August of 1944, the German attacks were reaching their zenith. In one twenty-four hour period, during the height of the launchings, 316 V-1's were aimed toward southern England. Twenty-five of these bombs crashed at launch sites and 107 actually crossed the English coast. Of the total V-1's launched from Europe, 184 Rockets had been shot into to the Channel by Allied fighter planes. In July of this same year, 2441 people were killed while another 7101 were wounded. Approximately 50% of these launched "Buzz Bombs" actually reached the English mainland.

Our first night in London proved exciting because of these new and different merchants of death and destruction. The civilians were rightfully frightened and the eerie sound of the air raid sirens constantly in use did little to alleviate this feeling. This would be entirely different from the blitz they had lived through and experienced for years from the German bombers droning overhead. These brave people had been through so much in the last five years that this new situation created what I would call a controlled concern.

The interesting thing about the V-1s, making it different from typical dropped bombs, was that you could hear it circle over the city. It would go round and round in a several mile circle and you could follow the sound. When you noticed the sound of the engine quit and go silent, you knew, after a ten or twelve-second delay, you would hear the explosion.

If the sound disappeared while this 'Buzz Bomb" was overhead, you could feel relatively safe since it would explode many blocks away from your position. It depended on exactly where you last heard this menace, whether you would make a dash to the closest shelter. Shelter locations were something you would constantly notice as you wandered about the city.

This first night and the next three nights we spent in London we got several glimpses of the bomb between buildings. We could see the tracers from the guns being fired arcing their way at this moving target. It almost seemed like a Fourth of July fireworks' display, except you realized that this was a tool of war.

The thought occurred to me, "what sense does it make to shoot these bastards down when they will only blow up everything within their landing area?" The British gunners soon came upon this same rational and moved many of their guns to the coastline. If the incoming V-1s could be hit near the coast, most would explode in less populated areas.

The 95th Bomb Group, along with other units, had been bombing these ramps along the French and Belgium coasts for many weeks. We were given the code name of "No Ball Targets" for these missions. The British and American Intelligence were aware of what the Germans had developed and our effort was to delay and hinder their operation. Our bombing did little to slow them up since the launch ramps were made of concrete. Any damage would be repaired by slave labor within days, putting the ramp back into production.

When "Waddy" and I returned to our hotel room, in the early hours of Friday morning, we discovered that one of these damn "Buzz Bombs" had exploded in the neighborhood, blowing out all of the glass in our windows. The beds and floor were covered with this flying glass. We immediately could see another advantage to drinking. It was the main reason why we were not in our room this night.

MY MISSIONS CONTINUE

We arrived back at Horham just in time to find out I was scheduled for a mission the next morning. This mission, on June 15th, would be my 12th credited one and would take me to Misberg, Germany. Though it was a rough and typical mission, we lost no planes, though seven had been badly damaged and these planes would have wounded aboard.

I now had settled down in my job as a Lead Navigator and I personally resolved how I would face up to combat in general. Fighter attacks by the Luftwaffe and any flak over targets were taken as another annoyance I would rather do without, but something I did not let emotionally destroy me. I knew I was compelled to do anything my superior officers demanded of me and I also knew I could do nothing about what the Germans had in store for the time spent over the continent.

My thirteenth mission, one everyone wanted to get out of the way, would be to the north central part of Germany, a few miles south of the city of Wolfsburg. Our target was an aircraft factor in Fallersleben, Germany.

Today's mission would have our formation fly a good portion of our flight over the North Sea and then we would turn into Germany prior to reaching the peninsula that joins with Denmark. We would turn southeast and enter Germany near Cuxhaven. We would continue to fly southeast between the large cities of Hamburg and Bremen.

I always liked this approach to Europe because we always received an accurate landmark while over the North Sea and prior to entering the skies over the continent. There is a small island called Hellgeland. This island was occupied and controlled by German forces throughout the war. If our formation of bombers flew anywhere near this island, the German Antiaircraft gunners would send up a barrage of flak, thus pinpointing the exact location of this isolated spot off the coast of northern Germany.

On most missions, we found a blanket of clouds below our formation, concealing the North Sea and the coastline. The concentrated smoke from the exploding flak shells would accurately locate the position of the island and as a Navigator, we would make note of this. If the results determined it, we could make the necessary changes on our charts, giving us an accurate latitude and longitude before starting on the most dangerous part of our mission to the target.

On this particular long haul we got the usual attention by Luftwaffe pilots, though their number was small. We seldom got attacked while we were over the Channel or over the North Sea. No pilot cherished bailing out of a crippled airplane over the cold water. Unless you could get into a dingy within a few minutes, your chances of survival were minimal.

We were hit by several ME-110 who stayed out of range and lobbed cannon or rocket shells into our formation. This is the first time I noticed this type of German fighter plane. Usually we were attacked by FW190s and ME109s. The Messerschmitt Bf110 was a twin engine fighter-bomber that had an extended twin tail. Most were powered by two 1475 hp Daimler-Benz 601E engines. This plane, if caught by our fighters, usually came out second best.

We experienced the ever presence of flak at the target. I truly do not believe a target worthy of an air strike can be found in Germany where you would not get flak thrown up at the formation. It was a constant and it only varied in the degree we would receive. All planes returned from this mission, unfortunately several had extensive battle damage and several crewmen were wounded.

Though I am not unduly superstitious, I was happy to have completed my thirteenth combat mission. Normally I would have been over half way through my tour but the number of required missions is now thirty-five instead of the twenty-five missions originally told each of us when we arrived in England.

The next several days found me going to Berlin; Fruges, France; and to Leipzig, Germany. I was beginning to make some inroads into the thirty-five missions in my tour of duty. I appreciated being busy, but of course there was the strain of the actual missions. Perhaps tension or pressure might be more appropriate words.

This stress was not the fear of getting killed, but rather the struggle of trying to do the best I could and to meet the challenges of each mission. I believed very sincerely that if it was meant for me to successfully complete my tour and come home in one piece it depended entirely on fate. We each knew we had no control over fate.

The duties required of a Lead Navigator or, for that matter, a Lead Bombardier are many times more complex and exacting than having the same position on any of the other planes in the formation. However, each participant on a mission was exposed to the same hazards and dangers.

The jeopardy we each were confronted with had nothing to do with the job or position we happened to have been assigned on the plane we flew in nor the location in the formation in which we flew. Death or injury could seek you out regardless of where you worked. Your exact duty was dictated by your aptitudes, past experiences, and perhaps some opportunistic series of events. Fate is the key word that we each rode with on every mission.

GERMAN RADIO

Many evenings, when I didn't fly, it was nice to just lie on your bunk and listen to the radio. Most of the time we had on a program that originated in Germany and was meant to be purely propaganda. I never owned a radio but many of my bunkmates did. We listened to this station because they had the best and latest American tunes.

There were, of course, British and American radio stations broadcasting each day, but it was more interesting to listen to the garbage from Germany, with interludes of nice music. The people who introduced each song and pumped out the propaganda was a gal called "Axis Sally" and the fellow who supplemented her efforts was known as "Lord HaHa."

Their technique was to quietly and softly remind you that, while you were in England and risking your life fighting Germans, your girl friend was home with your best friend. They, supposedly, were sitting in a bar, opposite one another and their eyes made contact. Slowly their hands reached across the table and suddenly they touched. In a dreamy state of mind they suddenly were grasping each other's hands. Now, in a very sincere voice, good old Axis Sally would then announce that she would play the song "Hands Across the Table."

Next they might go through a similar scenario with your best gal and a strange handsome guy, sitting in the park on a remote bench. Yes, it would be a dark night, but the moon would just be exposing itself over a distant hill. Each, of course, was smoking cigarettes. Yep, now they would play the recording of "Two Cigarettes in The Dark."

I never did hear or learn of any of my fellow Air Force personnel go AWOL because of this type of propaganda. It did, however, accomplish a certain amount of nostalgia and homesickness to sometimes creep into you thoughts. Not that you mistrusted your love at home but rather you wished you could have been there with her.

The theme song played each time this interesting program went on the air was the song "Lili Marlene." It was originally written in France, never caught on there and then, the Germans discovered it. The German Forces accepted this song as their own and it became very popular.

It did not take them long to find out that this song had the same effect on the Americans. Though it could be classified as their theme song, it was played a great deal more often than that. The following are the sentimental, beautiful words:

LILI MARLENE

Underneath the lantern, by the barrack gate.
Darling I remember, the way you used to wait.
Twas there that you whispered - tenderly
That you loved me - You'd always be
My Lili of the lamplight,
My own Lili Marlene

Time would come for roll call, time for us to part.
Darling I'd carress you, and press you to my heart.
And there neath the bar of lantern light,
I hold you tight - We kiss good night,
My Lili of the lamplight,
My own Lili Marlene

Orders came for sailing, somewhere over there,
All confined to barracks, was more than I could bear.
I knew you were waiting - in the street
I heard your feet - but could not meet,
My Lili of the lamplight,
My own Lili Marlene

Resting in the village, just behind the line,
Even though we're parted, your lips so close to mine.
You wait where the lantern softly gleams
It sweetly seems – to haunt my dreams,
My Lili of the lamplight,
My own Lili Marlene

This sentimental song was made famous by the voices of Lale Anderson and Marlene Dietrich. It's a song of parting and a song of the heart. In my humble opinion, it transcends language and the war itself. The words to the very popular tune touched the feelings of most of the fellows that took the time to listen. I know it held special meaning to me each time I heard it. Its mystical enchantment was difficult to put into words, but it left each of us searching our memories.

Nearly every officer and enlisted man was separated from a girl friend, lover, wife or someone very dear. I know I never tired of hearing this nearly ever day or evening at some time or other. My own Lili Marlene, was my Norma, who was back in nurses training so far away in Rochester, Minnesota.

I can remember my Father telling me about World War I and some of the songs that meant so much to those young men who were fighting in France. Such songs as "It's A Long Way To Tipperary", "Smiles", "Over There", and dozens of others. Music can do so very much to sooth the soul, especially when your lonesome or have other nostalgic thoughts racing through your mind.

Another interesting fact, worth mentioning, was the knowledge that the Germans seemed to know supposedly secret facts about our troop movements. The night that I arrived, with perhaps sixty others, the German announcer welcomed us to the 95th Bomb Group and Lord Ha Ha informed us that they would be waiting to meet us in the air. I do not know how they could get this secretive information so quickly and so accurately. "Hell, half of the time I did not know the where, why or reason of many of my assignments or exactly what was going on in and around my base."

July 4th found me on a mission deep in southern France. We hit a German airfield near Gien. By the 8th of July I will have an additional three credited missions in and will have reached number twenty. These targets were in Fiefs France, Kolleda Germany, and to Bernay France. The mission to Kolleda is near Mersburg, just south of Leipzig. Flak and German fighter planes lived up to their reputation.

FLETCHER

On this last trip to Germany I flew with another lead crew that had a most interesting tail gunner aboard. His name was Fletcher and he was young enough that his voice continually changed pitch. This erratic vocal tool became even more humorous over the intercom. On all missions, I encourage everyone on the plane to report in to me if they see anything that intelligence might want to know about. I can then make note of it by writing any information on my chart and report this info later at interrogation.

On this trip, while we were flying over the Netherlands, Fletcher spotted some boats on one of the numerous rivers or canals in Holland. I thanked him and noted time and location for these boats. A minute later, Fletcher called back and with his voice rising and descending, along with the crackling of the sound system, told me he now thought they were barges instead of boats.

"No problem "Fletch", I'll make the change." I had just crossed out boats on my chart, and written barges when Sgt. Fletcher again contacted me. In a very crackly voice that ranged through several octaves, he said, "Sir, I think those barges all were boats." I did not inform Fletcher what was going through my mind, at this instant, but I again crossed out barges and rewrote boats. Perhaps twenty minutes later our tail gunner contacted me once again and stated he was now sure they were barges and not boats.

By now we are nearly a hundred miles away and deep in Germany. I had other things to do and I needed this final piece of information like a hole in the head. Without making any further changes on my chart, I thanked Fletcher.

I knew this was Fletcher's way of covering over the fears he had about this mission and the pending attack by fighters. Despite Fletcher's seriousness about whether they were boats or barges, we all could appreciate the humor in this incident and each could use the break in the tension we all experienced.

Periodically, Group Headquarters would determine that it was time to give each of its fliers a mandatory leave to go to what was referred to affectionately as "Flak Shack." Early in July it happened to be my turn to be sent to the west coast of England to a small community called South Port.

I was given train tickets, along with twelve or fourteen other individuals, who I did not know, but were all from other Squadrons of the 95th Bomb Group. Because of my position as a Lead Navigator I seemed to always be out of synch, especially when entire crews would be assigned duties. I no longer had a crew I could call my own and by flying with so many other lead crews I really did not get to know any of the fellows I flew with.

Our place of residence in South Port was a lovely old hotel the 8th Air Force had requisitioned for just this purpose. I understand they had procured several other places very similar for rest and relaxation. South Port was an ideal place since it was on the west coast of England, midway between Liverpool and Blackpool, on the Irish Sea. We would be over 200 miles, as the crow flies, from Horham and all the air activity. There was a serenity here that our minds and bodies would suck up.

The Air Force knew that it was an absolute necessity to relieve the tremendous tension and pressure that combat placed upon each individual. I am sure that each of us had a breaking point where our nerves would yell "uncle." Before this point would be reached, some R & R would be therapeutic.

I suppose most of us were not entirely cognizant of the significance or the real substance of this brief pause in our daily routines of either tangling butts with the enemy or preparing to do the same. I know I was beginning to start on yet another mission as though it was just another day at the office.

I shared a nice sized room with two other Officers from another Group. This room had a view of the Irish Sea, looking toward Ireland. I knew, as I walked on the beach, I was staring toward Rochester, Minnesota and the feeling was good. When I would be on missions or preparing for one, I did not have time to get lonesome, nor did I dream just for the sake of dreaming. Here at South Port it would be different. I did not have to force myself to let it all hang out or to let it go.

I was a part of a large group here at "Flak Shack" and yet, I suddenly felt alone. Now that I thought I was getting well into my tour of duty, I began to believe, for the first time I may actually come through this experience alive. My waking moments were almost entirely spent thinking, dreaming and contemplating. Soon, if the possibility turned into a reality, I would be going home and I would be getting married.

Instantly tons of questions popped into my head. "What do I know about being married?" "Would Norma appreciate some of the odd ball things I thought were essential to me and my life, like hunting and fishing, like participating in contact sports, or just staying close to nature in general?" "What did Norma and I really know about one another?" "Would I get chicken at the last minute?" "What were her inner feelings and what hobbies did she enjoy?" "What about my dumb sense of Humor?"

One day, while loafing on a small grassy knoll overlooking the water, two young girls stopped to talk. They were perhaps eighteen or nineteen and I thought rather pretty. At this moment, I felt like I was years older than my actual age. I also felt particularly lonely. They asked if I minded if they sat and talked with me. With a question like that my first reaction was they must be stupid.

After the usual conversation with questions of where I was stationed?, what were my duties?, how many missions had I flown?, etc., we got onto some more serious discussions. Despite their many questions, I just enjoyed their distinct British accent. One of the girls, whose name was Ilene Mc Cladrigan, seemed to be the least giddy or more serious of the two. My confabulation was directed primarily toward her.

I did not realize it at this moment, but I think I was subconsciously picking her mind in order to learn more about what made women tick. I tried to analyze her thoughts and reasoning. I watched her reaction to statements I made and wondered if this English lassie could possibly be emblematic of the girl I loved now going to school in Rochester, Minnesota.

I know she must have thought it very odd, my asking such questions as: Do you like athletics and all sorts of sports? What do you feel about nature? Have you ever gone hunting for grouse or pheasant? What is the most important trait for a man to possess? Do you ever drink beer or other alcohol? To my amazement, Ilene had an opinion for each of these off-the-wall questions. She didn't always say exactly what I wanted to hear, but I now believed I was more aware how girls thought or reasoned.

I enjoyed these few hours with the perfect strangers and I'm sure they did not know how important this time was for me. I began to realize that the months and years ahead of me would present new and exciting challenges. My life would be changed and I would become a team, not a carefree individual who lived by one whim or another.

I would now be able to share my inner thoughts with someone who would care. This would be entirely new for me because I grew up with parents that never got to know me at all. I knew my actions had to be reasonable and considerate of my partner. It now seemed to me the most important word or criteria for a marriage to be successful was the word respect. Each had to have respect for the other.

BACK TO BUSINESS

Between July 12 and July 21, I flew seven additional missions, most assignments with different crews and all in a Lead Navigator position. These trips over the Continent would bring my total mission count up to 27, with 8 big ones still to go. My 21st mission was to Munich Germany, often referred to as Munchen. This trip is always rough because our target is located deep in the south of Germany, near the Austrian border. This part of Germany is known as Bavaria.

The 95th Bomb Group was attacked by Luftwaffe pilots just south of Frankfurt and again in the same area upon returning from our target. We saw one fighter plane roll over as it trailed smoke and we witnessed the pilot eject and float earthward. I personally was happy to see that he did not go down with his plane.

On July 14, my 22nd mission, I went to St. Medard France. This mission turned out to be most interesting and worthy of further comment. It was a trip to assist the French Partisans, known as the Maquis. These were the "Freedom Fighters" who risked their lives each day behind enemy lines. They harassed the German troops constantly, disrupting, destroying, and killing at every opportunity. They were like a thorn under a saddle blanket.

The 95th Bomb Group was able to parachute supplies, like small arms and other weapons such as hand grenades, we included medical supplies and various food items, and even some clothing items such as caps, mittens, and jackets. An American Special Service man followed the numerous barrels to the plateau high in the mountains by parachuting out of one of our planes.

This entire mission would be flown at very low altitude to avoid German radar and we were well escorted by fighter support. It was interesting following the beautiful terrain while flying across France. You could see vineyards and large estates with their castles. Gradually we followed the slope of the mountains to reach our rendezvous place and the drop zone where all 35 planes emptied their bomb bays.

On July 16 our 95th Bomb Group, with yours truly, flew to Stuttgart Germany. This is another large German city that has many important military targets and is very well defended. When we fly into one of these industrial areas, the Germans never let us down or disappoint us.

I did not know it at this moment, but my last and 35th mission would again be to Stuttgart. All priority targets in Germany were heavily defended with both fighter planes and batteries of flak guns. Today the 95th would send only 17 B-17s over the target.

July 17 the 95th B.G. flew (my 24th mission) to Cheny France. This was a target deep in southern France and a trip equal in distance to our flight to Munich. Flak is becoming one of our greatest threats because of bigger and better antiaircraft guns and because of all of the practice these German flak batteries get.

German fighter protection for targets deep in France seems to be diminishing, primarily due to the heavy toll our "Little Friends" are taking on the German Pilots and because of our advancing Allied troops. I later learned that the lack of aviation fuel was now critical in Germany for both of their major fronts they were fighting on. A lot of sacrifice had been made to destroy or damage their oil and gas facilities.

My 25th, 26th, and 27th missions were all flown to targets in Germany over a four-day span. The missions to the "Father Land" are never "Milk Runs." On the 18th of July we went to Hemmingstedt on a tactical mission. We put forth a maximum effort this day with 36 B-17s in our formation.

Our target was near Frankfurt in the heart of the Axis' remaining power. Our group sustained a moderate amount of battle damage, although one of our planes limped home severely shot up. It was proclaimed SAL (Damaged beyond repair and would be used for salvage value.)

Two days later I went to Lutkendorf, Germany. Our target area was near Halle and our bombs were dumped on a factory that made components for German fighter planes. We didn't lose any planes from the devastating flak, but we experienced a great deal of battle damage. We all managed to limp home with the 28 planes we started out with, although there were several wounded in different bombers.

On the 21st I went on my 27th mission to Regensburg Germany in a formation of only nineteen B-17s. Today we would not be so lucky. The Lt. H.L. Laird crew flying in Plane Number 4297120 went down at about 1040 hours. The aircraft left the formation with one engine feathered and was still under control. They had time to jettison the bombs and then were forced to bail out near a position of 48 degrees 40 minutes North and 11 degrees 25 minutes East, just south of Nurnberg. This was their 17th credited mission.

Pilot Lt. Laird, Co-pilot Lt. F. Clark, Navigator Lt. W.O. Gifford, Bombardier Lt. O.B. Gates, radio operator Sgt. P.C. Tortora, and ball turret operator Sgt. W.E. Shuster landed and managed to evade capture until rescued by the Allies. However, the engineer and top turret operator Sgt. R.C. McMinn, waist gunners Sgts. E.W. Jones and C. Kalil, and tail gunner Sgt. F. Gegg were all captured by the Germans and ended up as prisoners of war. One German fighter plane was seen blowing up with no sign that the pilot escaped his flaming FW190.

My 22nd mission, on July 14, having been eluded to previously, was deep in southern France. We knew at briefing that we were about to take part in a new phase of the war. Instead of blowing the hell out of some German target, we were going to provide direct aid to one of our beleaguered Allies. Now, on August 1st, I would again have the chance to go on a similar mission to once more assist the Maquis who are harassing our mutual enemy.

The purpose of this mission, like the one to St. Medard, near Cadillac France, was to again parachute out supplies such as medicine, food, ammunition, small arms, etc. The twenty-six Flying Fortresses that took off from Horham this beautiful morning carried no bombs, but each plane was loaded with canisters filled with the needed supplies.

THE FRENCH MAQUIS

The recipients for our unusual cargo were another group of the French Maquis, located a considerable distance away. The Partisan fighters were also completely surrounded by German forces. They lived in the southeastern section of France just south of Geneva, Switzerland. Their sanctuary was in the foothills of the Alps.

They defended positions on high plateaus and used the hit and run methods of gorilla warfare. The cost in personnel for the German Armies to wipe these fighters out would have been high. The cost in equipment and lives against the Germans by these brave fighters were also high.

The two major differences, between this flight and other more conventional missions, were we would fly to our drop area at a relatively low altitude and the supplies would be dropped at specific coordinates. In fact, the drop zone would be identified by a coded signal that the French Maquis would use, namely the burning of three large haystacks in a clearing on the top of this large plateau.

The early part of the flight was over occupied territory of France, since our troops had taken a sizable piece of land in the past five weeks. Our low altitude provided us with a new view of the landscape, something that we seldom saw from nearly five miles high and usually with a great deal of cloud cover below our formations.

As we watched the French farms and fields pass below us, it was hard to believe this beautiful country was at war, had been occupied by the Germans, and was a threat to our intrusion. We noted several large French chateaus with their huge beautifully landscaped estates as our formation roared its way over the countryside. Because of our speed across the terrain, we could not see signs of the front line between the Allied fighters and the German armies.

As we approached the drop zone we noted the beautiful Mt, Blanc on the French-Swiss border. We could still see signs of snow at the summit of this famous landmark. The view from the nose of my B-17 would have made a beautiful scene for a Christmas card.

The French Partisans we were about to help were a group of brave men, women, and even children. They had been fighting the German war machine long after the country had been captured and had surrendered. These people continuously harassed the Germans. They blew up staff cars, they wrecked train engines, they tore up railroad tracks, they blew up bridges, they destroyed or appropriated supplies and equipment, they helped prisoners to escape, and generally were a thorn in the German side.

Their missions were a hit and run technique and they would plan their attacks with the element of surprise on their side. It was gorilla warfare at its best. They all knew to be caught meant torture prior to being killed. The German Gestapo placed a priority on capturing anyone connected to these brave French partisans.

All of the above knowledge just made our interest to be of help even more important. Today we would be able to see results of our efforts, instead of just dropping our bombs, not knowing exactly what the consequences. Our role in this war was a lot less personal than that of the G.I. slugging it out with the German Army. We did not have to smell death like our brothers who fought and died on the ground.

The 95th Bomb Group found the plateau the French Partisans had selected for the drop and as we circled we spotted the three burning haystacks. The supplies were dropped and pushed from each bomber as rapidly as possible to keep the pickup in a small area for logical reasons. There were different colored silk parachutes used on the various barrels we had dropped. I could see them on the ground or still floating through the air during the drop. I do not know the significance of these various colors. Perhaps it was coded to identify the contents of each container.

As we turned away for our return trip, we could see trucks being loaded and the colored chutes lying on the ground. These people would use everything, the metal canisters and barrels, the silk parachutes, and of course the nylon parachute ropes. I did not see it, but was told later, that an American Marine jumped to assist these people.

It was a great feeling to take part in this operation and to see first hand the results of our efforts. These people would play an important role in the liberation of many of the French cities, including Paris, as the Allied Forces advanced. Our special flight gave them an added moral boost.

This day, hundreds of Partisans left their hiding spot in the surrounding woods and rushed out into the opening and formed the Cross of Lorraine, by aligning their bodies. They had one long line of figures and they had two shorter ones, each would be perpendicular to this first line. I had tears running down my cheeks, as did others in these B-17s. What an unbelievable sight. It was like a living Christmas Seal Cross.

On the return to our base, we again flew at a low altitude, racing over the terrain at about 170 mph. The beautiful French countryside exposed many people actually waving at this unusual sight as we roared overhead. The boldness of this type of operation certainly indicated that victory would not be long in coming to this section of France.

It took our formation of twenty-six planes, nearly two and a half hours to come within sight of the Channel. On the outskirts of Dunkerque as we approached the English Channel one of the gunners in our plane spotted a German gun tower dead ahead. All guns that could be trained forward were aimed at this unexpected target. This tower appeared to be about 100 feet high with many Germans racing around the upper deck. It immediately was apparent that other planes recognized this as an unexpected target.

As thousands of 50 caliber shells converged on this rapidly approaching target, we could see dozens of Germans leaping over the railing, falling nearly 100 feet to the ground, or trying frantically to climb down the diagonal bracing. We have no way of knowing how many of the enemies were killed or injured this day, but the sight will always remain with me, both because of its proximity and because of the brutality of war. This would only be a note on my card, later to be passed on at interrogation.

If a mission can be looked upon with positive memories, this particular day will be remembered with a great deal of fondness, by me. Today, for a change, we would lose no planes or crewmen from the 95th Bomb Group. This was one of the few times our actions seemed more personal because we did not traverse over Europe at a five-mile altitude, but rather from a humanistic vantage point, while skimming over the countryside.

From a personal standpoint, some thirty seven years later, this 29th mission of mine on this trip to Lac d'Anncey, France, was the unexpected visit my wife Norma had in June of 1981. She had been touring France, Switzerland and Italy with some friends, when another European friend took her to a National Monument built at Plateau Des Glieres, Haute-Savoice, France. At the very spot where I had been on August 1, 1944, the French Government had constructed a monument to those brave Maquis. It was titled "Monument National A La Resistance."

Norma had the chance to talk to some of these Partisans who were recipients of our dropped canisters. My wife had remembered my stories I had relayed to her, about my two missions that entailed parachuting supplies to these magnificent fighters. Many of these Partisans had been killed or tortured, but all agreed that it was necessary to resist this German enemy. One woman, who owned an Inn near this monument, told Norma how the German Gestapo had tortured her for information by ripping out each of her fingernails. She had told them nothing.

They told her of another middle aged man who lived and was forced to work in the castle the Germans now occupied in the valley below. Each night, while all were asleep, he would leave by a secrete door and would then run up the mountain side to make contact with the Partisans.

He would keep the French Maquis informed of what he had learned about the German troops, any news of pending shipments, or anything that might prove of military value. Before daylight this brave man would return to the castle, getting little or no sleep. He did this each day until the Germans retreated or were captured by the advancing Allied forces.

All who talked to my wife expressed their appreciation for the efforts the Eighth Air Force had made, especially the 95th Bomb Group who visited their special plateau. There was still evidence of the use of the metal from the barrels that had been dropped from our bombers. It was flattened out and used as roof material on several small buildings still being used on the plateau of this mountain range. The silk from the numerous parachutes and the nylon rope was especially treasured.

This mission is only noted in the record books as FON (Field order number issued by 8th A.F.) Number 508, also as GSN (Group sortie number credited to 95th B.G.) Number 185, and then noted as simply Target No. 13. It shall always be remembered, by this participant, as something far greater than a series of impersonal numbers.

CHAPTER 18

The day before this memorable mission, I had flown to Munich, Germany for my 28th credited flight and my second to this important German city. The mission itself turned out to be different since our orders were changed while in flight from the briefing we had received hours before.

Instead of hitting a specific target and have all thirty-two B-17 bombers drop their load when the Lead Bombardier dropped his, we were told to toggle our bombs out, one at a time, as we flew across this huge city. We even spread out the formation as these lethal and destructive, streamlined missiles were released.

The purpose of this treatment of a German city was in retaliation for some of the intentional random destruction of cities like Coventry, London, etc. The City of Hamburg received similar treatment by other bombers. The Eighth Air Force hit Hamburg by day and the R.A.F. hit it by night. The fires were so great that over 80,000 people perished in a huge park in the center of town from the lack of oxygen.

War makes no sense as these two similar incidents realistically point out. This state of armed conflict throughout the world ultimately caused the death of over fifty million human lives during World War II. This had to be a stupid and insane way to resolve whatever problem there might be between nations. Unfortunately, most of those casualties would be civilian and innocent people.

MILK RUN, MY ASS

On August 2nd I was to fly my thirtieth combat mission scheduled to be a tactical target. It would be beyond the invasion front in France, a short distance beyond where the Allied troops had advanced, near the outskirts of Paris. I had flown fourteen missions during the past month and today I felt like I had been scheduled for a "Milk Run."

Since gaining Lead Navigator status, short missions were the exception since they wanted to use us for more distant targets. For this mission I would be flying with the Lt. Besser Crew, a group of fellows I had flown several other missions with.

I use the term "Milk Run" because several factors indicated this very probability. Namely, our target would be a bridge, just east of Paris; the weather was to be excellent for the entire flight; we would be flying mostly over territory already taken by the Allied Forces; we would have fighter escort the entire trip; and a visiting high-ranking officer was to fly in our Plane.

The fact that an officer with a lot of rank was scheduled to ride in our plane did not necessarily mean it would be an easy target. However, when one of the Brass without flying status comes along you rest a little easier. On occasions, newspaper correspondents and other dignitaries would be taken on short and somewhat less dangerous missions. There were times, however, when photographers or correspondents went on more hazardous trips.

I never did know who this individual was, nor did I learn exactly where he came from. I only was informed that he would be flying in our plane as an Observer. This was to be his first experience on a mission so that he could witness what the life of a typical bomber crew was like. Perhaps it was only to be chalked up simply as an experience. This certainly had to be tagged a "Milk Run." Was I wrong?

This morning, with the sun now rising, with the sleep well out of our eyes, with the Observer aboard, we were all in high spirits. A great deal of joking was going on between the gunners as we each assumed our stations in the B-17. We were a Squadron Lead Crew, so each of the members had a great deal of experience and were accustomed to getting ourselves into the routine of doing our respective jobs.

Today, however, we were not to fly in the Group Lead position of the 95th Bomb Group but would be a Squadron Lead in the number two position. This meant we would fly to the left, slightly below and a short-distance back of Lt. R.O. Baber and his crew. A third of our planes would be in echelon formation behind us.

The take-off, the rendezvous over Buncher 8, our trip to Slasher 7 after the Group had assembled, and the flight of our entire formation toward the south coast of England went without incident. Because the forecasted weather in our target area was to be excellent, a Pathfinder plane was not required in our formation and headed toward the 100th Bomb Group and a different target, deeper into France. At this point we still had 32 planes in our formation.

As we approached the coast south of London, Lt. Curley's plane, number 42-31600, aborted because of failure of his number 2 engine. He turned back to abandon the mission. Shortly thereafter, Lt. A.P. Salvia's plane, number 42-97232, also had a failure in his number 2 engine and he peeled off to return to base. We were now down to 30 Fortresses from the 95th.

Soon after we entered France and were passing over the front lines below, holy hell suddenly broke loose. Without any warning or expectancy, we ran into a large group of flak bursts. We were to learn later that a crack German Artillery unit facing the advancing Allies had raised their 88mm guns skyward and had ascertained our altitude and range accurately.

Instantly the beautiful blue sky turned both black and threatening. At the same moment we felt a direct hit on our plane we could see that Lt. Baber's lead ship started to blow-up as he veered below us. As plane number 42-102700 went by us, it was a ball of fire.

The red and yellow flames, against the black smoke of the flak, were beyond description. I could feel the intense heat on my face as I watched this plane break apart. Small pieces of their plane were flying in all directions from the huge ball of flames caused by the explosion. At this same moment our plane began to fall away from the formation. I heard someone yell over our intercom that three crew members managed to leave Lt. Baber's plane and get their chutes open.

These were busy seconds trying to determine our own damage while being concerned about the fate of our lead plane. We knew we were out of control and might be going down and yet, we were aware that the men in the Lt. Baber's plane were in greater danger. Seconds seemed like minutes.

My window on the right side of the fuselage had been shattered by exploding debris. We had taken a hit somewhere on our right wing and our number 3 engine instantly had smoke streaming out of it. It made it very difficult for me to see if men were leaving the other plane. The gunners in our plane were screaming frantically into their mikes what each of their eyes were forced to witness. There was more concern by members of our crew for the fate of the Baber' crew, than our own fate during these first moments.

The three men who were lucky enough to escape this flaming wreckage were: Sgt. D.W. Phillips, the ball turret gunner; Sgt. B. Lipkin, waist gunner; and Sgt. W.J. Collyer, tail gunner. All would be taken captive by the Germans and spend the remainder of the war as P.O.W.'s. Killed in Action were: Lt. R.O. Baber, pilot, Lt. J.W. Kalor, co-pilot, Lt. R.D.Dallas, navigator; Lt. F.T. Sohm, bombardier; Sgt. O.C. Warod, top turret gunner; Sgt. R.V. Hill, radio operator; and E.E. Bockman, observer.

The hit that took us out of formation was under our right wing and it immediately knocked out our number 3 and 4 engines. Some smoke could be seen as the plane fell out of formation in a steep twisting dive to the right. Lt. Charlie Besser worked frantically to get the plane under control. Within a few seconds he had stabilized our plane so that we were now in a slow glide away from the formation.

During all of this confusion, we had the problem of this special Observer, who had come along to see what a typical mission was like, much to his dismay. He had been standing behind the seats of the two pilots when the sudden burst of flak was thrown up at our formation. I'm sure he was as surprised as the rest of us. He immediately came down or fell down to the area between my navigation compartment and the escape hatch on the floor.

The Observer was a six-footer with a large build. I quickly noticed in the interim, he had snapped on his parachute onto his chest harness, making him look even larger. As he moved into the nose area, it was apparent that there was not room for the bombardier, myself, and, on this occasion, this large person.

The one and only time in my military career I told an Officer, who outranked me several times over, to haul his ass out of the nose and go to the waist position of the plane. The Observer turned and started to head for the back of this B-17. He immediately got himself hung up as he was crossing the cat-walk in the bomb bay. His parachute harness got hooked onto some of the shackles that protruded and it appeared he could not free himself. I had heard a loud yell and quickly ascertained the problem.

All of this was taking place as our plane was sliding downward in a controlled glide. The noise level was tremendous. Once Lt. Besser got the plane under control, his first job was to feather the propellers of both Number 3 and Number 4 engines. Number four responded instantly as the three blades turning into the wind and came to a stop. However, the propeller on Number 3 would not acknowledge his efforts and kept on windmilling.

I got on the intercom and asked the top turret gunner, our engineer, to help free the extra passenger who chose to accompany us. By the time he left his position, the radio operator already had the "Big Boy" freed, through the bomb bay and into the radio compartment. I'm sure he was happy to only feel all the commotion and not have to witness it. The compartment that houses the radio operator has no windows and could even be called cozy.

We had lost a fair amount of altitude before the plane was brought under control. Lt. Besser had the difficult task of bringing this falling B-17 into a stable flight attitude. With only two left engines as an unsymmetrical power source, it took skill and control to get this plane into level flight.

The first turn of our plane was in a northwest direction to get over friendly territory as quickly as possible. Pieces of the housing kept flying off the number 3 engine with a force that actually made them missiles. These small pieces cut through or dented the aluminum skin on the right side of my small navigation compartment in the nose of our plane.

My primary duty was to determine our exact position and give the pilot a heading that would take us home. The quickest method to determine our immediate position was with my British Gee Box. This instrument was normally useless over occupied Europe because the Germans would jam it. Today we were in luck, primarily because we happened to be close enough to England and the signals had adequate strength.

As I bent down to work the equipment, it was necessary for me to turn my back toward the wind-milling propeller and the chunks of metal being thrown against the plane. Just a week ago, in the Stars & Strips, our service newspaper, they showed a picture of the same situation. In this case the plane landed with a discharged propeller sticking in the nose of the plane. When this propeller flew off, it drove itself into the right side of the plane's nose. It had killed the Navigator.

This picture was on my mind as I knelt down and made calculations from my Gee Box. Sweat was running down my spine as I finally got the information I needed to give the pilot. I now could get away from this perilous spot and try navigating visually behind the two pilots. There was a high degree of calmness on our plane considering what had transpired these last few minutes.

I had given a heading that would take us over the friendly occupied part of France and would provide the least amount of Channel to cross. We were going to head for the tip of Cherbourg, the huge peninsula that the Allies captured in the first days after "D-Day." We were still concerned that we would have to abandon the plane and wanted to parachute over land if at all possible.

In the meantime Charlie decided to dump our four 1000# bombs to lighten the plane and to be able to maintain altitude. Normally, when we had targets in France, Belgium or the Netherlands, we did not unload our cargo except on a specific target. Over the territory of these former Allies the bombs would be brought back to our base if a target area had been obscured by clouds, we did not have an alternate target, or if we could not be sure that civilians would not be killed.

Today our safety required that these bombs leave the airplane because of the loss of our two engines. We were not sure how badly damaged our landing gear might be and we did not want to have these bombs aboard while landing with only two engines. Though we were now flying over that part of France already liberated, it was necessary to drop these four bombs.

The bombardier was instructed to pick a clear area and release the load. When the bomb bay doors were opened and he pressed the trigger to release, only two of the four bombs dropped. Instead of the plane reacting to the lighter load, we hardly noticed a change.

The bombardier discovered he was unable to toggle any of the two remaining bombs free of their shackles. Apparently the explosion damage had extended to the bomb bay. Our engineer left his post, and with a screw driver, working over the open bomb bay doors, was able to force each bomb loose. One, unfortunately, hit near a French farmyard.

About this time, with our bomb bay doors open and the erratic bombs dropping on liberated French soil, we attracted a small group of four P47's. It was common knowledge that the Germans had several of our captured B-17s and used them to fly near formations, etc. to send back information to their fighter planes or flak gunners. This day we were fortunate to be a lead plane with the ability to communicate with these four "Little Friends." Lt. Besser convinced them of our problem and they escorted us to the tip of Cherbourg.

We all were very apprehensive about the windmilling No. 3 prop, which seemed to get progressively worse with each minute of flight. Each knew that if this propeller flew off, it could go in any direction. Cautiously we made our way across southern England and back to Horham and our base.

The last of the remaining B-17s from our Group were landing, after their completed mission. We shot off flares and announced our critical problem to the control tower as we came in for a landing. All precautions were taken should we have to crash land.

The control tower informed us that indeed our right landing gear was down and appeared to be okay. The jar of the touch down made the number three prop fly-off onto the runway. We were again very lucky when the three bladed propeller fell to the right. Our tire on that side of the plane did not have to run over it, possibly causing a ground loop or a crash.

Everyone left this plane with extreme gratitude, a feeling I learned to appreciate on many of my previous missions. The right side of the plane was a mess from the exploding flak shell. Two engines torn up, extensive wing damage, some damage to the bomb bay, and the right nose section completely battered. This plane would be out of actions for many days.

As I left the plane, I had completely forgotten about our Observer passenger. When he exited from the rear door of the plane and had his feet on the pavement of our hardstand, he made it a point to shake each-crew member's hand. He apologized for any problems he might have caused and informed all who would listen he had just flown his first and last mission in a B-17. Unfortunately, this was also to be the last mission for Lt. Baber and his entire crew.

I learned later, another volunteer observer on a B-17 mission, was War Correspondent Andy Rooney. He also experienced a mission with many problems and one that he will long remember. I had the opportunity of reading, with great interest, his account of his unforgettable experience.

Several days after this "Milk Run", I was appraised that this mission had some additional irony connected with it for the Lt. Besser Crew. The Lt. Baber Crew, who flew Group Lead, was assigned Lt. Raymond D. Dallas as their Group Lead Navigator. Lt. Dallas normally flew as the Navigator for Lt. Besser. This had to be an additional tragic blow to Lt. Charlie Besser watching Lt. Baber's plane blow up and knowing his friend and usual Navigator was in this unfortunate B-17.

On this particular day I replaced Lt. Dallas and flew Squadron Lead with Charlie Besser in plane number 2102427. This knowledge now gave me some dissonant thoughts. Why does fate pluck one individual away and spare another? Why does one particular plane get destroyed while another escapes with only scars? Why does one burst of flak blow a plane and its crew out of the sky while another burst only signifies its location? Why does one fragment of this exploding shell seek out a single person instead of falling to earth? Why? Why?

Perhaps these are questions we should not dwell on or even try to find answers for. I personally can relate nine or ten of these specific quirks of fate whose final determination resulted in my experiencing a full life while one of my brother fliers made the extreme sacrifice. For this I shall be eternally grateful. I know gratitude does not answer the question postulated above, but . . . . maybe there is no answer.

MOVING ON

On August 4 I received two special surprises. First I attended a special ceremony where I was one of several who received The Distinguished Flying Cross medal and another oak leaf cluster for my Air Medal. Next I was informed that I would again be sent to South Port, England to the "Flak Shack" for another week of R & R. After having flown fourteen missions in the last month, the strain was beginning to tell. The smell of the salt breeze would be both refreshing and relaxing.

While at South Port, another Officer and I decide to visit Liverpool. The port city of Liverpool was approximately twenty miles south of our hotel. We had been warned to stay away from the dock area of this city because of the rowdy seamen from every section of the world. Many Americans had been rolled and roughed-up.

A single warning was enough for the two of us.

We spent the day and the evening visiting various sights in Liverpool and, of course, a pub. We asked an especially interesting Englishman, who owned this pub and was behind the bar, if he knew of a hotel or room we could rent for the night. The hour was getting late and we were not to sure of transportation back to South Port.

He suggested that we not stay in any hotel in this area but instead he would call his sister on the "telly" as he called it. This sister and her husband lived a short distance from the pub and he believed they would be happy to put us up for the night. He received an affirmative answer. Our congenial pub owner drew us a simple diagram indicating the easiest way to find the home of his sister and brother-in-law.

My friend and I walked down some cobblestone streets and found this modest home with no difficulty. We met the kind couple that volunteered to let two tired American airmen have a place to stay. Their home, though small, was neat and very tastefully decorated. We were served hot tea and some type of cookies or small cakes.

The four of us talked for nearly three hours when the woman of the house announced she would like to be excused. She stated she wanted to prepare an evening meal for the four of us. It was now nearly 10 PM or 2200 hours our time.

While she was in the kitchen, her husband apologized to my friend and me because he felt his wife may have appeared unusually upset. He went on to state: "This very day the two of them had just been informed that their son, who was a gunner on an R.A.F. British Lancaster bomber, was indeed dead." They had known he was missing in action when the bomber had been shot over the Netherlands. For many weeks they had lived with the anguish of not knowing for sure the destiny of this lost son.

Finally, the Germans had let the Red Cross in Sweden know their son's body was buried in a cemetery in Arnhem, Netherlands. Today, right before we had arrived, would be the moment they had dreaded hearing, that their missing son was indeed killed in this terrible war. The only consolation was the knowledge that they finally knew the fate of their youngest son.

This English couple, about the same age as my mother and father, had taken in two strangers and airmen about the age of their son. They had displayed no emotion that would indicate that they had just received this horrible news. The husband had nothing to apologize for. I could not imagine an American mother or father, for that matter, concealing their grief so completely. The fortitude of the British people had astounded me on many other occasions.

After a very restful leave, I returned to the 95th Bomb Group and was prepared to finish up my tour of duty. On August 24th, 25th, and 26th I flew missions to Ruhland, Germany; Muritz Lake near Politz, Germany; and to Brest, France. I almost preferred flying every day so I could get my tour in and hopefully head home to Norma and my family.

An interesting event took place after I had returned from my mission to Brest, France. I was told to hurry down to a specific area where a historic picture was about to be taken. They wanted all the base personnel that they could gather for this very special photograph. Two B-17s had been placed wing tip to wing tip, forming a wide-open wedge shape. In front of these two planes, one hundred and twelve bombs were laid out in a pattern to signify the number **200**.

The numeral **200** was about 100 feet long and each zero was about 30 feet in diameter. The bombs were laid next to one another with the fins all aligned on the extremity of each zero. It was accurately designed and laid out. It was very impressive. This picture would commemorate the fact that the 95th Bomb Group had just completed its 200th combat mission with our Group's return from Brest, France.

All available personnel from the 95th then were positioned to fill the wedge with standing, squatting, and sitting bodies. There was a large group positioned in front of the bomb display. Over two hundred men were located along each wing of these two B-17s. Many were on the exposed nose of the fuselages and the four inside engine nacelles. There appeared to be bodies everywhere.

The purpose for this very special photograph was the celebration of the 95th Bomb Group's **two-hundredths combat mission against Germany.** At this moment in time, no one who managed to get into this photograph had any idea that our Group would fly an additional one hundred and twenty-one more missions before this terrible war would be over. Today though, this was certainly an accomplishment worthy of a celebration.

I had just landed after my mission to Brest, France and completed the necessary debriefing. I was driven out to the site just in time to get into this monumental endeavor. Since I was small in stature, I was told to assume a position near the point where the two wing tips touched. Smaller personnel or individuals were encouraged to get placed at the extreme ends of the wings for logical reasons. I still was in my flight suit and I had on my Maywest-Lifevest. I was helped up into position and I just had time to say "cheese" when the picture was snapped.

That night, in a cleared, cleaned up, and decorated hanger a special celebration was held for a slightly weary outfit who had just flown their 200th mission. The orchestra just happened to be Glen Miller and his famous band. There would be free beer, dancing, and plenty of fancy foods to eat.

The orchestra was on a raised platform with a huge 48 star American Flag as a backdrop. On either side of this 60-foot wide flag were placed a smaller American flag and a British Union Jack hung. Below each of these were two large signs with a large 200 printed on them. One had the insignia of the Eighth Air Force and the other the insignia of the 95th Bomb Group.

One only had to be of this generation to realize the thrill of being able to see and hear perhaps the greatest group of musicians during the Big Band Era. Captain Glen Miller and every member of his band were in a Special Services Group. They devoted their every effort to entertain the many different service groups serving in Europe.

I hung around as long as I could before fatigue finally caught up to me. My three missions in a row evidently had sapped my energy. I had heard the Glen Miller Band once while I attended the University of Wisconsin. Tonight though, I just needed sleep more than the sweet sounds of all those saxophones.

Unfortunately, soon after this engagement at Horham for the 95th Bomb Group celebration, Captain Glen Miller was lost in the English Channel on a flight to France. No one is certain exactly how this happened. There were reports the plane he was flying in had been shot down by a German fighter plane and there were reports that his plane met its end simply from mechanical problems.

The unfortunate loss of Glen Miller meant the world had lost perhaps the greatest big band leader who ever lived. His arrangements of all of the tunes of the day were never really challenged. Fortunately the German radio thought enough about Glen Millers talents because they offered us so many of his arrangements on their propaganda broadcasts.

On September 3rd I got credited with my 34th mission to Lanveoc, France. I have only one big one to go. The last mission usually carries the additional worry or strain. Everyone would hate to "buy the farm" so near the end of your tour of duty. Just as some crew met with misfortune on their first mission, there were occasions when crews went down on the very last mission required of them. We all were aware of these stories and we did not want to be the individual others would talk about. Superstition is one insidious thing.

On my return from my 34th mission, Captain Lyle Dallman, our Squadron Navigator, sent me a notice I was to report to him immediately. When I went into his office I was greeted with: "you only have a single mission to take part in and you will be shipping out. I hate to lose you. Should you sign up for another tour of duty in the 336th Squadron I could immediately pin your Captain's bars on. You would be able to return home with the higher rank. This is entirely up to you. Should you decide otherwise, we will understand." I asked permission to sleep on this suggestion and I would return an answer tomorrow.

This night, before my final mission, I had zillions of thoughts racing through my head. It now looked as though I might make it through this war, and yet, I knew each moment on a lengthy mission could be your last. I tried to project my thoughts into the future and imagine what life may have in store for me.

I knew should I be lucky to chalk up my 35th mission, my war would go on in some other phase. My country will still need my services elsewhere. I also knew that the rank of Captain would mean more pay and prestige.

I would be returning home to get married after my 35th mission and I was sure I could use the additional income to begin our new life together. Then I remembered my father's advice, "Whatever you do, DO NOT VOLUNTEER." The next morning, when I saw Captain Lyle Dallman, I only said "Thanks, but no thanks. If I could return after my 35th mission, I decided not to be mad at anyone. From then on I would become a lover, not a fighter.

STUTTGART, GERMANY

Two days later I flew my second mission to Stuttgart, Germany, returned safely, and had now completed my obligation of thirty-five credited combat missions. I would be returning home, with my body in tack and with all of my marbles. A single German fighter plane had been shot down by one of the 95th B.G. gunners this day and I knew his war was also over.

All that I have written was not intended as a personal manifest. These were the recollections and remembrances of a very young lad who was asked by his country to face harsh and brutal dangers and who then survived his baptism under fire. Many of my Brother Warriors would not be so fortunate and I grieve for them.

This last mission to Stuttgart would prove to have an added twist that I discovered many years later. In 1951, quite by accident, I met and became friends with a former German Fighter Pilot. We have been corresponding for over fifty years now and each has visited the other on three different occasions. Our friendship, which many have told me to be bizarre, has proven to be the most rewarding and interesting of any friendship I have ever had.

This friend's name is Siegfried Bethke, and his home before and after the war was Stuttgart, Germany. On one of his visits to my home, I showed him my list of thirty-five missions. He noted my two trips to his home city. When he read the date,

September 5, 1944, he exclaimed in his thick German accent, "Auk, mine Got, that is the day my house caught on fire." It seems his father-in-law had just finished impregnating all of the wooden beams and structural members with a chemical to keep the wood from burning. This probably saved the house from being totally destroyed.

My friend Siegfried Bethke had been in the war since 1939 as a pilot, flying primarily Messerschmitt ME-109s and Focke-Wolff FW-190s. Though we talked of the war in general terms, I personally never tried to pick his brains, to get him to talk about things that would bother him. Siegfried did tell me he had been shot down three times. Twice it was over Germany and, after time spent in a hospital, he was able to return to his unit. Much of his time spent during the war was in the Brest area of France. He was in the Von Richtofen Squadron.

Late in the war, he was shot down for the third time by a P-51 Mustang. He had been caught flying a small light plane. The P-51 made several passes, destroying the plane and wounding Siegfried. The American forces captured him and had sent him to a hospital. Upon his recovery he was then imprisoned, and they finally released him at the termination of the war.

Siegfried, who was a Professor at the University of Hollenheim, later worked for UNESCO of the United Nations. He was in charge of the Food Program for nineteen different African Nations for over 10 years. He operated primarily out of Ethiopia and Rome, Italy. He finally resigned from this important job, because of all of the mismanagement and corruption of the leadership of most of these nineteen nations.

On a visit to Germany, in 1989, Siegfried, Norma and I climbed a mountain of rubble that was cleared from the city of Stuttgart. Almost 90% of the large city had laid in ruin at the termination of the war. This mountain of bricks, twisted steel, and crumpled concrete, was covered with black dirt, trees were planted, and a monument placed on top of this lasting reminder of the futility of war.

The monument consisted of identifiable column caps, stone arches, broken sculpture, sections of once fluted columns, and thousands of pieces of a once proud city. A spiral road and walkway wound its way to the top, trees had grown on either side of this road that were now ten inches in diameter. On top of this wooded hill there was a huge cross and benches provided a solemn atmosphere to contemplate the stupidity of war.

One day my dear friend told me something, I shall always remember. In a conversation with him I inadvertently mentioned how rough it must have been, to be a German fighter pilot, those six years during the war. He told me he marveled at the bravery of the American bomber crews who flew through fighter attacks and intense flak. He noted we would not change course to the target, regardless of losses and danger.

Note:(There is no record of any bomber of the Eighth Air Force ever failing to drop their load on an enemy target because of German fighter planes or the unbelievable amount of flak they could throw into our formations.)

Siegfried stated: "we as German fighter pilots, if we experienced a situation that was more than what we wanted to contend with, we would lift up a wing and get the hell out of the problem." I had never thought about that. My experience of fighting my war, in the skies, left me with no bitterness toward the German pilots. There was a great deal of pride in what we were doing, but also an equal amount of respect for what our enemy did. It was called "es'prit de corps'".

Over the ensuing years I have revisited Europe on many occasions. I have met and become friends with several other Luftwaffe Pilots, exchanging stories and memories about a war none of us can ever forget. Some of these pilots had flown the ME 262, the very first turbojet-powered fighter plane.

On two occasions my Group had been attacked by a single jet that sped through our formation without a single shot being fired. I've had the fortune of spending time with another former Luftwaffe pilot who had flown a ME 163 Komet, the first rocket powered plane. The one thing we all had in common was the fact that we each were asked by our country to fight against an enemy.

CHAPTER 19

These past dozen hours before I would leave England, my tour of combat, and the many friends I had made, I began to have new and different thoughts racing through my mind. I found it necessary to extricate some of these feelings and emotions so better sense could be made of the myriad of ideas now tantalizing my brain cells.

I discovered I finally was beginning to appreciate the complexity of what we young rambunctious fliers were really doing. We had been brought together from every corner of the United States, we came from nearly every nationality or ethnic group, we had varying degrees of education or cultural backgrounds, yet they were somehow able to mold us into a well trained fighting unit.

We found that we were able to confront the *Luftwaffe*, the German Air Force, despite the fact that they had a dozen years head start. During all these years they were able to mold and develop an efficient air force. The German Fighter Pilots we confronted and those thousands of manned Anti-aircraft Guns were indeed a formidable opponent.

OUR ADVERSARY

Though military aviation was forbidden in Germany, in accordance with the Treaty of Versailles signed in 1919, Germany, because of their interest in aviation in general, managed to keep ahead of the rest of the world by devious methods and self-serving interests. As far back as 1926, the *Deutsche Lufthansa* was not only training civil airline pilots, it also formed a covert group of military aviators.

In January of 1933 Adolph Hitler appointed Hermann Goering as *Richskommissor* for the future *Luftwaffe*. They had already established many secret training fields, with combat planes, in several areas of Russia. This was not discovered until after WWII. During the Spanish Civil War, German "volunteers" arrived in Spain. In short order they became instant trained fighter and bomber pilots. These *Jagdfliegers* developed their combat techniques and tactics that would prepare them for the upcoming war in Europe.

In 1939 the *Luftwaffe* gave more than adequate support to the German Army, which had invaded Poland on September 1st. By the time the Americans entered the air war, the German *Luftwaffe* had over ten years to perfect their talents and the quality of their aircraft. This then was to be our opponent.

Once we entered the war, immediately after Pearl Harbor, we had little time to develop a true Air Force. Our military planes had to be upgraded and personnel trained. It was necessary to take raw recruits and train them to develop the required skills necessary to compete with our foe.

As I look back tonight on these early years, I believe the greatest prerequisite for a candidate in the U.S. Air Force was how fast you could learn or be taught, not how smart you might have been or how much you already knew about certain things. Probably over 98% of our flight crews were made up of personnel who had never been in an air plane in their life before enlisting.

Tonight, as I tried to handle the myriad of thoughts racing through my head, I began to realize an interesting fact. Probably over ninety percent of the young men who enlisted in the Air Force imagined themselves as a pilot. This would not be the case however.

By designed and sometimes erroneous screening, a majority of the candidates were weeded out of flying status and assigned to the many other essential branches of service in the Air Corp. The multitude of branches would have had few volunteers for the specialized job requirements, all essential to the entire operation. I was beginning to appreciate the true complexity of the entire problem.

While lying in my sack, for some reason or other, it became necessary to probe and search past thoughts and impressions. Since I now had completed my thirty-five combat missions, my thoughts took on a different temperament. In reality though, I never dwelled too long or hard on pending missions nor did I permit myself the license to let fear dominate my thinking.

I knew I was one of the lucky ones to have survived the ordeal of combat and it was time to appreciate just exactly what this all means. I wanted to put everything into its proper perspective. I now started analyzing the ten member crews on the B-17 Flying Fortress. I was sure there were many similarities between this plane I flew in and the B-24 Liberator Bomber, a newer creation.

It was not important to dwell on each individual's specific training or primary duty, but rather on what each of them had to endure during a mission. With a certain amount of redundancy, I now tried to analyze what each crewman experienced.

THE FLIGHT CREW

The Bombardier sat in the nose of this Flying Fortress, hunched over his Norden Bomb Sight. Most Bombardiers seldom used the full capabilities of this secret and protected piece of equipment, since they dropped their plane's bombs in synchronization with the Lead Bombardier. This crewmember sat on a stool that exposed him to more Plexiglas than any other member. This very same exposure also permitted him to see and witness more of the horrors that the unfriendly skies over Germany would sometimes present. One of his primary duties was to man the twin 50 calibre machine guns mounted below his position.

The design of the Plexiglas nose was to give the Lead Bombardier excellent vision to detect the target, track the target, to make adjustments in the formations course, and to release the bomb load at the exact moment. All of this exposure for the typical Bombardier or Togglier did little to shelter them from the mayhem going on in the skies around them. They could observe more flak than any other member in the plane. These bursting shells could be seen above, below, to either side and especially in front of his position.

On bomb runs, the view of flak and all that it entailed gave this member the best view. One only had to experience this on a single mission to know that having the best seat in the house was not an asset. This same member had to be constantly vigilant in order to spot enemy planes attacking from the front. His two guns, and those of the top turret gunner, were the key to protect this B-17 from a frontal attack, the choice of most *Luftwaffe* pilots.

Because most Bombardiers were never called upon to take on a Lead role, many were ultimately replaced with a trained gunner who would also assume the title of a Togglier. It would then be his responsibility to release his planes bombs at the same instant the Lead Plane dropped theirs.

Next to the Bombardier, in the nose of the plane, the Navigator had his "office." The Navigator could look over the Bombardier's shoulder and get a fairly good view of the black sky and the bursting of flak. During these moments, this Navigator had required chores that demanded his attention.

He had to check instrument readings and record this information on his charts. He noted the exact moment the bombs were dropped, and when the formation changed direction to escape flak. He had to note if any planes had been damaged, if any left the formation, if any planes exploded, if crew members left the plane, how many parachutes were spotted, and the coordinates of where any of the above took place.

Perhaps the most challenging thing the Navigator had to contend with was an environment not conducive to thinking and reasoning, something that was essential in order to do a good job. The plane was constantly jostled about; the noise level excessive; the temperature in the minus zero range; difficulty holding pencils, computers and working dials with gloves on or exposed cold bare fingers; and to move about with all of the umbilical chords attached to his person.

This was his office during rush hours. None of the above was conducive to making for an ideal workplace where thinking, calculating, decision-making, or just plain accuracy would be required. The position of a Lead Navigator required considerably more challenges.

If you were in the Lead plane of your Group you had dozens of critical rendezvous points to consider where time and location of the formation would be most important. It was essential to be at a certain point on your pre determined route so our fighter planes could locate us. You had to hit the I.P. (Initial Point) at the right time, at the right altitude, and be heading in the right direction into the target. You had to avoid flying over major cities where flak could be expected. You had to detect changing wind conditions, like direction and velocity, because this would affect all of the above.

This Navigator had two separate 50 calibre machine guns suspended from the ceiling by cables. They protruded through two small windows on either side of the nose of the plane, called cheeks. In my humble opinion, both of these guns should have been eliminated entirely for several valid reasons. As an avid hunter of geese, ducks, quail, pheasants, grouse and rabbits, I knew a successful hunter had to track the game with his rifle or gun; then, depending on the target's speed, lead this target; and at the right moment, pull the trigger to achieve any degree of attainment.

This was completely impossible with either of these two deadly weapons mounted in the nose of the B-17. The left gun had approximately a 15-degree swing with extremely poor vision. The right gun was only slightly better. I would be most skeptical if any Navigator was credited with a fighter kill using either of his guns, for all the mentioned reasons. To have any chance of success, an enemy fighter plane would have to be on an extended angle of attack almost aimed down the barrel of either of these guns.

The German *Luftwaffe* pilots preferred frontal attacks whenever possible because of the rate of closure. A *Focke-Wulf* FW-190A-8 or a *Messerschmitt* Bf –109G-6 could fly at well over 375 miles per hour. The B-17G flew between 150 and 180 miles per hour. The rate of closure during an attack from the front would be in excess of 535 miles per hour. The German pilot would be screaming past a formation of bombers at approximately 785 feet per second. It is obvious that a gunner had to have some time to move his sights a considerable distance in order to have a predictable lead on this German merchant of death and target.

The Government and the Air Force could have saved many millions of dollars by eliminating the 24,000 50 caliber machine guns installed in the 12,000 B-17 F's and G's Models. It would have lightened the dead load of the bomber by several hundred pounds, it would have increased the air speed because of this lesser weight and the lesser air resistance, and it would have eliminated a real hazard caused by these two guns constantly swinging on their cables. Oh well, I had been hired to be a Navigator, not an efficiency expert.

The two pilots above the Navigator position had their own unique problems confronting the German *Luftwaffe* and the accuracy of the Anti-Aircraft Batteries five miles below. Their primary job was to keep a mulish plane in formation while all of this was going on. They had almost as good a view as the Bombardier, except they had no guns to help relieve some of the ever-present tension. There were times that I'm sure they wished they could use their pistol to have the feeling that they were protecting themselves.

It was also important for these pilots to present some semblance of calm and decorum during all of this mayhem taking place before their eyes. The noise within the metal shell of this plane they had learned to master could be unbelievable at times. To the constant roar of the four powerful engines would be the screams and shouts of gunners on the intercom, giving blow-by- blow descriptions of where fighter planes were attacking. There would be moments when eight or ten 50-calibre machine guns simultaneously would make their presence known.

There were times, I imagine, these pilots even were able to hear their own hearts beat. Air turbulence during formation flying was a constant challenge. This became most critical while flying through flak since the concussion caused by exploding shells and the release of several tons of bombs threw each plane in all directions.

Directly behind the two pilots' seats was located the crew Engineer and Top Turret Gunner. His primary function during a typical mission was to protect the plane and the formation from *Luftwaffe* fighters attacking from any direction above and before him. He also had the skills required to handle minor problems with the plane's operation during flight.

Many times he would be called upon, while in flight, to leave his post and to apply these talents. He would also report major problems to the ground crew upon return to Base. He would help preflight the plane before the mission as well take on the role of being a leader for the remainder of the plane's gunners.

The Radio Operator was placed behind the bomb bay in a small, but adequate, isolated compartment. Above his work area was a small Plexiglas window that faced skyward. At one time it also held a worthless 50-calibre machine gun. It was finally removed early in 1944. This small opening to the heavens could only give the Radio Operator a glimpse or hint of the melee that was taking place around the plane. I never was sure whether it was better to be oblivious to the mayhem taking place all around you by not having visual contact or to have a ring side seat for the spectacle you knew you could live without.

He had the knowledge of knowing the formation was under attack by enemy fighters or that we were about to penetrate a wall of flak without visually being apart of it. It does not take much imagination to comprehend the emotions and feelings he experienced at these moments. With hell raging all around him he could only guess the degree of this mayhem.

Next in line would be the Ball Turret Gunner. He had several unique problems that gave him one of the roughest jobs on the plane. It was mandatory that he be small in stature because he would be compelled to ride in the movable ball turret with his two 50-calibre machine guns. This sphere had been designed to be small, because of its location and the fact that approximately half of it was suspended in the slipstream below the plane. If it had been any larger, it would touch the ground once the plane landed.

On a typical mission, this young man would be compelled to spend in an excess of six hours cramped in a fetal position within this rotating turret. It would be usually minus 40 degrees below zero temperature with an ample supply of fresh air finding every opening and crack in this unique environment.

If this gutsy little guy were smart, he would know that he could not drink any liquids for many hours prior to a flight, for obvious reasons. He did not have room to wear his parachute, something he would have to come out and engage with should it be necessary.

In my honest opinion, it took more guts and fortitude to be a Ball Turret Operator than any other position on the B-17 Flying Fortress. These brave little guys will have my undying gratitude and admiration.

The two Waist Gunners each had a single 50-calibre machine gun, one mounted on the right rear of the fuselage and one directly opposite on the left side. They spent hours standing behind their guns, looking out through their small windows for any signs of the *Luftwaffe*.

The first sign may be just a speck in the sky, but often times it would be a plane swooping down on the formation from a direction impossible to ascertain an attack. With the sun at their backs, the fighter could appear instantly in a lethal position.

At other times we would hear one of the gunners announce the sighting of some of our little Friends. With this proclamation, we would know that there might be some P-47 Thunderbolts; P-38 Lightenings; or some P-51 Mustangs protecting our formation from attack by the *Luftwaffe*. On some rare occasions, we had the feeling of security, when someone would spot some British Spitfires or Hurricans escorting our Group for several minutes.

The Waist Gunner's constant enemy was the extreme cold. With negative temperatures in the minus 40 to 50 degree range, frost bitten fingers and toes was a constant worry. Many times to get a jammed gun to work, it was necessary to remove their gloves, exposing the flesh to frozen metal. Their constant vigilance required them to stand at their window and gun for long hours, constantly being jostled about by the unpredictable movement of the plane.

The actual position for these two waist gunners was slightly staggered so they would keep out of each other's back pocket. Despite the fact that these gunners were only inches apart, once we put on our oxygen masks, they could only communicate with one another when it was information the entire crew had privy to. The Intercom was not to be used for casual communication.

The Tail Gunner was usually of smaller stature, for reasons similar to the Ball Turret Gunner. He was required to fly backwards while manning his twin 50-calibre machine guns in very tight quarters. The primary duty of these men was to protect their plane and the formation from attacks from the rear. The rate of closure from this approach would be about one third that of frontal attacks so was not usually preferred by the *Luftwaffe*.

If this gunner heard about fighters approaching from the front, he knew that they would streak away from his position at unbelievable speeds, giving him little time to react. The Tail Gunner would kneel with his butt pressed against a pad for hours on end. His position is not only a lonely and cold part of the plane to be so isolated, it also is a difficult place to exit the plane in any emergency.

Everyone on this B-17 Flying Fortress had some common things to contend with, besides those just mentioned. Each airman was restricted to a limited area in the plane because he was connected by umbilical chords or lines, namely the following: There was a double wire to the ear phones built into the helmet worn during the mission; there was a double wire to the throat mike which was worn around the neck with two sensors on each side of the larynx; a wire that provided heat to the flight suit, slippers and sometimes gloves; and finally the heavy one inch in diameter flexible tubing that provided the life sustaining oxygen to the mask worn at altitudes exceeding 10,000 feet. All of these connections restricted the movement of the airman, especially the two Waist Gunners and the Navigator.

If the oxygen line got accidentally unplugged or severed, the airman may not even be aware of it and could die within minutes. All of the lines, except the one connected to the heated suit, could become disengaged without the airman's knowledge. Constant checks would be made to ascertain if all could hear, speak, and were conscience.

Then there was the problem of normal body functions. If any crewman had to urinate, he would have to disengage himself from all four umbilical connections, hook himself up to a portable oxygen bottle, and then make a trip to the bomb bay, where a funnel was connected to a hose, which exited the plane. This was the coldest and noisiest place in the plane since the bomb bay doors permitted cold icy air to circulate throughout this compartment.

The most challenging part of this operation was progressing through several layers of clothing and finding the proper part of the anatomy to make this operation a success. Urine would instantly freeze should the airman miss the funnel. One can easily see why this effort was not looked forward to and was avoided if at all possible.

The other normal body function created a situation that is even difficult to imagine. Relieving of one's bowels moved the unfortunate airman to a new level. This task had to be accomplished by those men who consistently could not regulate this function.

To have a "BM" required this airman to resort to a portable bottle of oxygen, remove his parachute harness and May West life preserver, pull down his flight suit, drop his uniform pants, get through his winter underwear, and expose his *derriere* to sub zero temperatures. Only after this had been accomplished could he position his anatomy over an open, large paper sack.

Sometimes the planes movements only added to the difficulty. When he finally regained his composure, the airman would take the paper sack and place it on the bomb bay metal doors. This parcel would precede the dropped bombs earmarked for some German target. Because of the extreme temperatures, this unique package took on the characteristics of an unusual frozen missile.

Such things as a slight cold, a runny nose, or a simple cough became a major problem for one wearing an oxygen mask. Some individuals who were prone to develop excessive gas in their intestines and found it impossible to relieve themselves properly discovered a serious problem in the rarified air at 28,000 feet altitude.

To avoid an extremely irritated face from wearing the mask for many continuous hours, an airman with a heavy beard growth was required to shave shortly before each mission. Many crewmen were young enough that they had still to experience the growth of facial hair.

All of the previous disclosures gave ample reason why just being present in this plane during a combat mission was hell. Then, when you add the additional ingredient of intervention by enemy fighter planes and the ever-present German flak over all target areas, you were aware of an atmosphere and working environment that bordered almost on insanity.

Hundreds of thousands of Eighth Air Force fliers did this very thing each day because they were aware of the price that had to be paid to preserve freedom. Obviously, it would be difficult to convince combat crews that flying was glamorous. This illusion would have to be reserved for ground-gripping admirers,

Each man on the crew had a specific duty or function to perform. We had been brought together from every corner of our great country, from every type of background, and each with his own idiosyncrasies. Now we were a team that would man a complex piece of equipment, fly together as a complete unit, and challenge an enemy that was truly formidable and imposing.

THE GROUND CREW

One of the unsung group of men who kept our planes in the air, were the ground crew. They deserve all of the recognition one can muster for the task they were charged with. Many of these men had prior aspirations of flying a plane, but instead, were arbitrarily assigned a job or duty that was equally foreign or unknown to them.

Once a Fortress returned from a mission, the ground crew would be at the hard stand, the place where this plane would be parked, to greet and welcome the crew home. As tired as we may have felt, we could always read the faces of these men, usually older than most of the various flight crewmembers.

You could see and feel the sincerity of men who had been sweating our arrival out for hours. These faces expressed a multitude of reactions, mostly one of genuine gratitude that we returned safely. It would be kicked up a notch when it was announced that we had no deaths or wounded aboard.

Once the crew had been trucked off to Interrogation, these men immediately swarmed all over the plane and began applying each of their specialties they possessed. The pilots, the crew chief or any member of the flight crew had already made mention any irregularities they may have noticed.

A normal mission, without destructive damage by enemy action, could have produced symptoms of impending problems with any of the four 1200 hp engines. There could have been problems with the controls of the plane, an oxygen leak, a low tire, an oil leak, etc.

Battle damage from *Luftwaffe* fighter planes and the ever-present flak would keep this team of specialists working throughout the night, with the hope they could have their particular baby ready for tomorrows mission. There would be a point of no return when they had to inform the powers to be that more time would be required. Each member of this important group had both affection for the B-17 they were responsible for and they took pride in getting this plane back in service, capable of going once again to the "Fatherland."

Some days a complete engine may have to be replaced. This would require removal of the damaged engine and reinstalling a new or refurbished one. This entailed the complex job of supporting it; aligning it; and finally connecting the myriad of oil, gas, electrical, and bolt connections.

Most nights, while we lay in our bunks, we could hear these men starting up these engines, revving them up, listening for sounds that would mean nothing to me, making final adjustments, and finally, being sure it could carry its share of the load.

They may have to replace windows that had been shattered, or perhaps some control mechanism that could be damaged. Someone would clean out the plane from spent 50 calibre-cartridges or any other debris lying around. They had to check all of the moveable turrets to see that they functioned properly.

They reloaded each of the gun positions so that the proper amount of ammunition would be available to answer the call. They made sure each of the oxygen stations were working and that a fresh supply of this precious life saving gas was aboard.

They made sure that the plane was properly refueled with 100-octane fuel, enough for the impending mission, and that all required oil reserves were filled. Each day they would be notified, at the last moment, the type and number of bombs that had to be procured and then loaded on to the shackles in the bomb bay.

These bombs could vary in size from 100# incendiaries to 200#, 500#, or perhaps 1000#. Depending on the type of target selected for the next mission, these bombs could be adjusted with timers that determined if they would explode on impact, had delayed action for several minutes or perhaps hours, or they would explode just prior to impact. Care had to be taken that each bomb was protected with a safety device.

An appreciated job these dedicated men did was to greet us in the wee hours of the morning as we climbed down from the trucks with our equipment and just prior to boarding the plane for yet another mission. They did not always know many of these young fliers very well because, on different days, other crews may man this particular bomber, "their baby."

They were well aware that on the next mission some could come back wounded or perhaps killed. They also knew that their plane had the possibility of never coming back because it may have crashed somewhere in Europe, or in the North Sea. If this had happened, they knew they would be assigned a different plane to their hard-stand and new loyalties had to be cultivated.

OTHER PERSONNEL

Most of the time the Flight Crews lived in a very sheltered environment, namely because we had to devote almost all of our entire energies to over come all of the apprehensions our jobs required. Much would be taken for granted. There were many of us, who never took the time to appreciate all of the effort and work by others just to make any single mission a success.

Without all of the talents, from a long list of personnel, the B-17 crew could never have achieved the record that history now has recorded. The Eighth Air Force was the largest single air unit ever assembled in the world and hopefully this distinction will never have to be challenged. For every man in the Air Force who was on flying status it required eleven additional individuals to support him.

The following are names or titles of individuals that most of us never saw or rubbed butts with. They worked behind the scenes and their efforts were preparatory to the green flare going off to send the 95th Bomb Group on yet another mission. The following group of individuals is not in any order of importance, is not alphabetically listed, nor is it a complete enumeration of all who had a part of the whole:

Ordinance Officer * Operation Clerk * Photo Lab. * Medic * Intelligence
Line Chief * Base Refueling * Mess Sgt. * S-2 * Telephone Operator *
Cryptographic Section * Armament Officer * Fireman * Electronics *
Bomb Sight Mechanics * Transportation * Sub Depot * Munitions Officer *
Air Craft Armorer * Pathfinder * A/C Supply * Dental Technician *
Aerial Engineer * Draftsman * Control Tower *Communication Officer *
Chaplin * Sheet Metal Crew * Cooks * Flight Surgeon * Mickey Operator *
Air Traffic Control * Motor Pool * Bomb Loader * Air Engineer * S-4 *

The success of any operation will be determined by how well each of its parts functioned. A snafu or breakdown in any part of the whole could result in either partial or total failure. Each individual knew the importance of their function that they had been trained for and were aware of the ramifications should they be derelict in performing their duty.

What most individuals may not have appreciated was the pride and determination of all of the other branches in this complex fighting unit. All members of every branch of service, both in Europe and in Asia, can take pride in the legacy we gave the world. No price can be placed on freedom. Freedom is never free.

CHAPTER 20

For over seven months, I hid and protected a bottle of straight bourbon, whose sole purpose was to "hang one on", should I be one of the lucky ones to complete my 35 missions. My intention was to celebrate with all of my friends being left behind. Upon returning from my final mission to Stuttgart, Germany, an entirely different feeling settled over me. Drinking did not seem important right now and I had mixed feelings as to how I should express what was going on inside me.

I began to experience some real disbelief and became aware of conflicting emotions. I had actually flown 35 missions against our enemy and was now free to take a leave for home and all of the people I had left behind. Next, I would suffer a feeling of guilt because I had seen so many friends and brother fliers die or get captured and I am now going home in one piece. The mind and one's conscience creates a myriad of foreign feelings, many going on simultaneously. It is like having something important to shout about, but extreme modesty makes you content with just a quite soliloquy.

I naturally was elated, my tour was over, but I also was aware that all of my friends around me still had to fly against our enemy. I knew there would be some who would never make it back. In fact, several days before I was to finish my tour, Capt. Lyle Dallman, my friend from Wisconsin and the person who had offered me the rank of Captain, went on a shuttle raid that was to go from England to Russia; from Russia to Italy; and from Italy back to England. On each of these legs the 95th B.G. was to hit German targets. The day after my last mission we received word that the lead plane went down in Hungary. Captain Dallman was in that plane.

They were on their way from Russia and were to drop bombs on a railroad shop at Szolnok in Hungary. Their plane was hit twice by flak, requiring the crew to bail out. Capt. Dallman and the best Bombardier of the 95th Bomb Group, Lt. John S. Bromberg, plus the rest of the crew were all taken prisoners.

Cpt. Dallman happened to be from Antigo, Wisconsin, approximately twenty–eight miles from my hometown of Wausau. The day before I was to leave for home, Lyle had asked me to deliver some things to his wife and children. He had finished his tour of duty and was now the 336ᵗʰ Squadron Navigator.

He decided to go on what looked like an interesting and unusual mission. He had given me several of the decorations he had received and there were a few small items he had bought as gifts. I assured him that my trip to Antigo, even before I got married, would be one of the first things I would do, once I got home on leave.

I also received word, a little over a month after I left England, my best friend "Waddy", Lt. Dan Waddell, from Hendersonville, North Carolina, was wounded on his 31st mission. On October 17 he went to Cologne, Germany for the second time in three days. The flak was intense. Three planes were damaged severely, with one going down in target area. Lt. A.E. McCulley and his crew were taken prisoner, except the bombardier Lt. W.J. Kehoe, who had been killed.

The two other planes, one piloted by Lt. Dan Waddell and the other by Lt. J.M. Miller, made it to our lines in Belgium. "Waddy" had been wounded and the navigator in Lt. Miller's plane had been killed. This would be the type of situation I would be leaving behind. Somehow, when I was flying missions, I didn't dwell on these types of facts. Now it seemed to be different.

The night of Sept. 5, after my last trip, instead of celebrating, I decided to walk over to the N.C.O. Club (Noncommissioned Officers Club) to see some of the many crewmembers I had flown with. My tour consisted of flying with a total of nineteen different crews. I got to know many of these gunners better than their Officers, but never real well. Somehow it seemed important to me to say goodbye to some of the guys I remembered. The N.C. O. Club is normally off limits to Officers.

I was having a beer with the fellows, when an orderly instructed me to return to Headquarters immediately. They had been looking for me for nearly an hour, believing that I should be at the Officers Club, living it up. I had no idea what the hell was up since I had only been invited to report to Headquarters just once before, and that was two weeks prior when Captain Dallman offered me a promotion.

Tonight though, I had no idea of why my presence was requested at General Headquarters. While I hurried over to this remote building I thought that perhaps they were going to congratulate me on finishing my tour. As I entered the building and was ushered in to a large office, there were five or six High Ranking Officers awaiting my presence. I recognized most of them but really did not know any personally.

Before I had time to worry what this entire matter was all about, I had been asked why I led the 95th Bomb Group over the Belgium City of Oostende? I immediately got the complete picture since I knew we did fly over this city and had picked up some flak. Several planes received some battle damage, but our flight sustained no actual losses, nor injuries to any of the crewmembers.

They wanted my side of the story and I was now anxious to give it. On our return from my 35th and last mission to Stuttgart we returned on a coarse that would take us directly back to Horham and our field. A short distance from the English Channel I noticed, on my maps, that we would pass over Oostende. I notified the pilot of this and suggested we fly a double drift leg maneuver around this city, since it might still contain some German Forces.

The Allied Armies had over run most of Belgium and France by this time, but they avoided capturing many coastal cities. The intention was, to go back and clean out these few pockets of enemy troops later. They had surrounded them and offered no avenue for their escape. I had read all this in the Stars and Stripes, our service newspaper, the day before. There could still be some anti aircraft guns in these surrounded cities.

A double drift leg is a procedure Navigators use over water to ascertain the wind direction and velocity. It requires a plane to alter course by turning 45 degrees to the right for two minutes, then turn 90 degrees left for two minutes, and then turn right 45 degrees, to get the plane back on coarse. The four-minute procedure would only lose one minute of flight time from our actual coarse, had we initiated this maneuver.

When I suggested this over the intercom, I was told we would proceed on the course that was taking us directly to our base. I do not know if this was the first Pilot's decision or the Colonel who flew in the co-pilot seat. Their wish is my command. When I related my version of why we flew over Oostende, Colonel Truesdell surprised me by saying, "That's all I need to know, congratulation on completing your tour of duty Krueger, and good luck in the future." I left with the feeling someone would get his "tail chewed out."

The next day I spent handing in most of my navigational equipment and signing a variety of papers. I also was requested to talk to a group of Navigators from newly arrived crews. These replacement crews would soon take the places for members of the 95th Bomb Group who had failed to return from missions or for the few lucky ones, like myself, who completed their tour of duty.

I told them about combat, what to expect, suggestions for navigational procedures I found useful, and answered numerous questions that were thrown at me. When I looked into their anxious faces it was easy to find the cocky ones and the others with their pent up fears about the unknown. I recalled my feeling eight months ago when I was afraid that this damn war would be over before I got into it. The first mission usually dispels this attitude. As I looked into each of their faces, suddenly I felt older than my twenty-three years.

THOUGHTS OF HOME

My thoughts now began to be of home and the realization that Norma and I were once again going to be together. Suddenly, I became aware of the fact that all of our courtship had been via the mails. Before I left for combat we had become engaged, but all of our thoughts, promises, and dreams of the future were through letters. Because of censorship, others would read my every thought and expression I had put on paper, long before she ever opened one of my hundreds of letters.

I began to realize just how lucky I was to be preparing for this trip back to the States and loved ones I had not seen in a long time. I obviously was extremely grateful to have survived these thirty-five trips into Germany, the Netherlands, Belgium, Denmark, France, Poland, and even Czechoslovakia. I was particularly gratified to have participated in dropping supplies to the French Maquis on two occasions in different parts of France.

I had a cigar box filled with pieces of flak I had collected from my clothing, my boots, my navigational equipment, and from the immediate area around my work-station. I knew that each one of these pieces of spent metal came close to having my name on it, yet, I am able to carry these "trophies" home in an empty cigar box.

The only injury I had received during my entire tour was a face wound I received from flying plexiglas when my astro-dome was shattered by a flak burst. My face was a bloody mess, but once the Bombardier wiped it off, only scratches remained. I suffered from several bruised ribs when we crash-landed on May 24th. I also burnt my ankle from a fired 50-caliber shell casing that ended up in my right boot. Oh yes, there was the time I seriously injured my pride, when "Waddy" and I locked handle-bars on our bicycles on one of the many excursions we took to cultivate our knowledge of the English countryside.

Tonight it hit me for the first time that my friendship with Dan Waddell was going to be split up by my leaving and it would be a very long time before we would get to see one another again. My relationship with "Waddy" was more than two guys being thrown together by fate, one from North Carolina and one from Wisconsin, one from the south and one from the north.

Our friendship had been instant and genuine. It had come at perhaps the most important time in both of our lives. "Waddy" will never know exactly how important his friendship meant to me. I have tried to tell him, but words sometimes cannot express feelings that run so deep. As I listened to myself, my words took on a dissonant sound. ""Waddy", I truly needed you man." Sometimes words can get in the way of feelings and I'm sure the reciprocal has equal validity.

I knew, as I was about to leave, this dear friend had only reached his 24th mission and he still had 11 big ones to go. Thoughts and fears entered my head for this buddy of mine. I was realizing greater concern and worries for him, than I had for any of my own pending trips to Germany. Once again I had to rely on my fatalistic beliefs and let the matter rest.

My thoughts went back to Norma once again. I began to worry whether we knew enough about one another, what we would do after this war was over, where would the two of us end up living? . . . so many questions. Serious thoughts crept into these moments that made me realize that the touching, the hugs and kisses, the expressions, the deep inner thoughts and all of the many things that go into a normal relationship, had been missing.

There never was a doubt that I had discovered the person I wanted to spend and share my life with. Only this night, I wanted to know more about her dreams and wishes. I began to wonder what in the hell did she see in me to want to commit herself to this partnership. I recalled the high pedestal I had placed her on while in High School because of her warranted and deserved popularity.

I wanted to pick her brain and I wanted her to know about my idiosyncrasies. Was she buying into a "pig in a poke? There were many times I could be a person with a haughty attitude and moments later take on the persona of a sensitive "pussy cat." At this moment, I wish I could find complete absolution from these many doubts and fears that were racing through my head.

My experience in combat gave me insight into many of my limitations and I had also learned something about some of my strengths. How would all of these pluses and minuses fit into sharing one's life with another person? All of these new worries and thoughts now going through my head suddenly made my previous fears I had before each mission take on an illusion of only imperceptible dismay. Abruptly I turned off these damn cerebrations and found myself saying out loud, "Hell, I'm not going to be the first guy who ever got married."

Just about the time I thought I had control of my inner problems, an interesting picture suddenly popped into my head. I knew my days in the Air Force were not over just because I completed my tour in combat. The war continues and my services were still required. Where would I be stationed and what would my duties be? At this moment I only knew for sure I would not volunteer to return to the 95th and take on the obligation of a second tour.

I had been told of several options that might be available, but each depended on openings and being in the right place at the right time. I remembered the promise made to me when I was transferred out of pilot training and into the navigational school at San Marcos. I was told I could return to pilot training but did I want to be subjected to the life style of a cadet again? Yes, I shall always remember this lengthy night when a myriad of thoughts raced through my mind.

GOING HOME

On Friday morning early, September 8, 1944, I will leave the 95th Bomb Group Base at Horham for the last time. I have train tickets to take me to Glasgow, Scotland to board the Queen Mary for my trip home. I joined the Lt. Richard Harvey crew, who had just completed their tour with all ten crewmen safe and sound. They had flown their 35th mission together, in quess what? Yep, it was old B-17 number 42-97334, the plane I still affectionately call "HAARD LUCK."

Old 42-97334, our original plane named **"HAARD LUCK,"** would go down just eight days later with the Lt. Mooring crew aboard. They were on a mission to Ruhland, Germany on September 11th when they were hit by German fighter planes at 1220 hours. With their right wing aflame, all nine crewmen left the burning plane. Their target was to be the Ruhland Synthetic Oil Refineries near Brux, Czechoslovakia. How well I remembered the two missions I had to this remote objective.

The plane crashed just west of Leipzig in the proximity of the Czech-German border near the small town of Schmalsgrube in Germany. The entire crew parachuted safely. They were all taken prisoner and interned for the duration of the war. Pilot V.R. Mooring, Co-pilot C.R. Swanson, Navigator A.P.Janson, Flight Officer R.A. Moerke all became POWs and spent the remainder of the war at Stalag Luft I at Barth, Germany.

Engineer & top Turret Gunner C.P. Stein, Radio operator F. Alievto, Ball Turret operator T.H. Merriman, Waist Gunner W.P. Martin, and Tail Gunner J. g. Weber all were captured and they became POW and were interned at Stalag Luft IV near Stettin, just south of the Baltic Sea. For obvious reasons, this crew would not have the same sentimental feeling for Number 42-97334 as this author has. My favorite plane did not manage to bring them home.

Some fifty-eight years later I have gotten to know Charlie Stein, the Engineer aboard "HAARD LUCK" this fateful day. He informed me that they remained in Stalag Luft IV until February 6, 1945 when they were evacuated ahead of the Russian Spring Offensive. About 10,000 prisoners were marched for about 600 miles until rescued by the American 104th Division on May 6, 1945 near Halle, Germany. These prisoners were poorly fed, had little or no shelter at night, and were forced to walk the entire distance. This march became known as the Black March of Germany.

This was the 41st. mission for this faithful B-17G, a life span nearly ten missions more than the average fortress in the 95th Bomb Group. Now, some fifty-eight years later, I have a box filled with small remains from Number 42-97334, given to me by a Mr. Jan Zdiarsky from Kovarska, Czech Republic. Jan is the Director of a Museum in Kovarska devoted entirely to the famous Air Battle over Krusnohori on Sept. 11, 1944. I had visited this very target near Brux, Czechoslovakia on two separate occasions.

As a point of interest, on September 11, 2001, my wife Norma and I returned to Korvarska, Czech Republic for a Reunion commemorating this famous air battle that took exactly fifty-seven years before. There were over a dozen Luftwaffe pilots and there wives in attendance. Norma and I were the only Americans present since all other air line flights had been canceled due to the Terrorist attacks on the Twin Towers in New York and the Pentagon in Washington D.C.

On that date a book I had written regarding the complete and interesting history of the B-17 affectionately called HAARD LUCK, plane Number 42-97334, was issued. The title of the book "THE TRIALS AND TRIBULATIONS OF A LADY" had been published in the Czech Republic and made its debut. The book, ISBN 80-903030-4-8, relates the complete life of this bomber that flew 41 missions. The average life of a B-17 in the 95th Bomb Group happened to be 32.1 missions.

TIME TO GO

The eleven of us, The Lt. Harvey crew and me, were trucked to the railroad station at Diss, the small English town northwest of Horham. In less than an hour, we were aboard the train and heading toward Glasgow, Scotland. On this train, while we started to relax, each of us began to fully realize we had made it through our tour of duty and combat against the German war machine.

The tempo of our conversation and the excitement displayed by each of us certainly indicated that this moment was more than special. We each were aware that we had defied the Law of Averages and fate and would live to tell about it. Each airman also took pride in the task they had just accomplished. For one reason or another I had flown as Navigator with the Lt. Harvey Crew on one occasion. All of the Officers on this crew also lived in my barracks. I felt extremely fortunate I could enjoy this moment with fellows I knew, something that was not my usual experience or privilege.

Our train arrived in Glasgow late in the evening and we were then quartered in a small hotel the American Government had taken over. Our celebration continued into the wee hours of the morning. Sleep this night did not have a high priority.

Nearly every member of this grateful group of men had similar plans, once we reached stateside. Most plans were to meet our families first, quickly followed by plans to get married or to get engaged. We each knew that we were the lucky ones to make it this far and we had learned that each day is more than just precious. Many of our buddies, had all of their "tomorrows" flee or taken away. We had been away from home and loved ones for about a year now.

When we assembled early Saturday morning we were told that our entire group would not board the ship, the Queen Mary, until 8 P.M. that evening, giving us plenty of time to continue our celebration. I took time out to telephone our 95th Bomb Group Base to get the latest word on Captain Lyle Dallman.

I was told that all crewmembers parachuted safely from the falling plane somewhere over Hungary. This would be the extent of the information the 95th Bomb Group had. At least now I could inform Marion Dallman her husband was alive and a P.O.W. instead of the "Missing in Action" letter the government would be sending her.

THE QUEEN MARY

The 9th of September was an especially long day, even for a Saturday. We walked the streets, we drank, we walked some more, we drank . . . we did this until late in the afternoon. About 6 P.M. we all piled into two taxicabs and headed for the dock at Gourock. Many hundreds of American service personnel were already dockside when we noticed the ship.

The word ship seemed instantly inadequate to describe what was before us. This sucker was huge. It stretched out the length of three and a half football fields, approximately one-fifth mile long. As I stood there, trying to put this entire view into some perspective, I realized I was looking into a wall of black painted steel, which subtlety displayed the gentle curvature defining the hull of this ship.

Being from the isolated State of Wisconsin, most of my acquaintance with a vessel capable of floating was something slightly larger than a rowboat. To say that I was impressed would be a gross under statement. I had heard about the Queen Mary and a few other famous ships, but this was beyond my expectations.

The Mighty Queen was at anchor in the Firth of Clyde, at the mouth of the Clyde

River. Dozens of ambulances, with their red crosses, could be seen and we were told they had been loading wounded soldiers from the war for the past several hours. Excitement permeated the air. We were all going home. "God . . . . that sounded good."

Just before our group was to board the ship, some G.I., who was starting to go up the gangplank, offered me a whole, large, cooked red lobster. Being from the "boonies" I had never even seen one of these creatures before and could not imagine how it would taste. Much to his amazement, I turned down this generous offer. Before he got out of range, he tore off one huge claw and threw it to me and asked that I give it a try.

Hell, this thing looked like something dangerous, not something you would try and eat. I was not quite sure just how I should attack it. I finally and cautiously tasted this strange edible monster. It was succulent. I made a half ass effort to find the "lobster-man" but there was nothing but confusion about this floating city at this moment. I presented myself with an instant challenge. This would be the first meal I would order out in a restaurant, once I was Stateside.

I had been assigned, along with seven other officers, to a 1st class stateroom on the veranda deck. This was a huge room with twelve single beds in it. Only the eight of us were to share this ample space for the next six days. Later I was told, during peace-time, this particular stateroom would cost a family $2,000 for a single crossing.

In normal times, the Queen Mary would sail with 1904 passengers and have a crew of 1285. Now this famous ship was serving its country in the time of war. All or most of the luxury trappings had been removed. Six miles of carpeting had been taken up, 220 cases of china, crystal and silverware were in storage in a warehouse.

As a troop carrier, she normally would carry between 14,000 and 16,000 troops from the United States or Canada to England. This return trip would have approximately 3,200 passengers, made up of mostly wounded, several dozen Air Force Personnel, several hundred ground troops returning home on leave, and an unusual contingent of pregnant WACS, WAVES, and NURSES.

The Queen Mary was launched in 1934 and was one of the prime ships in the world. Her sister ship, The Queen Elizabeth, was under construction at the beginning of the war and would be twelve feet longer and slightly heavier than the 81,237 gross tons the Queen Mary weighed.

Four sets of single-reduction-geared turbines ran the ship. Each developed 160,000 shaft horsepower that drove the 18-foot propellers. Normal speed was about 27 knots per hour, which meant that the ship would consume over 1000 tons of fuel ever 24 hours. Instead of the normal crew of 1285, she now had a crew of only 200.

This beautiful ship went into service for the war effort on April 17, 1940. She had been refitted to bring American and Canadian troops to England as rapidly as possible. In all, she made a total of 89 crossings.

One of the wars most memorable brief log entries for the Queen Mary went as follow: "New York to Gourock (Clyde), 16,683 souls aboard. New York, 25 July, 1943, 3353 miles, 4 days, 20 hours, 42 minutes, 28.173 knots. The greatest number of human beings ever embarked on one vessel." The total of 16,683 passengers was later surpassed.

To be able to carry these huge numbers of troops, standee bunks were designed. They developed a tree of metal tubes, supporting six canvas stretchers, so as to accommodate six sleeping enlisted men. On the Observation Lounge, it was converted into a maze of five tiered bunks. Each cabin, which a couple would share on a normal crossing, was fitted with 18 triple tiered units for 54 men.

When 16,000 men were transported, three G.I.s rotated shifts in each bunk over the twenty-four-hour period. Meals were served 2,000 at a time, starting at 6:30 A.M. Thirty thousand eggs were boiled every morning, just to give some idea of the magnitude of the food problem.

We discovered the food problem went even deeper. As officers, we ate in the Dining Room and actually had a menu with choices. We learned that the enlisted men from the Lt. Harvey crew did not fare as well. These six men, along with all other enlisted personnel, were provided no choices and the food they were served was marginal at best. We started ordering food we had no intention of eating and then taking it back to our suite for these gunners. Rank should have no bearing on how our service men are fed.

My first impression of this majestic ship was that she was a floating city with restaurants, banks, hospitals, theaters, and all of the other pertinences. Since we were to have less than one fifth the number of passengers on this return trip, my impressions are bound to be somewhat different from those G.I.s that left New York for their war.

At about 11 P.M., we slowly moved away from the dock and were underway. We did not reach the open sea, north of Ireland, till early the next morning. Now was the time to explore this complex creation of man. I walked the decks every free moment I had, sticking my nose into any space that titillated my curiosity.

I managed to have several of the Queen Mary's crew tell me to haul my butt away from certain areas, on more than one occasion. In the next few days I think I explored every major section of this magnificent ship. Many times I got completely lost in the maze of corridors, different decks, and specialized spaces within the bowels of this huge vessel.

As a Navigator, I soon discovered, by watching the stars at night, that the Queen Mary was constantly changing course, in a very erotic manner. I later was informed that this was done, so no German U-Boat could intercept us. This ship was faster than any submarine, but it would have been suicide to head in a straight line for New York City, because it would certainly be intercepted.

It had been learned, Hitler had offered $250,000 and an Iron Cross to any U-Boat Captain who sank, either the Queen Mary or the Queen Elizabeth. Many submarine commanders made efforts unsuccessfully to accomplish this feat and several would later regret their attempt.

On Monday night, September 11, I went up to the Bridge and asked permission to take a peek at the ship's Navigator work area. I had informed him of my navigational skills while flying combat. Much to my amazement, I was invited in and offered the opportunity to work with this important member of the crew.

He permitted me to shoot several star fixes and actually plot them on his chart. The ability to use a sextant without being thrown all over the place, the degree of accuracy of each star shot, and time to make all of my calculations, made me feel confident of my work.

The room that the ship's Navigator had to work in was the size of a huge office in a large building. There perhaps was more square footage in this single space than in our entire interior of the B-17 bomber we flew in. He had cabinets used for storage and racks that he kept his many charts on. The most notable thing he had was a large comfortable stool to sit on, which was on carpeting. The room did have a rather low ceiling which perhaps made the room seem larger. This reduced headroom only added to the coziness of the entire space.

This ship was speeding through the water at about one tenth the speed of our B-17. Therefore, when I took shots for a three star fix, it was not necessary to advance two of the shots. The table I was working on was perhaps ten times larger than the one in my B-17. I appreciated this unique opportunity.

As one of a limited number of Officers aboard ship, I pulled an assignment on my second day out to sea. I was assigned to "Officer of the Day" duties, which meant that I would spend several hours below deck in the hospital sick bay area. Many of the seriously wounded, from the battlefields of France, were being shipped home and most of these were confined to beds.

I saw things I was hardly prepared for. There were men without arms or legs, faces partially blown away, various degrees of bandages and traction devices, some men were ambulatory, but most were confined to beds. Despite their broken bodies, these men were as elated as I was to be going home.

I suppose pulling this detail could be considered a rough assignment. However, I was grateful for the opportunity to truly see how fortunate I had been to make it through this damn war in one piece and for the chance to meet and talk to so many of the G.I.s in this special section of the mighty Queen Mary.

Despite this horrible and sad picture of these hundreds of wounded men, both they and I knew that an equal number of their friends were being returned home in hastily produced coffins. If the world's leaders, who involve their countries in war, could spend time in one of these sick bays, perhaps problems could be resolved in a more humane manner.

Most of the men, in the various bays I visited this day, were in high spirits. We talked and swapped war stories. They were more interested in my combat experiences and constantly reiterated that there was no way, you could get them up in a bomber or fighter plane. Many had seen planes shot down or witnessed the wreckage of fallen planes. I told them about the advice my father had given me, and how someone would have a hard time getting me into a tank, a submarine, or even a trench, for that matter.

My personal feelings were that if I had to go, I preferred to get it over with in the shortest time possible. In reality, most of us had little to say about the outside forces that would remove all of our "tomorrows." Anyone of us could have met our end by contacting a simple cold, by falling off a truck, by a malfunctioning aircraft, by ditching in the North Sea, by a 30 mm shell from a Messerschmitt Me 109, or a tiny fragment from a near by burst of flak.

It took all types of Americans to serve in the many branches of service and each of us, in our own way, did our very best to bring the Axis Powers to a halt. Many in the German High Command could not comprehend men from our country having the stomach to wage this type of warfare. Freedom is worth whatever the price requires to preserve it.

I had the opportunity to return to this sick bay on two more occasions. Though this duty had been assigned to me I have been forever grateful for the chance to be among young men who did all that was asked and expected of them. For most, their broken bodies will mend. There would be some that will have to endure many painful days ahead and even more difficult years living with their wounds and scars of war.

DEMENTIA TREMORS

Three days out from England, on September 12, two of my friends and I were standing along the rail, up at the bow, when we each concurred, we were getting the D.T.'s, (dementia tremors). Before we boarded, we had been told there would be severe disciplinary action taken, for anyone caught bringing alcohol on board the Queen Mary. The net result, we drank our entire supply prior to walking up the gangplank.

The Military Police did a good job checking each person as they boarded. If they saw a suspicious bulge under your uniform, you could expect a sharp rap from a leaded nightstick. Using this technique, they did not have to confiscate the loot. Those that were caught with a suspicious bulge had broken glass inside their shirts or pockets and a variety of precious liquid running down their legs. This could be considered a drastic measure.

As we stood along the rail, because of the horrible predicament of having no access to any form of alcohol, we were feeling sorry for ourselves. We began to wonder, "Did we have dependency on the stuff?" The fact that we were told we could not have any was probably more important at this moment than any addiction for whiskey, bourbon, gin or "you name it."

I cannot speak for the others, but when I left the service and went back to the University, I did not have a drink for several years. I couldn't afford it. So much for addiction.

When I was on duty in the sick bay, some of the men had told us Bing Crosby and Fred Astaire had put on a show for them the night before. We had known they were on board, returning to the U.S.A. after a U.S.O. tour for the troops in Europe, but we had not seen them.

Suddenly lights went on in our heads . . . "Let's find out if we can buy a bottle of anything with alcohol in it," each having the same spontaneous thought. We all felt certain that they had a supply or could certainly get their hands on some. It was decided the three of us would go on this important mission to procure some booze.

BING CROSBY & FRED ASTAIRE

We knew where their isolated suite of rooms was located and it didn't take us long to approach their door to test our latest theory. We knocked, stated our reason for being there, and waited for a positive reply to our request. Much to our amazement, Fred Astaire invited us in to their suite.

I could only tell it was the famous dancer by his voice. He had answered the door, minus his toupee and looked almost like a man twenty years older than I had imagined. If I hadn't admired his talents on the screen and recognized his voice (also the fact I was aware he was assigned this particular suite), there was no way I could have guessed the old man before me was Fred Astaire.

Bing Crosby, who looked almost as old, came over and introduced himself. There were two other men who were part of this elite group. I had never heard of them nor did I remember their names. We again explained our dire predicament and were immediately offered a drink of our choice. I did not choose buttermilk.

They had an actual bar set up in one corner of this living area, in perhaps, the best suite of rooms on the Queen Mary. They informed us that the bar was open and to just help ourselves as we felt the need.

In no time we three found it impossible to refuse or spurn their unselfish hospitality.

All four of these men kept firing questions at us about our experiences in combat, what it was like to be attacked by German fighter planes, and of course, the terrible flak we would be exposed to at each prime target. They wanted to know which Bomber Group we belonged to, and exactly where our airfield was located.

We were not given the opportunity to treat Mr. Crosby and Mr. Astaire, like the celebrities they were. They also did not put on any airs of importance that would make them look artificial or affected. They all were just plain, great guys, who happened to have what we needed most.

One of the four asked if we played poker. This had to be a facetious question. There were three things that each of us did these past many months. They were to fly, to drink, and to play poker for money. "Say no more." "Fred", "Bing", Lt. Gordon, Lt. Stevenson, Lt. Krueger, and one of the other men we had met, sat around a cleared large table. A deck of cards was produced and it was decided that the stakes would be modest: a dollar to open, a dollar to draw, a dollar to bump, and a maximum of five dollars to raise a final time. There would be no wild cards. This was to be a friendly, sociable game.

When we played poker back at the base, a typical game was played with English money and the basic unit for betting was the British pound. Sometimes we used an Irish or Scottish Pound. Back in 1944 the actual value of the pound was worth $4.035. We threw this paper pound around, like it was a dollar bill. I guess this might prove most things are relative. This night though, the game of poker being played, turned out to be, mostly talking and joking and very little astute card playing.

The most memorable thing about this special evening of September 12, 1944, was not the card game, nor the fact that our systems were getting the alcohol we thought it craved, nor the fact that I even made a few bucks from the game. It was not even the reality that we were actually in the presence of two of our countries most notable entertainers.

For me it was a lesson in learning that notoriety and fame can be both earthy and human. This most auspicious happening showed me that Fred Astaire and Bing Crosby came across as two plain, ordinary guys. Over the years I have the privilege and opportunity to meet other famous celebrities, many who were extremely shallow and arrogant.

These two famous men made us each feel at ease and comfortable and, on several occasions, expressed their admiration for the thirty-five mission we each had flown. All evening long we had called them Bing and Fred, not out of disrespect, but rather because we sensed that this is what they preferred.

Bing sucked on his unlit pipe all evening, and when he felt he might have a good enough hand in poker, he unconsciously would hum one of the little ditties he was famous for, thus tipping off his hand. Needless to say, when I heard these melodic sounds being emitted, I usually folded my hand.

Soon after we started the poker game, it became very apparent that these two men had more talent as actors, dancers, and singers. Their card sense left something to be desired. In any case, we were made to feel welcome, and the three of us did our best to express our appreciation for this most memorable evening.

We left this smoke filled stateroom, with an experience each will cherish and long remember. I also believe we left these two guys from Hollywood, with a similar feeling. I was now far enough removed from my home state of Wisconsin and my former humble way of living that I now almost felt worldly.

The next day I awoke, knowing that my motor was running on all cylinders, and believed I now could make it to New York, because of the sustenance of the night before. This may have only been a mental thing, but my body responded in a very positive manner. Each day the weather was absolutely perfect (not the usual conditions out in the Atlantic Ocean) and the nights were even more exquisite, with the uncountable stars ever present.

Nearly every waking hour that I could spend doing what I enjoyed most during this exceptional voyage was spent up near the bow of the Queen Mary. I watched the wake as this monster of a ship cut its way through the relatively smooth Atlantic Ocean. I was not aware that my A-2 flight jacket, with all of its ornate decorations, was being ruined by the invisible salt spray we both were exposed to.

Several months later, while on my leave, I noticed the leather was turning slightly white. I immediately took it to a cleaning establishment only to find out it was beyond repair. The goat-skin leather lost its flexibility and would tear upon the least little provocation.

It later had to be replaced and redecorated with our HAARD LUCK figure, our 95th Bomb Group Insignia, and 35 small bombs with their fins painted to designate which country they landed in. I had my A-2 jacket duplicated from five of my white tail deer hides I had tanned from previous hunting expeditions.

NEW YORK

Early on the morning of September 15, which happened to be a Friday, we entered the harbor in New York. This beautiful ship passed through the Narrows between Staten Island and Long Island and entered Upper Bay. The powerful engines were barely working as this huge floating city gracefully and silently moved along this invisible pathway in the calm waters off the shores of our own country. "God . . . . . what a feeling". As each moment passed, more and more passengers came on deck to witness this spectacle.

Small boats were darting around us, making evidence of their presence by the tiny wakes behind each vessel. There were many fireboats spraying water into the air. These streams formed lazy arcs of water that appeared as moving fountains. About this time several tug-boats were maneuvering next to the hull of this huge ship, and would disappear as they moved below the curvature that formed the graceful lines of the Queen Mary.

By mid morning we had crept to within sight of Ellis Island and the Statue of Liberty. Moist eyes and tears tended to diffuse this sight of the stalwart lady with her raised arm and torch. The generous gift from the French people had welcomed millions of immigrants.

Today it was not hard to imagine the significance of this beautiful symbol to those souls who arrived with nothing but hopes and dreams. Time and history divulged the reality of what these immigrants had to endure before getting established in these United States.

Sliding silently past this eminent statue of steel, copper and gold leaf, you get the feeling that this is a symbol that depicts only the positive. To those privileged to pass and observe this gift from the French, it is a visible sign, signifying the opportunity and hope this great country offered its people.

My heart swelled within my chest and I could feel tears running down my checks. I was not embarrassed for showing this emotion, an emotion generated by my pride of being an American, for being one of the chosen ones to return from combat, and a sight I had only heard or read about in books. I could feel my chest swell up with pride and I think I was even standing taller.

The bow of the Queen Mary gracefully parted the water as we slowly moved up the Hudson River. The skyline of Manhattan was on our starboard. Excitement was not the word for the feelings and emotions being displayed by the returning veterans along the rail. This fellow from a small town in northern Wisconsin was standing on the deck of one of the world's greatest ships, moving gracefully in the harbor of the world's greatest city, as we inched our way into Cunards Pier No. 89.

Horns and whistles on the many small boats made a background noise for the large band that greeted our arrival at the dock. Thousands of people had gathered to welcome home one of the first large contingents of returning veterans. I now knew what the expression, "popping your buttons" meant, when they referred to pride. Words alone cannot describe the thoughts and electricity that were within my body. I felt a very special kind of pride at this moment and I now knew what I had risked my neck in combat for.

The sight on the dock below us was unbelievable. The waving throngs, the brass band, the welcoming banners, and the complete atmosphere made our tear ducts spring into action once again. An old Irish expression described it as "your bladder moved just behind your eyes."

A sobering sight was apparent on the fringe of the crowd, where several dozens of ambulances were patiently awaiting their cargo. These wounded were equally happy to come home and they would be one of the firsts to leave the Queen Mary. The memory of this entire scene is the epitome of what my country is all about.

The able bodied veterans were told it would be many hours before we could leave the ship, but this didn't seem to matter. I soaked in all of the sights and sounds of this joyous welcome and moment. It was interesting to see the hatch covers to the hold removed and all of the cargo lifted out of the bowels of this huge ship. There seemed to be activity everywhere you looked, all going on simultaneously.

It took several hours to remove the wounded from the ship and get them secured in the dozens of ambulances and buses that had now been moved to the lower exits. Most of these men would be going to hospitals for specialized treatment. Many of the wounded, as well as others, had family waiting to greet them.

My loved ones would still remain far away, but at this moment, very close to my heart. They would not know I was even back in the States until I could get ashore and telephone them I had made it through this terrible war. Nothing mattered to me now. I was going home. "What a privilege it was to be present at this moment in time at this very spot and knowing you were an intricate part of the history being formed."

CHAPTER 21

By mid-afternoon it was my turn to walk down the gangplank and step on the good old U.S.A. once again. The Air Force had several buses waiting for us. Once a roll call had been completed, we were driven over to New Jersey to Fort Lee. This was a typical permanent U.S. Base, and vastly better than the collection of Quonset huts we left behind in England. We had the mistaken idea that we would be here a day or two and be shipped, as promised, to our hometowns. How wrong we were.

The very first news we received after checking into our barracks was that we would be at Fort Lee for three or four weeks. The time of our detainment would vary with different individuals. This news told me I had to call Norma immediately to relay this vague date of departure so that they could change our wedding date. I knew they needed an illusive and indefinite date for my arrival like a hole in the head. Despite all of this, it was my intention to "get me to the church on time."

It seemed that tons of paper work had to be processed, a complete physical had to be given, and it would be necessary to play the Army game of "hurry up and wait." The facilities on this base were nice and we would be given passes for any free time we wished to spend off the post. We were offered transportation to all public facilities such as buses, trains, and streetcars. We were made to feel that all personnel serving us was appreciative of what each had done while in combat.

The food was the best we had in nearly a year. German Prisoners of War waited on the tables in the mess hall. The service was excellent, due primarily to the pride these men possessed and their effort to display complete efficiency. They carried this efficiency almost to the point of being arrogant and pretentious. I have never been served during a meal with more skillful competence.

I had run across Italian prisoners, while I was over in England, who had been given jobs on British bases. These prisoners were indifferent and seemed eager to show their displeasure at waiting on tables. These German prisoners however, were in a league by themselves. They were so damn vainglorious, almost to the point of being cocky and insolent. It was interesting just to watch them. They seemed to be telling us that, though their war may be over, the German spirit lives on. "Hell, I almost felt like tipping them."

NEW YORK – NEW YORK

I got the chance to get into New York City several times. My first meal off the base, as I had promised myself, was a lobster dinner, with all of the complications of this type of entree. I was given hardware and tools to dissect this beast and I didn't quite know each of their functions.

Though I used to be adept at using a variety of woodworking tools, I now felt like a genuine bungling fool and inept with the crackers and picks to retrieve any morsels from this crustacean from the sea. Suddenly I felt like I had an audience just waiting for me to flip this strange looking creature on the floor. I noted its stalking beady eyes as I finally accepted some help from a waiter.

Ultimately I managed to get most of the meat out of the different anatomical parts of this creature. I guess I looked like I was from Wisconsin and a thousand miles from the sea. Hell, what does a hick from Wausau know about a Maine lobster?

On one of my several trips to the Big Apple, I happened to walk past a theater in which the stage play "Bloomer Girl" was prominently displayed on the marquee. I decided to buy a ticket to see the play, only to be informed that it had been sold out for weeks.

The only other live play I had ever seen was back in my home town of Wausau where a group, featuring Charles Winneger, a Hollywood movie actor, annually put on a play in the Schofield School Auditorium. He originally hailed from this very small community.

I did not know what this play Bloomer Girl was all about, but I thought the title had sounded interesting. The fact that it was sold out would turn out to be only a momentary setback.

As I started to leave a fellow came over to me and grabbed my arm. He informed me he was the manager of this famous theater. "Did you just return to the States?" was his only question. "Yes sir, three days ago." He told me to wait by the side of the main entrance doors. "There's the possibility I might find a seat for today's performance," he whispered. My wait would not be long.

Minutes before the play was to start this same fellow tapped me on the shoulder and ushered me into the theater. We walked to the edge of a huge lobby, up several stairs, down a lengthy corridor, and stopped before a door he said led to my seat. "Take any seat. There will be no charge young man. Enjoy the show, it will start shortly."

When my eyes adjusted to the light conditions I discovered I was alone in a special box that actually protruded out over the edge of the right side of the stage. It became obvious to me that this was a very special box that had two rows of seats, with only four seats per row.

I was alone in a section of the theater where normally eight people would be seated. I sat down next to the balustrade with a single railing mounted on the ornate cap. The cushy seat felt comfortable and I suddenly felt important and privileged as I started to relax.

Once the lights were dimmed and the curtain went up, I realized and believed I probably had the best seat in the house. Now, for the first time I felt very self-conscious sitting alone in such a conspicuous spot. Without much effort I could see many eyes from below directed toward the balcony box I now occupied.

Then, to make matters even worse, several times during the performance, several different pretty singers, dressed in gay nineties dresses, looked up and intentionally directed their song and gestures right at me. It was obvious that they may have been told to do this by the manager.

The audience had a better sense of humor than I did. I was so damn embarrassed by this attention I can honestly say I would have rather faced a Luftwaffe Fighter Pilot than what these pretty young ladies were doing to me. I'm sure I blushed and directed my eyes elsewhere, only to exaggerate my being rattled. All of my self-assurance and coolness developed during my thirty-five combat missions seemed to vanish as a spotlight found my lonely seat more than once.

The play and the songs were about a period of history that took place during the 1890s. It was about women's suffrage and their right to be treated as equals. This current war and the accomplishments of this gender proved to the world that the American woman could do anything asked of her. During the performance the management even had the ushers bring me refreshments.

This gesture on the part of the theater manager and certain of the actresses was the first of many more such experiences where I was made to feel very special. At this period of the war I happened to be one of the early returning veterans and I suppose I was being looked upon as a valorous person. I was sometimes treated with sincere magnanimity that I knew was meant for someone on a far away battle front or someone who was never coming home. My country and its people had gone through so very much.

Despite the fact that I'm usually very outgoing, I am basically a shy person who did not always appreciate this preferential treatment. I was to be overwhelmed, once I reached my hometown of Wausau, Wisconsin. I found the people of this place I had grown up in could not have shown their gratitude or appreciation more. I had left for my cadet training feeling lonely and now upon returning I found it nearly impossible to be alone.

HOMEWARD BOUND

On October 10th, I was finally given my orders for my next assignment and told I had a sixty day-leave-of-absence. I was given train tickets to my hometown of Wausau, and another set of train tickets from there to Miami Beach, Florida, each one via dear old Chicago.

This trip to Florida would be an effort by the Air Force to appraise the condition of each returning veteran from the rigors of combat. There obviously was not a single veteran returning from seeing action against the enemy that was not affected in some way. Each would have to be evaluated by specialists. At this moment I was not mindful of any problems this veteran might have or things the Air Force might be interested in.

I discovered that the train trip from the New York Grand Central Station to the Chicago Union Station seemed to take forever. My anxiety was beginning to kick in. Though I constantly looked out of the window, my mind was traveling faster than this iron beast could move my body. I kept thinking I knew what the word married meant, but I'm not sure I knew all of its ramifications. Again I found myself scheduled for a brand new mission I hoped I was prepared for.

Now that I was actually moving toward home, rail transportation suddenly offered all of the negative things I remembered. It was slow, it was jerky, it was dirty, and it was uncomfortable. At this time I would have enjoyed seeing my old friend George Cormack and listen to him elucidate on the merits of rail transportation. This day however, I would have disregarded his enthusiasm by expounding exactly what I thought of the American rail system I believed our country was letting go to hell.

I arrived in Chicago early in the morning of October 12, which gave me a whole day to kill. Every time I take the train to Chicago it always arrives at around six A.M. and my next connection is in the early evening. Twelve hours alone in this big metropolitan city is something I never cherished. I have never found the "Windy City" to be the most cordial place to be alone in.

I distinctly remember one windy day in Chicago when my officer's cap blew off as I rounded a corner on La Salle Street. My cap started rolling down the center of the street with me in full chase. Perhaps a dozen people up ahead could have intercepted my special grommet-less head gear. Instead, they appeared to enjoy the dilemma this serviceman found himself in. My cap rolled nearly three blocks before I could stop its forward motion. Now it needed to be dry cleaned. "Thanks Windy City, I don't love you either."

Thinking about seeing my family and friends and realizing I was about to take part in my pending wedding, made each moment of inactively seem like an eternity. I had the impatience of a little child waiting for Christmas or perhaps some destination after a long automobile ride.

Waiting has never been one of my great virtues. This trip home was to be no exception. I think I went into two different movie theaters to kill most of the time, but what had been on the screens has completely evaporated from my mind.

On Thursday evening, at about 1800 hours of the same day, I boarded the Hiawatha Train for my last leg of my trip up north to Wausau, Wisconsin. This trip was scheduled to be an all night ride with no scenery and the usual clickidy-clack of the metal wheels taking note of the spaces between each of the rails. All of the swaying and jerking would still be apart of this ride.

The hardest part is just getting out of the "Windy City" and all of the required switching that the system seems to deem necessary. The route would be through a slummier part of Chicago where you could look down from the elevated tracks into weathered brick dwellings. Each dwelling looked like they had long out lived their usefulness and should have been taken down. Broken windows and boarded up openings marred the faces of nearly every structure.

Entire neighborhoods of soot colored wood dwellings with porches tacked on and little or no space for yards seemed to be paramount along the tracks leading out of Chicago. Little children in tattered clothing would stand in silence as they watched this train move northward. This is an area that the poor were obviously relegated to live in. None were impressed as the daily evening train rolled past and out of their city.

I was so nervous and impatient I rode in the smoker car most of the way up to the north-central part of my home state. I really got to know the Porter who shined shoes whenever he returned to this designated section of the train. I remember he had asked me to call him Clarence. During this trip we would carry on a several hour conversation.

He was interested in the war and particularly the part I played. He also appreciated the company on this lonely night. Periodically he would be compelled to leave me for duties he had to perform, but each time he would return we would carry on our chit chat, both of us ignoring the several interruptions.

He informed me that his home was in Gary, Indiana and that he has been working for the Rail Road over thirty years. He stated he loved his job very much and it was important for him to meet and talk with many of his passengers. He also informed me he had a son in the service over in Europe who drove a truck delivering supplies to various armed services. This would be my first real experience where I felt I got to know a little about an African American man. He made this otherwise lonely trip a truly great happening and I now wished I had gotten to know him better.

In the early hours of the morning, I began to recognize some of the little towns the train passed through. This was the C.M.ST.P. & P. line, an abbreviation for the Chicago, Milwaukee, St. Paul and Pacific Rail Road. As we slowed down in the dark I would notice the dimly lit, typical long narrow weathered brown signs hanging from the eave of each of the small depots, spelling out the name of the rail station we were approaching. Each little station or depot were very similar like the little signs I squinted at through my dirty window.

From Portage on I kept track of our progress as I strained my eyes trying to penetrate the besmeared train window. Next would come Wisconsin Dells, Lyndon

Station, Mauston and then the New Lisbon stop. Here we would pick up and drop off several passengers because this was the junction with the Chicago and Northwestern Rail Line. We crept through Necedah and Babcock and made a brief stop at Wisconsin Rapids. As the sun was coming up and I could identify each of these little communities with a little more clarity, I felt almost like I had never left home.

Two more whistle stops at Junction City and Mosinee and I would be home. At Mosinee I instantly recognized the rotten egg smell of sulfur dioxide, a bleaching agent used by the local paper mill. It was a tell tale sign no one could forget. As children we were often told about Mosinee: "If you couldn't spell it, you could certainly smell it."

I had arranged with the Porter to have the train stop at the depot in Rothschild, several miles south of Wausau. It was a stop that the railroad seldom used. It was here I knew Norma, my fiancée; my parents; and her family would be waiting to greet the returning airman.

I had placed a call to Norma while I was in Chicago so she was aware of my being on this particular train, which rarely had a reason for even delaying, let alone stopping in little old Rothschild. I was almost certain I would be the only passenger leaving this single daily train heading north.

At 7:25 A.M., Friday morning on October 13, 1944, the train slowly squeaked to a stop. For the last ten miles I stood by the closed door between cars, waiting with the Porter. All the plates that made up the floor between the two adjoining cars were moving in every direction. This improvised floor squeaked and groaned as they rubbed against one another. It seemed like this damn train needed these many miles to slow down from an already snails pace. Sometimes I sound like I'm not too impressed with rail travel.

Finally, even though the train seemed to be hardly moving, the engineer managed to stop with a jerk, sending me against the end of the passenger car and a pipe railing that pointed to the ground. My entire luggage was a stuffed B-4 bag and an equally heavy duffel bag, all in olive drab. The Porter insisted he carry these two items, plus a heavy metal step to be placed on the ground.

As he left the train he fell to the ground with all of the bag and baggage mentioned. He was lying amid this heap with his limbs disarrayed in every direction and his porter's cap spinning on the ground. I glanced toward the tiny depot and recognized the aggregation gathered for my homecoming. Suddenly I saw Norma break from the group. She was racing toward me with open arms as I bent down to help this hapless Porter.

In the seconds that were ticking off I did not know what the proper etiquette would be for this peculiar situation. I found myself straddling this fallen porter with one hand trying to lift him into a sitting position while my other arm was extended toward my bride-to-be. I felt frozen in time.

Then, to add to my dilemma, a glance back at the passenger cars revealed dozens of curious eyes staring out of every window within sight. Noses had been placed up against these dirty windows by all of the passengers on the right side of the car.

The Porter must have informed all who would listen about a returning war veteran about to meet his new bride-to-be. To this day I do not know in what order I had mastered the moment. The final scene, as the train slowly moved northward, was one happy airman in the arms of his sweetheart.

We remained at the clearing just south of the petite little depot for about a half hour. I needed this time to receive the blessings of each of the many who honored me by arising early this morning for this greeting. I was home and it felt good. Tears of joy seemed to be leaking out of most of the eyes of the eight or more people who had welcomed me home. Though he tried to conceal it, I saw a tear or two trickle down my Dad's check before it could be rubbed away.

CHAPTER 22

My old room at my parents' house seemed almost estranged to me. I had been away at the University of Wisconsin for a year prior to my enlistment and now I was returning to a place I had spent most of my life in. In the interim, my Mother had rearranged and decorated this space so it did not welcome me as I had expected. My Father even had altered several areas of our house so it almost took on the appearance of an entirely different place.

I would not spend too much of my time at home these first days because Norma somehow took precedence in all my thoughts and emotions. It was not my intention to appear insensitive of my parent's wishes, nor hurt their feelings because of my current priorities. I know I spent a disproportionate amount of time away from 217 Weston Avenue, the address of my Parents.

There were many moments when I seemed to be living in a vacuum with people from all directions wanting my mind and time. Time began to take on a new dimension for me when I realized I could not be at several different places at the same instant to pacify desires from divergent sources.

About this time I suddenly realized and became aware of some unfamiliar and uncharacteristic sensations in my body. I would develop a cold sweat that may only last a few minutes. There were times my hands would start to shimmer and shake and it may force me to set a cup of coffee down because the rattling of the cup against the saucer.

I would find myself suddenly lighting a cigarette when I would notice one burning in the ash tray. I did not have to divulge these idiosyncrasies to Norma because her caring eyes and her training as a nurse had detected a problem developing.

Strange sensations made their appearance at the most awkward times and I began to feel others might notice it. I made it a point to drink a cup of coffee off by myself or I would use two hands to remove the cup from a saucer. I sometimes had trouble even lighting a cigarette. I would not point at something because of the involuntary movement my protruded index finger assumed.

The nerves I had control of on combat missions appeared to be leaving me. The more I tried to hide my dilemma the worse it seemed to get. Both Norma and I concluded that my nerves were going through a transition and needed time to react to a completely different life situation. Within the week we both noticed an obvious improvement.

I later was to learn, when I attended the University of Michigan and in their Infirmary, my entire nervous system had been compared to a large spring similar to one in an alarm clock. This spring (my nerves) had been wound up very tight and it remained in this condition for a long time (my tour of duty in England). Now that I was relieved of the stresses and strains, this spring was trying to unwind and assume its normal function. It would take some time before everything would settle back to some normalcy.

WHAT ABOUT THE WEDDING

The first major decision had already been made prior to my arrival. The wedding had to be postponed one-week, until Saturday, October 21. Wishful thinking had selected the date of October 14th, the day after my arrival. The primary reason for selecting this specific new date was the requirement, in the State of Wisconsin, requesting a blood sample be taken by a doctor and sent to Madison, the State Capital. This had to be done prior to receiving a marriage license. This would take several days.

I felt really bad I had been unable to give Mrs. Schmidt a more accurate time and date for my arrival home. However, this had been entirely in the hands of the military. I'm sure the Schmidt Family appreciated the additional time for this very special wedding. As for me, I would have taken my bride-to-be up to the courthouse and a judge or talked some minister into stepping out on his porch and hitching us. Anything that Norma wanted was the way it would be.

My part in the actual planning was practically nil, though I found out there were some matters I had to take care of. Somehow, the only real significant thing that mattered to me at this moment in time was I now was home at last and I had managed to arrive in one piece. As for the wedding, I would go wherever they pointed me and do whatever anyone wanted of me.

Just being home was only a small part of my feelings. I now was with the one person in this world that had represented my many recurring dreams and thoughts these past six months. She now was beside me and I could ask or tell her anything. I could reach out to touch or hold her and I could expect responses to my own consciousness. My Norma Ann had waited and, despite a courtship that relied on the inefficiency of the overseas' mails, she wanted to share her life with me.

This fact may not seem like a testimonial for some kind of commemoration, nor will it go down in the books as a record. I knew many of my buddies who had received "Dear John Letters" and had their dreams shattered. I knew of some of my fellow crewmen who had sweethearts waiting for them and they constantly broke the bonds of trust and fidelity. These were difficult times that constantly tested individuals' strengths and weaknesses.

Our country was going through a war, people were forced to be separated for long periods of time, and the paramount feeling of only relying on the moment and not the future, caused potential couples to drift apart or be overwhelmed by unfaithfulness.

These were not my problems. I had been brought up and raised to believe and respect the virtues of trust and faithfulness. These same qualities would be paramount when I would consider an individual to become a friend of mine. Though courtship and romance were relatively new to this novice lover, I knew that a marriage to succeed had to be built on trust and respect for one another. You did not have to be an Einstein to realize this.

I found out later, after we had been married, that Norma had been exposed one evening to a situation that could have proved embarrassing, if not a total disaster. In the ensuing weeks while I was still at Fort Lee awaiting my sixty day pass to return home, Norma had overheard a mutual acquaintance, a young girl who lived only two blocks from my home, tell another person that Lt. Lloyd Krueger was on his way home from combat and that they were going to get married.

Nothing could have been further from the truth since I had never even had a date with this person. I only knew her because of the proximity of her home and that of my parents. In actuality, I probably hadn't seen or had any contact with her for three years or more. I was so very sorry Norma had to be subjected to this kind of cruel fabrication and erroneous groundless gossip.

Though I believe I knew what the real world was like, I never had doubts or worries about our own relationship. Our continuing letters each contained only positive thoughts, about what would or should lie ahead for the two of us. The word L O V E is such a nebulous thing, but its basic connotation has primarily to do with feelings and trust.

As I look back to these early days in the war I now know that the strict and regimented way I had been brought up and raised in a German oriented family was more conducive to withstand the exposure to combat than to be a romantic or amorous person. I wondered if it was possible to make up for all the time I seemed to have misplaced or that had vanished.

While growing up it was a rarity to see my Mother and Father embrace or kiss one another, yet I knew that they both deeply loved and respected each other. Though it may have happened, I do not ever remember a kiss from either of my parents or a hug to assure me that everything was okay or I had done something they might have been proud of. All these things would have to be taken for granted. At the same time I always felt I belonged and was accepted 100%, even though I sometimes was not understood.

I suppose love can be expressed in a multitude of ways. Tender passion can be replaced by solicitude and compatibility and still be recognized as affection. The words sweaty pie, honey, precious, and darling would not carry as much weight in my world as such words as admire, esteem, appreciated or to be devoted to. There were so many nights I would lay on my cot and reflect on what all of this really means and just how much of it I understood.

I grew up believing it was necessary for me to be very masculine, where such words as brave, valiant, muscular, athletic, strong, courageous, self-reliant, gallant, and chivalrous are paramount in my development. Now, suddenly I am lying on my back and staring up in to the darkness, deep in my own thoughts about words I was aware of but hesitated to interject into a sentence or thought.

Such words as affection, tenderness, devotion, unselfishness, and benevolence came to mind as to their importance. I knew words like admiration and common interests as words with significance because they could relate to anyone of my buddies.

I also knew I personally was a very sensitive person toward all things in nature and more particularly people. I also was aware I had much to learn, but I knew I had the desire to be worthy of this young woman who waited for me. Perhaps, we both would find that it might be necessary to do some adjusting and this we would learn together.

While I was in England and separated from my "love" I ran across a poem that both captured my deep inner feelings and the moment. I sent Norma a copy of this poetic endeavor that I appreciated so very much. It was my belief she would appreciate this poem as much as I did.

Purely by accident, I discovered a battered and torn magazine thrown along the pathway on one of my solitary walks. Debris in England was a rarity. This must have been done by some disrespectful G.I. In this magazine, on one of the few legible pages, was a poem that caught my eye and heart. It said everything I wish I had the talent to express at this period in my life. Periodical I would remove this battered clipping of this poem and read and reread it several times at night. It was perhaps my surrogate prayer. Now I desire to preserve this poem and make it apart of my story.

WAIT FOR ME

(by Konstantin Simonor, (Russian)
Wait for me - I will come back.
only wait . . . and wait.
Wait though rain clouds glowering black make you desolate.
Wait though winter snowstorms whirl,
Wait though summer's hot
Wait though no one else will wait and past forgot;
Wait though from the distant front, not one letter comes;
Wait though everyone who waits sick of it becomes.
Wait for me . . . I will come back.
Pay no heed to those who'll so glibly tell you that it is vain to wait.
Though my mother and my son think that I am gone,
Though my friends abandon hope.
And back there at home rise and toast my memory, wrapped in silence pained,
Wait. And when they drink that toast, leave your glass undrained.
Though from Death's own jaws
Let the friends who did not wait
Think it chance, no more.
They will never understand
Those who did not wait
How we, your waiting that saved me in the war.
And the reason I've come through we shall know, we two;
Simply this, you waited as no one else could do.
No one else could do.

KEEPING A PROMISE

One of the first things I had to do, once my feet were planted on the terra firma home in Wisconsin was to borrow my father's car and drive to Antigo, about forty miles northeast of Wausau. I had to first locate and then to see my friend Lt. Lyle Dallman's wife. I wanted to let her know that fellow crewmen spotted her husband's parachute open and that he was alive.

I knew that the War Department had notified her, simply stating that her husband was MIA, "Missing In Action", and I knew it would be months before any update on his condition would be made. I was right, the only news Marion had was the telegram informing her that Lyle was indeed a MIA. Norma and I made this trip to also deliver medals, war mementoes, and several small gifts I had been given by Lyle to take to his wife Marion and children.

On the way to Antigo, while we were in serious conversation, I managed to gradually let the car migrate over to the left side of the road. I was driving along, big dumb and happy and was not aware of my mistake. Evidently part of my mind was still back in England since this is how everyone drove in the British Isles all of the time.

When I spotted a car, that looked like it had a bead on me, my first reaction was to cuss him out. "Look at that crazy fool . . . he's driving on the wrong side of the road." A scream from Norma tested my reflexes as I quickly swerved my vehicle into its proper lane. What the war had not managed to do my stupidity almost succeeded in accomplishing.

We met Lt. Dallman's wife Marion for the first time. We sat down with her for several hours, both to get to know her and to give her all of the information we had about her husband. I explained the type of shuttle mission he had gone on. I was able to tell her what target they were on during the second leg of this special type of bombing raid and I knew that ten parachutes had been spotted by crewmembers in other planes.

Marion was a beautiful woman who was raising two little boys by herself. One of the youngsters had been diagnosed as a severe diabetic. She did not need this insufferable uncertainty. I was happy I could remove a little of the mental and emotional load she had been forced to carry. Though Lyle was now a P.O.W., at least he was alive and would be liberated soon, once the Allies over took the remainder of Germany and its satellite countries. Now it would only be a matter of time.

Lt. LYLE DALLMAN

Several years later, Lyle paid a visit to our home in Madison, and I was able to find out more details about his crew that went down on September 6, 1944. On their bomb run at Szolnok, Hungary, they were trying to knock out a railroad shop. Their plane received two direct hits from flak and they were forced to bail out.

All ten members of the crew immediately were captured by Hungarian peasants, who beat them and perhaps would have killed them, had not the German troops come to their rescue. They were all sent to various prison camps except one particular individual. His story is incredible and almost unbelievable. It may put a strain on the credulities of any who might be reading this account.

Lt. John S. Bromberg was considered the Ace Lead Bombardier of the 95th bomb Group. He had been a professional wrestler prior to joining the Air Force and, as a result, he was distinguished by having both of his ears damaged to the extent they were extremely cauliflowered. He was built like a brick outhouse and all knew he was as hard as nails.

The following account was taken from a book published by the 95th Bomb Group, simple called "CONTRAILS". I believe this account of what happened to Lt. Bromberg is important to recount here, because many others, who did make it back, paid more than their just dues.

LT. BROMBERG

"He was the Lead Bombardier on this plane that took two hits. The second burst of flak knocked him off his seat out onto the catwalk at the escape hatch. He crawled back to the bombsight and released his bombs. All other planes in the formation now released their loads. A road convoy took pot shot at him as he floated down. He landed in a cornfield and managed to hide for some time."

"He had been hit several times in one foot. A small group of SS men and Hungarian soldiers discovered him and kicked him around. They then chained his wrists and dragged him to one of their vehicles. He was next taken to a farmhouse and put under guard, but not before several women and children struck him repeatedly with fists and sticks. He next was locked up in a village cell without windows, lights, bed or chair."

"With no medical attention, he was taken by trolley and train to Szeged near the Rumanian border, a trip lasting until midnight. He was again locked in a similar cell. All of his personal belongings were taken from him. Two days later, without food or water, he was taken to Budapest."

"During that incarceration, a Luftwaffe Major interrogated him for hours. He refused to divulge any information other than his name, rank and serial number. The Major then threatened to turn him over to the Gestapo, and demanded information on captured equipment which they showed him, such as bombsights, radar sets, and aerial cameras. Once again Bromberg would not talk."

"He then was taken into another room where two young men beat him up with rubber hoses and the liberal use of fists and feet. He lost consciousness and suffered a broken rib and clavicle. He was given no medical attention and had no food or water for seven days."

"Finally he was given some thin black ersatz coffee and put on a railroad prison car with other prisoners. This train traveled for several weeks because of bombed out tracks. His only food was black coffee and occasional thin soup."

"At Dulag Luft in Oberursel he was put into a cell with no ventilation. A large heater was turned on to make the room unbearably hot. Then it would be turned off and the room became intensely cold. He was again interrogated but would divulge no information. The next day he was sent to Wetzlar P.W. Camp. Here he was offered some food but was unable to eat."

"He was sent to an infirmary and fed liquids. Next he was again put on a train. At Fulda an air raid warning was given and Bromberg and his two guards went to a shelter. A bomb hit nearby, killing the two guards and knocking Bromberg unconscious, with metal fragments buried in both of his legs. He was picked up by stretcher and loaded on a train."

"Near Eisenbach it was strafed by American P-47s and wrecked. He finally was taken to an Allied hospital, run by the British, with German guards. There he received his first medical treatment since he had bailed out. The hospital had been liberated, by the 11th Armoured Division on April 2, 1945, six months after Lt. Bromberg's ill-fated 34th mission."

"Soon after his release the rugged bombardier went into action with tank and infantry units. On one patrol he killed a German General who tried to shoot him as he entered a house."

Note: The above account was taken from the 95th Bomb Group's CONTRAILS, a book published about the history of our Group. This story is related here, because it is an actual example of the total dedication on the part of one individual, who I was happy to call my friend and who I had flown with.

WEDDING PREPARATIONS

Little by little I was exposed to some of the myriad of decisions that had to be made when planning a wedding. I was not proxy to most of this, but on occasion, when I made the mistake of hanging around, I sometimes ventured a suggestion or reply for something I knew nothing about. Like "How many of your relatives would attend the wedding?" "Hell, most of them didn't even talk to one another," I remembered.

I wasn't even sure how many relatives I had. Since my mother had come from Iowa, her side of the family was scattered in every corner of the "Corn Husker State." My Mother assured me none of these relatives would come because they could not afford to make the trip.

My father's tribe all lived in the Wausau area, but family disputes had most relatives not having contact with one another. Much of the dissension was precipitated by the actions of the dozen or more male cousins. Nearly all my aunts and uncles on my paternal side had three or four sons, just like our household.

I recalled that when some of these paternal relatives got together the first line of business was to get the boxing gloves on several of the boys. We would beat the heck out of one another until someone got a bloodied nose or said he'd had enough. The only satisfaction gained from one of these debacles appeared to be solely by the fathers.

The wives blew a fuse when they saw their son with a bloodied nose and his clothes in disarray. Usually they would get pissed off and insist on being taken home. Say no more. For some reason or another my parents seemed to be the only ones who had and maintained contact with all of the other relatives. I grew up looking at all my cousins in Wausau as pugnacious off springs of each of my aunts. We grew up to be bitter rivals and competitors in all the sports where we competed against one another.

This now would be one of the few chores I was asked to do for the pending wedding. They expected me to inform them of how many of my aunts and uncles they could expect to attend the ceremonies. I tried picking the minds of my Mom and Dad and got conflicting guesses of who would or would not come to this wedding.

This one would show up if that one stayed home. They went through a myriad of combinations and possibilities. All this was conjecture obviously. Finally I said we should just divide the total of potential relatives by two and this number might be somewhat realistic. Using pure logic finally resolved this most difficult current problem.

DECISIONS – DECISIONS

Now I was asked something directly that seemed to have a personal touch to it. The simplest question I had to answer was; "Who do you desire to be your best man at the wedding?" This would be the easiest decision I would have to make. George Cormack would fill this position. I had never spent a moment, since our engagement, thinking about what constituted a wedding party. I only envisioned the two of us saying "I do" in front of a minister and that would be it. However, this decision immediately created an instant argument with my Mother and Father. As it turned out, the final resolution would be neither simple nor easy.

My quick determination, as to who would be the Best Man at the wedding, became a major family problem. My parents told me that my brother Robert, who was exactly one year and one day younger than me, should be my Best Man. My Brother Bob was taking no part of this earth-shaking problem now being kicked around. He could have cared less.

Once I understood the symbolic role of the Best Man at a wedding I could not possibly image having anyone but my friend George. I now took a firm and immediate stand on this major point of contention. Bob would be in the wedding party but he would not be the Best Man. I guess they term his position as the Groomsman. I now had two unhappy parents. This was a role both of my parents were accustomed to since many of my important decision these past few years were in direct conflict with their beliefs or understandings.

At this point I got an instant quilt feeling. I realized my parents had taken a back seat for my attention since I came home. Though I slept in their home and ate a few meals, otherwise I was gone. All of my interest was now focused on one person, Norma.

My folks were sort of left out of perhaps one of the most important things about to happen to me, the wedding. I was also the eldest son and the first to get married. Without realizing it, some of my priorities were changing right before my eyes. Waging war in the skies over Europe seemed to require fewer resolutions.

Most of the planning and details were in the hands of the Bride's parents. Fortunately, and purely by accident, Norma and I had both gone to the same church, so this did not develop into anything consequential. I knew I would marry her under any roof where a marriage ceremony could be performed. If Norma had merely said she wanted me, it would have been the only bond I would have needed to make us a team forever.

I did not know the protocol for all the nuts and bolts of a wedding. Hell, like I said, I had never attended a wedding ceremony. Taking part in a shivaree did not make me an expert in anything. The fact that we could bang on an old circular saw with a hammer or perhaps a pan, until someone gave you a desert, or probably a drink, and just because this was a traditional thing to do, did not qualify me as being adroit at anything. All of the knowledge collected regarding the several shivarees I had been at would not help me now.

I finally told my parents that they may think me stubborn or bull headed, but I only expect to get married once. George Cormack would be my Best Man and my Brother Bob would be my Groomsman. I knew my brother Bob did not give a damn, one way or the other. He also had been a member of our shivaree parties. After several hours of heated discussion, things finally settled down and my parents will once again attend the wedding.

BEYOND THE WEDDING

I now realized a major problem that I would be confronted with. THE-LACK-OF- MONEY. I had lived my life in combat knowing the odds of coming home were about fifty-fifty. I spent my meager flight pay like there was no tomorrow. Now, for the first time, I was aware that my future required an entirely different fiscal attitude. I had to analyze what my potential was in the restrictive position the military had me in.

I knew my base annual salary, as a First Lieutenant, was $2000.00 per year, or $166.67 per month. As a flying Officer, I would get an additional pay increase, amounting to 50% of base pay. This would increase my monthly pay to exactly $250.00. Then there is the subsistence allowance for a dependent, my Norma. This would increase it by another $42.00 per month. Finally, we would get $75.00 per month rent allowance, making a grand total of $367.00 per month. Hell, I almost felt like a king. However, this monthly allotment would only take effect once I got married and would have my wife with me.

My problem, at the moment, was to borrow enough of the green stuff to buy a ring for Norma and to have some money to go on a short honeymoon. My friend George came through and loaned me a small sum of money. His Scotch ancestry determined the extent, or rather limitation, of our honeymoon plans. The monetary problem was ultimately given a shot in the arm. I later discovered attendees at weddings usually bring gifts. Some of these gifts fortunately were pecuniary in nature and came to our rescue.

In the process of all the financial computations I was beginning to realize the responsibility one assumes when you have to be accountable to another person. This would be my biggest challenge. My first big expenditure would be the two dollars required for the marriage license. Norma obviously was worth this modest disbursement and I found I could handle this expenditure without tapping friend or family.

About this time I again became aware of a somewhat serious problem with my nerves. I was unwinding from a life of intense excitement and danger, to a life more laid-back. Again my hands shook when I tried to light a cigarette or pick up a cup of coffee. These were feelings I had never had before I returned home and I wasn't quite sure how to handle them.

I obviously had to cut back on my drinking for a multitude of reasons. I thought that this may have something to do with these tremors. I did my best to conceal my current affliction by a variety of tricks. I would not light cigarettes in front of people, or I would pick up my cup of coffee with both hands and simply sip.

Just before the wedding day I was told to show up late in the afternoon at a large shower given by friends of Norma. I was to help open gifts from all those in attendance. Mistake. Big mistake. I had spent the afternoon at the "Glass Slipper" bar. I had been talked into playing a drinking game that was new to me and would not help my present situation.

The first player to roll a twelve, or "box cars" suggested a concoction of various alcohols for a single drink. The next unlucky roller to hit this same combination had to pay for it, while the third one to hit the twelve, had to drink it. Actually, the same person could accomplish all three of these losses.

Though I was one of the luckier players of this stupid game, I really left for the shower with a great deal of apprehension, but feeling no pain. My assumptions proved accurate. I fumbled with tape and ribbons in front of about fifty or sixty giggling women, who seemed to cherish this position I seemed to have found myself in. "What in hell is so wrong if you accidentally damage a piece of decorated wrapping paper?" The final hour of this shower had moments when I started to compare my current situation to facing up to some of "Jerrie's" flak.

Over at the Schmidt house everyone had dozens of jobs and things to get done. Wedding dress and dresses for the bridesmaid, the maid of honor, the flower girls, etc. were things I was only aware of. I stayed away. I had planned to get married in my uniform so what did I have to worry about.

Fortunately, my mother had scrutinized the condition of my uniform, the garb I had intended to get married in. The sleeves of my Officer's blouse, on the underside, were coated with scum collected from hundreds of bars in British pubs. I had rested my arms or elbows on obviously soiled surfaces, picking up whatever might have been on them. I had been completely unaware of the soiled condition of this, my Officers blouse.

When I took this mess to the dry cleaners they assured me they could make it look just like the day it was issued. They were right. They had removed all of the buttons, brass, ribbons, medals and insignia from this blouse before it was cleaned. They then sewed or attached all of these removed items to their designated position.

My pinks (shirts and trousers), my ties, and the blouse looked new and unworn. Besides the fantastic job the cleaners did on this uniform, they refused to take any pay for their services. This is just another example of appreciation shown this airman by the people I had come home to.

A few days before the wedding, Norma and I picked out simple wedding rings for the pending ceremony. We had very limited choices because of the amount of money I was capable of spending. We agreed that the symbol and spirit of these rings were more important than the intrinsic value. We both possessed nothing but positive thoughts and had confidence in our future.

THE FADING MOMENTS OF INNOCENCE

Saturday, October 21, 1944 had now arrived. The wedding was scheduled for four P.M. at the St. Paul Evangelical Church and I had the greater part of a day to walk the floor, smoke endless cigarettes, take nervous pees, and wondered what I was getting into. This entire scenario was like my memories of the time my folks forced me to play my saxophone in front of a large Christmas audience. I had not mastered the instrument, I was extremely shy, my audience appeared to be indifferent, and it was the last place on earth I wanted to be. "Surely, this wedding couldn't be more difficult than combat?"

The moment of truth finally arrived, George, my brother Robert and I waited up at the front of the nave with Pastor Ortwein. This large church seemed to have every pew filled. Women, who didn't even know either of us, came out of curiosity. Neighbors from each of our families found it necessary to see the spectacle about to take place. I couldn't believe or understand why.

The organ had been playing for some time, but now with a slight pause, the wedding march started to slowly fill the air. All heads turned toward the narthex. This show was going to be bigger than "Bloomer Girl" and I again felt like the spot light was about to find me. Each of us at the head of the church altered our position so we faced the throng who occupied every space on all of the pews.

The bride and her entourage had been waiting also for this moment. Little Kay Johnson, the Flower Girl walked down the aisle defined by gawking faces turned toward the back of the church. She was completely oblivious of the packed house. She advanced with more confidence than I felt at this moment.

As she held a dainty basket with one hand she nonchalantly scattered small colorful flower blossoms along the carpeted path with the other. Casually she approached the sacred territory where the Minister, along with the three bewildered stooges, are each patiently waiting.

Some distance behind little Kay I now noticed Elain Poore, Norma's special friend from nurses training at Rochester, Minnesota. She also would stutter-step her way toward the sanctuary as the Bridesmaid. "Why do they have to drag this thing out?" Now Nathalie Johnson, Norma's roommate while she attended the University of Wisconsin, made her presence. She also was taking her good natured time getting up to the front of the church. Nathalie would be the Maid Of honor.

Norma came into view as she left the Narthex of the church on the arm of her Father, Edwin Frederick Schmidt. He turned out to be the best father–in-law anyone could ever have, and he will always be remember by me as just plain "Ike", his nickname. As she entered the Nave of this rather large church, the carpeted aisle seemed like a mile long.

Ever pew was filled, not only by relatives and friends of both families, but by the multitude of curious strangers. There did not seem to be enough room for each to twist around, snap photographs, and get their first view of the Bride. The confusion of this moment created sounds that were in conflict with Brahms' Wedding March being emitted from the organ pipes that covered the entire rear wall of this church.

My arrival home had been written up in the Wausau Daily Record Herald. Inquisitive old women discovered a place to be entertained and had filled this large church to its capacity. Once I had spotted Norma, I glanced around the Nave very quickly, only to realize I hardly recognized a face in this huge ecclesiastical place.

My bewildered eyes looked upon hundreds of people I had never seen before. On three side of this large Nave was a balcony in which there were about six rows of additions pews filled with the curious. I was going to play before a packed house.

THE WEDDING

The scene I was witnessing looked like it had been cast for a movie. Norma had concealed her athletic appearance beneath a beautiful wedding dress. There was a crown on her blonde hair and she carried a large bouquet of yellow roses. The usual bounce in her stride was replaced by a stutter-step down this mile long aisle and her personality was concealed somewhere within this satin wedding gown and her veil made of Italian lace. It became apparent she was in no hurry to get on with it because she and her father took forever to arrive at the front of the church.

This was "Ike's" baby and youngest daughter about to get married and all of the deep wrinkles on his face were arced in the form of an unmistakable smile, all the while he tried to look somber. Much to my amazement he also had mastered that damn stutter-step that meant they would take forever to reach my side.

Finally "Ike" proclaimed that he would give his youngest daughter away after being prodded by Reverend Ortwein. Norma and I were now standing together and the show was about to begin. The usual ceremony was nearing the climax when I knew I had one obligation yet to perform. As the good Reverend raised his hands above us to formally pronounce us Man and Wife, I leaned over toward Norma's left ear and whispered "Oh Bullah." This was an "in-house joke", between the two of us.

While in England, for no known reason, the exclamation of "Oh Bullah" was expressed if anyone wanted to avoid using profanity or some diabolic word. It got to be sort of a stupid habit I suppose. When I arrived home, it seems I had unconsciously abused this simple remark during the long and trying week. I had promised her never to say it again after we were married.

This then, was my last chance to get in one more "Oh Bullah." Norma tried to conceal her laughter and only managed to shake and shimmer. Everyone in the church believed she had broken down and was crying. A touching and sentimental moment this was not.

When Rev. Ortwein said, "you may now kiss your wife", I closed my eyes, puckered up and leaned forward to give Norma a kiss. In this brief moment of hilarity, Norma decided it was time to move on out. She had already turned and started down the aisle, with her husband a step or two behind. Our embrace had to wait until we reached the Narthex.

THE RECEPTION

Immediately after the ceremony, Norma and I had to go across the street to Lemke Photography Studio to get some formal pictures taken. After the pictures had been shot and I was making arrangement with the photographer for payment, Norma let out a scream. I turned around as two large fellows, dressed in gay nineties garb, were pulling Norma out the door.

I could recognize them as Norma's Uncle Roy and Walter Drew, a friend of the family I had previously met. Just at that moment I was also ushered out to the street and forced to get into a rejuvenated freshly painted black 1928 Model-A Ford.

While they were awaiting my return from combat and the pending wedding, Norma's Uncle Roy Hanson, along with Norma's brother-in-law Cliff Johnson, her father "Ike", and my Dad worked on this old car. Uncle Roy came up with the idea that they could get an old car from the dump and put it into some sort of working condition. Roy went out to the dump and resurrected a junked old car he thought had possibilities.

He worked on it until he barely got it running. Now this small group spent the next several weeks giving the piece of junk a quick paint job and a little dignity.

The broken windows were removed and the torn upholstery covered with blankets. The project would be complete once they mounted an old horn on the driver's side, which was operated by squeezing a rubber bulb.

At about 5 o'clock on Saturday afternoon, just as people were leaving work for home, this vehicle, with Norma and I perched high in the back seat, was driven up and down Third Street, the main street in the heart of Wausau. Uncle Roy, a 5ft. 8 inch 280 pound farmer and Walter Drew, a tall slender sixty year old, occupied the front seat of the passé escapee from the dump. This moving object was about as streamlined as an old packing crate. It had the sound of a laboring threshing machine and it traveled at a maximum speed of approximately 5 miles per hour.

As if this sight did not draw enough attention, the antiquated horn assured we would have everyone's glances. Both Norma and I had mixed emotions while riding in this auspicious vehicle. We had just been pronounced man and wife and now perfect strangers were looking at us in astonishment, wondering what in hell all the commotion is all about.

What seemed like an eternity, we finally pulled up in front of the Hotel Wausau, where the reception was to be held. The sad part of this entire incident is, not a single picture was taken of this revived car. Our professional photographer is still kicking himself for not capturing this moment on film.

He had not known about this unique project the fellows had worked on for so long. Their efforts to make our wedding something really special vanished when the car was returned to the dump. Norma and I personally do not need a picture to recall their appreciated efforts. This would be but a single moment in the many memories we have of this special day of October 21st, 1944.

The reception, in one of the large dining rooms of the Hotel Wausau, was a large affair. Family, friends, relatives, and many people who would be perfect strangers to me attended this banquet. From here, the entire entourage left to go to a building next to Norma's home, in the Village of Rothschild. For this special wedding, they had fixed up this unused old structure, cleaned and decorated it, and waxed up the floor for dancing.

My parents and I had believed only about half of the relatives on our side of the family would show up. We were so very wrong. Every last one of these relatives, who seldom spoke to one another, where going to the dance.

During the Flying Dutchman Dance, one by one my four aunts, tried to out do one another on the dance floor by nearly tearing my arms off. By this time I was completely out of uniform, with my blouse stashed somewhere and my tie pulled off. There were times I felt like I had been in a wrestling match.

Just about the time that the evening got perking on all cylinders, an unexpected hush suddenly came over the crowded dance floor. We all moved away from the center and formed a circle of astonishing eyes to watch my 85 year old Grandfather, waltz across the floor with my new wife.

Heinrick, Friedrick, Wilhelm, Krueger and Norma Ann Krueger were flowing across this unique dance floor to a Viennese Waltz. It was beautiful to witness this young bride, in her wedding dress, and this proud old German, with his handle bar waxed mustache, glide effortlessly, within the tight circle of spectators and admirers. If there had been any dissension between my relatives, they now had forgotten what it was. They not only were talking, they were dancing with one another.

It was nearly 1:30 in the morning when Norma and I stole away from the party, which was still going on. The orchestra had been paid to remain and the bar was kept open. Norma and I had secretly registered at the Hotel Wausau, supposing that we had fooled everyone as to where we would spend the night. We found our room and so did others. Our bed had been short sheeted and mothballs had been placed under the mattress. My only Sister's perverted sense of humor would not spoil this night.

THE HONEYMOON

Early the next morning we took my father's car and headed north on a one-week honeymoon. We had made no reservations. Our plan was a simple one. We wanted to rent a nice clean cottage that had to be on a lake, it had to have a fireplace, and it had to have electricity. The plan sounded simple.

During these years in Wisconsin, prior to snowmobiles and the interest in cross-country skiing, we discovered, to our astonishment, all cottages were closed for the duration of the winter. Some might open up during deer hunting season, but that would not be until the later part of November. This was only October. We pulled into and stopped at nearly a dozen locations, only to find them shut down for the season.

We finally arrive at a town about 100 miles north of Wausau, called Minacqua. Norma and I ended up in Barnie's Bar at about 4 P.M. with no place to spend the night or for that matter, the week. Barnie's Bar is noted for only one thing. That single shot at notoriety was having the longest bar in the State of Wisconsin, approximately seventy feet in length. The place had only a few customers and the far side of the room was without lights, making the long bar appear to vanish into the darkness.

Norma and I talked about our situation but neither of us had pressed a panic button. We both could see the irony of our predicament, but what the hell. We had a few drinks and during the hour we were in there, we kept playing "our song" which was "Till Then" by the Mills Brothers. No one else seemed interested in the music box so we felt no competition when making our special selection, over and over again.

Barnie finally said, after listening to repeated versions of the same song, "Do you guys have a problem?" "No, we are just up north here on our honeymoon and have not found a place to stay." There was no anxiety or apprehension in our retort. A now concerned Barnie called his sister and she agreed to open up one of her cottages that are normally used only during the summer season.

Norma and I had first heard the song "Till Then" right after we had gotten engaged. Instantly we both recognized that the words to this song had been meant for our exact situation. Special hope, belief, conviction, and optimism would be required by the two of us during my tour of duty over the skies of Europe. This song would fill that special need.

There would be many moments during my stay in England when either the BBC (British Broadcasting Network) or Axis Sally of the German Propaganda Network would play "our song." I was not able to ever listen to the words of this song without thinking of Norma and the hopes and dreams we had for the future. By letter, Norma informed me that these words gave her equal hope for our tomorrows.

"TILL THEN"

Written by: Guy Wood, Eddie Seiler, & Sol Marcus
Sung by: The Mills Brothers, John, Herbert, Harry & Donald

TILL THEN, my darling please wait for me,
TILL THEN, no matter when it will be,
One day, I know I'll be back again,
Please wait TILL THEN.

Our dreams, will live tho' we are apart,
Our love, I will keep in our hearts,
TILL THEN, when all the world will be free,
Please wait TILL THEN.

Although, there are oceans we must cross,
And mountains that we must climb.

I know every gain must have a loss,
So pray that our loss, is nothing but time.

TILL THEN, let's dream of what there will be,
TILL THEN, we'll call on each memory,
TILL THEN, when I will hold you again,
Please wait TILL THEN.

Although, there are oceans we must cross,
And mountains that we must climb,
I know every gain must have a loss,
So pray that our loss, is nothing but time.

TILL THEN, let's dream of what there will be,
TILL THEN, we'll call on each memory,
TILL THEN, when I will hold you again,
Please wait TILL THEN.

OUR APPRECIATED COTTAGE

It took many hours to get the cottage on Mid Lake to warm up. We had no fireplace but we ended up with two out of three of our desires. The beautiful log cabin was on Lake Minoqua, but actually we were within canoeing distance of Lake Tomahawk and Mid Lake. A short river or stream connected all three of these beautiful lakes. This was awfully nice of these people to open up a cottage and their hearts to a newly wedded couple.

We were invited over one evening for dinner with the Wilsons, but for this we paid the exorbitant price of having to look at over 2500 slides of the building of the Alaskan Highway. Our host had worked on this major road-building project for two years and it now was apart of his life.

My recollection of this endless supply of 35 mm slides was that over ninety percent of them showed nothing but mud, huge rocks, and heavy road equipment. Once, when we thought he had projected all of his boring slides, he discovered another box full of those suckers.

Frank "Mopey" Morman, and his relatively new wife, Marlys, joined us later in the week. Marlys came from my neighborhood and both Norma and I knew her. Frank was an Officer in the U.S. Navy so he also was in uniform. I had not known he was home from sea duty or that he had actually attended the wedding. We two old married couples spent several days together, enjoying the north woods with all of its autumn beauty. Like most honeymoons, this one seemed too short and before we knew it, we had to return to reality.

The one important thing I did learn during these sunny autumn days in Northern Wisconsin was that Norma had the same intense interest in nature. What I had hoped for was in fact a reality. The woods with all of its large and minute creatures intrigued her as it has always done for me. Becoming one, with the out-of-doors, would forever be apart of our lives.

When we got home, Norma had to start making plans for her return trip to Rochester, Minnesota and her nurses' training. It was very hard to have to say goodbye and know we would once again be separated. I had a week before I would be required to head south and resume my flight duties. An added regret at this moment in time was the realization I would have to get on that damn train again.

The most difficult thing we had to content with is the lost opportunity for Norma to join me down at Miami Beach, Florida for several weeks in the sun. I knew neither one of us had ever been there, but I also knew she had no option but to return to her classes in Rochester, Minnesota. Each of us knew how to face up to these difficult moments and we knew we were capable of making yet another sacrifice. We had agreed before the wedding that this separation would happen.

During the several weeks I had remaining in Wausau I had several demands on my time. Since I was one of the earlier returning veterans, I had been asked by several organizations to speak to their members. It was next to impossible to go into a bar or a restaurant and pay for anything.

I had agreed to be interviewed by the Daily Record Herald, the cities only newspaper, and I also discovered it very difficult to get accustomed to all of the positive attention I was receiving. Everyone was just expressing appreciation to a returning war veteran, but this was attention I did not ask for, nor really desired.

CHAPTER 23

The few weeks dragged by since Norma left for school in Rochester and I finally was glad I could get on the Hiawatha Train and head for Chicago. As usual I had an eleven-hour layover before I could once again get on the train that would take me to Miami, Florida. Without my new wife I knew that the main purpose of this stay in a nice hotel, on the beach in sunny Florida, was going to be wasted. When I checked in, nearly all of the Officers were with female partners, which I assumed were their new brides or wives to be.

The Air Force mandated that returning veterans go to one of several pleasant resort type places, primarily to rest, but also to be evaluated by several psychologists and medical doctors. Many of these returning veterans were demonstrating that they had some real problems from the strain of combat. While we were in New Jersey, the first of these evaluations had taken place.

Once these individuals had been screened for special symptoms they would receive additional consideration. I'm not sure what treatment was given, since I was simply told to relax and enjoy my stay at this facility. I had not told them of some of the minor things I started to discover when I first arrived home because I had attributed these symptoms to drastically reducing my alcohol intake and the fact that my nervous system had more time to adjust. I sincerely believed I now had things under control. I also did not divulge my feelings regarding one missing wife here at the edge of the Atlantic Ocean down in sunny Florida.

In the middle of the week I decide to get away from all the swooning other couples and get on a train and travel north of Miami to a small town called Hollywood, Florida. There was a Naval Base there, but most importantly this is where my friend Frank Morman was stationed. Right after he and Marlys spent those few days with Norma and me up at Minoqua, midway through our honeymoon, he had to report back to duty. "Mopey", and his wife Marlys rented a small, picturesque, little house

338

near the Naval Base. Their temporary abode was very nice.

We spent the day just jawing and reminiscing about old times and what we would do once the war was over. I had the thrill of being able to pick my first orange by simply lifting up the kitchen window and grabbing one. This trip was therapeutic for me because it afforded me with many hours of not feeling sorry for myself. It was interesting to discover how our normal conversation had changed since the two of us had gotten married. Kidding and joking about insignificant things were not apart of this days discussions.

I had reached the conclusion I would leave this nice hotel that fronted on the Atlantic Ocean and the other officers and their wives early. It was difficult watching all of the cooing and aahing going on with these newly wedded couples. I couldn't remember if Norma and I had acted like some of the pairs down here in Florida. Maybe it had something to do with the latitude.

Frankly, I was jealous and once again I started feeling sorry for myself. I now wanted to get on with it and to head for my next assignment. I talked with some of the officers in charge of this nice R & R place and explained my desires to them.

I was issued orders that would get me out of Florida early the next morning. These orders read that I was to report in to Ellington Field, just outside of Houston, Texas. I got on a train early in the morning and headed due west, across the width of Florida, the southern portions of Alabama, Mississippi, and Louisiana, before crossing into Texas. Within an hour or two I ascertained that a southern train is as bad as one jerking its way across northern states.

Most of my time was spent just looking out of the window and trying not to think about anything in general. I finally convinced myself that I was traveling through the armpits of America. Most of the views framed by my large and as usual dirty window were swamps, failing small farms, dilapidated shacks and houses in disrepair, or the marshalling yards and industrial complexes in larger cities. Perhaps my eyes were looking as though they were just a half pair because of Norma's absence and I now dwelled on more negative things.

When I checked in several days early at Ellington field I was given a room in the B.O.Q. The facilities were very nice, in fact, the best I have received since joining the military. I was immediately informed we would be here for quite a few weeks.

It seems that they were not prepared for the first of the returning veterans and would have to play it by ear. This information did not shake me up, since I had gotten myself in a perfect mood to do nothing. The B.O.Q. was practically empty since they were not expecting most of the Officers for another several days.

I decide to take a trip into Houston and just walk the streets, looking in shop windows. I had not been too enthused when I noted on my new orders that Ellington Army Air Force Base was in Texas. Since I had taken my entire cadet training, both pilot and navigational here in this huge state, I had hoped to have the opportunity to see more of the entire country by being shipped to California or one of the other western states.

At least it was not Nashville, Tennessee.

I found Houston to be a large city without the congestion that both Chicago and New York have. It did not have the tall skyscrapers and it seemed to be both spread out and rather flat. The center of town was only about eighteen miles northwest of Ellington Field so it was no big deal to find transportation into the city.

I discovered, though the heart of Houston is about twenty-five miles from Galveston Bay and the Gulf of Mexico, large ships were at docks within the city. These ships slowly moved up a stream called the Houston Ship Channel. When I looked from a distance and saw the silhouette of a large ship slowly move past houses and buildings, I first couldn't believe my eyes.

I found out there were several colleges and universities in Houston, namely Rice University, University of Houston, Texas Southern University, Houston Baptist University, University of St. Thomas, and San Jacinto College. I usually enjoy going on various campuses, however, in my present mood they suddenly seemed too dispersed and difficult to find. I now decided to head back to the Base at Ellington. Damn it . . . . I sure am missing Norma.

"SNUFFY"

One of the first individuals I got to meet on the Base turned out to be one of my best friends during the weeks we were to remain in Texas. His name was "Snuffy" Albaugh. I do not know if I ever knew Lt. Albaugh's first name or not. If I had heard it, it has long since become history. From the moment I met this interesting new officer I felt comfortable with him and enjoyed just sharing the many free hours we were going to experience.

He had picked up the moniker of "Snuffy" because of his love of the wad of pulverized tobacco he constantly had between his front lip and gums. Though I believed this to be a ridiculous habit, with this new friend I found it tolerable, even though it is still most disgusting.

"Snuffy" informed me that he also was sorry he did not bring his fiancee' to Miami and then get married. They had talked about it, but finally gave it up as a bad idea. He thought they would be one of the only married couples here at Ellington

Field. This would be one of the many things "Snuffy" and I had in common. Now we both could feel sorry for each other.

"Snuffy" came from Iowa and served his tour of duty in the Pacific. He was slight in build and perhaps only five foot six inches in height. His physique might even be termed skinny. He had a very dark complexion, had very deep-set eyes, delicate facial features, and there was a fine, well-trimmed little mustache exactly where it belonged.

A feature that immediately became apparent was the yellowish hue his skin seemed to have. I found out later that most individuals who spent a long time in the Pacific Areas, where malaria was prevalent, had to take adabrim tablets. This daily treatment ultimately created the yellowish hue or tint that attracted my earlier attention. In time this affliction would leave him and all the others.

Several weeks after we arrived at Ellington, "Snuffy informed me that his sweetheart was coming in by train from Iowa. Since the predominance of Officers had their wives along, they had changed their minds. He had just talked to his Iowa girl friend last night and they had decided to be married on the Post here at Ellington. In fact, he had already set up a wedding for Saturday afternoon in the Chapel on the Base. An Air Force Chaplain would unite these two. "Snuffy" was not letting any grass grow beneath his feet.

The next surprise I was to receive was when "Snuffy" asked me if I would be the Bride's Maid for this planned marriage. I made him repeat what he had just asked me because I thought I had misunderstood his request. Since I'm an old married man, I now know all the nomenclature for the participants in a wedding. He repeated the request. "Snuffy" told me he knew of no women he wanted to take on this role and he doubted if anyone but me would consider his unusual request.

I gave him an affirmative answer. After all, I'm an established married man and who else is such an authority on weddings. I told "Snuffy" to "bring it on." I was relieved to learn I did not have to dress for this unusual role. His best man was someone who stayed across the hall in the B.O.Q. and obliged 'Snuffy" by also saying yes to taking on his role at the impending wedding.

We met Louise at the depot in Houston and he informed her of all of the arrangements that had been made. Louise was a petite and very fair blonde girl. She did not appear to be shy and she impressed me as someone who had just made the long trip to Texas primarily to get hitched. I never was sure just how much she agreed on "Snuffy's" selection for the Bride's Maid for the upcoming wedding, but I did not discern a negative reaction.

Friday I accompanied them to a dress shop where "Lu", the nickname of Louise, was going to purchase a dress for the occasion. While they were doing their thing, yours truly was snooping around. A terrific idea rang a bell and I decided I would also buy a dress for my wife. Even though I hadn't screwed up so far, it doesn't hurt to earn some brownie points.

The young woman who waited on me began to ask the damnedest questions, like: "How tall is she? What is her bust size? Would you say she had broad shoulders? Do you know what size her waist is? Is she long "waisted" or short "waisted"? What about her hips? "Well then, if you do not know any of that, tell me how much does she weigh?"

"How in the hell should anyone be expected to know all these statistics." I only knew my height and age, and was never sure about my own weight. I looked around the establishment and could see no one who appeared to be Norma's size. I thought I could just simply point at someone who appeared to be the size of my wife and resolve all of her questions. Using my mathematical skills I thought I could state something like she is 7/8th the size of her or she is about 8.5 % larger than this one. Sorry, no one was buying.

Fortunately, I had a few drinks before venturing into this dress shop, so my mind was "sharp" and I did not get too flustered. I did not want to appear as a royal neophyte about just who I happened to marry and completely in the dark about all her essential credentials. I was shown dozens of different styles, colors, and materials. I personally had no idea just how dumb I was about this entire matter and how I was completely out of my element.

"Hell, I never really picked out a pair of overhauls for myself." I also wasn't honestly aware of any of the clothes Norma had worn on most of the occasions we were together. I only saw her as a person. I knew she was beautiful, had an unbelievable personality, and was the single person in the entire world I enjoyed being with the most. I never felt the need to analyze her proportions or scrutinize her anatomy.

I finally narrowed my choices down to three or four dresses. The sales gal was truly not very helpful and I had the feeling she may have been amused by the stupid decision I was about to make. Still, my inner sensibilities were being tantalized by what I simply would call a "gut feeling" as I settled on two garments, each different styles and both with distinct colors.

During this entire transaction I was to receive no help from "Snuffy", "Lu", or the sales person who was supposed to be interested in my problem. In reality the gal waiting on me was already eyeing the next customer. I paid the store extra to carefully package the apparel that was finally chosen and address it to Mrs. Lloyd

Krueger in Rochester, Minnesota. Was I acting like a Husband or what? In less than two weeks I was to find out the errors of my way.

It seems Norma received the surprise package from me, opened it and discovered two dresses, of two different sizes, two different styles, none of which would have fit her. The added element to this bizarre story is the fact she was not particularly pleased with the design, style, color, or cut of either dress. It was obvious that my sincere and well-intentioned act brought an element of levity into her dorm room. I was glad that I just happened to be about 1400 miles from Rochester.

Fortunately two different girl friends living in her dormitory bought the dresses for approximately what I had paid for them. Norma proceeded to write her mother

343

about the ridiculous thing I had done, how she wasn't particularly thrilled about the ill fitting garbs, and how she lucked out that two of her friends, who obviously had poor taste, purchased these dresses. Next she wrote a wonderful and grateful letter to me, expounding on the thoughtful overture she had just received through the mail from her new considerate husband.

The major twist to this story is that my letter was mailed to her mother by mistake and I received the letter not meant for my eyes. The entire gesture of purchasing personal clothing has never been forgotten and has been chalked up as a lasting lesson. In the past fifty–eight years I have never had the nerve to buy anything resembling clothing for my wife. I venture my opinion when ever she buys something, but only if I'm asked. This first experience in Houston taught me to never tread in dangerous waters.

ANOTHER WEDDING

Saturday afternoon we all gathered at the Chapel on the Base with the Chaplain. I stood to the left of "Lu" as her Bride's Maid while another friend of ours stood to the right of "Snuffy" as his Best Man. These four characters were all mentioned on the wedding certificate, which "Lu" and Snuffy" will cherish forever. In the distant future I'm sure there may be a snicker or two when someone notes that there once was a girl named Lloyd. We all went to the Officer's Club and made the most of a simple, but very nice wedding.

Lt. Albough and his wife had rented a small home that was completely furnished in Texas City, on the Gulf. It was about 24 miles south of Ellington. I've heard about whirlwind affairs, but "Snuffy" was a master at pulling all of the strings together in a matter of literally hours. I do not know of anyone who could get his girlfriend on a train, arrange a wedding, rent a house, and look like an old married man in less than three days.

Several days after this momentous wedding I received a notice that I could get an unexpected 10-day pass. It was apparent that this Base was not entirely ready to process the returned veterans. I got on the telephone that evening and was fortunate in catching Norma in her room.

She was most excited, first that I just received a pass and secondly, because she had something important to talk over with me. She said she had received some good news, something we could talk about once I got up to Rochester, Minnesota. "If you don't tell me what the news is, how can I know for sure it is good news?" was my question to her. "I can handle all of good news you can throw at me, I only have a problem with bad news."

I finally got her to tell me what this good news was. Her Nursing School had granted her a Leave of Absence to be with her husband. This was done primarily because of the few credits and classes remaining for her to complete her work at Rochester, Minnesota. This was both thoughtful of the nursing school and welcomed by both Norma and me. This was a turn of events I had not expected or counted upon. Now I would have my wife with me until this damn war is over.

ROCHESTER - HERE I COME

The long trip, once again, via the railroad, would be tolerated. I was again going to see Norma. Lt. Albaugh also received this same ten-day pass so "Snuffy" and "Lu" took the same train as I did, except they would get off at St. Louis, Missouri. They had to transfer to a different train for their remaining trip to Iowa. This would give them a chance to celebrate their new commitment with both of their parents.

When we got on the train a small group of Merchant Marines greeted us and asked if we would join them. They were gnashing at the bit to celebrate their return to the United States after nearly two years at sea. "Snuffy" thought about it for one instant, but "Lu", with a single glance, gave him the answer. This was the exact moment I realized "Snuffy" had been put on a leash, even though he did not realize it this day. Time will ultimately inform this friend of mine.

My initial intention was to have a single drink with these happy sailors and then go sit down with "Lu" and "Snuffy". There was a lot of railroad track between Texas and Rochester, Minnesota. I had made arrangements for a lower bunk in a Pullman car, thus hoping this would make the trip more tolerable on this jerking, noisy, mode of travel.

For one reason or another, I was to remain with these merchant seamen until it was time to have the porter make up my bed. There would be an elapsed time of many hours between when I got on this damn train and when I was to see my bed. This was not the smartest thing I had ever done. Time has a way of teaching all of us.

I was aware of the role these merchant seamen played during the war. They were truly silent heroes and most of the American people knew little about the important role they played in this conflict. They sailed the North Atlantic Ocean delivering supplies to both the British and the Russians. These brave seamen had been doing this since 1939, long before we formally entered this terrible mess.

They traveled in convoys, protected by a minimal of Naval vessels. On some crossings they did not even receive this support. Many convoys lost over half of their ships, sunk by German submarines. Nearly all of the unfortunate seamen would perish in the cold waters of the North Atlantic. On rare occasions a few may have lucked out by being rescued by another ship in the next convoy

They were not a part of the Navy, they got no special perks for being in the war, and they would never be entitled to insurance and the educational benefits of the GI Bill, which would ultimately be put into place. Their ships were constantly threatened by German submarines and the loss of live was unbelievable.

I found it near impossible to break away from them because I respected what they did. I knew what I had done during my time in combat took guts, but I also knew that a fifty-fifty chance of survival is a hell of a lot better than perhaps only 10% like these merchant marine sailors were facing.

Each of the sailors had been paid at the end of their long venture at sea so they felt flush and exuberant. Like me, they were glad and appreciative to be alive. The very first drink I had with these men started out to be a most legitimate one. I had some whisky poured over a few ice cubes, with a generous amount of mix to dilute the drink. My problem started when I noticed that each time I took a sip of my drink, someone would pour more whisky into my glass.

Their numerous stories about the experiences they lived through had my utmost attention. I discovered that, just as I would never had served on one of those tramp steamers that carried war material, neither would it be possible to get anyone of the sailors into a bomber on a combat mission. This war required all types of individual efforts, each of which had equal importance.

These Merchant Marines were on ships that traveled in large convoys and would make these long journeys only as fast as the slowest vessel. On every trip they expected to lose many of their ships to German submarines. Each was aware of the fact that less than half of the members of their crews of these sunken ships could expect to be rescued primarily because of the cold frigid waters of the North Atlantic. The submarines had no room for these seamen floundering in the water.

Before I realized it I was told that the porter was making up our berths so we could retire for the night. I left these interesting Merchant Seamen and spent an hour with "Snuffy" and Lu before going to my Pullman car. "Snuffy" was most interested in what I had found out about these Merchant Seamen and I know he would have liked to join the bull session that had gone on for hours.

When I finally found which berth I had assigned to me, I sat on this lower bed looking into the aisle and pondering if I really wanted to "hit the sack." I knew I had made a smart decision of purchasing this lower berth for the long ride up to Winona, Minnesota instead of stretching out on the usual uncomfortable passenger car seat.

About that time a fairly young women approached and said she had the berth above mine. She looked at the difficult situation of getting up to her bed for a few moments. Just then I decided to become a gentleman and an officer by replying in a chivalrous manner, "Why don't you take this lower berth and I'll climb up to the upper." There was no hesitation on her part.

I made the journey toward the ceiling of this Pullman car and pull a thick curtain closed across my little cubicle. By squirming and contorting myself, I finally got undressed. I lay back, with the ceiling of the sleeper only a short distance from my nose. The instant I laid my head on the pillow I realized I had made a big mistake by volunteering to exchange berths with the young and now happy women below me. I only hoped she was not down there laughing at me.

The ceiling of this Pullman car had a perforated metal liner only a few feet above my bedding. Each time I looked at one of these 1/8th inch diameter black holes the entire train seemed to rotate around it. No matter which black dot I picked, this stupid train would go into its gyration.

If I closed my eyes, a new and nauseous motion fortified my conviction that I had made a stupid and blundering mistake. I believe the young woman in the bunk below me did not truly appreciate the consequences of my original gesture, nor was she aware of my immediate predicament.

The only way she could fully appreciate the magnitude of my gesture was if she had ever traveled at night in the upper berth of a Pullman Car. If she had, I have to believe she would have been smart enough to have purchased a lower bunk before boarding this train.

About this time my next realization hit me. "What if I had to get up and go to the bathroom? I don't have a bathrobe. Would I have to get dressed each time that trip would be necessary?" "Oh God..............What if I throw up." I managed to get dressed and spent the night in a section they call the smoker.

Some of the merchant seamen were there, but I had enough sense to reject any more drinks. Suddenly my head told me it was easier to just sit quietly and not get involved in a conversation. Fortunately all of the Merchant Seamen had reached this exact stage so all of us sort of stared at one another wondering if they felt as bad.

Later that morning I departed my train at Winona, Minnesota, along with a first class headache. I had several hours to kill before I would board a milk-train for the last leg of my journey to Rochester, a city I had never visited. Only three of us got off and were momentarily standing on the covered apron along the tracks. It was quite apparent that none of us knew one another nor did we seem to know exactly where to go.

I HAVE A PROBLEM

A well-dressed businessman, of middle age, evidently made some remark to the nice looking and tailored young woman. I could see she was most uneasy with the attention he was paying her and the entire situation. Since it was nearly noon, I suggested that we all go together to have lunch at a café within sight of the depot. While we slowly walked across the street she whispered that I not leave her alone with this other fellow.

After we had lunch I excused myself to go to the restroom. The other fellow left the table and followed me. As we were standing at the urinal, this character reached over toward me, made an overture and a remark that told me he probably was a homosexual, but in any case certainly had a problem.

I grabbed his wrist and damn near twisted his arm off. I was perturbed even more when I realized that this was the second time something like this had happened to me in the last couple of months. I had heard that certain people attract more mosquitoes than others. Maybe I have a problem.

My previous experience occurred on my way to Miami. The eleven-hour holdover in Chicago afforded me the opportunity to attend a movie, to pass some of the time I had to kill before heading off to Miami. The time is seven o'clock in the morning and I enter a large, ornate, impressive theater, only a few blocks from the Union Station. I had never seen a movie in the morning in all of my life. "Hell . . . I seldom ever saw a movie."

At this ungodly hour I intended to see "Mrs. Miniver" with Greer Garson. As I enter the darkened theater I can see it is almost entirely empty, except for six or seven sailors from the Great Lake Naval Station. These fellows were all sleeping, probably from the drinking they had done the night before.

I find a seat in the center section, three quarters back from the front, and settle down. In less than five minutes another fellow sits next to me on my right. The theater has probably a thousand vacant seats and this turkey has to sit next to me.

I passed it off by giving him the benefit of the doubt. He may have bad eyesight and in the darkened theater he didn't realize his many choices of empty seats. "Perhaps he will move, once his eyes get accustomed to the conditions," I mistakenly thought.

In less than five minutes I feel a hand on my right thigh. As soon as I felt him move his hand I made a fist out of my right hand and protruded my index knuckle. With all of my strength I planted this missile in the back of his bony hand. He let out

348

a yell that damn near awakened the sailors. I told him, as he grabbed his injured hand, "Get the hell out of here or the next one will be aimed at your face." He couldn't move fast enough. I saw him leave the theater just as the movie was getting interesting.

What perplexed me was the fact that two times, in a little over a month I was to be confronted with something I knew nothing or certainly little about. This person's problem was only a word to me. I do not know if I handled either of these unfortunate incidents properly, I only reacted to something that I was not familiar with, something that did not fit into the way I had been raised.

The train ride to Rochester was devoid of any consequential new adventures. Norma met me at the depot and once again it was nice to hold her in my arms. She had already registered at a hotel and informed me she had purchased tickets to a concert for that evening. She had thought of everything.

Who should be sitting two rows behind us, but the individual who made the earlier mistake in a rest room in Winona. He appeared to be sitting with someone who looked like she could be his wife. I could see my glances made him squirm so I had reason to feel elated. I decided that three different momentary glimpses evenly spaced out would be sufficient to spoil his evening.

Norma and I talked into the night as she explained about the opportunity of being with me while I completed my military obligation. I did not know at this moment exactly where I would be heading, but I was sure wherever it might be I would be permitted to bring my wife.

We decided we would head up to Wausau, say goodbye to our families and pick up some things so it would be possible for this newly wedded couple to set up some light house keeping. At this moment I was not sure exactly what the term house keeping implied.

The next day, the two of us boarded a Greyhound Bus and headed for Wausau. We had several hours that we knew we did not have to share with anyone. Each of us hardly noticed the bus passing through Eau Claire, Chippawa Falls, and Abbotsford. This trip gave us a chance to talk about the many things we felt important. We obviously wondered what the future would hold for us and when the darn war would be entirely over.

We finally arrived in Wausau late in the evening and took a taxi to the south end of town. That night we would stay at my parent's home. Early the next morning we proceeded to tell all who would be interested of our plans and what we thought would be essential or more importantly, what we could realistically take with us on our trip south. We proceeded in making a list of a variety of things to collect for our trip back to Houston.

Both my Mother and Mrs. Schmidt were kind enough to part with certain of their pots and pans, plus some silver, dishes, linen etc. A single large suitcase accommodated all of the utensils and other sorted items that would start to make a dwelling into a home. We knew in time we would gradually procure any other essentials we believed necessary.

The following evening we said all of our goodbyes, packed our bags, and once again headed for the depot and the now familiar Hiawatha train. We would be required to take several different rail lines for this trip to Houston, Texas. Lt. and Mrs. Lloyd O. Krueger are now heading south to an entirely new experience and an unknown future. Oh yes, I had purchased tickets for, not a lower berth, but an isolated compartment on the Pullman car.

For the first time when we boarded the train to head for Texas, I felt like I was moving my family. First of all, Norma was coming with me and secondly, we were taking along some items to facilitate setting up a simple way of life. Basically, we were moving ourselves and just about everything we owned.

On this first leg, down to St. Louis, Missouri, we were very fortunate that we had made the arrangements for a sleeping compartment. We were hardly underway before my Norma got sick. This would not add to the usual discomfort of riding the rails, but we appreciated having our own compartment and bathroom for what turned into a long and restless night. It was most distressing for me to see my wife sick. I felt so terribly helpless.

The train out of Fort Worth, Texas for the third and last leg of our trip looked and rode just like it had come out of an old western cowboy movie. This particular train had wicker seats and most of the couches were more than half empty.

It was extremely hot so all the windows were open, thus permitting each of us to smell the dusty outside air permeating each passenger car. The sooty air also carried with it the many sounds that only an antiquated train can conjure up. This entire contraption we had bought tickets to ride truly should have been on a movie lot.

To add humor to the situation, we had a tall slender conductor whose face had deep and twisting wrinkles while his voice was rough and raspy. He wore the usual garb of a porter but it appeared both the pants and coat could have been two sizes larger. The dark rimmed glasses did little to add to his appearance. He sort of reminded me of a carnival barker who would use every trick with words to convince you that it would be prudent to purchase whatever he was trying to sell.

About once an hour this unique person would walk through the six or seven swaying railroad passenger cars and start hawking a variety of items. Sometimes he would remove his official conductor's cap and adorn his head with a variety of attention getting headgear. You could start to hear his snorting and growling two cars back.

During each of these trips through our car you could not help watching this character, with his two-foot square tray strapped to his bony shoulders, with the frayed yellow straw hat he now saw fit to wear, and the heavy dark brown rimmed glasses he kept adjusting on his oft broken nose. In each of his attires he took on the appearance of a skinny version of Harold Lloyd, the movie comic.

Sometimes we would have the rare privilege of purchasing snack items, but most of the times he would twist his mouth to one side and expound of the merits of owning something everyone could easily learn to live without. He was loud enough that we could catch his pitch even before he entered our car. He should have been a barker for a sideshow at a funky carnival where I'm sure he could have made a better living.

As we approached the noon hour, suddenly the entire train pulled off on a siding, out in the middle of nowhere. We squeaked to a halt in front of an old dilapidated shack, modified to take on the appearance of a stand. Weather beaten boards that had never been in contact with paint, appeared to be the material of choice. A rusty tin roof covered this unusual kiosk type structure.

If you looked at the underside of this weathered roof you could see tiny shafts of sunlight find their way into the depths of this unexpected dispenser of food. This now would be the place where we could walk up and purchase our lunch. It had everything but appeal.

Since there were no tables, it was standing room only for the forty or so passengers that gradually left the train. It was instantly apparent few passengers had made this trip before, judging from the humorous retorts and looks of amazement on most faces.

Once each person had gotten over the initial shock of standing in the heat of an overhead sun, in the middle of nowhere, before this dilapidated shack, they found they had few choices or selections for morsels to purchase. What there were was almost overshadowed by the entire situation.

Within a short time you learned the art of holding a paper plate with some potato chips and a sandwich, juggling a flimsy paper cup filled with some type of juice or soft drink, and a small carton that held ice cream that was melting right before your eyes. This moment in time should have been captured on film. Though the year was 1944, the scene we were all witnessing should have been happening over sixty years ago.

The last several hours we had been exposed to a world that is almost beyond description. It was so humorous and ridiculous you could find a spot, such as this, where time seemed to have passed it by. All who left the train found it hard to believe this had actually happened. It would be a memory worthy of telling to some interested soul down the road.

Once we pulled into Houston and got off this unique train, Norma and I toted our heavy bags to the Rice Hotel. We had just gotten settled in, when we got a phone call from "Snuffy". He and "Lu" were down in the lobby. I do not know how he knew we had arrived nor where we would be staying, since I had not been in contact with him.

After I introduced Norma to my new friends, "Snuffy" informed us that there was another furnished little house across the street from them in Texas City. He said he had put our name down as being interested. In fact he practically rented the place for us.

Two days later Norma and I formally rented our first home, which was completely furnished. We needed this extra time to recoup from our trip south. This new development consisted of very small houses, economically constructed, but certainly adequate for the new occupants. It was a perfect size for the two of us.

We settled in like any old married couple and each day soon developed into a ritual. "Snuffy" and I reported into Ellington each day while our wives slowly developed their own routines. I became very proud of the early resourcefulness that Norma was displaying. She very early chanced upon a special butcher, who would bend the rules, so that it became possible to get rationed items, with insufficient food stamps.

I do not know if it was her contagious smile or an opportunistic wink. During this period of the war most food and gasoline was being rationed and required the exchange of the proper stamps before a purchase could be made.

Norma also discovered a place at the docks where she could buy fresh shrimp each day. This was something neither one of us had ever seen, nor tasted. We soon developed an addiction to these little rascals. Neighbors had shown Norma how to prepare them and how we could drown the little devils in a special sauce she learned to make.

Norma had also met several other wives of airmen from the Base. Many of these couples owned their own automobiles so there was more than adequate transportation available. She had the opportunity to take some trips, like to Galveston or into Houston.

We spent many nights with the Albaughs, either at their house or at ours. The first evening we visited "Lu" and "Snuffy', we witnessed something we had never believed possible. Each night "Snuffy" would actually eat a dishpan-sized container of popcorn. It is something they raised in Iowa and Lt. Albaugh was doing everything he could to help their State's economy.

I couldn't believe this little guy could put away this quantity of anything, let alone popcorn. When they visited us, he brought along his own popcorn. I would estimate he consumed four times the amount the three of us desired to nibble on.

MARRIAGE BLISS

Several weeks had transpired and the Base still did not seem to know exactly what to do with us. We would report in each day and then be told to await further orders. Some days we only had to call in, instead of making the long ride into Ellington Field. It seems so much effort was put into rushing the newly trained men into combat that no plans had been developed once the fortunate ones returned to the states.

"Snuffy" and I spent a great deal of time together, mostly comparing our different experiences, both across the Atlantic and the Pacific. All the while the two of us were together, Lt. Albaugh continued his habit for which he had gained his nickname, chewing or sucking on snuff. The exception would be when he was at home or in Lu's presence.

Several times during this interim I had warned "Snuffy" about an impending crisis I could sense was on the horizon. When he and "Lu" got married he had made a promise to give up chewing this horrible stuff. Now though, the only time he would indulge in this filthy substance, was on the Base and away from home.

He carried a day's supply in one of his former Adabrin containers. Pure logic would indicate it would be only a matter of time before he got caught. We would not have long to wait.

In the middle of the night Norma and I were awakened by a knock on our bedroom window. It was about three o'clock in the morning. We pulled back the curtain and saw "Snuffy", with his two bewildered eyes, staring up at us. We could not hear or understand what his lips were saying, but I knew instantly what his problem was.

When I opened the door to let him in I was greeted with, "We've been arguing for the last six hours. "Lu" threw me out because she found out about the snuff. Could I sack down here until this blows over?" There was obvious concern in each of his deep set eyes.

The next morning, at a more reasonable hour, Norma walked over to have a talk with "Lu". She explained to this petite, some-what shy girl, who in the past few weeks was being transformed into a very domineering, strong willed, marriage partner, that "Snuffy" had a habit that would take realistic time for him to break.

She told her that each of us in the service, after being thrown into combat situations, developed our own way to handle fear and stress. Norma mentioned I did an excessive amount of drinking and cigarette smoking, and I lived as though there may be no tomorrow. She tried explaining to her of the men who had mental and physical breakdowns.

Norma, with all of her nurses' training, was able to finally put the entire incident into a better perspective, where "Lu" would be more tolerant. When she told "Snuffy" that the coast was clear, he sheepishly walked back home. The concerned look on his tawny face more than expressed his gratitude for what Norma had done this morning.

During the ensuing months "Snuffy" made a conscientious effort to overcome this disgusting habit of chewing snuff. On one rare occasion I caught him depositing a wad behind his lower lip. The shake of my head was enough for him to go to the closet "john" and remove it.

MY PERSONAL DENTIST

I happened to be fortunate in that I was born with both an excellent and healthy set of teeth. This was something I inherited from my Mother. However, I did have a slight problem with all four of my wisdom teeth. For some reason, they grew in large and were very close to the hinge part of my jaw. Occasionally I would experience a problem because of the apparent lack of room for this set of choppers to function. In any case, with nothing better to do, I went to the infirmary and checked in with the Dentist on the Base.

The Dentist, some Lieutenant, checked me over and agreed it would be a good idea to get these wisdom teeth removed. While he was pondering on what would be the first order of attack, his superior, a Captain, entered the scene. He went to the blackboard and drew diagrams in front of both of us to explain just how the lower left wisdom tooth should be removed. He explained that there were three roots and by using a chisel, he would crack the tooth into three pieces and just twist and roll each of these roots out. He would demonstrate for the young Lieutenant

This very cocky Captain proceeded to freeze my jaw and then took up hammer and chisel. On the second blow with the hammer, the tooth split and a stream of blood shot out of my mouth. This stream of blood actual made a hissing sound as it arched its way to the face and white jacket of my high-ranking Dentist.

He immediately got pissed off and truly acted like it was my fault. He ranted and raved at me and literally was pulling his rank on this lowly, First Lieutenant, who was just sitting there, with his mouth open and wondering exactly what sin I had committed. The other dentist had left the scene for obvious reasons.

After some minutes, I caught the Captains immediate attention by asking him, "Doc, did you happen to flunk out of Med. School?" "Get the hell out of the chair" he shouted. My remark, plus the bloody mess, obviously got him slightly perturbed.

After what I had gone through in Europe, I wasn't afraid to continue this conversation. "My jaw is frozen, I've got a cracked tooth, I'm bleeding, and I'm sitting here until someone takes care of this damn mess," I managed to mumble.

In a few minutes this Captain calmed down and even apologized. He proceeded to remove the entire tooth and put a packing into what I thought was a huge cavern. As I left the Dentist office and got out into the fresh air I began to realize I didn't feel all that great.

Normally Lt. Albough and I would ride from Texas City with one of our neighbors and late in the afternoon we would again get a ride home. It's now 10:30 in the morning, I'm not feeling too great, so I decided I would hitch hike home to Texas City.

I walked off the Base to the road heading south. Something I had not counted on was my tooth extraction would start bleeding profusely. I had not planned on having this tooth removed when I left home that morning, so I happened to only have one handkerchief in my pocket. Soon, this small piece of cloth was saturated with blood and it was running down my right arm.

Usually in the early hours of the morning and again late in the afternoon this road was well traveled. Right now vehicular traffic was practically nil. After a half hour of elapsed time, I begin to wonder why anyone would stop to pick up a hitchhiker looking like a bloody mess. My summer uniform was beginning to look like hell and I'm out on the U.S. Highway 45 trying to thumb my way to Texas City.

The fact I was in uniform probably helped, despite its appearance. I finally got a ride. A truck that had seen better days slowed down and with his brakes squeaking, came to a stop some distance beyond me. He had a large mottled colored hound dog riding in the back of the truck, along with a variety of junk. Despite the appearance, I felt elated that at last I could move toward home.

This farmer saw my predicament and seemed to care less that my blood might soil anything visible in his front seat. He told me he was going all the way to Galveston so it would be no problem to take me to my front door in Texas City. This farmer told me he had most of his teeth taken out, but he couldn't understand why anyone would let a Dentist remove a perfectly good tooth. This was not a point of contention worthy of further discussion. I thanked him and waddled into the house. Now my personal nurse could take care of me.

A CULTURAL SHOCK

On the base one morning I accidentally overheard someone mention that Jose' Iturbi, the great pianist, happened to be present and was going to put on an impromptu concert in a particularly large room. I called in to Norma in Texas City and really lucked out. She happened to be with another friend's wife, who owned a car. They would arrive on the base within the half hour.

This rare opportunity was something both Norma and I will always cherish. Jose' played for nearly two hours to this attentive audience. No one can imagine how this moment was for two young people, born and raised up in the boon docks, to be able to listen and see this great artist.

This would be another plus for our marriage, liking and having similar tastes for music. Though the nearly two hundred officers and their wives sat on metal folding chairs, you could have heard a pin drop in this room. This was another example of so many of our country's great artists giving of their talents. Many found the time to entertain the service personnel all around the world at the various Military Bases, Airfields, or even on Islands in the Pacific.

Several days later, to everyone's surprise, we were informed that Ellington Field had received orders offering various opportunities to interested returning veterans. There were duties, such as going to flight schools as an instructor, there were various types of office jobs, you could enter certain training programs to develop new skills, and there was the chance to get into a completely different branch, such as the Air Transport Command.

This later branch, the Air Transport Command, appealed to me because the duty would offer the opportunity to ferry planes all over the world. That night I could come home and tell Norma that we were to report into Rosecrans Field at St. Joseph, Missouri on or before March 14, 1945. I would now be in the Air Transport Command. I do not believe she was completely cognizant of just how much I would now be away from home, but I was confident she would adapt to whatever was necessary.

Once again we boarded a train, along with several other couples, to make the trip northward to our next assignment. St. Joseph is a fair sized city in the northwest corner of the State of Missouri. I do not know why they put an airfield in this area other than to disperse them for political reasons. We spent two nights registered in the Ruebedoux Hotel until an apartment could be found. While I was out to the Base getting oriented to an entirely different operation, Norma finally found a second floor apartment near the center of town.

At this period of time in St. Joseph, finding rooms, apartments, or temporary accommodations was next to impossible. In order to secure the apartment Norma had finally discovered she had to agree that the two of us would paint several rooms in this place for the landlord. Mrs. Haber stipulated that this was the only way she would rent out the apartment. It was part of the deal. She said they would furnish the paint and brushes but we would be required to do the work. Norma agreed and we fulfilled our obligation.

We discovered there were six funeral homes within a block of our apartment. St. Joseph was a city where local farmers moved into town, to not only retire from farming, but to retire permanently. There were several funeral homes within sight of our new abode.

Our apartment did not possess the uniqueness of our little home in Texas City, but it would do until I was discharged from the military. The house would be only a short taxi ride to the Base and would be within walking distance for groceries, etc. The Habers would be our landlords.

This apartment had a huge, ill shaped kitchen, which consisted of perhaps half of the space we were renting. Our bedroom was also large and it appeared it might have been used as a porch or sunroom at one time or another. This bedroom had three walls of glass, which overlooked several of the funeral homes, in the neighborhood. It also had windows opening into the kitchen, along with an access door.

Our bathroom had to be entered by leaving the apartment and traveling down the hall. It was being shared with a single old man, who fortunately, did not require it use, except on one or two rare occasions. The tub, in this small bathroom, required a certain amount of athleticism, just to park your body in it. An antiquated lavatory shared the back wall, opposite our kitchen sink. Despite the numerous windows, the place maintained a dark and dreary appearance. Despite all of the above, we lived, we entertained, and we even survived intense summer heat with zero air conditioning.

Each day Norma and I were together I discovered how very adaptable and capable she was. She not only found this apartment, she had already located the essential stores in which to shop, like the grocery, the butcher shop, a drug store, etc.

She never complained about my many trips and the indefinite length of time I would be gone, complaints I heard from so many other wives. On top of all this, I found her to be a most worthy prize to come home to each time I made a trip somewhere in the world. She now was a significant part of my being.

CHAPTER 24

AIR TRANSPORT COMMAND

The first week at Rosecrans would be spent on learning what was to be expected of us. I had the opportunity to meet many new Officers. It soon became obvious the atmosphere on this Base was somewhat relaxed. The "Spit & Polish" attitude or temperament did not appear to be paramount here at Rosecrans.

We were told our primary new duties would be ferrying new airplanes to bases all over the world and on some occasions, we may have to bring back war weary planes to the United States for disposal or storage.

We were informed that the length of these trips would vary, but once we reported in, we were to be assured of a three-day pass. We also would be issued a Priority No. 1 Travel Pass, which would get us on the next commercial or military transport flight. Later, I would wonder, just why we were issued these special Priority Passes since we only hurried home to wait.

There were several Air Transport Command Officers living in our apartment building here in St. Joseph, some with cars. This simplified getting out to the base each morning because all of these individuals soon became our friends and insisted we ride in with them. Norma and I also met other officers and their wives at the Officer's Club on the Base. The entire group was very congenial and we discovered these guys had served in almost every theatre of operations and the group was made up primarily with Pilots, Co-Pilots, and Navigators.

FIRST TRIP

I received notice of my first trip within days of reporting in for duty. I would be apart of a group ferrying four B-17H's to the Hawaiian Islands. These new bombers had been converted for air-sea rescue work and they would be modified. The ball turret had been removed and a Higgins lifeboat was mounted underneath the fuselage.

This boat could be dropped from the air. The chin turret had been removed and was replaced with a radar bubble. The top turret also had been removed as well as the two guns from the Navigator's position and the guns from the waist and tail positions.

I was elated and thought it quite a coincident that my first assignment would be a B-17, a plane I had flown in for over 300,000 miles. My enthusiasm did not go unnoticed. That night the three other Navigators, who had been assigned to the other B-17s on the upcoming trip, paid Norma and me a surprise visit at our simple abode.

They showed up with their wives and plenty of beer. They immediately dropped an interesting and unexpected problem before me. All three of these Navigators had served in the C.B.I. Theatre and they each admitted to not remembering a darn thing about celestial navigation. Their duty, while in the China, Burma, India Theatre, was to ferry supplies over and around the hump, to various bases.

They usually flew down the same valleys to avoid the world's tallest mountain peaks. In these valleys radio stations and beacons had been set up so most of their duties relied on the radio compass. These crews assigned to ferrying made the same trips so often the pilots knew where to go and did not have to rely on their navigators to assist them. The news I was receiving from these three new cohorts of mine was something I found hard to believe. Despite all this, I agreed to give them any information I could.

Several of these navigators noted my reaction when we were told of our assignment and that the plane we would be ferrying would be B-17s, my favorite bomber. These fellows had been flying on transport planes, such as the C-47, C-46, also known as the DC 5 and DC 4. After a brief bull session among themselves, all agreed they had some reservations about their celestial skills.

They told me they could remember very little about the use of a sextant, but specifically how to use the Navy Star Tables to calculate positions by determining the altitude of specific stars. "Hell, I can't remember one star from another," Mike stated. I noted the other two nodding their heads in approval of this last statement.

While the wives were off in another room getting acquainted, we Navigators were drinking beer and trying to resolve the current problem. Though I had not used my training and knowledge of celestial navigation since my trip to Iceland and England on my way to combat, I knew what and how to do it. I tried to break this phase of navigation down into its simplest components, but it did not take long to realize that my efforts were not being assimilated.

I recognized the difficulty of the situation after about an hour and a half. I ascertained that all three of these fellows, while at the various Navigational Training Centers, never were good at celestial work. With their lack of interest or proficiency, they now had been away from it too long.

Each of these Navigators freely admitted to having a certain amount of fear set in because of the up-coming trip. Finally and, perhaps the main reason, we all were drinking beer. It was apparent they also had a negative span of attention.

Finally, one of them just plain admitted why they showed up this night. They had learned I had been a Lead navigator and had flown 35 combat missions in B-17s, the sole reason why they were at our apartment this night before our trip. They also had reservations about the type of airplane we would be delivering and the thought of crossing the Pacific Ocean didn't help matters.

So as not to further interfere with our socializing and drinking, I finally said: "When we get to Sacramento and pick up our planes, I'll fly lead and we will all take off at one minute intervals. This will keep us close to one another so that we should have visual contact, but most certainly we will constantly be in radio contact.

I'll periodically check with you and update our actual position so you can keep track of our progress on your chart while flying over the Pacific Ocean, just incase we run into a problem. I suggested that they make every effort during the flight to take shots of stars they can identify and plot them on their chart. Somewhere down the road this may prove very helpful on any future flight they may be assigned to. I was now drinking with a happy group of new friends.

The next morning, four pilots, four co-pilots, and four navigators boarded a DC-3 and headed for California. We had a day and a half to recover from the bucket seat ride over the Rockies. Once we got to Sacramento, five of us rented a convertible car and drove to San Francisco, a city where none of our group had ever been before. Though we had never set eyes on Sacramento either, the Capital of California did not appeal to any of us.

We drove around several hours, saw the Golden Gate Bridge, the Fisherman's Warf, China Town, and thousands of sailors. The traffic we were confronting finally made us turn northeast and find our way back to our Base. The next day we were informed we would start our mission in early evening so the major part of the flight would be at night, making celestial navigation the best way to keep track of our position.

All four planes got off as planned and were in a very loose formation. Our small group of B-17s would have made a German Fighter Pilot laugh. In less than a half hour it was still light enough so we could see the Golden Gate Bridge off our left wing. It was a beautiful sight. Now we had one hell of a lot of water before us.

While it was still light I was able to take a shot of the sun before it set in the West. I thought it would be a good chance to reorient myself with the sextant, get a line plotted on our westerly course that would be almost perpendicular to our plotted course and still be within sight of a landmark on the coast of the United States.

This would be a quick check on the accuracy of the sextant I had been issued. I found I had no trouble remembering celestial navigation, even though it was nearly a year since I last had to depend on this skill. The night was beautiful, the sky was clear and free of clouds, and the stars began to flicker like diamonds on black velvet. "Bring it on."

We were all heading toward the Island of Oahu, our final destination. This trip should be routine and I anticipated it would be fun to get back into celestial navigation again. I was not expecting the type of problems I experienced on my flight in the northern latitudes on my earlier trip to Iceland over a year ago.

I noted our air speed was only slightly affected by the lifeboat we had mounted below our fuselage. This was a concern I had when I first noted the type of plane we would be flying. The elimination of the top and nose turrets from this B-17H evidently compensated for the addition of the Higgins boat mounted and exposed below the fuselage.

It was a beautifully clear night and would have many choices of finding the stars needed to calculate the many required fixes before the morning sun came up. I knew my sky would constantly change during this long night so I would get to see many different constellations.

I purposely plotted a course that would be just south of the direct line to the Island of Oahu, almost aiming for the Island of Maui. The string of Hawaiian Islands are lying in a West-Northwest direction and it would not be difficult to miss Oahu should you be in err to right of course. I had instructed each of the other three Navigators of my intention so we each started out with similarly plotted courses.

As we approached our final destination we would have the island of Hawaii off to the left of our plotted course. This would be over an hour before we would land. It would be at this time that I would give the pilot a slight course correction to take us to the proper assigned field on Oahu.

It was fun keeping track of my three cohorts. I wanted to have them make every effort to follow what we were doing, not to just sit back and follow the plane I was in. I knew they were most appreciative of the way we were making this particular trip, but I wanted them to bring their talents up to the standard necessary for future trips over the great distances in both the Atlantic and the Pacific Oceans. All our ferrying assignments would require trips of great distance over water.

This would be the first and last time I would fly in a group with these three CBI navigators. Over the next several months I would have the opportunity to fly many missions out over the Pacific Ocean. I got to such places as the Islands of Guam, Saipan, Iwo Jima, Tarawa, Tinian and many times to the various Hawaiian Islands.

Many trips would also be made that would take me to the Caribbean, South America, Africa, and of course back to Europe. Guam and Tinian Islands were part of the Marianas, Tarawa belonged to the Gilbert Islands, while Iwo Jima was about 600 nm south of Tokyo.

In every case, when I ferried planes to the many different pacific Islands, we would land first on the Hawaiian Islands, usually on the Island of Oahu. On one occasion we did land on the Island of Hawaii at John Rogers' Field near Honolulu. Our next leg would then be a relatively short one to Johnston Island, west of the Hawaiian Chain. This Island, or atoll, was just large enough for a single long runway. It was a precautionary measure to shorten any flights to the islands that our other forces had liberated, such as Guam or Iwo Jima.

In keeping with the same decision I had made regarding each and every combat mission I had flown, I will only refer to a few of these oversea trips that are similar and had become most routine. The ones I will enumerate on would be typical, but would have some special interest to them. I had not been in the Air Transport Command very long before I realized it was not necessary to join the Navy in order to see the world.

An unauthorized, but apparently tolerated system already developed and practiced by the many officers Norma and I socialized with, was explained to me. The practice was, under normal conditions, when you returned from an overseas trip, you would be granted a three-day pass. These men deviated from this by simply not reporting in immediately upon their return. After two or three days they would check in and then be issued their customary three-day liberty.

In reality, I don't think we were ever fooling the Brass. I believe they knew and never called us down on this minor point of contention. We had all served time in combat and appreciated not being treated like boy scouts.

On one of my trips in the Pacific area, when we returned on a Military Transport, we were dropped off at Denver, Colorado. From there we were to catch a train to St. Joseph, Missouri. Our problem surfaced, when we discovered we had just missed the daily train leaving Denver by only a few minutes and another would not be heading East for twenty three and a half hours. We checked on the possibility of getting a ride on some other Military plane and it was about the same story.

Another officer and I decided to hitch hike back to our wives. When we inquired on what highway we could take out of Denver to head East to Missouri we were informed it would be Highway 76. The guy then said, "Hell, it's only three or four miles from this Base, I'll drive you out to the edge of town and get you on the correct road." With all of our baggage, we appreciated this jester.

Our timing was perfect because a salesman picked us up almost immediately in his relatively new Chevy. He then proceeded to drive like mad. Our driver was a guy about forty years old, constantly had a cigarette in his mouth while he proceeded to inform us he wished he had been younger so he could have been a fighter pilot. He assured us he would have made a good pilot because he loved speed. We did not tell him that 95% of all Air Force personnel thought they too would be excellent fighter pilots.

He raced across Colorado and into western Kansas. This was as far as he was going, but he was kind enough to go out of his way and leave the two of us off on a Highway 70, the road we wanted and need to get home. He wished us luck for the remainder of our trip. The first thing both of us noticed was the absence of his constant chatter.

We were happy to get out of the speeding car and onto the Highway since we had been literally flying at nearly 70 miles per hour since we left Denver. The happy salesman never stopped talking and never had more than one hand on the steering wheel the entire trip. We needed a definite change of pace and a chance to breathe some fresh air free from the cigarette smoke. We both agreed our chauffeur would not have been a good candidate for pilot training, but perhaps he could have used his love for speed in the postal service where it could have been used.

We spent several hours waving our thumbs at the few cars on the highway before we took a trucker up on his offer to drive us all the way to St. Joe. He was driving a relatively new and huge semi tractor-trailer, which had two levels of nothing but squealing pigs. This would be my first ride in an eighteen-wheeler.

Driving up front with him drowned out the shrill sounds of these unhappy porkers. As this trucker raced down the highway, the smell of the hundreds of swine could fortunately not catch up to us in the cab. Occasionally when we were compelled to slow down the aroma from our other passengers would find its way to our nostrils. Night had set in and he was now driving down secondary roads to get these pigs to their new home.

What the driver hadn't told us was he had to unload these little rascals on a large farm near Atchison on the Eastern edge of Kansas, prior to getting to St. Joseph. At two o'clock in the morning our trucker drove into a beautiful farm yard and backed his rig to a gate leading to a large fenced in area. The back gates on this semi now turned into cleverly designed ramps.

We now watched hundreds of these pigs run down the inclines to freedom, each one sounding like they were being killed, or at least tormented. It was at this point the smell became almost intolerable. This was a moment when it truly was enough to test what your stomach could handle.

Fortunately the farmer had several additional hands to help with the unloading. These men had been waiting for the truck with its squealing cargo. Because of this, only about a half hour was required to empty this huge double-decker 18-wheeler. The squealing and the smell from these hundreds of young pigs however made this a long half hour interlude despite trying to position myself up wind of the entire operation.

It was about three in the morning when I slipped quietly into our apartment, hoping I could carefully awaken Norma without frightening her. Despite her surprise, she immediately reciprocated by telling me, "Guess what? My mother came today." I was the one who almost went into shock, not because Mrs. Schmidt was visiting us, but what would happen early tomorrow morning? "What about tomorrow morning?" I whispered. "We'll think of something. How was your trip?"

What we were alluding to was a daily ritual we just knew she would not approve of. On one of my trips I had discovered an unbelievably good recipe to make Old Fashion drinks. Each morning, about nine o'clock, the gal next door would come over with a full glass of pure scotch while Norma and I would join her with one of our new Old Fashion drinks. My dear Mother-in-law, Mrs. Schmidt, might be led to believe our friend merely had a glass of water, but our drinks would certainly give us away.

I ultimately resolved this matter by mixing her drink with all of the fruit in tact, but only a trace of bourbon whisky. I even left out the Angostura bitters. Hell, it was like lemonade. It was in the middle of summer and St, Joseph got very hot. My problem now was I had to keep mixing these mild drinks for my mother-in-law who was consuming them just like pink lemonade. We had to move her up from a small old fashion glass to a large tumbler.

I don't believe she ever knew what her youngest daughter and new husband were doing. As years went on and we visited her, just outside of Wausau, in the little town of Rothschild, the first thing she would ask of me was to mix her an Old Fashion. She always made my day by this special request.

While she was visiting us though we did receive a scolding and a reprimand because we used oleo for cooking and on our toast. We were doing this because we found the only butter we could purchase in St. Joseph always tasted rancid to us. "No one from Wisconsin, the Dairy State, eats oleo," she informed us with a degree of sarcasm. I do not believe we ever convinced her of our line of reasoning.

GEORGE TAKES THE PLUNGE

On June 1st, late in the evening, Norma and I received a telephone call from our dear friend, George Cormack. It was not difficult to know he was very excited concerning the news he was about to unload. He and Marge had been going with one another for several years and they were going to get married. Marge is a schoolteacher in northern Wisconsin and comes from a very small community called Bruce. "Would you and Norma come up to Bruce for the wedding, Krueeeeger? I want you to be the Best Man." He blurted out. "It's going to be a church wedding with all of the trimmings. Can you two get up here?"

By now I am standing back on my heels and the mind is racing a mile a minute. "George, when the hell is this big wedding suppose to take place?" Immediately he replied, "This coming Saturday!" I shouted back into the phone, "that's only a week away. I'm not sure if I can get even an hour off, the way we've been flying."

I could sense his disappointment over the phone and how my reply was letting air out of the high he was on when he placed this call to St. Joseph, Missouri. My mind was racing a mile a minute as I stood there only shrugging my shoulders. I was trying to resolve an impossible situation without any of the required answers available.

"George, let me call you back tomorrow morning about ten o'clock. I will talk to my commanding Officer and see what I can come up with. Don't be surprised if I am denied any time off. Hell, we're fighting a war Buddy.

Start thinking of someone else to be in your wedding party should I get turned down. We'll know by mid morning." George hung up, but I knew he did not truly understand.

I don't think he even remembered the time he visited me down in San Antonio, when I was in S.A.A.C.C., the cadet center. He unexpectedly called me from San

Antonio and wanted me to take a week off so we could be together. On this occasion I felt fortunate and blessed to get an eight-hour over-night pass to spend with him.

Early the next morning I went to Headquarters and tried to explain my predicament, never expecting to receive a sympathetic ear. I explained how this special friend of mine was the Best Man at my wedding when I returned from combat, how he had tried everything to get into the service (including the Red Cross), but was rejected because of his 20/400 eyes, and how our friendship has been going on through high school and a year of college. The later statement, about the length of our friendship, was more than a slight prefabrication, it was a damn right lie.

While the Major was listening, he was thumbing through a file that I noted my name on. He finally said, "Lt. Krueger, take you wife and head up north to get your friend married. I will issue a ten-day pass, starting noon today." I simultaneously popped to attention and gave the Major a smart salute, followed by "Thank you sir." I was so flabbergasted that I almost forgot to give Norma a call to start packing. George was by the phone, impatiently waiting to hear from me. "Everything is A – OK, we'll be at your wedding Cormack."

The only practical mode of travel, once again, was the darn train. These were the times Norma and I wished we could afford some kind of a car. We had to take the bus to Kansas City and then get on a train to Chicago. We had another transfer to the Hiawatha train that would take us north. This now familiar all night ride once again was tolerated so that we can step out at six A.M. in the morning at Wausau.

My Mom and Dad picked us up at the depot and we had been invited to stay at their home while on this leave of absence. We four would be traveling together since they also had received an invitation from George and Marge to this special wedding ceremony to be held in Bruce, Wisconsin, a small community in the northwestern part of the State.

My parents had known George for many years. While I was in England, George stayed at their home for many months. His folks had sold the family home and had permanently moved to Florida. Though my Mom and Dad believed they knew dear old George, I know they never really knew him at all. George took a certain understanding and patience to get to acknowledge all of his attributes, and to not get pissed off over some of his idiosyncrasies.

Early Saturday morning Norma and I jumped into the back seat of my Dad's car and the four of us headed toward Bruce, Wisconsin. The distance was less than a hundred miles had we been crows, but there were no direct super highways to this remote little town in this corner of Wisconsin. As we approached our destination, you could see how the former lumber barons and lumberjacks had stripped the forests of trees. They left behind a wasteland that now looked both desolate and depressing.

In some respects, the landscape took on the appearance of a war torn piece of wasteland, with mile after mile of tree stumps, about six or seven feet tall, the only visible remains from a former day. The reason for the size of these tree stumps was because this section of land had been cleared during winter when the snows were five or six-foot deep. Wisconsin is one of the most beautiful of our states, but this isolated and somewhat depressed area, stands out like a sore thumb.

We tracked down Marge's home and got to meet the almost married couple about 10:30 A.M. The wedding was to take place in a little over an hour so my Father, George, and I were kicked out of the house for many different but obvious reasons. We walked over to the church, only a few blocks away. In fact, everything in Bruce is only a few blocks away.

The three of us were standing on the lawn under a huge maple tree in order to take advantage of its shade. Suddenly George surprised our small gathering with, "I don't really think we should have this wedding. I'm not sure I'm ready to get tied down." Knowing George, I instantly knew this was not said in jest or some type of joke.

I didn't let him proceed with more of what I considered negative talk. "Bull crap, knock that kind of garbage off. Norma and I came over 500 miles just to get you married, and by God, I personally will tie you down and drag you inside the church if that's what it will require to get you and Marge hitched."

Over the years I got to know all of the nuts and bolts about this unusual friend. His Scotch ancestry made him analyze nearly everything in dollars and cents, in positive or negative terms, amount of freedom or restrictions, or by plus or minuses. During these final moments before his wedding I knew this once more was how the wheels in George's head were spinning. I also knew his remark was said in dead seriousness and not just to pull my chain. He finally simmered down and agreed that this was no time for that kind of reasoning or talking.

While his mind was in its spinning mood, George came up with another surprise. This was to be a Catholic wedding, as we all knew, but now my friend informs me that their church is without a regular Priest. George believed it necessary for each of us to know that the Priest who is going to perform the ceremony should not be considered a typical Priest or Man of the Cloth. This individual is traveling between several small parishes and agreed to perform today's wedding.

FATHER HURLY

George hardly had gotten this latest tidbit of news relayed to us when an obvious Man of the Cloth came waddling up to our small group assembled beneath the boughs of the large maple tree near the rear of the church. George introduces me to Father Hurly, both as his good friend and also as his Best Man. Instantly I noticed some of what dear old George was eluding to. I'm glad I had been fore warned.

This Priest had a large red nose, which appeared to be swollen to twice its normal size. His face had red veins radiating out from this distinct proboscis or what I would term a drinking nose. His eyes were obviously very blood shot. This person had all the symptoms of being an alcoholic of the first order. Even my sympathetic nose could detect the spirituous nature of the morning breeze as he approached.

Father Hurly reminded me of W. C. Fields, except he did not seem to possess the sense of humor nor was he wearing a cocked straw hat. This dumpy little man had on a black frock that looked like it contained potatoes. His black shoes were scuffed and appeared to have seen much better days. His two hands looked swollen with pudgy fingers much too small for the size of the palm. What little hair he possessed seemed to be missing a part and had not seen a comb in some time.

As we made small talk, Marge's younger brother approached with a white robe, a tie that was not properly pulled up, and a look of a typical boy who was actually on the high school football team and one who wished he could have been elsewhere. He had a bruised left eye that was actually becoming on his youthful face. He was to be the Alter Boy for the impending ceremony.

When Father Hurly saw the less than perfect necktie on Mike, he reached out and pulled it up tight, with zero finesse. "Leave that God Damn tie alone. You look just like hell," shouted the Priest. I was shocked and yet not really surprised by the words coming from his mouth. My friend George was happy he had fore warned us. My Dad just stood there with his mouth open. He had been caught between a laugh and a gasp.

Though I am not a Catholic, I had made up my mind to do everything up at the head of the church as though I was. I would kneel, bow my head, I would mimic anything that George did, except prematurely kiss the bride, take any vows, or kiss the Priest's ring. I did not want to attract any attention toward myself, although I did stick out like a sore thumb with my officer's uniform on.

The ceremony was relatively short with none of the sincerity that took place at Norma and my wedding. I noticed Mike, the now attentive alter-boy, periodically passed Father Hurly a small bowl that was suppose to contain Holy Water in it. I could see that it was bone dry. It had nothing but dry flacks of lime deposited on the bottom. Yet dear old Father Hurly would dip his fingers below the rim, feign to shake off any excess "water" and pretend he was crossing himself with dampened fingers.

He appeared to be completely oblivious of the congregation, parents, or just spectators that were watching from below the alter platform. He also seemed to depend on Mike to guide or give him clues for what would be the next part of this special ceremony. Inept, a klutz, an actor, a joke were all words that could describe or profile this character posing now as a priest.

In the church that I had attended as a youth, when we part took in communion, we each would be presented with a wafer and a small sip of wine. During this ceremony, the only one who received the wine was Father Hurly. He managed to find six or seven different parts of this wedding ceremony where he felt it necessary to drink wine as a symbolical gesture prior to the ritual about to take place. The wine vessel was not empty like the Holy Water container.

Oh well, George and Marge were pronounced man and wife and everything was now kosher and legal. The most significant thing about these two friends of mine being wed this day was that they had exchanged their wedding vows they made promises to one another, and were now legally considered man and wife before God and Country.

It now occurred to me that I had never thought or considered my friend George as a married man. He always appeared to be a proverbial bachelor candidate because I knew him to be very content doing many things as a loner. Most of his travels and trips would be solitary excursions.

I know my soul mate was justifiably embarrassed about good old Father Hurly. None of the unique Pastor's antics did not really distract from the solemnity of the occasion. It might have even been better than one of those quickie ceremonies performed in Las Vegas, in a tiny fake chapel along the strip, by some turkey that could have made Father Hurly look dignified.

When we arrived at Marge's house, everyone stood around like they had just attended a funeral. I did not know at the time, but did learn on the trip back to Wausau, that good old Father Hurly had been making a hit on my wife during this awkward part of the wedding day. This crafty old man tried to convince Norma that she should be in the movies, that she looked younger than her 22 year, etc. etc. etc. Had I known, I might have checked out the sensitivity of his proboscis.

Once I noticed the solemn and somber atmosphere of the gathered people at the house, I asked George about opening a bottle of something and let's celebrate.

George replied, "We can't until Father Hurly goes home with the two nuns after we have lunch."

I came back with my retort, "To hell with Father Hurly, this is the time to make with a celebration. You may not realize it, but you just got yourself hitched. If you don't want to get a bottle of something out of its hiding place, I'm going out to my Dad's car where I know there is a bottle of some prime liquor, a bottle of Korbel Bandy. Besides, I've got strong suspicions Father Hurly is not a foreigner to lifting a drink for whatever the occasion might be."

I started to mix some drinks by putting a couple of ice cubes into each of several glasses now placed on the kitchen counter. At the same time I asked George if he had anything for a mix I could use besides water. I was informed there was only a case of coca cola out on the porch. It would be a shame to ruin this good brandy or scotch with coke. Perhaps I could convince most to just use water. When some insisted on the coke it now became apparent I needed a bottle opener.

Before I could ask, Father Hurly pulled on a long gold chain that was wrapped around his waist, dangling down his right leg and curling back into his right pants pocket. At the end of this beautiful chain was a bottle opener, along with several other trinkets. There was a very large gold crucifix attached at the bend of this ornate chain. With the motion of a pro, he had the caps off several coke bottles in the blink of an eye.

When I started to pour coke over the brandy and ice cubes, again Father Hurly intervened, taking the bottle of coke from my hand. With the assuredness of a pro he put his right thumb over the bottle opening, shook this glass container three or four times past his right ear and the length of his body, aimed the opening of the bottle at the glasses on the counter from about a foot away, and a stream of coke unerringly hit the ice cubes. I was truly impressed. This guy was gooood. I now was sure he missed his calling.

Father Hurly did not disappoint me at the large and beautifully set dinner table where the food was about to be served. All the food was first passed to this crafty old Priest before anyone one else was to be served. I was not sure the good Father deserved this honor or distinction, but under the circumstances, it was a protocol that would be adhered to on this special day for Marge and George.

This unusual Priest, who seemed to find more ways to attract unfavorable attention, proceeded to eat with the same finesse he performed the wedding ceremony. He had zero table manners. He talked with food falling from his mouth, he was dribbling over his robe each time he drank coffee, and he reached across people for food instead of asking them to pass it.

Good old Father Hurly was noticed by all, even though no one tried looking at him. Most at the table were embarrassed for him. He was in character from the minute I met him until we finally bid him farewell.

I told George to not worry about Father Hurly. "Look upon him like I am remembering the antique car at Norma's and my wedding. Both of these things will be recalled as something interesting, very special, and certainly different." With each passing year, as we look back, both of these antiques, Father Hurly and the 1928 Model "A" Ford car will only be a small but significant part of all the memories we will have of the days when we four got married.

George and Marge told us that they planned to take a vacation later to extend their honeymoon and they wanted to come to St. Joseph, Missouri to visit us. They would do this prior to Marge having to start teaching at school for the next semester. I was not surprised when George mentioned they would take the train. Both Norma and I agreed that this would be perfect. The important thing about the honeymoon excursion plan was to time their visit at a time when I would be home.

We had a few days to spend in and around Wausau, visiting relatives and friends, before we would again get on yet another train. I'm beginning to believe I am recording more miles via rail transportation than George ever dreamed of. The only problem was I wish it had been my friend, the train buff, who had to suffer all of these precious moments traveling on the railroad.

In all honesty though, traveling with Norma seemed to keep my mind off from the negative things about our rail system that has always bothered me. It provided the opportunity to talk and plan about the future. Each of us seemed to have so many voids in what we knew of one another and these trips provided the time to enlighten one another and do our reminiscing.

CHAPTER 25

LORAN

Shortly after my return to Rosecrans Base at St. Joseph, Missouri, I was informed that I would be apart of a large group of Navigators who would be flown to Wilmington, Delaware. As a means to provide continuing education or training, we were to attend several days of classes that would teach us a new system of navigation to be used primarily while flying anywhere in the Pacific.

This system, called LORAN, was an abbreviation for Long Range Navigational Systems. Several operating places throughout the world had been selected and signals were emitted that could be picked up by this newly designed equipment. It had limitations because we depended on the few islands or land that we controlled at this time. Most of the signals would be deflected by the troposphere, a portion of the atmosphere, which extends outward about seven or ten miles from the earth's surface.

Stations had now been set up in such places as Alaska, Hawaiian Island, Okinawa, Australia, and the west coast of the United States. By triangulation we could interpret these signals and plot them on our special charts. When the system worked properly, you could ascertain your location very rapidly and with a high degree of accuracy. This would truly be a blessing for my three Navigational buddies who had been in the C.B.I.

When we had a day off from classes, a good friend of mine asked if I wanted to hop a commuter train and go into Philadelphia with him. Lt. Sydney Kaplan just happened to be Jewish and I personally felt he received unwarranted treatment at times from many of the others at our Base. He acquired the nickname of "One Meatball," a title that never made any sense to me.

Though Kaplan was anything but handsome, you had to get to know him before you discovered him to be a most sincere human being. I happened to like him. I accepted his friendship and present offer to go into Philadelphia as a token of the way our two relationships had gone.

Lt. Kaplan was from New York and it was obvious he knew his way around the East Coast. We boarded a commuter train that had few similarities of most of the trains I had the misfortune of riding on. In what seemed like only an hour or two, we were in Philadelphia. We got a taxi and it was then I found out what the purpose was of this trip. We were going to a park to hear a concert.

We arrived at a place known as Robin Hood Dells and found a grassy knoll to sprawl out on. Tonight Andre Kostalonis would conduct his Orchestra under the stars and as added attraction we would have the pleasure of hearing his wife sing. His wife happened to be the famous Lili Pons, the French born but American soprano. These were names I had only heard of on the radio. Tonight I could sit and listen in this gorgeous setting. This would be one of the most enjoyable evenings I can remember. The only thing missing was not having Norma by my side to share in this very special moment, something I knew she also enjoyed.

Most of the other flight crewmembers, those who never got to know this side of Lt. Sidney Kaplan, were the losers. This small, but significant experience, fortified my belief in being tolerant of others. If, for some reason, I found I did not like an individual, I would just write him off, leave him alone, and ignore him. I only teased and gave attention to those I liked.

The next day the entire class was informed that our contingent of Navigators would fly in a special C-54, complete with desks and LORAN equipment and go to Bermuda. This would provide us with a hands-on situation by using this new development in a realistic setting. The trip seemed to be over before we wanted it. Practicing using Loran it immediately became obvious that we could arrive at fixes in a fraction of the time that it took with the stars and a sextant.

The pilot landed and we were informed we would have about six hours to spend anyway we wanted before flying back to Wilmington. Lt. Kaplan suggested we might go down to the beach and just loaf around. I noted while we were circling to land the unusual scene below. All the little houses were snow white and all had red clay tile roofs. It was very picturesque'.

Most of the fellow decided the in thing to do was to go swimming. I had not brought a suit so it was necessary to purchase one. My friend Kaplan did not desire to go into the water but elected to sit on the beach and watch the sun baked bodies walk by.

I remember my surprise when I discovered the white sand below the shallow water was like a gentle washboard with curved ribbons of sand that looked like small uniform gentle waves. It seemed like I had to walk nearly the length of a football field before the depth of the water was up to my shoulders.

I had not gone swimming since before I entered the service and I almost made a tragic mistake. First of all, ever since I was eleven years old, I have had a certain phobia about swimming. Back in 1932 a group of us kids went on a long hike in the country. When we arrived on the banks of the Eau Claire River, a place called Yellow Banks, we decided to go skinny dipping.

At the time I and several other guys were going to the YMCA and taking swimming lessons. We were at the early stage of just learning how to swim using the preliminary system of mastering the simple dog-fashion stroke. Our friend, Wally Schmidt, wasn't permitted to attend the Y for some religious reason and didn't know how to swim. We all knew this.

We were at a shallow part of the river where several of us had gone with the Boy Scouts on numerous other occasions. The deepest part of the river at this bend was only about six feet deep and less than eight feet across. There was a large island less than thirty feet on the other side of the river bank and it had a beautiful sand bar. The object was for each of us to get to the other side, across the narrow obstacle and play on the sandy bank of the island. I helped the two youngest members of our group, who could not swim, by supporting them under one arm pit and helping each over the deepest water.

Wallace Schmidt, who was a few months younger than me, however was about three inches taller. We told him all he had to do was bounce his way across the deepest part and get to the other side. For one reason or another, Wally pressed the panic button and just thrashed around in the water and stayed out in the deepest portion. He had pulled his legs up, perhaps from a cramp, and just floundered in the water.

I tried four or five times to grab him and pull him back to the bank. Each time he would wrap his arms around my neck and arms and pull me under with him. I would break free when we were submerged and then try again with no success. My brother had searched for a branch or pole to no avail. Finally it was too late.

Unfortunately the other fellows were of no help and they stood around helplessly and frantically watching their friend drown. I slipped on my blue jean pants and ran nearly a mile down the railroad tracks to the closest farm. I made contact with a young farmer who carried me back on his shoulders. While I stood on his porch I now realized that my feet were a bloody mess from running over the cinders along the tracks. I had not been aware of the hundreds of cuts I had accumulated.

The farmer's wife had called the fire department and they were at the scene about the same time I arrived on the shoulders of her husband. Wally was pulled from the river. They tried using what was called a pull motor on our friend, to no avail.

The Fire Chief had me collect all of my clothes and he drove the two of us back to our neighborhood. He parked and then he and I went to the door of Wally's house to confront his Mother. She took one look at me and screamed. She knew there had been a tragic accident with her only son. Why this Fire Chief insisted I go with him I will never understand. This entire incident left a lasting scare. Most times since then when I go into the water I sometimes find myself hyperventilating.

BEAUTIFUL BERMUDA BEACH

Today, with the sun over head and the white smooth sand pushing its way between my toes, I decided I would go into the water. Once I started wading I noticed the floor of the ocean to be wavy, with each small curved ridge about two inches apart. It was like a sine wave we would use in mathematics or like the waves on the surface of the water when a pebble or small object is carefully dropped in. It was unique and comforting to wade across this unusual surface. I had never seen sand like this before, forgetting that this was my very first swim in the ocean.

I slowly walked out away from the shore, probably about a hundred yards or more. I now was up to my arm pits and sort of getting pushed about by the movement of this warm sea water. The surface of the water was relatively calm so I kicked off into a swimming plane and decided to swim out some distance in the deeper water.

I swam for several minutes, enjoying my very first adventure in an ocean. It had not really occurred to me to make allowance for the energy I would require for the return trip. I had swum approximately 50 yards and just as I decided to swim back toward shore I noticed something black below the surface of the water and it felt like some substance had rubbed against my leg.

Without waiting to analyze what I had seen or felt I pressed the panic button and began racing toward the shallow water. I was expending my energy at a rapid rate, I was hyperventilating, I was sucking in salt water and I knew I was quickly running out of steam. Periodically I would stop swimming, believing I could touch bottom.

When I discovered the water depth was too deep I would struggle to get back into a swimming plane. Again I was squandering my remaining strength. I had imagined the dark object in the water might have been a shark or some other sea urchin I had only read about. What the hell did a kid from Wisconsin know about this damn ocean.

I made the mistake of trying to touch bottom six or seven more times with my toes searching out the safety of the sand. Each time I would swallow water and I was now finding it nearly impossible to stretch out on the surface. My arms were like lead and I no longer could even feel or know what my legs were doing. I found myself thrashing in the water instead of swimming. I was almost at the stage where I felt like quitting and giving up.

When I finally reached a point where I could bounce forward without submerging my head I discovered it was next to impossible to inhale or exhale. There was an awareness I was close to drowning and no one seemed to notice. I was somewhere between yelling out for assistance and trying to be macho, hoping no one would notice this klutz struggling to make shore.

Somehow I gradually made enough forward progress where the surface motion of the salty water did not tend to tip me over. I coughed up water and phlegm until I once again could get air into my lungs. Finally I struggled to shore and dragged myself over to where Lt. Kaplan had been sleeping on a towel.

This would be the second time since I returned home from combat that I damned near killed myself by doing something stupid. I should have known better because I was aware of a problem I always had when I got into unknown waters. Today, over twelve years later, I once again thought of Wally Schmidt.

My trip back to St. Joseph from Wilmington, Delaware made me feel a great deal had been accomplished in a little over a week. I had learned how to use the newest and fastest navigational aid in the form of LORAN, I came close to drowning, and I had the unexpected opportunity to go to a real concert in the park and hear Andre Kostalonis and Lili Pons.

I was reminded of a particular incident my Father had told me of his experience in World War I. About the only positive thing he related to me was the night he happened to see and hear Madam Schumann-Heink, the world renown contralto who was born in Austria. She had sung in France to the American troops who were on a rest leave from the front. I now can relate to my Dad and the importance he also placed on this precious moment in time.

I was especially appreciative that Lt. Kaplan saw fit to invite me to come along as his guest to the various places in the New England States. He knew his way around perhaps the most diversified place in the country, with so much going on and with the possibility to commute to the various adjoining states. Thanks "One Meat Ball."

I had much to tell Norma when I arrived back on our Base. Each one of these special trips I get scheduled on leaves me with the empty feeling that I wished I could have shared these many new experiences with my wife. Both of us had led a fairly sheltered life by barely getting out of our home State of Wisconsin. Up until this war Norma had only ventured down to Chicago and of course to Minnesota. I had only been to the Upper Peninsula of Michigan.

During the next month I had the opportunity of ferrying several Mitchell B-25 attack bombers, one to Africa and the other to the Island of Guam. This was an entirely new plane for me though I was cognizant of the important role it had been playing both in Africa and later against the Japanese in the Pacific.

The Mitchell B-25 was named after the very controversial early champion of air power, General Billy Mitchell. He was one of the first to claim that air craft, properly equipped with guns and bombs, could sink ships at sea. He even advocated it was capable of sinking a battleship. Time proved him correct.

The B-25 went through many revisions during the first years of the war because it was thought to be a plane that could fill a certain niche. The first one was flown on August, 1940 and then during the next few years this plane went through many revisions and improvements.

One version known as B-25G had a 75 mm US Army field gun mounted in its nose plus six 50 calibre machine guns. It was designed and used against primarily Japanese shipping. The later Model H had the M4 75mm cannon plus 14 112.7mm (0.5") or 50 calibre machine guns. There were a few planes ultimately equipped with 18 of these guns.

This special attack bomber became famous on April 18, 1942 when 16 of these specially prepared bombers took off from the Aircraft Carrier USS Hornet. Lieutenant Colonel James H. Doolittle, along with the 15 other B-25s flew off the carrier, something never before attempted, and headed 800 miles toward Japan.

They attacked targets at Kobe, Nagoya, Yokohama, and Tokyo and then went on to land in China, mostly crash landings because many planes ran out of fuel. Some of the crews became prisoners of the Japanese while others were ultimately rescued by Chinese Nationals and were returned to the United States.

This entire operation was only important because for the first time it let the Japanese people know they could be bombed and some of their cities destroyed. It perhaps was more psychological than effective. Time would get our Forces closer and we would develop the planes to get the job done.

Lieutenant Colonel James H. Doolittle became a General after this mission and then was put in charge of the Eighth Air Force over in England. Because of this man I was compelled to fly five additional missions after General LeMay had also added five more. Within a few weeks my tour had changed from the required 25 missions to 35.

The interesting thing about the B-25Js that we were ferrying to Africa was that they had been painted with French markings and insignia. Four crews picked up these attack bombers in Kansas City. We all were surprised to see both the destination for these four aircraft and also how they were painted. We had heard there was a terrible shortage of this particular bomber in the Pacific Theater so we were surprised to know they were to be given to the French and to be delivered to Africa.

The B-25 Mitchell is a two engine attack bomber with a maximum speed of approximately 270 miles per hour. It had two 1268 kW (1700 hp) Wright R-2600-92 Cyclone radial piston engines. It had a service ceiling of about 24,000 feet and a range of nearly 1400 miles.

The plane was designed for a crew of five. It had a top turret with twin 50 calibre machine guns. It was approximately fifty-three feet long with a wing span of 67'-7". This particular J Model had a total of 12 - 50 calibre machine guns.

Our trip to Africa was via South America over to Recife, Brazil, then we all landed on Ascension Island out in the middle of the Atlantic Ocean and finally to the Continent of Africa. I will go into further detail about this much used route to ferry planes in a later story. Thousands of planes flown by combat crews and by personnel such as the Air Transport Command used this route because they had control of bases that provided short legs for the long trip to Europe and ultimately to India and Asia.

Our orders were to deliver these four B-25Js to a Base in Tunis, which is in Tunisia. This is a rather small country just to the east of Libya. After we left Ascension Island we all landed at a rather nice air field and facility at Dakar on the coast of Senegal. This leg really made us sweat out our fuel supply since the trip would be over 1300 miles. A one day flight got us to Marrakech where we had a day of rest.

When we took off from Marrakech we knew we would again be pushing our luck because the route to Tunis was almost the same distance as our previous one. My big surprise came when we landed and were told to line the four B-25s along side a long row of other similar new planes. They all had French markings identical to our planes. Next we were told that these planes had not been used for many months and none were in a condition to be used without extensive overhaul work.

The reason for this is that because of all the blowing fine sand from the desert, each engine would have to be pulled and cleaned thoroughly. Each engine on these planes had been exposed to these desert conditions for months. The men who flew these planes and been reassigned many months ago and were now stationed in England.

Our planes had been on some old manifesto and were scheduled to be shipped to this very designation, come hell or high water. This was an obvious snafu because all of these planes were needed desperately out in the Pacific by our American fliers.

Our group was flown back to Casablanca in a DC3 to await a flight back to the States and our Base. We had a day to roam around this ancient city in Morocco. Thursday morning we boarded a commercial plane that would get us to New York and ultimately home to St. Joseph.

The other B-25 I had the opportunity to ferry would finally be delivered to our own Air Force out in the Pacific. Six Pilots and six Navigators again went to Kansas City and were each assigned a brand new B-25 Mitchell Bomber. All six planes took off in a matter of fifteen minutes and our first destination would be a field near Berkeley California, a short distance north of San Francisco.

Two nights later we took off for the usual flight to the Hawaiian Islands and landed on Oahu. The next morning we hopped over to Johnson Island, refueled and were on our way to Guam, an island in the Marians Chain. Our six planes were received with open arms. The only question they asked us was when were more B-25s going to be forthcoming? The shrug of our shoulders said it all.

When we landed, we were witness to something that proved difficult to accept. A lone soldier, with his rifle laid horizontally across his two extended arms, was bringing in a Japanese prisoner. This nearly naked man looked emaciated and frightened and each time he was about to stand up he was kicked by this soldier, only to fall forward once more.

It seemed that the Marines stationed on this Island would go out and hunt Japanese soldiers just like I used to hunt deer in Wisconsin. The Island of Guam had been captured but there were isolated men in caves and in the jungle that perhaps did not know their situation was hopeless. I looked and could make a quick judgment. I also knew the fellows who had to take this Island saw too many of their own get killed. I was not the person to assess this treatment.

I talked to a Navy seaman who was apart of a torpedo boat crew stationed on Guam. He told me an interesting story worthy of being related. The Lieutenant in charge of this particular TB Boat had a brother who was a pilot of a B-25 in the Air Force, also stationed here on Guam at the time.

One night, when a group of fellows were exchanging stories about recent escapades, the Navy brother mentioned about how the Japanese still held or had control of many islands in the Mariana chain of islands. He mentioned that when they were on patrol with their Torpedo boat, the Japanese would tolerate their craft to proceed to a point just beyond the range of the machine guns aboard.

Periodically these Torpedo boats would linger in this tolerated zone only to check on any new activity on the various islands in the Northern Marianas. The Americans now controlled the sky and the water ways in this area so the Japanese were literally confined to their own little refuge. In many of these situations the Japanese military could no longer supply these remote spots in the Pacific.

The Navy brother mentioned if they could locate a heavier gun they could create havoc from the very distance they were permitted to roam. The Air Force brother said he believed they could procure a M4 75mm field gun from a B-25H that belly landed on a beach nearby a few days ago. The plane was to be rescued and ultimately repaired. "If a group of guys got on the stick, like tonight, we could appropriate this gun and get it mounted on the nose of your Torpedo Boat"

Within hours their mission had been accomplished, the attack bomber was missing one cannon and one PT Boat had this powerful new weapon proudly displayed on the bow. Several days later on a routine patrol mission they had their moment of glory. At a distance when both enemies supposedly were out of range of one another, the Navy opened fire with the new 75mm gun. They caught the Japanese by surprise. Many small boats, buildings, and personnel were hit.

Each trip I had been schedule to take ferrying new planes also gave me the opportunity to see new places, meet many new men, see different situations, and to get a broader view of what the entire war was all about. The Pacific Theater was entirely different from what I had experienced while in Europe.

On one of the islands we had delivered a plane you could see, upon making a landing on a newly installed runway, the aftermath and the price paid to capture this island from the Japanese. Below the surface of the Ocean were sunken ships, LSTs, tanks, and debris. Signs had been posted telling about certain events or action taken. There were temporary grave sites with their own markers.

The CBs had quickly installed metal perforated pads on a graded site so that we could land safely. On one island they had scooped out a huge hole about twenty feet inland from the edge of the ocean. It then filled with water that percolated through the ground. This now was a swimming facility for swimming and free of the dangerous sharks.

I was always happy to return back to my home base at St. Joe, Missouri and Norma. There was always much to tell and I also knew each passing day was bringing us closer to the end of this long and terrible war. I knew what I was doing had a certain amount of danger connected with it and now that I was married I was aware of the consequences should something happen to me.

CHAPTER 26

POLIGNIANO, ITALY

Once I reported in to Operations, I was immediately made aware of an interesting trip I had been assigned to. There were to be eight crews, each one consisting of a Pilot and a Navigator. We were to deliver eight A-26s, known as the INVADER, to Poligniano, Italy on the outskirts of Naples.

On Monday I had to leave our apartment especially early in order to get out to the Base, pack my gear, and then catch the bus for Kansas City. I knew or recognized over half of the other fifteen fellows making this trip and I knew between each leg of this long journey I would get to know the others. This would be my first meeting with Captain Greg Hillman, the Pilot of the plane I would be Navigator for. He was from Camden, New Jersey and extremely handsome.

I only mention this last fact because everyone who saw us together made the comment they thought we were brothers or even twins. In our uniforms, this likeness was even more pronounced. Several guys had come up to me, when Greg and I were apart, and started a conversation that made no sense to me. Later, our wives got to see the two of us together and came to the same conclusion. God, I'm glad he was so handsome. One obvious difference though, he out-ranked me and he was over an inch and a half taller.

Our flight from Kansa City to Savannah, Georgia gave us all a chance to get better acquainted and consequently the flight went rather fast. We each had high priority passes so we had no trouble getting on the first available commercial airline flights. We lost an hour because of the time belt change and an additional hour driving from the airport to Hunter Army Air Base.

Once we were settled, we were briefed that our job was to ferry the eight A-26 Attack Bombers to a destination just outside of Naples, Italy. We were all to take off at approximately 1000 hours on Wednesday, April 10th.

The type of plane that we were ferrying was completely new to me. Captain Hillman had previously been checked out in this new attack bomber, as had all of the other Pilots who would be making this trip. The A-26 had been hurried out of the design stage and into production.

THE INVADER

The A-26, referred to as the "Invader", looked a great deal like the A-20 "Havoc", except it was slightly larger and a great deal faster. It also carried more armament. The word "Invader," by definition, means to enter in quest of plunder or to permeate. Once you set eyes on this beautiful creature, you know it is aptly named.

The plane was being rushed to Italy to be ready for the final stage of the war in Europe. It was believed, that as the war wound down, Hitler and most of his cronies, would make a last ditch stand in the Alps. The final battle was thought to be at his famous Berchtegaden Retreat in Bavaria near the Austrian border. This plane had been designed with all of this taken into consideration.

The A-26 had a long narrow fuselage that terminated in a high thin graceful rudder. The stabilizers were set well above the plane of the wing, thus making it next to impossible to bail out should one be required to leave the plane. The other end of the streamlined fuselage ended up with a nose containing six 50-calibre machine guns, mounted in two vertical rows of three each. There were two remotely controlled dorsal and ventral turrets, each with two 50-calibre machine guns.

Mounted in the wings on each side of the cockpit were two huge engines, each the size of a large automobile. They were 2000 horsepower Pratt & Whitney R-2800 engines and the plane could reach a maximum speed of 571 km/h or over 355 mph. This new model A-26 would be the fastest U.S. Bomber in World War II.

It was meant to be a low altitude, high performance, twin-engine attack bomber designed for specific targets. It had no provision for oxygen. This meant that it would be operational below 10,000 feet. The plane looked extremely awesome parked on the ramp and it looked even more terrifying as you watched it streak across the sky. You felt most insignificant sitting in the cramped cockpit, yet you knew you were surrounded by raw power.

We had all day Tuesday off before we would leave so Greg and I went into Savannah and did some sight seeing. At a remote corner on the outskirts of this very old city, quite by accident, we stumbled onto a run down little shop that sold liquor.

We stopped in to by a bottle of anything worth drinking for the upcoming trip, but to our amazement, the proprietor had two cases of straight bourbon whisky. It was labeled "Old Mill Farm", a name that meant nothing to me. We were assured it was the very best bourbon made. Besides, it was next to impossible to even find the stuff during the war.

Within minutes, 12 bottles of "Old Mill Farm" belonged to the twins. This particular brand of bourbon could be sipped directly from the bottle and one could honestly feel, as it dribbled down the throat, this truly was the "nectar of the Gods." The next morning we had to sneak this precious cargo of liquid gold onto the plane.

Finding room on this A-26 would be the major problem we would be confronted with since compactness was the guiding word the designers at Douglas Aircraft Factory were influenced by. We had to distribute our cargo into smaller units to find adequate space. We were motivated by the desire to get this precious cargo back to St. Joseph, Missouri, a trip that would be in excess of six thousand miles.

It was mutually agreed by the entire group that our ship would be the lead plane on each leg of the journey for two major reasons. First, Captain Greg Hillman was the highest-ranking officer among the sixteen making this trip. We were all 1st or 2nd Lieutenants, with a single Flight Officer. Secondly, it was recognized, that I had the most experience as a Navigator because of the number of missions I had flown in a Lead position during my tour of duty with the Eighth Air Force over in England.

A few minutes after 1000 hours on Wednesday all eight planes were all lined up and took off in one-minute intervals. It also had been decided it would be less stressful if we didn't fly in a tight formation, but rather as a loose group with radio contact maintained. This decision turned out to be a very important one on our third leg of this long journey.

The feeling in the cockpit of this A-26 was one of being very crowded. The entire nose of the plane was completely filled with armament and the two huge engines on either side of the small space called a cockpit shut out most of the view to the sides.

We knew it would be next to impossible to bail out in an emergency situation and we had been briefed, should it be necessary to ditch, this sucker was expected to float for less than eight seconds. These were sobering statistics, especially since we were flying this brand new prototype that had been manufactured by the lowest bidder.

The first leg of our trip was approximately 1300 miles to a field in Boringuen, Puerto Rico. Nearly all of the legs on this long journey will be at least 1000 miles or slightly longer. On this clear day though, we would be able to see a continuous string of islands off our starboard side. These constant landmarks would make navigation very easy, almost like being on a sightseeing tour.

About a half hour after takeoff from Savannah we could see the skyline of Miami, Florida in the distance off our right wing. I started to fool with the radio in hopes I could pick up some nice music. Suddenly the cockpit was filled with the sounds of Morse Code being tapped out. Our first thoughts, "someone might be in distress," caught our immediate attention and concern. I use and emphasize the word "our" because of how this story ends.

I had a small clipboard and a pad of paper strapped on my right thigh, so I immediately started to take this code down. As a Navigator in training I was exposed to this code at San Marcos, Texas. We had to reach a moderate scale of proficiency before we graduated, like twelve words per minute. We were not expected to have the talent of the radio operators, but this was something someone felt we ought to know. That was long ago and I had never found a need to use it since my early training.

Occasionally I would miss a letter, but I was catching enough to spell out the the the words: **"da dit da, dit da, dit da da dit, da, dit da, dit dit, da dit, — — da da, dit dit, da dit da, da dit, dit dit,, da da dit, Dit dit dit dit, da ********: Just as I was beginning to write down these letters, C A P T A I N – M I D N I G, a voice shouted out: "Captain Midnight." It was an old radio program for children and these were the opening remarks prior to the current serial starting.

I now felt like a damn fool. Suddenly the cockpit seemed too large to hide me. During the course of this trip, Capt. Hillman made a point to relate this story to anyone who would listen. This incident certainly was embarrassing to me, though I personally was proud that most of my twelve words per minute skill had not left me.

GREAT DISCOVERY

I made an important discovery the day I first saw this awesome A-26. By nosing around the entire plane, trying to find suitable spots to stash our bourbon, I uncovered a ridiculous looking funnel. It was obviously a specially designed vessel to pour oil into some remote and hard to reach part of the engines on this particular airplane.

There were four or five offsets in the spout as it narrowed down to the spigot of this odd looking Rube Goldberg contraption. I could not believe a beautiful streamlined work of art like the A-26 would have this ugly piece of contorted copper aboard.

This peculiar looking funnel would play a most important role on the remainder of this trip. The only facility to relieve oneself on this INVADER, a plane that cost hundreds of thousands of dollars, was a single cardboard two-quart ice cream carton.

It was about four inches in diameter and about eight inches tall, with a cover. It had been constructed using heavy duty cardboard in a spiral laminate. Despite what some powerful minds had reasoned, this container was only good for a single use and then should be discarded.

Both Greg and I urinated in this petite container and also emptied our ashtray contents into it. Greg stated, "I wish we could dump or empty this damn thing out somewhere. We have to be careful we don't tip it over in the cockpit. We'd have a real mess."

"EURIKA." I shouted. I now remembered our funnel. I twisted myself around and finally procured this odd looking beast. Greg looked bewildered and said, "what in hell is that contraption?" By simply opening my side window a small amount, I could get the end of the funnel out into the slip-stream.

I poured the contents of our carton into the funnel and was soon going to pollute the Caribbean Sea. Our paper urinal instantly began to dry out and would be ready for the inevitable use later on. Greg began to realize just how important his Navigator turned out to be.

When we landed, the most paramount thing discussed or mentioned concerned their soggy carton and how they could hardly handle it while trying to empty it onto the ground. Both Greg and I decided, at least for the moment, not to inform them exactly how we handled this delicate problem.

We believed they could probably milk one more leg of this journey out of each of their paper urinals. In fact, the next day, just to exasperate this problem, when Greg or I had radio contact with one of the other planes, we would offer an exhortation of how nice it would be if we could get out and make a pit stop. We both were aware of the power of suggestion.

Once we checked into operations at the Base in Boringuen, our large contingent headed for the Officers Club. There was a local native Puerto Rican who happened to be on duty as the sole bartender. Regardless of what you asked him his first retort would be, "No problum Mon." He had a smile that was larger than his face. Though he was not a very large person, he more than made up for it with his personality. He had black flashing eyes and hair to match. The shirt he happened to be wearing was the loudest thing I had ever seen.

It didn't take long to discover that he could mix a mean Old fashion. It was a treat just to watch him at his art. He flipped his tools, he chopped fruit, he poured from a great distance, he twisted rinds and he would shake the contents in a rhythmic fashion. It was apparent he had done this many times. In fact, you could say he was showing off.

Greg and I mentioned to him of the treasure we had discovered in Savannah, our straight bourbon. He then offered to divulge his formula or recipe by using some of our precious liquid in one of his Old Fashions. I wrote it down on a paper napkin and think it worthy of including here with the notes of this trip.

BORINGUEN OLD FASHION

° lump sugar
2 dashes of Angostura bitters
2 dashes of water to cover sugar
(muddle well with right hand)
1 medium size ice cube
2 oz. Of OLD MILL FARM bourbon whisky stir in clockwise direction w/ pinky of right hand protruding.

Add twist of lemon rind and gently drop into glass.

Decorate w/ slice of orange and ° slice lemon. Carefully place one cherry in center.

Serve w/ stirring rod——sit back and ENJOY.

Greg and I, before we left this interesting and beautiful island, had the chance to buy and to split a case of the best, (as per our new found friend the bartender,) Puerto Rican Light Rum. With the addition of these six rum bottles, each of our B-4 bags, besides being heavy, are now developing a shape they were never designed for.

SECOND LEG OF JOURNEY

On Thursday morning we got briefed and into the air with no problems. We would be heading south from Puerto Rico on a heading that would take us to an airfield just south of Georgetown, British Guiana. British Guiana is a small country on the north central coast of South America. It lies just east of Venezuela and a short distance above the equator. This would be one of the shortest legs we would fly and it also provided us with an interesting string of islands to assist my navigation.

As we progressed after taking off I made note of many of the picturesque little islands we either passed over or could see off our right or left wing. There was St. Croix, St. Martin, St. Kitts, Antigua, and Barbuda Islands in the Leeward Islands.

Next we could find Dominica, St. Lucia, St. Vincent, and Barbados Island in what is referred the Windward islands. This entire chain of islands is called the Lesser Antilles. Just before we got to Georgetown, British Guiana we could see in the distance, off our right wing, the islands of Trinidad and Tobago.

That evening Greg and I each opened up one of our bottles of OLD MILL FARM, and treated the others as we sat around jawing. None of us knew tonight that four of our members would die the next day. Midway into the evening we were about to learn that President Franklin Delano Roosevelt had just died at Warm Springs, Georgia.

We, of course, were saddened to learn this news of our President, who was now in his fourth term of office. He, of course, was our Commander In Chief. It took some time for one of us to finally come up with the current Vice President.

We had kicked around the name of John Nance Garner. I was able to offer the fact that he was our 32nd V.P. and was definitely not a current one. I knew a little about him since I had taken my primary flight training at Garner Field, Uvalde, Texas. This particular field was named after ex Vice President John Nance Garner since it was his hometown.

Finally the name of Henry Wallace and Harry Truman were remembered. Despite our drinking and joking, we all agreed that it was indeed Harry S. Truman who was now our current Vice President and it would be he who would now be our Commander In Chief.

Before the night was over, Greg and I had the chance to purchase a case of top shelf (we were assured) exquisite Dark Rum. This we also split.

Normally I have never been a lover of rum, but the quality of our latest purchases made the rum taste like an entirely new drink. We had had the opportunity to sample both types of rum when we were at the bars in Boringuen and now here in Georgetown.

We were now using our t-shirts, handkerchiefs, and shorts to wrap around these precious bottles to keep them from breaking or making noise. This insatiable urge to purchase this high quality alcohol these past several days may seem somewhat off . . . . . we were only caught up in the moment.

TRAGEDY STRIKES

The third leg of our journey was to be entirely over jungle. Because of the eventuality of bailing out over this mass of vegetation, we were issued linen maps of the entire area. We were told that normal paper maps would disintegrate within a day or two, while the linen ones would survive the extreme heat and moisture of the jungle for several weeks should they be needed.

During our briefing we were also informed of the difficulty or near impossibility of surviving in this jungle. We were told and shown pictures of the many species of poisonous or deadly snakes, poisonous spiders, hordes of insects, a variety of carnivorous animals, and the many deadly plants growing in this unexplored rain forest.

To make the picture complete, we were also informed that any natives we might encounter probably had never seen white men before and most of them practice cannibalism. I believe this was information each of us could have done without.

As I sat there listening to all of these encouraging words, I was almost glad that it was next to impossible to bail out of this damn airplane. Suddenly this interesting trip took on a more serious outlook. To make matters even worse, we were now given some bad news about the weather. There would be a cloudbank covering most of our route that would be 10,000 feet thick.

The weatherman briefed us with the assurance that the bottom of this cloud cover should be 2000 to 3000 feet above the jungle. Visibility, however, would be a maximum of less than a mile. They gave us an altimeter setting, the wind direction and velocity, and wished us well.

I had hoped we would have a clear day with unlimited visibility, like the previous two legs we had just completed. We mutually agreed to increase the interval that we would fly in because of the weather. Greg and I took off first on a southeasterly heading. The other seven A-26s would takeoff at three-minute intervals.

The map I was now using for navigational purposes indicated nothing but vegetation, no towns, no cities, no roads of any kind, not even rivers.

The trees covered everything. It was as if man had never put his imprint on this section of the world.

Not long into our flight we noticed the distance between the bottom of the cloudbank and the tops of the tallest trees was rapidly getting less, along with our visibility. We also noted that periodically an extremely tall tree would grow nearly a hundred feet above the jungle roof.

If one of these suckers would be directly ahead of us we would have to pull back on the stick or lift one our wings to clear this unforgiving obstacle. It was getting darn right hairy. Greg increased our altitude a little as we now were getting into tufts of clouds from the mess above us.

Our course was headed for the Amazon Delta and a town called Bele'm, in Brazil. We were about a third of the way along this leg, approaching the eastern border of French Guiana, when one of the crew flying behind us shouted over the radio, "One of our planes crashed into the jungle, I saw him go in and explode. God help them." Within thirty seconds a second plane, of our small contingent, met the same fate, evidently running into one of those damn tall trees that were now touching the bottom of the cloudbank.

Our first inclination was to circle back but logic and common sense made us immediately realize there wasn't a thing we, or any of the other five remaining planes could do. We knew that we could not even find out where they went into the jungle because of the thick canopy in this awful impenetrable thicket of vegetation.

The weather was now so bad we had to climb up into the soup and fly instruments, just to get the hell out of this mess. We knew we could not climb high enough to get above this crap since we had no oxygen. The ever present fear of running into one another was ever present. Greg informed those behind us of the altitude he had chosen and suggested every other plane, in the order we took off, increase their altitude by an additional 500 feet.

I had made an entry on my log of the coordinates where these two planes went in and the exact time the accidents took place. These fellow airmen disappeared at 1019 hours, approximately 2 degrees 20 minutes North Latitude and 54 degrees 10 minutes West Longitude. They went down almost at the juncture of three small South American countries, namely French Guiana, Amapa, and Surinam. It was in the middle of nowhere.

"I wonder who went in Greg? Did you hear who it might be?" Once we climbed up to an altitude several thousand feet above the highest terrain on the course ahead of us, we leveled off. We would be on instruments until we could fly out of this damn soup.

Finally Lt. Lyons called out over the radio that it was Lt. Butler's and Lt. Nitzel's planes that crashed into the high protruding trees and exploded. I hardly got to know these two Pilots and their Navigators. "Why?" was the only word I could utter. I guess there are no answers to some questions.

In combat I had witnessed many planes go down. Sometimes we might know if they were able to escape an explosion if we could count chutes, but usually there would be fewer parachutes than the number in the unlucky crew. As often as I witnessed these stupid disasters I discovered you never really get used to it.

Despite our gut feelings about what had just transpired, we had things that demanded our immediate and constant attention and concentration. We all had to maintain our agreed about air speed since there were still six planes flying in this turbulent cloud and piss poor weather. There would be no time for evasive action should two planes get near one another.

Just as we approached the southeastern border of Amapa, the clouds rapidly dissipated. As we let down to our predetermined altitude, we could see the Amazon Delta up ahead. Bele'm would still be a little over 200 miles on our heading of 124 degrees.

Off our left wing we could see this huge delta, still in the process of being developed by the famous Amazon River as it flowed and was about to become a part of the Atlantic Ocean. A quick calculation informed me, at the location where we were flying, this delta was over 100 miles wide.

This was an unbelievable sight— — —the world's greatest river dumping all of its silt that had been picked up during its nearly two-thousand-mile journey. Some of these droplets of water started high in the Andes Mountains of Ecuador, Peru and Columbia and made their way ultimately to the Atlantic Ocean after depositing their silt, mud, and rich soil in this huge delta.

Up ahead we could see the Tocantins River and the airfield just north of Bele'm. We had just completed our third leg, but we all were landing with heavy hearts. Silence seemed the best remedy for each to handle this tragedy.

Because of the tragedy of the four killed airmen, we were given the following day off to relax. Several of our group took this whole unfortunate accident extremely hard. For some, it was their first experience of being so close to death and having a friend or someone they were just beginning to know, have their time "to buy the farm."

I don't know if you ever get used to the finality of this sort of thing, but my experience of combat over Germany and the Continent had somehow steeled me not to dwell on these moments. My strong fatalistic attitude led me to believe that when your number was up and you had to cash in your chips, you had no choices. I also was aware that only by a quirk of fate it could have been our plane.

Today though, someone in Operations decided we would get a day off so that we would overcome our grief and then be better able to get on with the business of delivering these A-26s. We had been trained to accept death as part of this whole damn war.

The impersonal side of our role almost dictated that we did not need a day off.

The reality is that no amount of time can completely heal or make up for the loss of not only a friend, but also a brother airman. Today we lost four.

Later during the day I wandered off to be by myself. I walked down a defined path into the jungle near our Base. It had its own sort of beauty. I was so busy looking at the various types of vegetation I had never seen before that I was unaware my path was beginning to dwindle away.

Leaves the size of washtubs and vines dangling in all directions caught my eye. I saw insects that were five times the size of bugs I had learned to examine. Then, as I listened, I could hear the squeals and the howls of monkeys or other small animals I could not see.

Suddenly I felt completely isolated except for this strange and bizarre environment I now found myself in. By looking and gawking at all of this fascinating foliage, I had completely lost my sense of direction. The foliation did not permit the sun to find this area I now found myself in. There was not one thing I could orient myself to. I could not see a path, my footprints, the sun, — —-"Hell, this Navigator was lost."

Unexpectedly I felt my heart begin to pound and I noticed how I quickly felt the heat around me. Then I caught myself breathing heavily and now I knew I had to put my brain into gear. I stood very still for almost five minutes and just plain listened for any sound that might be foreign to usual jungle noises but something I could identify with back at the Base.

Finally I distinguished a manmade sound off to my left and slightly behind me. As I cautiously started walking slowly in that direction, I intentionally mutilated leaves and made marks at eye level on some vines. Finally I spotted the original path I had taken. I could not see it until I was within only a foot or two of the worn trail.

I had previously experienced moments when I was temporarily lost in the northern woods of Wisconsin while deer hunting. This however, was an different emotion and experience I could have lived without. The next morning at briefing we all got the chance to see a boa constrictor that had only recently been mounted in the office building.

It was nearly 20 foot long and perhaps seven or eight-inches in diameter. The coloration of this enormous snake was beautiful, with obvious large diamond shapes the entire length of this creature. I was most curious about it so I started asking questions of where and how they had caught it.

I was informed that the local natives made a small enclosure out of numerous stakes they spaced just wide enough so a small pig could not escape. They lashed the top of these stakes with vines, about two feet from the ground. This snake crawled in during the night, swallowed the pig, tried escaping between the stakes, and then, in the morning, was killed by the natives.

It appeared the snake did not have enough know how to simply crawl over the enclosure with its prize. "Very ingenuous." I was glad this baby had not been out along the path I got lost on. I do not know, but I would guess it probably weighed twice what I did.

On Monday morning, the 15th of April, we headed for Natal, Brazil. This important city is about 1100 miles from Bele'm. This would be our last stop before crossing the wide Atlantic Ocean. The one thing I had heard about Natel from others who had passed this way was the size and quality of the PX on the Base.

This Post Exchange had almost anything you might desire, especially things manufactured by people in South America. This was a departing point for many U. S. troops and other personnel on the way to war zones. Thousands of planes would cross the Atlantic at this point.

Not to profit from past experience (two dresses purchased in Houston and mailed to my wife), I decided it would be prudent for me to procure some genuine silk stockings for Norma. I knew these were impossible to find and afford in the States because of the war.

"What size stockings would you desire sir?" said a clerk. "Here we go again. How do I know what size stocking or lingerie Norma would need?" I ended up purchasing twelve pair of silk stockings in three different sizes. "Surely one of these sizes would turn out to be correct." This decision seemed to me to be a no lose situation.

I also a procured what I thought was a beautiful and impressive alligator handbag for Norma. I had let this sales girl convince me every woman would die for this unique purse. The purse was beautifully made and truly reeked of quality and good taste. "There is no way in Hell that this decision would let me down."

One of my flying buddies insisted I buy a bottle of Channel No.5 Perfume. He assured me there wasn't a woman who wouldn't go berserk for the world's most famous perfume. This last purchase was to earn some sure fire Brownie Points once I got home. Perfume does not have to worry about size, shape or color.

For myself I bought a pair of the famous Natal Boots, something every officer and Enlisted man desired if they came through this part of the world. Finding a way to cart this back home was harder than parting with the money to buy the stuff.

AFRICA

Arriving at Ascension Island, about 1500 miles from Natal, would be our next challenge. This tiny island is about midway between South America and Africa and is only large enough to have a single runway carved into its volcanic makeup. This would be a navigational exercise requiring accuracy.

Once again we Navigators were reminded that a single error of only a degree would result in being off course a nautical mile for every sixty nautical miles we flew. This simple err alone could have us missing the damn island by forty nautical miles. The reality is the possibility of being off by more than a single degree.

Ascension Island was a mere dot on any map, but it also proved to be a welcome sight once you spotted it. In some respects, as we approached the field, I had the feeling this landing would be more like a typical naval landing on an aircraft carrier. The runway occupied most of the island and there was a high cliff at each end of this narrow band of concrete.

The takeoff from the relatively short runway was a little hairy on the morning of the 16th. This time, however, instead of aiming for a little dot, we would have the entire Continent of Africa before us. Our destination was an airfield just north of Dakar, Senegal.

My problem, as a Navigator, was not being able to find Africa, but to locate the only military airfield at a specific spot within the several hundred miles of the African coastline before us. Fortunately I had been through here before and was aware of what we had to look for.

A noteworthy thing, I shall always remember about this particular stop on our journey, were the natives who waited on us in the mess hall. They were the most polite, willing, and efficient waiters I had ever come in contact with. They spoke perfect King's English with that strong British accent, and each one of them seemed to have a bubbling personality. I truly enjoyed talking with some of them and simply watching their enthusiasm and their efficiency.

DAMN NEAR "BOUGHT THE FARM"

Our trip today, April 18th, would be partly over desert and partly over mountains. The course we had been given to follow took us over Mauritania and the Western Sahara Desert. This first portion of the trip was not too pleasant since we had to contend with haze, caused by blowing sand. At times we could hardly see our wing tips. The last third of this leg of our journey would take us through the Atlas Mountain Range to Marrakech, Morocco, our final destination.

Because of the almost constant amount of haze in this part of Africa, planes departing Dakar were told to fly down a specific valley until a radio signal would indicate a turn on a predetermined course, taking you down another valley. Once you heard this radio signal and your radio compass turned to 180 degrees, you had five seconds to alter course to the prescribed heading.

What we didn't find out until later, we had been cleared to take off, despite the fact that there was a problem with the radio transmitter and signal. Once we were airborne we were not aware of what was to follow. Suddenly, all of our other planes had been told to return to the hard stand until further notice. They would be notified when this radio beacon had been made functional.

Unknown to Greg and me, this radio signal was not functioning and the control tower had unintentionally let us take-off in our A-26. Unfortunately our lead position with the remaining six planes was not an asset this day.

Greg and I were flying down this canyon, big, dumb but happy, not knowing that our lives were in jeopardy. We were on the signal telling us that our heading down the valley was correct, even though it was very difficult to see because of the haze. I was trying to keep track of our position by air speed and time so that we could anticipate ahead of time when we would be signaled to turn by our radio compass.

Finally I yelled to Greg, "We should be picking up the turn signal right now. What's wrong." Suddenly everything seemed to get dark as I felt like I was being pressed into my seat. Captain Hillman had pulled the wheel back into his lap and pushed the throttles full forward. The A-26 was pointed vertical as we passed within a few feet of the wall of rock that made up the face of the Atlas Mountains.

The engines roared as they labored to pull up and over the peek of this range. We had been shoved hard against the back of our seats by a centrifugal force I had never experienced before. The strain put on the plane and our bodies temporarily made it seem like we were out of control. Body parts were momentarily forced out of alignment.

The centrifugal forces distorted our faces and made it next to impossible to move. Captain Hillman had just performed a miraculous job of saving our lives. As soon as we cleared the highest peak, Greg lifted up our right wing and turned west to head out toward the Ocean. About twenty minutes later we could see the ocean so we turned on a northern route to parallel the African coastline.

We had been within inches and a fraction of a second of getting splattered on the side of this damn mountain. Greg's reflexes had made the difference of becoming the third casualty of this trip. We each now had to get our hearts out of our throats as we sat in silence, the two of us, for many minutes.

We both were deep in our own thoughts. With the throttles now cut back we flew level along the western coast of Morocco trying to regain our composure. Nearly ten minutes would go by in complete silence. Once again I thought about how narrow is the margin between life and death? How many times can I expect to luck out?

What seemed like an eternity of listening only to the purr of our two engines, we simultaneously broke this uncertain tranquility. All at once we both started talking at the same time. We had been scared to death and I know our hearts were pounding out our anxieties.

We damned near got splattered on the Atlas Mountains because some son of a bitch wasn't on the ball and saw to it that our plane would not be permitted to take off. We both knew it had not been done intentionally but certainly someone was derelict in their duty. Once they made the mistake of letting us take off why didn't they radio our plane to return to Dakar?

This would be the third time since returning from combat that my luck had nearly run out. There was the confused mixed feeling of not knowing if I was unlucky to have these hairy incidences pop up or if I was fortunate to have survived them. This is primarily the reason war has the tendency to age each of its participants prematurely.

We continued to fly North along the African coast until we were slightly South of Safi, Morocco. We then flew East until we could make a landing at the Air Force base near Marrakech. When we reported into Operations they were shocked to see us. "How in hell did you guys get through the valley? No one is expected to make the trip North until tomorrow," They looked like they were seeing ghosts. They damn near were.

We told of our near miss and asked that Dakar be notified of their huge mistake.

Somebody's ass had to be chewed out for this stupid mistake that nearly cost our lives and would have eliminated the third crew and plane from our original group. This was as close as I'd ever come to cracking up in over two years of flying and several hundred thousand miles I had logged.

The other five crews of the A-26s would now be several days behind us because of the fouled up radio beacons and worsening of the weather. From here on Greg and I would be moving on without the rest. This is no big deal since we are now close to our destination.

Our next leg would take us from Marrakech, Morocco to Tunis, Tunisia, about 1200 miles, and it would all over land. After our take-off we would have to gain altitude in a hurry since we would be required to fly over some of the highest peaks of the Atlas Mountains, the same one that damn near claimed us.

As we flew into Algeria the mountain range kept dropping until it reached a large plateau. We now could see signs of green grasses and indications that there was some fertile tillable land below us. For perhaps an obvious reason, Greg and I spent a good deal of this flight discussing the question, "If we had an emergency and had to leave the plane, would you prefer it to be over the jungle, over the ocean, or over the desert?" Each of these three choices had some very negative connotations.

Assuming you could survive a bail out in this A-26 because of the high stabilizer, my choice was over the water. I chose this knowing that this plane would sink in eight seconds and knowing all about my personal love for the water.

I told Greg, " I'll take my chances over the ocean, because in eight second I can do one hell of a lot of moving. Once I get free of the sinking plane and get into a life raft, at least I feel some search plane or ship could eventually spot me." Greg's final decision and chicken answer was, "I prefer not to have an emergency."

About 45 minutes before we reached Tunis we could see Algiers to the North of us. I noted on my map that once we reached the airfield at Tunis, we would be too far South to see the Mediterranean Sea, even as we were now getting glimpses of it from the air. This pleasure would have to wait until tomorrow's flight. Our final leg of this ferrying mission to deliver this A-26 to its final destination would be only about 400 miles, or a little over an hour flight time.

For some unreasonable logic we had been scheduled the next day to take-off very late in the afternoon. In fact we could see the sun just getting ready to set off our left wing. This meant we would arrive at our destination in Italy in the dark.

When we were finally cleared for take-off, in all of the confusion and perhaps our desire to get the show on the road, Capt. Hillman was to learn later that a switch had not been energized. It had to be activated while we were still on the ground. It was for IFF, a device that sends out a signal that receiving equipment will recognize an incoming plane as being friendly. The IFF stands for Identification Friend or Foe.

Once we became aware of this error Greg decided to drop our altitude to just being on the deck of the Mediterranean. We would skim only a few feet above the water so radar would not pick us up. Flying at this altitude, just above the beautiful Mediterranean Sea, felt like we were skimming over the water at six hundred miles per hour. Most things were only a blur.

Occasionally we had to lift up in order to avoid the sails of some small fishing boats. Though we could not see behind us, we might have capsized some of these crafts from our prop wash. Now our only intent was to get this plane over to Poligniano and finally head home to our wives.

It was dark as we approached Naples and we still had to find the field we were assigned to land at. Supposedly, there were three fields northeast of the city and our map did not identify the names of these landing strips. It was too dark to see any pattern to the runway layouts.

Greg was in contact with the tower at the correct airfield and it happened to be some English operator who only could communicate with a thick British accent. He sounded like he had a mouth full of marbles. "Oeu soy, do belav kin harr yoo. Do yoo shee the towwa? Cum on baack plaz. Ovah."

After seven or eight-minutes of this crap, Greg brought the plane down on one of the three airfields, all within sight of one another. Luckily, he picked the right one. We had gotten in and over Allied territory without our IFF and no one challenged us.

We could have blown the whole damn place up, had we been an enemy aircraft. We later were informed that captured Italian prisoners were operating some of the radar equipment and some even manned certain antiaircraft guns. At this late stage of the war they had switched sides.

The first and most important job Greg and I had to do was to locate and retrieve all of the wrapped bottles of liquor we had collected during our long journey. This precious liquid had been pushed into every available tiny space we had access to. We had to repack our B-4 bags so this heavy load could be carried without making tell tale sounds as we picked them up or set them down.

Next, Captain Greg Hillman had to get many papers and orders signed so that this valuable airplane, our A-26 INVADER, could be properly turned over. After an hour of this kind of dittling around, we both were ready for the sack they had assigned us.

We had a free day before we would be flown out of here so we took a bus ride into Naples. We could see the famous Mount Vesuvius off to our left. This trip into Naples turned out to be very disappointing experience for me in several respects. In all of my reading and studying architectural buildings I had envisioned this city to be one of the most beautiful of all the cities of Europe.

It turned out to be a disaster for me. I knew the war had gone through this part of Italy almost a year ago and I expected to see battle damage. What I couldn't comprehend was the mess that still remained. It almost looked like the Germans had been forced out only a few weeks ago.

In London, for example, when whole city blocks were destroyed, within days the streets would be cleared of debris so traffic could move about. The entire area would be cleaned up and this rubble would ultimately be put in the holds of ships as ballast, returning to the United States for more supplies. It would then be unloaded and dumped into the ocean, prior to docking.

In Naples, people and animals walked around mounds of debris and in some cases, over these obstacles. Entire fronts of buildings, which were inhabited by people, were still exposed and laid open. No effort was made to use temporary construction to make the living conditions safer and more private. As I looked up into these structures, knowing entire families occupied these rooms opened to the world, I wondered how they could keep little children from falling out onto the rubble below.

The remains of shot down fighter planes would be just where they crash landed. A blown-up tank could be seen at one of the intersections of several busy streets. You could see the millions of tiny pieces of ground up glass glisten as sunrays reflected off of them. Many shops were void of whatever they formally sold while others had their merchandise on tables next to the sidewalks. It was now very obvious that this part of Italy was extremely poor and very desperate for aid and assistance.

The second and perhaps the most disappointing experience were the many times Greg and I had been approached by desperate men willing to selling the sexual services of their wives or daughters. To this day I find this hard to live with. War does not only destroy, mutilate, and kill, it can take away the dignity of its survivors. My memory of these few hours spent in Naples will remain with me forever.

HEADING BACK TO ST. JOE

On Monday morning we boarded an Air Force C54 Transport Plane for the long flight to Casablanca, Morocco. On this trip we would sit back and leave the flying to others. We had been told that we could expect a delay of several days in returning to the United States due to a large backlog of personnel. Casablanca was the key center from which returning personnel would depart in this part of the world.

Once we settled in on the Base in Casablanca, we were given the bad news that all Air Transport Command personnel would be put on a standby list to ferry war weary planes back to the States.

We were informed that they had a list of all ATC crews and names would be added as they arrived. If a specific war weary plane was scheduled for return, they would take the men on the bottom of this list that had been qualified for the required duties to ferry it home.

I had seen over a dozen old B-17s lined up at one end of the runway as we came in. I immediately believed my destiny was sealed. The thought even occurred to me that perhaps I could bribe myself off the list by parting with several bottles of my bourbon.

As much as I liked flying, returning war weary planes to the United States, just so they could be destroyed, made no sense to me. In the relatively short time I was in the Air Transport Command I had two occasions where I swapped flights with another Navigator. These two frightening experiences happened, once prior to this trip to Poligniano and once just before I got my discharge from the Air Force.

On each occasion I was approached by a Navigator who had formerly been assigned to the Pacific Theatre of Operations and who had never been to England. Because they knew I had flown my combat mission with the Eighth Air Force and they were scheduled for a ferrying mission back to some Pacific Island, they asked if I would exchange with them. It did not matter to me so I found no difficulty going to the various islands in the Pacific.

Once again I was challenged with the problem of trying to understand fate. On two of these exchanges the flights proved disastrous and both crews had been killed while flying the Atlantic. One crew went down while delivering a new plane while the second one met their end while returning a war weary B-17 from Scotland. By a strange quirk of fate I did not make these two flights that turned out to be fatal to these brother flyers.

While we were sweating out the entire situation in Casablanca, I felt Greg would not have to worry about those B-17s since he had never been checked out in them. Ultimately my worries were in vain regarding those tired Fortresses sitting out there on the ramp. I was sure my name was on a crew who would be required to fly it back to the States.

A large group of other ATC crews blew in shortly after we arrived and I moved up and off the list for this crap detail. Many of the new crew members were some of our friends who delivered their A-26s to Poligniano, Italy. I was specifically informed, by the "powers-to-be", there would be no chance I would be given this undesirable detail of navigating an over the hill B-17 back to the States just so it could be destroyed and scraped. The cost in lives and the waste of personnel to return this junk did not make sense to me or my fellow Officers.

I was to spend five days in Casablanca before I was scheduled to fly out on a Military Transport on April 27th. Captain Hillman had already been scheduled to leave on the 25th. This indeed was a busy place.

Greg and I decided to walk around and see some sights in bustling Casablanca, perhaps we might stumble on Rick's Place that Humphrey Bogart made famous. We had been told of a special market place worth seeing and also a zoo that was unique for this part of the world. We asked directions for the market place from young Arab lads who volunteered to show us the way.

As we proceeded down winding narrow streets, we noticed that the number of kids was increasing rapidly and the direction we were being taken began to look like a rough part of Casablanca. Both Greg and I began to suspect that we might be victims of getting rolled, something we had been warned against on several occasions.

On a given signal, Greg and I slammed our way through these kids and ran like hell for several blocks. We both had played football and by lowering our head and using one shoulder or the other we plowed into these twenty or more kids like they were bowling pins. We caught them completely by surprise. Many were screaming after us as we finally found a main street and some MPs.

After Greg left for the States I met one of the other Navigators from our Base at St. Joe and we decided to visit the zoo. This zoo was completely different from the several zoos I had seen in Milwaukee and Madison Wisconsin. Obviously they had many of the animals from Africa, but the main difference was the amount of pens and space they devoted to American farm animals. They also had many of the wild animals from the North American continent.

While approaching an American bison that was standing next to the metal enclosure, I decided to rub its head. On farms in Wisconsin I had learned large bulls appreciated having their skulls rubbed by pressing hard with one of your knuckles. For some dumb reason this now seemed like the thing to do.

I reached through the thick metal bars to apply this same technique to the large hairy buffalo in front of me. This critter either did not know what he should like or he just didn't give a damn for my adroitness. He twisted his head sharply to one side, catching my arm between the metal bar and one of his horns.

Midway up my right arm I had a slight abrasion that ran diagonally for six-inches. It was not bleeding, but the bruise instantly turned dark blue. I had not broken either bone in this arm though it hurt for some time. I now have another wound for which I could not expect a purple heart.

GOING HOME

Shortly before 1200 hours on April 27th we filled all of the seats in a Lockheed Constellation for the trip back to the United States. It turned out to be a beautiful Saturday morning and we were going home. Our first stop would be in the Azores, a group of islands about 1000 miles west of Portugal and Spain.

We were able to get off the plane, have dinner, and get some walking in while the plane was being refueled. The entire group of military personnel again boarded the C69 Constellation and our assigned seats for the all night trip to New York and La Guardia Air Port.

It wasn't very difficult to get some much needed sack time in during this flight. Mentally, I knew we were crossing time zones continually, thus moving the hour hand backward on our watches. I always wore two wrist watches, one for local time wherever I might be in the world and one for the time back at our Base. I also carried a third watch, my chronometer on which I meticulously kept Greenwich, English Time used exclusively while doing celestial navigation.

Something I did not know, while I was relaxing in my seat, that my bottle of Channel No. 5 was losing all of its perfume because of the altitude we were flying at. I discovered, after the fact, that I should have had them cover the top of the bottle with wax in order to seal it.

In a way I'm glad I wasn't aware of this evaporation going on while flaked out in my seat. The perfume was in my B-4 bag somewhere in the storage compartment in this huge plane and I couldn't have changed a thing with all this new knowledge I previously knew nothing about.

Early Sunday morning on April 28th we landed at La Guardia International Airport in New York. My next exposure to the degree of my unworldly knowledge occurred when I had to meet the requirement of once again going through customs. My B-4 Bag caught the immediate attention of the custom official.

The first clue he noticed was the weight and the second thing that got his curiosity was the sound the bag made when I placed it on the inspection counter. I was immediately informed that the law specifically states only four quarts or five-fifths of alcohol can enter the country without a special tax.

In all honesty, I pleaded complete ignorance of this law. I immediately envisioned the confiscation of most of my precious bottles. "Rum would go first." The fact that

I was in uniform, had multiple rows of decorations on my blouse, and did not look like a "Rum Runner" did not hurt my cause. In reality, this Custom Inspector was really swell about the entire matter.

In all sincerity, this custom official offered to take me to his home for supper, suggesting I bring a bottle of the straight bourbon along and then he would drive me back to La Guardia. I thanked him and told him I would have to renege. My pilot, Captain Greg Hillman, had returned two days ago and my Base was now expecting me home on the first flight.

I showed him my No. 1 Priority Pass we had been issued. This serious looking man said he was only pulling my leg and that I should not worry about getting my treasure through customs. He hadn't noticed anything unusual, he stated. I offered him a bottle of the bourbon, but he refused this offer for obvious reasons. "Could I accidentally forget to pack a bottle of boubon?" I stated. "No.....I would just have to turn it in." He immediately winked and gave me permission to pass on through. His last word was "enjoy."

I got myself involved in another problem less than an hour later. Lt. Atkins and I were in the huge airport's toilet room taking a sailors bath at the lavatories. We had stripped down to the waist and were washing ourselves up with the warm soapy water in each of the basins.

It was then we noticed a General walk into the large rest room and immediately tried to use one of the two pay toilets. The coin he was attempting to use in the slot did not work after repeated attempts. There happened to be nearly a dozen other toilet stalls along this same wall that would not require a single coin.

He then asked if one of us could exchange a dime for his, since he thought his might be bent or something. "Yes sir," I said. I have a pocket full of change." He took my dime and used the facilities without any further difficulty.

Soon after he left, while we were still washing up, I dropped a small pocketknife and was kneeling on the floor to pick it up. A very young looking Lieutenant from the Infantry walked in and asked if he could help find whatever I had dropped. In what I thought was a joking manner, I closed one eye and stated, "No thanks, my glass eye had rolled off the lavatory onto the floor, but I would find it."

A short time later, while still trying to finish my sailor-bath, I noted this guy on his hands and knees, crawling on the toilet room floor. "He was looking for my damn eye." I bent down and feigned like I had just found it, and yelled out. "I got it." "I got it." At the same time I pretended to wash it off, opening my closed eye and made like I was inserting this fictitious glass eye ball back into its socket. I thanked the guy and made a meaningless promise to myself that I would never crap around like that again.

About a half hour later, while waiting for my flight, I sat on a bench in the large waiting area of the terminal. I had been talking with a grandmother and her grandson who was about to leave for an Army Training Camp. I noticed this same General who I had given a dime to in the "John." He was alone and he seemed to be just wandering around and passing time.

The elderly woman said, "Oh, there goes General James Roosevelt. You know his father was the President." I didn't say it, but I could have told her, "That guy owes me a dime."

In another two hours I was on a commercial flight heading for Kansas City. Once again I was racing with the sun and the hour hand was moving in my favor. As soon as I arrived I called Rosecrans Field and transportation was sent to return several of us from the Kansas City airport to our Base.

Once the Air Force Bus got near town I asked the bus driver to drop me off uptown. I exited the blue bus only a few blocks from my apartment. Though my B-4 bag was heavy and I was tired, I also was excited.

BACK WITH MY NORMA

I climbed the stairs to our apartment and Norma. She was waiting for me with open arms and it was truly good to be home. This had been the longest absence she experienced because of the length and time of my trip to Italy. We sat up most of the night while I relived the many happenings along the nearly 10,000 mile journey.

It was with a great deal of enthusiasm when I finally got around to unpacking my strained B-4 bag. First we unpacked the many bottles of Old Mill Farm bourbon and then the two kinds of rum. I did not lose a single container of this precious liquid. Next I brought out the three packages containing the special gifts meant only for Norma. I just knew she would be thrilled with my selection of gifts for her. Maybe this would compensate for the two dresses I purchased so long ago in Houston. Was I mistaken?

First we opened the smallest package that contained the Channel No. 5 bottle of perfume. Instantly we both could see that the ornate exquisite bottle was empty, all the perfume was gone. At this moment I did not surmise the reason for the perfumes absence since the glass stopper had been on tight, it still looked sealed, and there was no indication of anything having leaked out.

I would learn later, in relating my problem, that at high altitudes the perfume would merely evaporate into the rare air. Our flight home on the C69 Constellation did just that. I can only guess but in the pressurized cabin of the Commercial Airliner they probably flew at an altitude in excess of 25,000 feet. My B-4 bag was below in storage.

We both realized the world had not come to an end. As I was reaching for the second package, Norma informed me that she could not have worn this type of perfume because the oils in her skin were not compatible with this expensive fragrance from France. She had sampled it several times unbeknown to me. Right now I'm batting zero. "Will I ever learn?" "One down, two to go."

I next grabbed the small package that contained the dozen pair of individually wrapped silk stockings. Before Norma had a chance to analyze the gift before her, I quickly interjected that I wasn't sure of her size so I bought three different models of this rare item of clothing. "I hope one of these sizes will be just right for you Hon."

The contents of this package spread across the table and it was most obvious what this gift was. The size that fit my darling wife was the one I had bought the least of. Out of the twelve pair of hose she would end up with only two pair of silk stockings. (The next day she did not find it difficult to sell the other ten pair of these impossible to get silk stockings.) I now, deep in my heart, feel like I am still batting zero. "Two down, one to go."

Finally I handed Norma the wrapped Alligator Bag. First she displayed a look of surprise, this was followed by one of contemplation, and finally she volunteered the following: "I think this purse is beautiful, but I do not possess any clothes to wear with it. This elegant purse would go with a fur coat or something more sophisticated than I own."

It appeared that the only true gift I would give her this night was my return from the three-week trip. I'm not sure all the bottles of bourbon and two types of rum could begin to compensate for my disappointment concerning those gifts for Norma.

I now know my choice of gifts had been selected by a husband who had not figured out his wife's likes, desires, wishes, and certainly dimensions. This would be something I would need more time to master. This *faux pas,* over time, was transformed into a family joke, with you know who as the innocent culprit.

The constant regret I dwelled on was the fact that we could not make these interesting trips together. There was no way I could take Norma on these trips with me to the far corners of the world so we could share those unusual sights and all the different cultures. I had figured ways I could get her out of the country with me, but then there was always the impossible problem of getting back to the United States and through customs. It might have been possible if I could count on getting the custom inspector I had at La Guardia International Air Port the day before.

Many of the planes we ferried had room to stow away another person. Now that I was married I wanted to share all of my experiences with the one person in the world who meant so very much to me. Hopefully, when this stupid war finally is over, we can then find it possible to do just that.

This last lengthy trip covered a great distance and touched many countries. For the first time in my life I think I finally appreciated the size of this old world. I was exposed to many different nationalities and their unusual customs.

We all are so different, and yet, there is a thread of similarity in each and every country I was fortunate to visit. I just had flown over oceans, jungles, mountains, deserts, and even a tranquil sea to deliver a single airplane, the A-26 INVADER, whose sole function (getting Hitler out of the Alps) was never realized.

After several days of rest, I once again reported in and inquired where I would next be sent. Every corner of this old globe is so different and I was getting the chance to see a great deal of it. The anticipation of flying to these various remote spots made my days in the Air Transport Command very exciting.

The A-26 Invader was a fine plane that never really got a chance to prove itself because of the pending end of this long and terrible war. Jets were soon to take over flight. However, I shall always have fond memories of the hours I sat in this plane's cockpit and I will forever be grateful for the A-26's power. Without this capacity Captain Greg Hillman could never have pulled this plane away from the wall of rock in the Atlas Mountains.

Five days after my return I had to leave for another trip to Scotland. This did not fall under the category of discovering new lands since I had been there several times. Returning a war weary aircraft was almost a constant at this stage of the war.

On our way to the British Isles we landed in New York City. When I left St. Joseph on this trip, I had no way of knowing that this would be my final assignment for the Air Transport Command. Several of us just happened to be in Times Square when we heard the war in Japan had ended.

WAR IN PACIFIC ENDS

Hundreds of thousands of excited people were going wild. I got hugged and kissed by dozens of perfectly strange women. These excited and elated people took their exuberance out on anyone in uniform. All the body contact and unwanted slaps on the back, butt, arms, the unrelenting handshakes, and moments when you felt like you were about to be smothered by the throngs pressing around you made me believe I truly was a victim of an uncontrollable mob situation.

I felt most uncomfortable and continually tried to retreat to areas with fewer bodies. I had gotten separated from my friends and now decided to get entirely away from Times Square and head for the Airport. When you passed a bar or tavern, drinks of every description, were handed to anyone in uniform. I had never been a part of any celebration or excitement of this magnitude like I experienced this night.

My two friends seemed to react similarly to this melee. Once we found one another, we mutually decided we had to leave this happy mob and go on our scheduled flight to Europe. The next day we discovered this rumor of the war having ended was actually premature. It would not officially end for two additional days.

We were in Stornaway, Scotland when the war with Japan official came to an end. The war in Asia did not hold the same esteem for the people of the British Isles as the one that had gone on in Europe, for many obvious reasons. To us Americans, both theatres of war had always held equal importance.

While in Stornaway, we experienced absolutely no enthusiasm from the British personnel on this Base for this very important moment in time. The eight of us decided we would create our own exuberance.

"TOJO - PUTT DOUN UR ZWARDD – DA VAR ISS OVAR"

We just happened to be quartered in a large Quonset hut when we mutually agreed that this moment required a celebration. Several of us took out our 45 caliber revolvers and proceeded to perforate the ceiling of this metal structure.

The noise that was created inside this tin can was almost unbearable to our tender ears. Our war was now over and these eight American veterans, in this tin can of a building, had unbridled emotions that needed to be liberated.

What we did may seem childish and immature, but strong feelings had been kept at bay long enough. Tonight we would go to sleep with tiny shafts of light finding their way through the roof of our Quonset hut. This we discovered had been an emotional way to filter in moonlight.

A little over a week later we returned to St. Joseph, Missouri and were told, "if you had accumulated enough discharge points, you would be sent to Sioux Falls, South Dakota and be processed out of the Air Force." I knew I had nearly twice the number of discharge points required so I did not anticipate a problem in becoming a civilian once again. I knew I would be leaving the Air Force.

Sioux Falls was one of many Discharge Centers scattered around the country to immediately return the millions of veterans back to civilian status. For our group stationed in St. Joseph, Missouri we only had a short distance to go to be formally discharged from the service and the duties we now were performing.

I immediately sent Norma home, via the usual train trip, knowing I would follow within the week. On October 23rd I arrived in Sioux Falls. I was aware that though the war was formally ended, much still had to be done by our Government throughout the world. I knew I had to make a decision of whether I wanted to remain in the military or become a civilian once again.

At Sioux Falls we were given complete medical examinations, loads of instructions such as the value of the $10,000 life insurance policy the government had taken out on each of our lives, and various programs like the G.I. Bill for education, etc. We were shuffled around to various individuals who were making sure the Air Force would be covering their butts before letting us go.

Because of my experiences during the time I served as a Lead Navigator, I was offered the opportunity to reenlist or I could receive an Honorable Discharge. I chose the latter. I had more than enough discharge points by this stage of the war so the Air Force could not insist on my remaining in the service.

As a final gesture, my grateful country saw to it that I received a small pin. This little pin would be forever designated as the "Ruptured Duck" by all those fortunate veterans who were honorably discharged. The pin was only about 3/8th of an inch in diameter with an eagle flying through some sort of a circle. It looked like it was made of gold, but there remains some doubt as to its intrinsic value. A special note was inserted on my Discharge Papers that I had been issued a "Lapel Button."

It somehow did not seem an appropriate or even a significant gift to be given to someone who had devoted over four years of his life to the Air Force. These last moments in Sioux Falls seemed so very impersonal.

GOING HOME FOR GOOD

Because I would travel home in my officer's uniform, I found it hard to leave this Base in Sioux Falls, South Dakota on October 25, 1945 feeling like a civilian again. So much had happened to this lad out of college so long ago. I now felt more matured and aged, but I was receiving mixed emotions.

There was a conglomerate of sensations racing through my head. I felt both elated and somewhat sad. There was a feeling of gratification and also disappointment. Now I wanted to hurry home, yet I could sense the despondency of having my part in the war completely over.

I soon discovered I could not get a train out of Sioux Falls until almost midnight. It was now 0900 hours. I made the decision I would hitchhike home to Wisconsin, keeping ahead of formal transportation that I could always use if I found it necessary.

A single ride with a traveling salesman raced me across Eastern South Dakota and Minnesota. The salesman fired questions about the war and I told him stories he found hard to believe. Time seemed to race by. He finally left me off at the bus station in La Crosse, Wisconsin.

I was most fortunate to get on a bus going to Wausau within the hour. I now decided that bus transportation isn't a hell of a lot better than the train my dear friend George is so fond of. The bus driver would not only stop at some certain spot in the smallest of towns, they would even stop along the highway to pick up passengers.

I finally arrived at the Greyhound Bus Terminal in my home town of Wausau just about the time I could have boarded a train in Sioux Falls, South Dakota. I walked over to the first taxicab I saw and stated I needed a ride to Rothschild. Once I settled down, the driver asked if I was Lloyd Krueger. "Affirmative" I stated. "How did you know that?" "My son knows you. I'm John Buhler and we only live a few blocks from your parents."

I was left off in the Schmidt driveway in Rothschild and Mr. Buhler refused to take neither the fare nor a tip. Though the hour was late, all the lights were on in the kitchen and the room was filled with my new family who I would now get the chance to know better.

In less than an hour I brought everyone up to date on my exact status with the military. Norma had actually been home for several days and had informed most of what the two of us had been doing. Despite the late hour, we all had one of my notorious Boringuen Old fashions. This was by a special request of my new mother-in-law, Mrs. Olga Schmidt.

I am home, my war is over, I think I have all of my marbles, and I am once again an ordinary civilian. Because I nearly met my demise many different times after I had flown thirty-five combat missions, I now began to realize the moving feeling of extreme gratification. I am now going to be a lover, no longer a fighter.

EPILOGUE

An epilogue, by definition, is a concluding addition of a book or novel and is usually meant to be an addendum, codicil, or supplement to the words, which preceded it. The concluding thoughts, recorded in this section, are justifications for why I believe this era should be inscribed for posterity. It should not only be recorded, but as many participants as possible, should relate the part each played.

Though I am now eighty one years old, the years I spent during World War II turned out to be an epoch moment in my life. I, of course, am grateful to have survived this destructive and devastating period in our current history. I also feel beholden and obligated to add my wisdom to these moments in time.

I was only one of over two million Americans who answered the call to arms. My account should be considered rather typical of the hundreds of thousands who were apart of the Eighth Air force. Any war, which cost the unimaginable loss of 50 million lives, cannot be ignored. American involvement came at a heavy cost with the burden of more than a million casualties, including 292,000 combat deaths.

I am particularly proud of the 95th Bomb Group I served in combat with. Of the 41 heavy bombardment groups stationed in England during WWII, the achievements and recognition of the 95th bomb Group are unequaled. This outstanding group was known for its dedication to mission, its pride, comradery and leadership in combat.

The group began operations at Alconbury, England on May 13, 1943 and later moved to Horham. From this date, until beyond the end of the war in victory, the 95th Bomb Group participated in every major campaign and air battle, earning honors of highest order. It was because of the undaunted courage of the aircrews and the dedicated, faithful, professional service of the ground support units.

A BRIEF SUMMARY OF THE ACCOMPLISHMENTS
OF THE 95TH BOMB GROUP (H)

- Flew 321 combat missions: dropped 19,769 tons of bombs.
- Flew (seven) 7 "Chowhound" missions.....low-level food supply to the starving Dutch Nation.
- Flew (four) 4 "Revival" repatriation missions.....to return Downed POW's and forced laborers from France, Belgium, and The Netherlands.
- Flew a total of 8,903 credited sorties.
- Utilized a total of 359 B-17 Flying Fortresses in action; 156 planes lost in combat, 36 planes lost in other operations, 61 planes were forced to land on the continent, 42 planes landed at home base, but were damaged beyond repair.
-   1,336 planes were repaired from major battle damage.
-   Consumed more than 35,000,000 gallons of gasoline.
- Lost 611 men killed in line of duty.
- Lost 851 crew members as Prisoners of War.
- Had 171 crew members returned to base as severely wounded.
- Lost 65 crew members interned in Switzerland and Sweden.
- Had 61 crew members evade capture after being shot down behind enemy lines.
- There are still 5 crew members listed as "Missing In Action".
- The 95th Bomb Group claimed 425 enemy aircraft destroyed, 117 probables, & 231 damaged.
- The 95th Bomb Group led the first daylight bombing mission to Berlin, on March 4, 1944.
- The 95th Bomb Group was the only Group in the 8th Air Force to receive three (3) Presidential Distinguished Unit Citations,—These were for leadership and valor on missions to Regensburg, Germany on August 17, 1943, Munster, Germany on October 10, 1943, and Berlin, on March 4, 1944.

I am sure each of the men who flew and served in the various Bomber Groups throughout England had pride for their units, similar to the justified pride I possessed in my 95th Bomb Group. It was this conviction that permitted the Eighth Air Force to accomplish its fundamental role in taking the battle back to Hitler's Germany. The Mighty Eighth became the largest air unit ever committed to battle.

I believe I would be remiss if I did not express my admiration and strong feelings for the British people. I have nothing but esteem and praise for the people of this relatively small nation who defied and held off the might of the German war machine. They endured the constant bombing by the Luftwaffe for nearly six years, while accepting all of the sacrifices required during the time of war.

I particularly experienced both the acceptance and the congeniality of all of the people around our Base in Horham, in the Suffolk area of East Anglia. They welcomed the Yanks who had inundated their small but beautiful island and made us feel at home.

In 1989, my wife Norma and I returned to England to attend a reunion at Horham. The principal speaker, at a noon luncheon attended by 39 former 95th Bomb Group members and our friends from the Suffolk area, was Roger A. Freeman.

Mr. Freeman is one of the leading authorities on U.S. warplanes, the airmen who flew them, and the Second World War operations in which they were involved. He has written numerous books and is best known for his perpetuating the memory of this unique piece of history.

The following is the complete text of Roger's remarks. It epitomizes the mutual feeling of the British people and the American Yanks:

"As a young schoolboy in 1943, I visited the airfield at Horham on several occasions and I saw the SQUARE B Fortresses of the 95th Bomb Group. You were young men in a strange land, complaining that the beer in the pubs was always weak and too warm. And you wondered if, and when, it was ever going to stop raining. All that was a long time ago. The old world has taken several whirls since then, but here we are. . . .our youth is gone, we are all getting a bit snowy on top, some of us have nothing on top at all and our old bodies aren't what they used to be. They stick in where they should stick out, and the stick out where they should stick in. But don't worry, because I might have been just a kid then, but I'm sliding past middle age just like you gentlemen. And as I said, it's a long time ago; and since then there have been many, many changes.

You have all been just down the road to see some other changes at your old airfield. It's not the Horham base that you remember of nearly fifty years ago. You saw so yourselves: "Is this really the place where there were 150,000 takeoffs and landings? Is this the place where we sent nearly 20,000 tons of bombs to Adolph Hitler and his cronies? Is this the place where the B-17s of the old SQUARE B took off at dawn from the runway which was the highway to battlefields far away?

Is this the place where we sweated in a machine shop, or where we froze on a cold winter day out on the airfield as we tried to change the spark plugs on a Wright Cyclone engine? Is this the place where we spent long and sleepless nights in those tin can Nissen Huts while hearing the mechanics out on the field winding up our B-17 engines in preparation for tomorrow's mission?

Is this the place from where the Fortresses of the 95th set off for the first daylight raid over Berlin? Is this the place where the gunners of the 95th were credited with more enemy aircraft destroyed than any other outfit in the 8th Air Force Bomber Command? Is this really the place where we spent our youth—- perhaps two days—perhaps two years?

Horham is the same place, and as everything else, it changes. But there is one thing that hasn't changed; and that is the feeling of the people of Horham and Suffolk County for what you Americans did and what you are. That has not changed!

It may surprise you after half a century that you are even remembered. But you are, and you can see that you are. Why are you remembered? You have faith in what you did, and you have faith in what your are. You have faith in the 611 who left this airfield and never returned home. You have faith in the old SQUARE B.

We are an old nation, and appreciate people who have faith in the past and do not forget—because we don't forget either. Welocme back 95th and please come again."

Roger Freeman is the author of The Mighty Eighth, The Mighty Eighth War Diary, Epics of Aviation Archaeology and several other books.

Norma and I spent several days with the people who lived and grew up in the Suffolk area. During our visits with these British friends, I seldom had a dry eye, primarily because of the acceptance and sincere welcome we experienced. Over and over these special new friends expressed their gratitude for what "you YANKS have done."

Though Norma and I have had the good fortune to return to Europe several times during the ensuing years, a memorable one worth mentioning took place recently. On September 11, 2001 we attended a Reunion being held in Kovarska, Czech Republic, commemorating the 57th Anniversary of a famous air battle that took place on the German-Czechoslovakia border.

As it turned out, we were the only Americans who were in attendance at this three day Reunion because of the Terrorist attack against the Twin Towers and the Pentagon. All other planes leaving the United States had been canceled. We flew out of Chicago on a direct flight to Frankfurt, Germany on the evening of September 10th and were in mid-Atlantic when the tragedy occurred.

On Sept.11, 1944 the 100th and the 95th bomb Groups attacked a synthetic oil refinery near Brux Czechoslovakia. In the air battle that took place over the Ore Mountains, the 100th B.G. lost 14 of its 36 bombers and the 95th B.G. had one of its 21 planes destroyed. The single B-17 from the 95th happened to be HAARD LUCK Number 42-97334 and it was flown by the Lt. V. R. Mooring crew. This would be the 41st mission that my very special Fortress would have flown.

In attendance at this Reunion in Kovarska were twelve Luftwaffe pilots and their wives. Norma and I were so very proud that we were able to represent the entire Eighth Air Force these three days. There were many Americans I had hoped to meet for the first time at this Reunion but fate dictated otherwise.

There is a wonderful Museum dedicated to this single important air battle on A.E. Trommer Str. 696 (Named after one of the American pilots who gave his life this day), Kovarska, Czech Republic. The only school in this modest sized town was renamed after a Sgt. Klugger who also gave his life. One of the B-17s crashed into the school roof on Sept. 11, 1944.

Though I have periodically made mention of the missions I had flown in combat, I have included a complete list, by number and date.

LIST OF MISSIONS FLOWN

Lt. Lloyd O. Krueger participated in the following Missions,
as confirmed by the C.O. of the 95th Bomb Group (H):

No. Date Target

1 5-09-44 Loan Athies, France
2 5-12-44 Brux Czechoslovakia
3 5-13-44 Osnabruck, Germany
4 5-19-44 Berlin, Germany
5 5-20-44 Brussels, Belgium
6 5-25-44 Brussels, Belgium
7 5-30-44 Brussels, belgium
8 5-31-44 Osnabruck, Germany
9 6-05-44 Boulogne, France
10 6-06-44 Caen, France (D-Day)
11 6-12-44 Vitry-en-Arteis, France
12 6-15-44 Hannover, Germany
13 6-20-44 Fellersleben, Germany
14 6-21-44 Berlin, Germany (Basdorf)
15 6-24-44 Fruges, France
16 6-29-44 Leipzig, Germany (Bohlen)
17 7-04-44 Gein, France
18 7-06-44 Fiefs, France
19 7-07-44 Kolleda, Germany (Leipzig)
20 7-08-44 Bernay, France
21 7-12-44 Munich, Germany (Munchen)
22 7-14-44 St. Medard, France (French Maquis)
23 7-16-44 Stuttgart, Germany
24 7-17-44 Cheny, France
25 7-18-44 Hemmingstedt, Germany
26 7-20-44 Lutkendorf, Germany (Halle)
27 7-21-44 Regensburg, Germany
28 7-31-44 Munich, Germany (Munchen)
29 8-01-44 Lac d'Anncey, France (French Maquis)
30 8-02-44 Invasion Front (Tactical Mission)

31 8-24-44 Rhuland, Germany
32 8-25-44 Muritz Lake, Germany (Politz)
33 8-26-44 Brest, France
34 9-03-44 Lanveoc, France
35 9-05-44 Stuttgart, Germany

I want to apologize to my Norma, (the wife, the mother, the friend, the pal, the nurse, the buddy, and the companion) for nearly fifty-eight years of patiently listening to most of these related memories, over and over these many years, as they came up in conversations with friends and fellow veterans. I have always appreciated her understanding, support, constructive criticism and caring.

I also want her to know of my deepest appreciation for her faithfulness, loyalty and understanding during the many months I was in England. I need to let her know how much her almost daily letters meant to me during those trying days of combat.

Then during the many months I served in the Air Transport Command and would be away from home sometimes for weeks on end, she waited patiently for my return and made me feel guiltless from those prolonged absences. Most of what I have accomplished these past fifty-eight years I owe to this single person I have always felt fortunate enough to have wed.

PERICLES

Something written over twenty four hundred years ago by the Athenian Statesman, Pericles, seems as apropos today as the moment it was spoken. The following is this pertinent thought:

"Each one, man for man, has won imperishable praise, each has gained a glorious grave, —not that the sepulcher of earth wherein they lie, but the living tomb of everlasting remembrance wherein their glory is enshrined. For the whole earth is the sepulcher of heroes; monuments may rise and tablets be set up to them in their own land, but on the far off shores there is an abiding memorial that no pen or chisel has traced, it is graven, not on stone or brass, but on the living heart of humanity. Take these men as your example. Like them, remember that the prosperity can only be for the free; that freedom is the sure possession of those alone who have the courage to defend it.

Many of my fellow crewmembers from the 95th Bomb Group and from the many other Groups of the Eighth Air Force are buried in the American Cemetery near Cambridge, England. The following is an Inscription at this Cemetery whose words are worthy of mention:

> **"The Americans whose names here appear, were part of the price that free men for the second time in this century have been forced to pay to defend human liberty and rights. All who hereafter shall live in Freedom will be here reminded that to these men and their comrades we owe a debt to be paid with grateful remembrance of their sacrifice and the high resolve that the cause for which they died shall live eternally.**

> **"In proud and grateful memory of those men of the United States Army Air Force who flew from these Friendly skies and flew their final flight and met their God. They knew not the hour, the day nor the manner of their passing. When far from home they were called to join that heroic band of airmen who had gone before. May they rest in peace."**

Finally, I would like to delineate more precisely this special person I have dedicated this book to, Mrs. Elsie Louise Weinkauf. Mrs. Weinkauf lived in my neighborhood during all of my youthful years. Ultimately she and her family moved next door to my parents from the time I was only ten until long after I left the military.

I will refer to her as Elsie, not out of disrespect, but rather from admiration and affection. There was no time during my developing years that our friendship would prove to be the single most important source for the expansion and broadening of most of my hopes, dreams and desires. She made me believe that all things are possible. She taught me pride.

Over the years she and I had hundreds of conversations covering almost every subject. I cannot recall a single statement she ever uttered that did not possess some important significance or precious advice to this famished young neighbor of hers.

I never had the chance to formally express my gratitude for what she meant to me or for the many values she instilled in this young rambunctious lad. Yet, I know she was aware of the important role she played in my life. She was able to touch me by stimulating my spirit, my hopes, and all that I would be.

Thanks dear Elsie.

ENJOY, LEST TOMORROW *FLEES*

ISBN 155395108-5

9 781553 951087

ger